American Aurora

"Grieve-Carlson has centered *American Aurora* on a re-examination of the life of Kelpius at the dawn of the eighteenth century, which he uses to re-interpret the challenge of the paranormal in early American history. In this elegant analysis of the community, he detects influences that resonate with modern controversies at the juncture of science and religion. By replacing these strands of ancient speculation into a new framework, the author argues powerfully for a re-examination of the ancient roots of a very modern and lively spiritual current."—**Jacques Vallee**, author of *Trinity: The Best-Kept Secret*

"Here we have it. The first book of a major new historian of religions, here setting his sights on Pennsylvania and early American history, ecological crisis as religious event, science fiction before there was science fiction, and what will become the paranormal. I am not sure how one could ask for more."—**Jeffrey J. Kripal**, author of *How to Think Impossibly: About Souls, UFOs, Time, Belief, and Everything Else*

"Timothy Grieve-Carlson's *American Aurora* is an innovative and fascinating treatment of the life, work, and influence of the enigmatic Johannes Kelpius, a thinker, author, and theologian of the seventeenth century. Known variously as a wizard, a pagan, a Lutheran Pietist, or as an influence on an American tradition of esotericism, Grieve-Carlson, with remarkable skill, allows Kelpius's work to finally speak for itself. What emerges is not only a groundbreaking study of an important theologian, but a pioneering treatment of esotericism from the perspective of environmental studies.

As Enlightenment rationalism appeared to displace an enchanted cosmos amidst environmental catastrophes, Kelpius wrote about "living through the end of a particular world." Grieve-Carlson reveals a "Hermetic Protestant" hermeneutic where the world and creation are alive with sacred presence that invites interpretation and relationship, rather than inert material to be defined. Grieve-Carlson's writing is fresh and urgent—he notes that he reads Kelpius because he wants to learn what he has to say about apocalyptic times. *American Aurora* captivates, but also serves as a powerful catalyst for introspection and action. Grieve-Carlson identifies Kelpius as a cosmotheist and thus contributes to important discussions about theology and space today. A must-read for those seeking profound insights into the pressing matters of our time."—**Diana Pasulka**, author of *Encounters: Experiences with Nonhuman Intelligence*

OXFORD STUDIES IN WESTERN ESOTERICISM

Series Editor
Henrik Bogdan, University of Gothenburg

Editorial Board
Jean-Pierre Brach, École Pratique des Hautes Études
Carole Cusack, University of Sydney
Christine Ferguson, University of Stirling
Olav Hammer, University of Southern Denmark
Wouter Hanegraaff, University of Amsterdam
Ronald Hutton, University of Bristol
Orion Klautau, Tohoku University
Jeffrey J. Kripal, Rice University
Michael Stausberg, University of Bergen
Egil Asprem, Stockholm University
Gordan Djurdjevic, Independent Scholar
Peter Forshaw, University of Amsterdam
Jesper Aa. Petersen, Norwegian University of Science and Technology
Manon Hedenborg White, Malmö University

CHILDREN OF LUCIFER
The Origins of Modern Religious Satanism
Ruben van Luijk

SATANIC FEMINISM
Lucifer as the Liberator of Woman in
Nineteenth-Century Culture
Per Faxneld

THE SIBYLS OF LONDON
A Family on the Esoteric Fringes of
Georgian England
Susan Sommers

WHAT IS IT LIKE TO BE DEAD?
Near-Death Experiences, Christianity, and
the Occult
Jens Schlieter

AMONG THE SCIENTOLOGISTS
History, Theology, and Praxis
Donald A. Westbrook

RECYCLED LIVES
A History of Reincarnation in Blavatsky's
Theosophy
Julie Chajes

THE ELOQUENT BLOOD
The Goddess Babalon and the Construction
of Femininities in Western Esotericism
Manon Hedenborg White

GURDJIEFF
Mysticism, Contemplation, and Exercises
Joseph Azize

INITIATING THE MILLENIUM
The Avignon Society and Illuminism
in Europe
Robert Collis and Natalie Bayer

IMAGINING THE EAST
The Early Theosophical Society
Tim Rudbog and Erik Sand

MYSTIFYING KABBALAH
Academic Scholarship, National Theology,
and New Age
Boaz Huss

SPIRITUAL ALCHEMY
From Jacob Boehme to Mary Anne Atwood
Mike A. Zuber

THE SUBTLE BODY
A Genealogy
Simon Cox

OCCULT IMPERIUM
Arturo Reghini, Roman Traditionalism,
and the Anti-Modern Reaction in
Fascist Italy
Christian Giudice

VESTIGES OF A PHILOSOPHY
Matter, the Meta-Spiritual, and the Forgotten Bergson
John Ó Maoilearca

PROPHECY, MADNESS, AND HOLY WAR IN EARLY MODERN EUROPE
A Life of Ludwig Friedrich Gifftheil
Leigh T.I. Penman

HÉLÈNE SMITH
Occultism and the Discovery of the Unconscious
Claudie Massicotte

LIKE A TREE UNIVERSALLY SPREAD
Sri Sabhapati Swami and Śivarājayoga
Keith Edward Cantú

FRIENDSHIP IN DOUBT
Aleister Crowley, J. F. C. Fuler, Victoria B. Neuburg, and British Agnosticism
Richard Kaczynski

THE UNKNOWN GOD
W. T. Smith and the Thelemites
Martin P. Starr

AMERICAN AURORA
Environment and Apocalypse in the Life of Johannes Kelpius
Timothy Grieve-Carlson

American Aurora

Environment and Apocalypse in the Life of Johannes Kelpius

TIMOTHY GRIEVE-CARLSON

Oxford University Press is a department of the University of Oxford. It furthers
the University's objective of excellence in research, scholarship, and education
by publishing worldwide. Oxford is a registered trade mark of Oxford University
Press in the UK and certain other countries.

Published in the United States of America by Oxford University Press
198 Madison Avenue, New York, NY 10016, United States of America.

© Oxford University Press 2024

All rights reserved. No part of this publication may be reproduced, stored in
a retrieval system, or transmitted, in any form or by any means, without the
prior permission in writing of Oxford University Press, or as expressly permitted
by law, by license, or under terms agreed with the appropriate reproduction
rights organization. Inquiries concerning reproduction outside the scope of the
above should be sent to the Rights Department, Oxford University Press, at the
address above.

You must not circulate this work in any other form
and you must impose this same condition on any acquirer.

CIP data is on file at the Library of Congress

ISBN 978–0–19–776557–9 (pbk.)
ISBN 978–0–19–776556–2 (hbk.)

DOI: 10.1093/oso/9780197765562.001.0001

For Bridget Hovell

Contents

Acknowledgments	xi
Introduction: "Strange Things Happening Every Day"	1
"Phoenomena, Meteors, Stars and Various Colours of the Skei"	5
The Crisis of Piety	9
Environment and Apocalypse	12
Global Crisis	17
1. "No Wisdom in Nature": Esotericism, Enthusiasm, and Ecology in Early Modern Europe	23
Extraordinary Heavenly Phenomena	23
The Crises of Early Modernity	27
Enthusiasm, Esotericism, and Ecology	30
Hermeticism and Alchemy	31
Hermetic Protestant Environmental Knowledge	34
"Nature Is the Interpreter of Scripture"	42
"No Wisdom in Nature"	47
Metamorphosis of the Metaphysics	49
Vita I. "Strange Things of the Invisible Worlds": Kelpius in Europe, 1667–1693	53
2. "Gone into the Ancient Forest": Hermetic Protestantism and Environmental Knowledge in Early Pennsylvania	62
Pastor Schuhmacher's Apocalypse	62
Early American Hermetic Protestantism	66
"All of It Is Only Forest"	68
Holy Experiments	72
"Every Plant Praises and Extols God"	74
"Moves Nature in a Jumping Fit / According to His Pleasure"	78
"The Genius of the Americans Is Bound Another Way"	88
Vita II. "I Cannot Pass beyond My Homeland": Kelpius in Rotterdam, London, and the Atlantic, 1693–1694	90
"The Poor People Call'd Pietests"	93
"I Cannot Pass beyond My Country"	99
3. "The Woman in the Wilderness": Kelpius and Company on the Ridge of the Wissahickon, 1694–1707	101
The Woman in the Wilderness	104
"For Wilderness Signifies Hidden"	106

X CONTENTS

The Wissahickon Hermits	111
The Keithian Schism	114
"Everything Too Spiritual and Too Heavenly"	117
"The Rooms in My Father's House"	119
"Contemplation of the Stars"	121
The Lamenting Voice of the Hidden Love	123
"An Antient Hermit Who Lives in a Lone House"	126

4. The Threefold Wilderness State: Ascetic Alchemy and the Technology of Self-Negation — 133

The Threefold Wilderness State	141
The Sources of the Threefold Wilderness State	151
The Technology of Self-Negation	155

Vita III. "Delay Not Longer the Blessed Day": Kelpius in Germantown, 1694–1703–4–5–6–7 — 161

5. The Long Shadow of the Enlightenment: Memories of Kelpius in Charles Brockden Brown's *Wieland* (1798) — 163

The Long Shadow Falls	163
An American Tale	167
Effects without Cause	175
"Hermes Never Taught Thee"	177
The Great Derangement	184
Long Shadow Fallen	189

6. "Weird as a Wizard": History and Literature in the Emergence of the American Kelpius Legend — 191

Mühlenberg's Report	192
The Philosopher of the Forest	197
Chronicon Ephratense	200
The Spiritual Travel of Conrad Matthai	201
The Method of Prayer	204
The History of Human Folly	207
"Weird as a Wizard"	209
"Rosicrucian Vestiges"	215
All Folk Songs Are True	222

Conclusion: An Unmute Gospel	226
American Aurora	230

Notes	233
References	283
Index	301

Acknowledgments

My first thanks go to my dissertation committee, who encouraged and shaped the research and writing that eventually became this book.

I am profoundly grateful for Jeffrey Kripal's careful guidance, generosity of imagination, and personal warmth over the course of my graduate education. There are very few PhD advisers who can give solid advice on the history of Christian mysticism, the history of UFOs and psychical phenomena all at once, which is what this project really needed. Jeff's attention to my writing and thinking really made this project possible. I can't thank you enough, Jeff.

Claire Fanger has been a great teacher and mentor to me since my first year, and she deserves special thanks for being willing to mentor me in Latin and allow me to join the medieval Latin reading group in the Department of Religion at the eleventh hour.

Timothy Morton in the Department of English has been a great teacher and mentor since the beginning of my graduate studies, whose hyperobjects, realist magic, and controlled doses of OOO are the hidden DNA of this project.

I am profoundly grateful to the medieval Latin reading group in the Department of Religion for constant guidance and assistance in translating Kelpius's merciless early modern neo-Latin. Dr. Anne Parker, Arina Zaytseva, Stanislav Panin, Mai Lootah, and of course Dr. Claire Fanger deserve the all of credit for any of the insight in the Latin translations of Kelpius that appear in this book. Any errors are all mine. Thank you all for saving the Tim-bits for me.

Beyond the Medieval Latin reading group, my colleagues and classmates at Rice were a source of endless encouragement and inspiration. My deep gratitude in no particular order to: Sam Stoeltje, Justine Bakker, Tommy Symmes, Justin Kelly, CJ Schmidt, DeAnna Daniels, Blake McAlpin, Benjamin Mayo, Clancy Taylor, Learned Foote, Stefan Sanchez, Waleed Rikab, Oihane Iglesias Telleria, Naamleela Free Jones, Gregory Perron, Christopher Senn, Cindy Dawson, Erin Prophet, and Simon Cox. Thank you.

A small army of archivists, librarians, and others deserve thanks for special insight and assistance along the way. In no particular order: I am grateful to Tom Carroll of the Kelpius Society for pointing me toward many hidden corners in my research based on his deep knowledge of the Kelpius community and to Catherine H. Michael of the Kelpius Society and the Library at Ithaca College for her extensive bibliographical assistance. Alvin Holm, who welcomed me to Philadelphia on my first research trip in 2018, took me to the

xii ACKNOWLEDGMENTS

original Wissahickon hermitage site, and demonstrated the occult magnetic powers of the fortieth parallel and the energetic resonance of the columns of the Philadelphia Museum of Art. I thank Joel Fry of Bartram's Garden for sharing his files and planting the seed of the second book, and the archivists and staff of the Pennsylvania Historical Society, the Free Library of Philadelphia, the Library Company of Philadelphia, and the Library of the Society of Friends in London.

A number of archivists, librarians, and clergy in Europe were willing to help my research during the pandemic by locating and sending copies of various essential primary documents while I was locked down in Texas. I am grateful to Dr. Susanne Rieß-Stumm of the University of Tübingen for her assistance in locating Kelpius's matriculation record, Dr. Petra Hesse of the University of Leipzig for her assistance in locating Kelpius's other matriculation record, Mr. Nicolae Teşculă at the Museum of Sighişoara for searching his parish, and Dr. András Bándi of Casa Teutsch-Haus for gamely putting up with my incessant requests for the 1667 Denndorf baptismal record.

So many essential pieces of this puzzle would be missing were it not for Bettina Hess and Dr. Frank Trommler of the German Society of Pennsylvania, who assisted during and after my term as a Fellow with the Horner Memorial Library for the German Historical Institute. I am also grateful to the German letters transcription group of the GSP, who did their very best to teach me how to read German handwriting. Vielen Dank!

I am very grateful for the support of the McNeil Center for Early American Studies at the University of Pennsylvania. The careful and kind feedback of Emma Hart, Laura Spero, Daniel Richter, and the other Fellows were essential each step of the way.

It would not have ever occurred to me to pursue graduate school without my undergraduate teachers and mentors at Drew University, in particular Marc Boglioli, Joslyn Cassady, and Karen Pechilis, who read term papers and advised theses on things like UFOs, ghosts, and Bigfoot with exceptional generosity of imagination and teaching skill.

I am very grateful to my colleagues at Westminster College, including Russell Martin, Angela Lahr, and Patricia Clark in the Department of History. I am also very grateful to President Kathleen Richardson and Dean Jamie McMinn for their support of my research.

My parents deserve as much credit for this work as anyone, for their love and support, their constant encouragement of my interests, generous patience, and weekly trips to the library. I am sure that keeping a set of the Time-Life *Mysteries of the Unknown* books in the house didn't hurt, either.

I would also like to thank my chihuahua terrier companion Twig, who accompanied me on long walks around the neighborhood and quiet writing sessions on the couch where most of the essential thinking and working of this book took place.

My final and by far my most important thanks go to my wife Bridget Hovell, who supported me during each step of the way of this entire process. I can't imagine how I would have gotten any of this done without you, Bee.

Introduction

"Strange Things Happening Every Day"

Oh, we hear church people say
They are in this holy way
There are strange things happening every day

On that last great judgment day
When they drive them all away
There are strange things happening every day
—"Strange Things Happening Every Day,"
Sister Rosetta Tharpe (traditional)

It was too late in the evening for many to see it as it shone across the night sky of Philadelphia in July 1829, but a few lucky night owls caught an extended glimpse. One witness wrote to the editor of *Hazard's Register*, a local almanac and news magazine, to describe the event:

> Mr. Editor: –A meteor of rather singular character made its appearance in the heavens last night, between the hours of eleven and twelve o'clock. As a great number of your readers, owing to the lateness of the hour, had not an opportunity observing it, I shall endeavour to give some description of it.[1]

The author of the letter went on to give a thorough description of the object, identified as a "rather singular" meteor. The description makes it almost immediately clear that the object seen over Philadelphia that night was not a meteor in any common or contemporary sense of the word.[2]

"It arose apparently from the neighborhood of the Schuylkill," wrote the correspondent, referring to the area just west of the city where the Schuylkill River proceeds toward the Delaware after converging with the Wissahickon. "A long trail of light, like that of a shooting star was seen to follow it in the beginning of its ascension." In addition to its trail, the object emitted "large sparkles" that descended slowly in its wake. In the author's description, then, the object seems to arise vertically from somewhere in the area of the rivers, emitting both a trail

American Aurora. Timothy Grieve-Carlson, Oxford University Press. © Oxford University Press 2024.
DOI: 10.1093/oso/9780197765562.003.0001

2 INTRODUCTION

of light and falling, sparkling objects beneath it. The movement of the object was also very much unlike the linear path of a meteor: "Its motions were rapid, irregular, and wavering, like the fluttering of a kite or the rocking of an air balloon." The object seemed to tremble and sputter in the air, and the references to kites and balloons seem to suggest a windblown pattern to its movement. Its color was no less extraordinary than its motion: "Its appearance was of a deep red colour, and remarkably brilliant, seemingly of about half the size of the moon." As it arose, the object passed over the city of Philadelphia and crossed the Delaware before descending in a fashion no less dramatic than its ascension:

> It arose until it crossed the Delaware; when it appeared but an inconsiderable speck scarcely discernible, and then descended with astonishing velocity until within short distance the horizon, where it remained ary for a few moments. Suddenly it became exceedingly large and brilliant, sparkles again separated from the main body, and descended as before. It soon after became dim and disappeared behind the trees.[3]

With its trembling motion, clear pattern of terrestrial ascent and descent, shining displays of arrayed lights and rich color, the nocturnal object of 1829 was not likely a meteor: but it was certainly a beautiful night to be out in Philadelphia.

As extraordinary as the object was, the readers of *Hazard's Register of Pennsylvania* would have been aware of a number of similar events in the skies over Pennsylvania over the previous few years. Just a few months earlier in the year 1829, *Hazard's* ran a description of the aurora borealis for readers. In one column, the author seems to refer to the frequency of such phenomena as common knowledge to a contemporary Pennsylvania audience: "The frequent appearance of these lights . . . so unusual within our latitude, is probably within your recollection."[4] The kinds of phenomena that *Hazard's* calls auroras are, perhaps expectedly, just as strange as its "meteors." Their descriptions include enormous perpendicular columns of white light that arrange and rearrange themselves as they cast themselves across the sky, and shimmering dark clouds that move through sky-wide arches of brilliance. And perhaps most telling of all, the "auroras" of nineteenth-century Philadelphia continued to appear throughout the bright light of day.[5] Again, it seems unlikely to our contemporary sensibilities and meteorological knowledge that the Northern Lights shone over Passyunk in the broad daylight of the 1820s, but these are the sources we have.

Sources like *Hazard's* can be confounding to the contemporary reader, who might be forgiven for assuming the skies of the twenty-first century are free of such strange brilliance. If one cares to look, celestial phenomena like those reported in *Hazard's Register* can be found throughout early American publications, especially those written for an audience of farmers, who largely based their planting schedules on close and careful attention to the movements and patterns of the stars, the phases of the moon, and the spinning signs of the zodiac.

The small, rocky, and metallic bodies that pass through the earth's atmosphere and occasionally strike the surface of the planet were a matter of severe scientific debate among the Enlightenment intelligentsia in Europe and the Americas at the turn of the nineteenth century, in the decades leading up to Hazard's Philadelphia "meteor." In fact, the acceptance of the meteorite (the rocky body itself, as opposed to the meteor, which is the rather poetic technical term for the far-more-easily-ignored visual event in the sky that accompanies its falling) as a scientific fact dated only to 1803, a few decades before Hazard's published its account of the object over Philadelphia.[6]

By 1804, meteors were largely and begrudgingly accepted as fact by the transatlantic scientific community. This rather belated acknowledgment was the subject of an editorial in the Edinburgh Review, which reflected on how such a widely witnessed and well-known celestial phenomenon could have been rejected by scientific authorities for so long. Why were "many well-supported testimonies" being "treated by the naturalists . . . with perverse incredulity?" asked the Review.[7] In other words, why did the scientific community seem to willingly blind itself to a phenomenon so obvious—and even the word "obvious" here does not feel obvious enough—after the fact?

As Simon Schaffer has written, scientific acceptance of meteorites was hindered specifically by the low social class of the people who reported them. From the elite perspective of professional scientists, knowledge of meteorites relied on "Plebians [who] were reckoned superstitious."[8] In the eighteenth century, as surely as today, there were deep class divisions and outright animosities between forms of knowledge. Enlightenment meteor-denial was the denial of a specific form of knowledge rather than a simple factual denial of the reality of lights in the sky. Rare celestial events like meteors required an environmental knowledge: a knowledge that was slow, observational, locally and temporally situated, and thus largely reliant on rural people, who were often poor and thus lacked access to formal education. Hence, meteors were the knowledge domain of "superstitious Plebeians." This kind of environmental knowledge was almost uniquely unsuited to the sciences, especially the localization of observations and the temporal need for a phenomenon to repeat itself in order to be experimentally verified.

Despite its extraordinary appearance and "singular character," the sources documenting the 1829 manifestation over Philadelphia do not suggest that it was an event of religious interest at all—rather, for all its mysterious beauty, it was only ever a "meteor." This interpretation, simple as it was, represented a tectonic change in how modern human beings experienced their environment. An interpretation of a similar event in previous decades can illustrate the significance of

Figure I.1 Daniel Schumacher, "Up to the Judgment" (Auf zum Gericht), 1769. Courtesy of the Free Library of Philadelphia, Rare Book Department.

this transformation. One manuscript depiction of a celestial event in southeastern Pennsylvania in 1769 included the following text: "Up to the Judgment; Up, do not miss it. A comet star of very pale color appeared in Pennsylvania in the year 1769 in August. You people, ask yourselves what this star may mean, whether God wants to punish you. O, do penance while there is still time" (Figure I.1).[9]

These two extraordinary celestial events took place in roughly the same area of the world, separated by only about sixty years—but within that separation was a vast gulf of understanding, of knowledge, of the *meaning* that people made of their cosmos. And while it is tempting for a historian to describe this shift as one from simple "religion" to simple "science," it is worth pausing for a moment to reflect on the operational difference between these two forms of knowing.

The first manifestation, the "pale comet" of 1769, was an event that demanded, above all else, an interpretation. Specifically, the author writes, "Ask yourselves what this star may mean." The pale comet called for introspection, for personal reflection; it called for an essentially hermeneutic process of knowledge. The meaning of the comet was not a question for the natural sciences: rather, it was an introspective process with a largely personal outcome, in this case, a kind of moral self-determination. The second event, the 1829 manifestation over Philadelphia, was an event that, so far as we can tell from reading *Hazard's Register*, did not even demand an act of explanation, much less personal reflection, so wide and deep was our understanding of the cosmos. The identity of the object as a meteor, as an *identified object*, was so embedded in its appearance that it seems the Philadelphians who saw it may have ignored a genuine celestial anomaly. With only sixty years between these events, the separation between the *ways of knowing* that separate them seems vast. Why?

"Phoenomena, Meteors, Stars and Various Colours of the Skei"

This book explores the history of this modern transformation of environmental knowledge. The early modern period was, among many other things, a time of profound change in the human understanding of and relationship with the cosmos. Throughout the pages that follow, I am interested in recovering an early modern sense of the cosmos as a site of hermeneutic knowledge—as a vital, intelligent presence to be communicated with, rather than a passive object to be dissected. In 1699, a Christian ascetic living outside Philadelphia explained the sources of his religious worldview:

> No wonder then, if your continual Gazing upon this Supercaelestial Orb and Sphier from whence with her Children, causeth you to observe every new Phoenomena, Meteors, Stars and various Colours of the Skei, if peradventure you may behold at last an Harbinger as an Evidence of that great Jubelee or Restitation of all things.[10]

For the author of this letter, celestial phenomena were a window into God's mind, and the sky itself was a living, animate text that could be read, interpreted, and understood. The author was not a scientist, although he was conversant with the cutting edge of European philosophy and science, having written academic critiques of Descartes and traveling with a copy of Newton's *Principia Mathematica*. Nor was the author uneducated; in fact, he a was university-educated theologian who received the equivalent of a PhD one of the leading German universities of the time. But he was not a noble or even wealthy: he was the son of a country pastor from an impoverished rural region of Europe, the Transylvanian mountains in what is now Romania. Writing from Philadelphia at the turn of the eighteenth century, this author claimed that the environment was God's first and most reliable text, and literacy in this book yielded a sense of personal meaning and spiritual knowledge that neither the sciences nor orthodox Christianity could hope to match.

In this book, I examine this modern transformation of environmental knowledge, not through a comprehensive history of Enlightenment philosophy or the natural sciences, but through the life and influence of the author of this

6 INTRODUCTION

letter. Johannes Kelpius (1667–1707) first appeared to me in a dimly lit cave between the covers of Leigh Eric Schmidt's *Restless Souls: The Making of American Spirituality*, which I read as I prepared to apply to graduate school. There he was again in Catherine Albanese's *A Republic of Mind and Spirit*. And again in Jon Butler's *Awash in a Sea of Faith*. None of these masterful books really attended to this mysterious figure: he was mentioned in passing as an important character, a mysterious presence, and he was variously referred to as a Pietist, an alchemist, a Rosicrucian, a Theosopher, a wizard, and even as the leader of a community of witches. True to his form as a hermit, he never really came up to me and spoke: all those books seemed to offer were fleeting glimpses from between the trees as he retreated further up the cliffs along the Wissahickon River.

In the book where I first spotted Kelpius, Schmidt's *Restless Souls*, the author devoted an entire chapter to the subject of solitude as a religious virtue in American history. In particular, Schmidt pointed out that solitude, both as a literary novelty and as a social virtue, *erupted* in the popular imagination of Americans in the nineteenth century. Including but not limiting his scope to the literary figures of the Transcendentalist movement in New England, Schmidt outlines a burgeoning popular literature on the exploits, suffering, and piety of American hermits. A very early example of an American religious hermit was Kelpius, whom Schmidt points out as being of both "necessarily limited influence" and having "left little by way of an institutional legacy." This did not impede the appetites of a voracious audience for popular hermit literature in the nineteenth century, and Schmidt describes how a "latter-day chronicler" of Kelpius's community reconstructed a vibrant image of the Wissahickon hermitage out of little more than "wistful memory."[11]

> In nineteenth-century memory, the pious souls of this Chapter of Perfection [the Kelpius community] became part of a larger dreamscape of mystic lore and solitude. Through the rosy lens of nostalgia, they became the Hermits of the Romantic Wissahickon. Mining this vein, lovers of solitude found their gold.[12]

The "latter-day chronicler" of the Wissahickon hermits that Schmidt refers to was an amateur Philadelphia historian named Julius Sachse (1842–1919), whose 1895 book *The German Pietists of Provincial Pennsylvania* indeed appears to contain as much opinion and embellishment as it does historical detail.[13] As Schmidt points out, popular hermit literature often straddled the boundary between legend and fact. Although hermit narratives and poems were often based on individuals whose existence is substantiated in historical records, it is usually impossible to tell where history ends and legendary profile begins. Hermits are always hard to find, whether one goes looking for them in the mountains or in the primary sources.

INTRODUCTION   7

Schmidt is pointing out a more serious problem, however. Our historical understanding of Kelpius and his community has been almost entirely overwritten by enthusiastic antiquarians and amateur historians, whose writings tangle with the primary sources of the period to produce a slush of literature in which Kelpius appears at once enormously legendary in profile and largely invisible as a historical figure. In response to the difficulty of distinguishing legend from historical fact, many scholars have chosen to bypass Kelpius and his community entirely in their analyses of adjacent historical or religious material. In 1999, Arthur Versluis noted that Kelpius's life and work "still awaited a full scholarly examination," and this remains the case today.[14] In 2003, Jeff Bach, perhaps the preeminent contemporary historian of early Pennsylvania sectarian and communal groups, simply concluded that "Kelpius is difficult to assess."[15]

Some less cautious scholarship has compounded the issue, blending and blurring the historical Kelpius with the more legendary details that have sprung up around him. Rather than point an accusatory finger at a number of otherwise admirable intellectual projects, here is a single example: in the leading undergraduate textbook on American religious history, Catherine Albanese's *America: Religion and Religions*, Kelpius and his companions are described as practicing "witchcraft . . . the religion of nature that had once dominated Europe and had only gradually yielded to Christianity."[16] Albanese's characterization of Kelpius as a witch has appeared in all five editions of *America*.

Our dim historical memory of Kelpius and the hesitation of scholars to cut back against the strata of folklore and legend have turned him into a kind of tabula rasa for an American occult tradition in search of an origin story from the earliest period in American history, a uniquely American spin on Wouter Hanegraaff's suggestion that esotericism is always grounded in a discourse of "ancient wisdom."[17] The Wissahickon hermitage of Kelpius and his followers has been the Edenic blank page in history books where generations of American occultists could write their own legitimizing Genesis story. Throughout the nineteenth and twentieth centuries up until the present day, practicing Rosicrucians, Kabbalists, and occultists of all kinds have rushed to claim Kelpius and his companions as their institutional heritage and, perhaps more interesting, the source of their unique national and religious identity as *American* occultists.

Kelpius and company are a vibrant memory in a number of American esoteric religions. In a creative and endearing twist on the more typical children's pageants commemorating the Pilgrims' arrival at Plymouth Rock, the Church Universal and Triumphant (best known for constructing and inhabiting bunkers in Montana in the 1980s in anticipation of a nuclear war) used to put on an annual children's pageant commemorating the arrival of the Wissahickon hermits in Philadelphia.[18] This was not the only twentieth-century pageant commemorating the Kelpius group—in 1908, a historical pageant commemorating the founding

Figure I.2 An engraved stone monument next to a root cellar in Wissahickon Valley Park, erected in 1961 by the AMORC. The information on the stone is largely derived from the work of Julius Sachse. Author's photograph, June 2021.

of Philadelphia included the "German Mystics and Pietists" among other groups like "the Scotch-Irish" and "Lenni Lenape Indians."[19] In 1961, the modern Rosicrucian Order AMORC (Ancient Mystical Order Rosae Crucis) erected a stone monument outside of a small root-cellar near the original Kelpius site, claiming Kelpius and the site as AMORC's first arrival in America (Figure I.2). The site itself has since become a location for legend-tripping, as a quick glance at the geotag "Cave of Kelpius" on any social media platform will confirm. The Johannes Kelpius Lodge of AMORC can be visited in Massachusetts today.

I frankly do not blame scholars who have misrepresented Kelpius in their work. The depth of misinformation is so overwhelming and the mixture of legendary and historical literature is so complete that it requires a book-length approach to the material to adequately sort it. But the situation is far from hopeless: despite the overwhelming volume of legendary material that encases the memory of Johannes Kelpius, there is a significant amount of primary source material from his own pen. We have a short diary, mostly in Latin, in which he details the circumstances of his journey to Pennsylvania. We have about ten letters of his correspondence (in Latin, German, and English), in which we can most vividly discern the outline of a brilliant young radical living through the tumult of the seventeenth century. We have a voluminous collection of original hymns and poetry, held in archives throughout Philadelphia. From his time in Europe, we have his dissertation on natural theology *Natural Theology, or, Metamorphosis of the Metaphysics*, an essay on the church fathers written with his teacher Johannes Fabricus (*Scylla Theologica*), and a long essay on Aristotle, *Pagan Ethics*.

Kelpius's influence and legacy are in fact vast, and the historical evidence from his own hand is far more abundant than it is for figures about whom much more has been written. Jeff Bach is correct when he writes, "Kelpius is difficult to assess," but this assessment should really not be so difficult, especially in a situation where a modern Protestant is portrayed as a witch in a leading textbook survey of the field, despite abundant and available evidence to the contrary. The historical Kelpius was, I think, much stranger and much more interesting than a colonial witch or the original wizard of the American occult tradition. Johannes Kelpius appears so warped and distorted in the lens of history not by accident, or malice, or lack of source material. We misremember Johannes Kelpius because the Enlightenment tradition that shaped our disciplines of knowledge has rendered the form of knowledge that Kelpius practiced profoundly alien to our modern sensibilities. And beneath the strata of wishful thinking, popular occultism, and folk memory, there exists a clear picture of an immensely influential religious ascetic in early America.

The Crisis of Piety

Without foreclosing constructive debate, the historical details of Kelpius's life are fairly straightforward and well documented, especially for a figure who has been the subject of such intense speculation. Johannes Kelpius was a theologian from Transylvania, from an ethnic community of German-speaking Lutherans, the Transylvanian Saxons. He moved to Germany as a young man and received an education in theology (a very broad topic at the time, including training in astronomy, math, and music) and achieved the high rank of Magister, the equivalent of a PhD. He authored numerous academic books and articles, and he could have easily taken on a fairly cushy post as a teacher, scholar, or minister. But at some point around or shortly after 1690, something in his life shifted dramatically.

Kelpius lived in a time and place in which new and fiercely pious forms of Christianity were flourishing, and orthodox church authorities found themselves facing emboldened popular Christian movements and vernacular theologies. In the broader historical scope of the period, Kelpius was born at the height of what historians increasingly recognize as a period of "general crisis," in which extreme climate change in Europe triggered wave after wave of famine, war, disease, and social unrest. The radical Protestantism of the seventeenth century was directly connected to the wider environmental crisis of the period.

10 INTRODUCTION

"Radical Protestantism" in the seventeenth century is a label with a wide scope. Throughout this book, I use the label "radical Protestant" to refer to truly dissenting Protestant factions, whose religious commitments put them in dangerous opposition to state and orthodox authorities. The early German Pietists, the English Quakers, and the English Philadelphians are the three main radical Protestant groups that appear in this book, but many other factions could be placed under the label. Each of these groups can be understood as responses to what historians call the seventeenth-century interdenominational "crisis of piety," a deep divide between the Christian life and practice of the laity—everyday people—and the increasingly academic and hierarchical theology of the orthodox church authorities.[20]

Kelpius was an early adherent of Pietism, which began in the seventeenth century with Kelpius's own denomination, German Lutheranism. Pietism, which will be explored more fully in the first chapter, was an early evangelical movement that responded to the consolidation of hierarchy and orthodoxy in the Lutheran church by emphasizing a deeply personal and emotional connection to God. By the eighteenth century, later Pietist leaders like Gottfried Arnold would take steps toward a reconciliation with orthodoxy, bringing their evangelical perspective into the ranks of Lutheran theology, where it remained influential right up to the work of major Pietist-educated theologians like Friedrich Schleiermacher. But during its origins in the late seventeenth century, Pietism was a truly radical movement that incorporated the alchemical and Hermetic thought of figures like Paracelsus and Jacob Böhme into its own Protestant worldview. During this period, radical Pietists published their criticisms against the church openly, accusing Lutheran leadership of hypocrisy and sin. In the most extreme corners, seventeenth-century radical Pietists accused the Lutheran church of being the Antichrist on earth: an accusation that could result in imprisonment, banishment, or execution. Although the primary record does not preserve all the details of Kelpius's affiliation with the Pietists, one thing is clear: by 1693, Kelpius was publicly associated with the most extreme Pietists in Europe, with whom he made arrangements to flee the continent under threat from orthodox authorities. Kelpius was a deeply devoted Pietist, a title that he identified with in print and would defend throughout his life and correspondence.[21]

This early stage of Pietist religion and philosophy, during which the influence of alchemical and Hermetic literature was at its height, was a unique period in the history of Protestant Christianity. Many of the figures and texts that centered so prominently in Christian life during the period are studied today under the rubric of Western esotericism, a relatively recent scholarly field that has made great strides in understanding the history and literature of movements typically relegated to the "cultural wastebasket," as Wouter Hanegraaff puts it. In addition to Platonic and Neoplatonic literatures of the ancient world, Hermetic literature

INTRODUCTION   11

and ideas, translated and interpreted by Renaissance humanists, along with older European forms of alchemical Hermeticism derived from Arabic sources and Neoplatonic mysticism in the Catholic tradition, proved deeply influential in European popular culture and Protestant thought throughout the early modern period.

Early modern Protestantism was a cultural amalgam of interrelated ancient and contemporary texts and ideas, read and reread through the circumstances of the people who practiced them. And in the seventeenth century, Christians were trying to understand their changing environment. Throughout the period, the effects of what historians now call the Little Ice Age had wrought unprecedented changes to the environment of Europe. Geoffrey Parker, the leading historian of the global cultural impact of climate change in the seventeenth century, summarizes its effects during the period: "Around 1618, when the human population of the northern hemisphere was larger than ever before, the average global temperature started to fall, producing extreme climate events, disastrous harvest failures and frequent disease epidemics."[22] At the very same time, perceptible celestial and earthly phenomena began to change: the century was a period of increased meteor activity in the earth's atmosphere, and more frequent comets and eclipses. Increased volcanic activity during the period darkened the sky for decades and even changed the color of the sun to pale red.[23] As we might expect, these dramatic environmental phenomena were consistently interpreted in religious frames of reference in sources from the period. For the people who lived through them, the environmental changes of the seventeenth century demanded religious attention.

Hermetic literature and ideas offered a perspective on these environmental changes that prevailing orthodox philosophies often did not. We can understand this Hermetic perspective, in part, by reading the orthodox heresiologists who criticized it. The German Lutheran theologian Jacob Thomasius singled out what he saw as the dangerous influence of Hermetic and Platonic literature, "paganism," as he called it, on proper Christian thought. The first was the Hermetic belief that God was really present in the cosmos—specifically, that "the world was co-eternal with God, as opposed to the doctrine of *creatio ex nihilo*," as Wouter Hanegraaff writes. The second error of these Platonic and Hermetic Christians was the belief that God's presence in the cosmos allowed for a sensory, experiential contact with divinity, both in the cosmos and in the microcosmos of the human body.[24] As Hanegraaff points out, Thomasius's heresiological perspective—biased as it is—was historically and philosophically accurate enough that it "may still furnish us with the fundamentals of what can usefully be called Western esotericism."[25]

Wouter Hanegraaff followed the Egyptologist Jan Assman in describing this worldview as *cosmotheism*: the "fundamental assumption," he writes, of the

Hermetic writings that the "divine is at home in the world."[26] Compared to orthodox Lutheranism, the religious perspective of these ancient pagan sources was decidedly worldly: it was, as the historian Frances Yates called it, a "religion of the world," in which the cosmos and the body were not excluded from divinity. This religion of the world seemed to land directly "in a Europe devastated by the awful wars and persecutions arising from the conflict between Reformation and Catholic reaction," as Yates writes. In addition to the wars of religion she describes, we can see how the shifting extreme environmental changes of the period would have made the environmentally attuned religion of the Hermetic literature interesting to people living through the early modern period: "Men were turning to the Hermetic religion of the world to take them above these conflicts," Yates writes.[27]

Once the basic resonances are noted, the connections between the environmental circumstances of the seventeenth century and the proliferation of popular Hermetic and alchemical ideas becomes clear. I think this is a missed opportunity for scholars of esotericism, who do not often locate their analyses in the history of environmental thought, since this is exactly where many environmental historians locate the very same subjects. Phillip Blom spends a good deal of time with Giordano Bruno and John Dee in his 2017 book *Nature's Mutiny: How the Little Ice Age of the Long Seventeenth Century Transformed the West and Shaped the Present*, showing how a changing environment shaped novel religious attitudes toward the cosmos. The single most important example of this is Carolyn Merchant's *The Death of Nature: Women, Ecology, and the Scientific Revolution*, a monumental intellectual history of early modern European attitudes toward the environment that relies overwhelmingly on the analysis of leading Renaissance and early modern authors (Marsilio Ficino, Pico della Mirandola, Giordano Bruno, Heinrich Cornielus Agrippa, Paracelsus) who resisted an increasingly mechanistic philosophy on the basis of essentially Hermetic and Platonic ideas. In a period of drastic environmental change and popular suspicion of orthodoxy, it is small wonder that Hermetic ideas became so popular.[28]

Environment and Apocalypse

This book is not only a history of Kelpius and an analysis of his thought in light of new trends in the study of early modern climate change and Hermetic spirituality. These histories form the basis of a theoretical framework through which I interpret literature from across the early modern Atlantic world, from seventeenth-century Hermetic Protestantism in Europe and Pennsylvania, to the body of American literature centered in and around Philadelphia that tried

INTRODUCTION   13

to make sense of one particular Hermetic Protestant, Johannes Kelpius, through the centuries that followed.

Throughout this book, I refer to a particular form of knowing that appears in early modern Protestant literature as "environmental knowledge," an original phrase by which I mean something specific. The concept of "the environment" and the English word we use today were not in use during Kelpius's lifetime nor for more than a century after.[29] I use the anachronistic phrase "environmental knowledge" to refer specifically to these early modern practices of Hermetically inflected contemplation and interpretation of the cosmos, "the world" that Yates sees at the core of Hermetic literature and the Christians who made use of such literature. Although largely elaborated in an alchemical context by authors like Paracelsus and Johann Arndt, this environmental knowledge was distinct from the modern sciences in precisely the ways shown by the difference in interpretation we have seen between the "extraordinary meteor" of *Hazard's Gazette* and the "pale comet" in the same area a few decades earlier. Hermetic Protestant practices of environmental knowledge treated the cosmos as a vital, sacred thing that contained real knowledge, like a dream inviting interpretation, rather than an object passively inviting one-sided scrutiny in the scientific mode. I will explore the genealogy of this form of knowledge and its use among seventeenth-century German Pietists more thoroughly in the first chapter. For now, it suffices to say that when Kelpius invites his reader "to observe every new Phoenomena, Meteors, Stars and various Colours of the Skei," he is not asking for scientific observations: he is inviting a process of contemplation of the cosmos, a hermeneutic process that yielded personal meaning and religious insight. I call this Hermetically inflected form of early modern Protestant knowing "environmental knowledge."

Within this rubric of knowledge and in the writings of Kelpius and his immediate milieu, certain environmental phenomena invited more interpretation than others. In a period when the sun changed color and comets and eclipses blazed in the sky, certain environmental phenomena seemed to *beg* interpretation. The world itself seemed to be trying to communicate. These environmental wonders in the macrocosm of the world had their mirror image in the microcosm of the human body and soul. In one 1699 letter, Kelpius sees the relationship between environmental wonders and inner revelation as an essentially alchemical reflection of the analogous relationship between the human and the cosmos: "As the Miracles wrought by God through the Hand of Moyses was for the main part in the outward Creation or Macrocosm, the Miracles of Jesus the Messia on the Bodys of Man or Microcosm," he writes, "so these in our days was wrought (much like unto them in the days of the Apostles) on the Soul and more interiour parts by Ectases, Revelations, Inspirations."[30] Kelpius and his radical Pietist colleagues were obsessed with signs of God's presence and goodwill,

14 INTRODUCTION

which might take the form of phenomena in the macrocosm of "the Skei" just as they might ripple through the microcosm: the human body, and the "interiour parts" like the soul.

The experience and interpretation of miraculous phenomena is a central theme in Kelpius's own writings and the writings of later American authors who would try to make sense of his memory and legacy. The early Pietists appeared during a period in which the very existence of the supernatural (a concept codified by medieval scholastics with an interest in visible confirmations of phenomena beyond the order of nature for the purposes of verifying beatific claims) was in question in some corners of Enlightenment Europe.[31] On one end of the spectrum were Protestants who saw all supernatural manifestations as signs of demonic influence. Cotton Mather argued as much in *Wonders of the Invisible World* in 1693, published the same year Kelpius left Europe for Pennsylvania.

Early radical Pietists had a completely different perspective on supernatural phenomena, both environmental and interior, which they interpreted as meaningful signals of divine attention, intervention, and goodwill. Their reasons for doing so were simple: they noticed that such phenomena were of deep personal significance to the earliest Christians, whom they saw as practicing a form of Christianity uncorrupted by orthodoxy. Early Christian histories like the Acts of the Apostles were relatively clear in their sanction of miraculous phenomena. As Kelpius wrote of his own experience among the early Pietists, not "since the days of the Apostles" have "such Miraculous Powers and operations . . . been manifested as in a matter of 3½ years among [the early Pietists]."[32]

The early Pietists were by no means unique in paying special attention to these phenomena. During my research for this book, I noticed a consistent refrain among the major historians of this particular period regarding the sheer volume of primary source material on supernatural phenomena. C. V. Wedgewood saw such phenomena as a crucial backdrop to early modern Europe in *The Thirty Years War*: "Miracles once again made the life of everyday bright with hope," she writes of seventeenth-century Europe. "The changes of the material world, the breakdown of old tradition and the insufficiency of dying conventions drove men and women to the spiritual and the inexplicable."[33] Bernard Bailyn notes the same of seventeenth-century colonial sources generally: "The environment, human and physical, was unpredictable, threatening, and miraculous." Life in the seventeenth century was a "struggle against hidden, occult forces," a struggle that cut across boundaries of nation-state and class.[34] Jill Lepore's history of King Philip's War, *The Name of War*, finds New England colonists overwhelmingly concerned with interpreting supernatural patterns in the world around them as their war with the Algonquins persisted. The only reliable source of knowledge for many of these colonists came through "the world of the occult," as Lepore writes. "Supernatural messages in the natural world," Lepore finds, were the only legible clues to the meaning of their sufferings. As war and climate change persisted, extraordinary environmental phenomena were crucial reservoirs of meaning and relation in the seventeenth century. As one of her colonial sources, Mary Pray, wrote: "We . . . know not what to do; but our eyes are upward."[35] Kelpius would have known *exactly* what Mary meant.

I could go on and on, but the major historians of the period have already confirmed this phenomenon abundantly in their sources. In a period when elite perspectives and interpretations of such phenomena ranged from the infernal to outright denial, common people were surprisingly consistent, taking extraordinary environmental phenomena seriously as a matter of religious interpretation and personal reflection. Amitav Ghosh has recently pointed out this exact phenomenon during the seventeenth century in his 2019 novel *Gun Island*: "It would seem that the intellectual titans of the Enlightenment had no inkling of what was getting under way. And yet, strangely, all around the earth, ordinary people appear to have sensed the stirring of something momentous."[36] Wedgewood, Lepore, and Bailyn's archives seem to confirm Ghosh's claim: intellectual trends in orthodoxy and Enlightenment had little bearing on the attitudes of ordinary people, who overwhelmingly interpreted extraordinary environmental phenomena as "supernatural messages," as meaningful signals to be interpreted and understood. The cosmos was animate, intelligent, and ready to talk: people like Mary Pray and Johannes Kelpius were listening.

We see a variety of perspectives on such phenomena throughout this book, and the medieval and modern taxonomies of the miracle, wonder, supernatural, preternatural, and anomaly are on vivid display.[37] Without erasing the meaningful differences between these ways of understanding these events, I use the word "paranormal" to describe them when they arise in my sources. Like my use of the word "environment," my use of the word "paranormal" is an intentionally anachronistic analytical category, meant to reflect the real ambiguity of these phenomena in the sources. I do so following the scholar of medieval Icelandic literature Ármann Jakobsson, who argues that "the term *paranormal* is fitting precisely . . . because it cannot be taken for granted, dismissed as a traditional or conventional term that can be deployed without intense scrutiny."[38] As the findings of historians like Wedgewood, Lepore, and Bailyn make abundantly clear, paranormal phenomena may have been common in the early modern period, but they were *never* mundane, everyday, or taken for granted, especially by the common people who found in them such deep wells of meaning. The line between a miracle, an anomaly, and a yet-to-be-understood natural phenomenon was blurry in the early modern period, and a harsh anachronism like "paranormal" preserves those ambiguities while still describing the basic content of the phenomena for those who experienced and wrote about them. It also helps to relate to later cultural trends some of the phenomena that Kelpius and his colleagues describe: as

16 INTRODUCTION

we will see, the very earliest descriptions of what would later be known as telepathy appear in the writings of Kelpius and his closest friends.

Even as Kelpius uses the word "miracle" when describing such events in English, his overwhelmingly interpretive approach to the subject strains a straightforward understanding of such events as "miracles." Biblical miracles, as a rule, were *rarely* ambiguous. A biblical miracle was self-evident: the Son of God feeding the multitude, calming the storm, or healing the sick does not require much introspection. These New Testament miracles carried no interpretive challenge; indeed, their lack of ambiguity was the whole point: they presented Jesus Christ wielding an unambiguously divine power over the environment.

The appearance of, say, a comet, or an apparition of any kind, was more complicated. The event itself is phenomenologically abundant and yet the meaning is secret, embedded in the text of the Book of Nature rather than some other scripture. The environmental phenomena in this archive of early modern Protestantism are often ambiguous. As Daniel Schuhmacher recommended to his readers after describing the pale comet over Pennsylvania in 1769: "ask yourselves what this star may mean." There is a deep difference between meaning presented on an ancient page and meaning presented in waking life. In the interpretative challenge of paranormal phenomena in early modernity, we can see how the environment functions like text or art: it comes alive in the connection between event and witness, phenomenon and observation, performance and critique, object and subject.

This interpretive act is the basis for the third and final aspect of my theoretical framework in this book. Kelpius and his colleagues have often been remembered as "apocalyptic" in their attitudes: that is, they were concerned with the decline of the cosmos and the end of history. While popular retellings of Kelpius's life drastically overstate the precision of their expectation for this event, Kelpius was certainly motivated by an understanding that his period in history was, in some sense, an ultimate period in history, and that a climax of some kind was approaching. But Kelpius shared this perspective with almost every living Christian since Paul the apostle. Kelpius's eschatology is much too complex to suggest that he simply expected the world to end imminently: instead, he openly hoped for a universal restoration of creation, a "great Jubelee or Restitation of all things," as he called it, following the Pietist author and visionary Johanna Eleonora Petersen.

There is another, more accurate way of describing Kelpius's religion and philosophy as essentially apocalyptic. The early Pietist and Hermetic Protestant milieu of the late seventeenth century was overwhelmingly concerned with the interpretation and understanding of the environment, particularly paranormal environmental phenomena, as a meaningful source of divine knowledge. Its participants also prized special states of revelatory consciousness in which such knowledge required no environmental sign: special states they called "ecstasies" in which the body and mind became a vessel for direct communion with God. As we will see, many of Kelpius's closest friends and colleagues were well known as ecstatics with paranormal powers among the early Pietists. This form of revelatory knowledge is, historically, the basis for the biblical genre of *apocalyptic*, special discourses of secret divine knowledge acquired in revelatory states of consciousness. As the author of the biblical book of Revelation, wrote: "I John . . . was in the isle that is called Patmos, for the word of God, and for the testimony of Jesus Christ. I was in the Spirit on the Lord's day, and heard behind me a great voice, as of a trumpet."[39] John connects his knowledge directly to this special state of awareness, to being "in the spirit," in which he could hear the trumpet-voice.

The historian and scholar of mysticism Eliot Wolfson defines "apocalyptic" as "the revelation of divine mysteries through the agency of visions, dreams, and other paranormal states of consciousness."[40] In this book, I follow Wolfson's definition, but I supplement his useful definition with Kelpius's own understanding: that such "visions, dreams, and other paranormal states of consciousness" are one side of the apocalyptic coin. For Kelpius, the revelations in the Hermetic microcosm of the body and soul were reflected in the macrocosm of the environment, the cosmos itself, plants, animals, and the sky, in which Kelpius and company found an equal source of special knowledge, of profound personal meaning, of a waking dream inviting contemplation and understanding: the world was a living apocalyptic text that demanded interpretation.

These interlocking themes of environment and apocalypse, interpretation of the cosmos through special hermeneutic attention to those extraordinary events that seem to call for it, form the basis of my analysis in this book. As we will see, these themes occur and recur throughout the milieu, life, and legacy of Kelpius and his immediate colleagues. As the seventeenth century closed and the Little Ice Age ended, the eighteenth century would bring entirely new disciplines of knowledge to the forefront of intellectual culture: disciplines that often demand the excision not only of paranormal phenomena but of *any* form of ambiguity or hermeneutic interpretation. This tectonic shift in the human understanding of and approach to the environment is, I argue, the central reason that Kelpius— and the form of knowledge that he practiced—remains so stubbornly "difficult to assess," as Jeff Bach writes, why he continues to thwart clear scholarly understanding despite his active pen and straightforward biography.

Global Crisis

It is difficult to avoid reading echoes of our present moment into the environmental and social conditions of the seventeenth century and the life of Johannes

18 INTRODUCTION

Kelpius. As Geoffrey Parker and others have shown, the seventeenth century was a period of "general crisis," in which extreme climatic conditions led to economic collapse, social unrest, and global conflict.[41] I will explore some of the more specific manifestations of this general crisis in southwestern Germany in the first chapter, in particular how the devastation of southwestern Germany (the Palatinate and Württemberg) led to a surge in Pietism, the radical devotional movement within Protestantism in which Kelpius was swept up. But as Kelpius himself notes, Pietism was one manifestation of a much more general religious awakening throughout Europe during the period: "If now this late Revolution in Europe," he wrote in 1699, "which in the Roman Church goes under the Name of Quietism, in the Protestant Church under the Name of Pietism, Chiliasm, and Philadelphianism."[42] Even for those living through it, the specific manifestations of the seventeenth-century crisis felt like moving parts of something much bigger, an ambient state of unsettlement that shook human institutions even as it shook the firmament of the earth and the stars out of the sky.

Kyle Harper notes a similar pattern during a completely different period in his 2017 book *The Fate of Rome*, in which he points to hints of a changing climate in connection with economic collapse, religious fervor, and a global pandemic. As Harper writes, "A precociously global world, where the revenge of nature begins to make itself felt, despite persistent illusions of control . . . this might feel not so unfamiliar."[43] Indeed, it certainly would not have felt unfamiliar to Johannes Kelpius, who consistently noted environmental and cultural phenomena as signs of the general crisis unfolding around him.

The connections between these periods and our own seem so simple that my instincts tell me that it *must* be more complicated. It *is* more complicated. Andreas Malm, writing in 2020, warns us against such simple historical arithmetic, pointing out that "this time is qualitatively different," because "non-anthropogenic climate change cannot be compared to global heating, any more than a pub crawl to a genocide."[44] And Malm is right: the scale of historical, technological, and climatological difference between these periods seems almost to defy comparison.

Malm is right to caution us that this time is different, and yet we might still see something of ourselves in Kelpius: a refugee, a radical, a desperate individual working to hold a community together while the climate changed, institutions failed, and both global and local crises multiplied. As I write this introduction, I am reminded of C. V. Wedgwood's remark at the beginning of *The Thirty Years War*:

> History reflects the period in which it was written as much as any other branch of literature. Although the historian's material is much more rigidly

circumscribed than that of the novelist or poet, he, like them, has to bring to the understanding of presentation of his material his own experience of life and the imaginative equipment peculiar to him and his time.[45]

It likely is not a coincidence, then, that as I turned to this particular archive while living through catastrophes like Hurricane Harvey in Houston, and first wrote the bulk of the material here under lockdown in Texas during the coronavirus pandemic, that the themes of environment and apocalypse loomed large in my thought and writing. But the opposite is true, too. As I pursued topics for research, one of the things that kept bringing me back to Kelpius was precisely his particular attention to themes of such contemporary relevance: environmental catastrophe, institutional decline, and the looming sense that one is living through a transitional period in history, to put it mildly.

None of this is to say that Kelpius's particular environmental knowledge is directly applicable to the current ecological crisis. I am interested in reading Kelpius today not because reading him might lead us to strategies for mitigating catastrophic climate change—we already have those, and merely lack the political will to implement them. I am interested in reading Kelpius to see what he might tell us about living through the end of a particular world, and what comes after.

This book is divided into six chapters and three shorter sections each called a "vita," which offer supplementary biographical information about Kelpius. These vitae appear between Chapters 1 and 2, 2 and 3, and 4 and 5, sketching out and filling in the details of the life of Kelpius amid my broader analysis of his world. These shorter sections let me scratch the itch of writing simple biography without letting the narrative of Kelpius's life overwhelm the analyses that take place in the main chapters.

The first two chapters serve as literature reviews and contextual analysis that offer their own arguments. The first chapter, " 'No Wisdom in Nature': Ecology, Enthusiasm, and Esotericism in Early Modern Europe," sketches the history of German Pietism in the wake of the Thirty Years War and the general crisis of the seventeenth century before turning directly to a series of authors whose work forms the basis of what I call Hermetic Protestantism in Europe: Paracelsus, Johann Arndt, Jacob Böhme, Johann Zimmerman, and Johannes Kelpius. This chapter argues, simply but originally, that early modern authors sought out Hermetic ideas and teachings for their insight on their environment during a period when the cosmos itself seemed to be subject to inexorable decline.

The second chapter, " 'Gone into the Ancient Forest': Hermetic Protestantism and Environmental Knowledge in Early Pennsylvania," follows these texts across the Atlantic to the English Quaker colony in Lenape territory that became Penn's

20 INTRODUCTION

Woods in the seventeenth century. Drawing on a deep archive of colonial literature including manuscripts, almanacs, and the writings of public figures like Francis Pastorius and Daniel Leeds, this chapter argues that a vernacular undercurrent of Hermetic Protestantism flourished in Pennsylvania beneath the elite religious and philosophical trends of the period.

The third chapter, " 'The Woman in the Wilderness': Kelpius and Company on the Ridge of the Wissahickon, 1694–1707," is an analysis of the surviving primary record of Kelpius, his companions, and their lives in Pennsylvania at the end of the seventeenth century and the early eighteenth century. This chapter does not offer a single argument like the previous two, but rather serves as a sustained response to the centuries of speculative scholarship, antiquarian reconstruction, and occult enthusiasm surrounding the life of Kelpius and his community in Pennsylvania. In this chapter I simply read the primary sources, locate them in context, and try to let them speak for themselves.

The fourth chapter, " 'The Threefold Wilderness State': Ascetic Alchemy and the Technology of Self-Negation," is a deep dive into the late theology of Johannes Kelpius through a close reading of a 1706 letter in which he outlines a tripartite system of spiritual development he calls "the Threefold Wilderness State." This text, which was copied, reprinted, and distributed among the more radical scenes of Philadelphia Quakerdom during the eighteenth century, reveals Kelpius's mature religious thought, the culmination of more than a decade of ascetic labor on the cliff of the Wissahickon, a deeply alchemical and ascetic reading of the Bible, his body, and his environment, with an eye toward spiritual and bodily transformation and eventually self-negation. As the great nineteenth-century scholar of German literature Oswald Seidensticker noted, Kelpius's late religious thought was at times "more reminiscent of Plotinus than Christianity."

The last two chapters turn a corner in the narrative, attending to the memory of Kelpius in the decades following his death in the eighteenth century, following his legendary and historical profile as it swells and distorts beneath layers of folklore, fiction, and memory. The fifth chapter, "The Long Shadow of the Enlightenment: Memories of Kelpius in Charles Brockden Brown's *Wieland* (1798)," focuses entirely on what I consider to be the most robust and influential posthumous appearance of Johannes Kelpius: the Philadelphia Quaker novelist Charles Brockden Brown's 1798 novel *Wieland; or, The Transformation: An American Tale*. This chapter explores the ways in which Brown recovers and portrays Kelpius's memory in his novel, a profound twofold critique of traditional religion and the hubristic excesses of Enlightenment rationality in the eighteenth century, in which the challenge of interpreting paranormal phenomena was placed at the center of early American life.

The sixth and final chapter, " 'Weird as a Wizard': History and Literature in the Emergence of the American Kelpius Legend," is a genealogy of Kelpius's afterlife in print, excavating his posthumous appearances in religious literature, popular fiction, and poetry, and by the nineteenth century, popular occult literature in which Kelpius and his companions were portrayed as the founders of and legitimation for an American occult tradition. This chapter shows how the historical sources remain remarkably accurate and consistent until they collide and blur with a more imaginative literature in the nineteenth century, leaving us with the image of Kelpius we meet today in popular *and* scholarly literature: at once a Pietist and a witch, a Christian and a wizard, a character in Romantic poetry who really existed: ultimately, an ambient, spectral presence in the city of Philadelphia and the historiography of American religion.

Johannes Kelpius identified and advanced a consistent religious and philosophical position throughout his body of work, a position that is as worthy of consideration by contemporary readers as it was to early modern religious radicals. One does not need to commit to an ascetic regimen, witness miracles, or even be a Christian to identify with the basic impulse behind much of Johannes Kelpius's life and thought, a way of knowledge that he derived from ancient pagan sources and from texts of the Christian tradition, like the Acts of the Apostles and the letters of Paul: that the cosmos encloses and discloses real hermeneutic content, that contemplation of the environment can yield moral and metaphysical meaning for the human subject, *that the world is actually communicating right now.*

Today, human minds are the only location where meaning is created, from which we distribute this finite resource throughout our lives, works of art, and in our experience of the world. In the cosmotheist Christianity of Johannes Kelpius and his colleagues, meaning flowed in the opposite direction, *originating* in the cosmos—where the observations and interpretations of human beings could locate and understand it. Following the Enlightenment's location of the human intellect as the source of meaning and knowledge, this kind of knowledge has fallen so far out of vogue as to be incomprehensible. But it was never entirely lost. As the work of Brett Grainger makes clear, early American Protestants retained a strong capacity for environmental knowledge through the eighteenth and nineteenth centuries, inspired in part by many of the same authors who inspired Kelpius and his colleagues: Paracelsus, Arndt, and Böhme.[46]

In the same way that Freud, centuries later, saw the content of dreams and the practice of dream interpretation as a "royal road" to insights and wisdom locked in the unconscious, Kelpius, his colleagues, and his intellectual forebears saw the waking world, the cosmos, their own environments, as a book *meant for us to read*, and as a source of knowledge, beauty, wisdom, solace, and meaning. The stations of the stars and the paths of the planets, the eruptions of comets and pale terror of the eclipse, the potency of plants, the behavior of animals, the physical

22   INTRODUCTION

sensations and awareness of the body, and especially those special phenomena or experiences that seemed to be beyond the ordinary course of nature, were all moments that merited special attention, contemplation, and introspection as sources of knowledge. Following the Egyptologist Jan Assman, I cannot help but wonder: "Perhaps the ancients not only saw much that is important to us today but also knew much that we, in the meantime, have forgotten."[47]

1

"No Wisdom in Nature"

Esotericism, Enthusiasm, and Ecology in Early Modern Europe

The heavens declare the glory of God;
And the firmament sheweth his handywork.
Day unto day uttereth speech,
And night unto night sheweth knowledge.

—Psalm 19

Extraordinary Heavenly Phenomena

It was late in the month of November, in 1680, in the city of Nuremberg, and Johann Jacob Zimmermann (1642–1693) was looking at the sky, which had torn itself in half. He was frantically adjusting, readjusting, and looking into his telescope, while writing: "On November 23, after the seventeenth hour according to astronomical calculation; or on November 24 in the morning after five o'clock, according to the common calculation, it [the comet] appeared slightly later than yesterday. . . . The distance of the comet from the bright midnight stars in Libra was measured."[1]

Zimmerman went on to systematically measure and record every detail of the comet that he could: tangents, radii, times, dates, and locations. His observations and measurements were so systematic and precise that they would appear decades later in the third edition of Isaac Newton's *Principia Mathematica* as detailed records of the appearance of the object that today's astronomers call C/1680 V1, the Great Comet of 1680: "Nov 23, O. S. at 5h. morning, at Nuremberg (that is, at 4 1/2. at London), *Mr. Zimmerman* saw the comet in [scorpio] 8° 8′, with 2°3′ south lat., its place being collected by taking its distances from fixed stars."[2] And so Johann Zimmerman, a provincial astronomer, pastor, and religious radical, permanently entered the history of science. But it was a science that, as we will see, he both admired and ultimately resented.

Paintings and illustrations of the comet, composed contemporaneously in Nuremberg, recorded the sight as Zimmerman would have seen it. In one local depiction, the comet's tail arcs at a close angle with the horizon, cleaving

American Aurora. Timothy Grieve-Carlson, Oxford University Press. © Oxford University Press 2024.
DOI: 10.1093/oso/9780197765562.003.0002

Figure 1.1 *Illustration and Description of the Wonderful Incomparable Comet.* Nuremberg: Schollenberger, 1680. Munich, Bavarian State Library.

the dark sky in two with an impossibly wide ray of white light at a steep gradient, as though the very dome of heaven was opening overhead. A crowd of onlookers jostles from their position somewhere in the countryside beyond the city: one of them is looking through a small handheld telescope (Figure 1.1).[3]

Lieve Verschuier's painting of the Great Comet of 1680 illustrates the scene from Rotterdam, which was (astronomically speaking) quite close to Zimmerman's position (Figure 1.2). Verschuier depicts a clutch of Dutch astronomers crowded around the edge of a canal to get a better look. In Verschuier's rendition of the comet, the great sungrazer's tail cuts almost straight up from the horizon, carving a nearly perpendicular rent in the night sky: a shining tear on the pages of the Book of Nature. A crowd of men holding cross-staffs, a handheld navigation tool, are crowded around the edge of a canal, from which they can see the aurora unencumbered by buildings. Their instruments seem to teeter, unwieldy in their hands, suggesting perhaps the latent absurdity of their purpose in Verschuier's portrayal: How could such little creatures really know something so awful and great? How could a human being presume to read God's mind?

Zimmerman's measurements appeared in his 1681 book *Cometo-Scopia, or Observations on the Heavens*, in which he offered some interpretation of the meaning of events like the Great Comet of 1680, alongside the data that so interested people like Newton:

Figure 1.2 *Staartster (komeet) boven Rotterdam*, Lieve Verschuier, Museum Rotterdam 11028-AB. https://museumrotterdam.nl/collectie/item/11028-A-B.

> The sky, says Daniel, proclaims God's glory and the strength of his handiwork (Psalm 19). How often now it is the same, in the ordinary course of nature, for God is powerful at all times, wisdom and goodness be praised, that God lets justice shine through extraordinary heavenly phenomena.[4]

Despite being a work of astronomy, *Cometo-Scopia* offered extensive theological reflections on the meaning of the Great Comet and of "extraordinary heavenly phenomena" generally. Zimmerman read scripture through his astronomical data, taking cues from a long biblical tradition of prophetic and apocalyptic sky-watching. Finally, he offered a conclusive moral and religious analysis of the Great Comet of 1680: that the appearance of the comet spelled the doom of "the spiritual Babylon of Europe" and a prophecy: that something terrible would happen in the year 1693.[5]

In his observance of the Great Comet of 1680, Johann Zimmerman drew on a deep heritage of Christian techniques for deriving religious insight from environmental knowledge. Zimmerman was far from the only Christian interpreter of this particular event.[6] Celestial phenomena generally were a matter of severe religious importance across Christendom: and indeed, for German-speakers like Zimmerman and Kelpius, "sky" and "heaven" are simply synonymous: *die Himmel.* The skies are always the heavens, and a German conversation about the sky will always sound religious.

But the German language is not unique in this association. Throughout the history of Christianity, the sky has been recognized as a place where lights could serve for symbolic communication between people and divine intermediaries. This particular pattern of environmental knowledge stretches back far earlier than Christianity, to the authors of Genesis, who indicated a belief that the *purpose* of the sky itself was for "signs," for meaningful communication between divine and human beings. As the King James Bible put it, "God said, Let there be lights in the firmament of the heavens to divide the day from the night; and let them be for signs."[7]

In his 2011 translation of Genesis, Hebrew Bible scholar Edwin Good translates this passage in a more contemporary and illuminating idiom: "Elohim said, 'Let there be lightgivers in the bowlshape of Sky to make division between Day and Night, and let them be for portents and for set times and for days and years.' "[8] In Good's translation, Elohim purposefully designs the sky as a place of "lightgivers," who serve two complementary roles. First, the lightgivers organize earthly experience temporally, into units like days and nights, months and years. Lightgivers lend structure and coherence to life on earth by arranging time into intelligible patterns. Second, lightgivers act as "portents," or as media of important or significant information that is either directly from God (like the postdiluvian rainbow) or prophetic information: knowledge of the future. In the Hebrew Bible, lightgivers both arrange time for human beings and allow them opportunities to actually transcend their temporal limitations by accessing future information, all by witnessing and interpreting luminous forms in the sky. From the writing of Genesis to the seventeenth century, the sky has consistently been understood as a location for communication between human beings and divinities.

But why was *this* German theologian, sitting between the cutting edges of the natural sciences and natural theology at the end of the seventeenth century, looking up at a light in the sky and working to decipher what God meant? Zimmerman was not unique in his religious focus on the sky and on "extraordinary heavenly phenomena." However, his particular approach to these phenomena *was* unique and radical for his time. Zimmerman's interpretation of the heavens, including the Great Comet of 1680, was overwhelmingly shaped by the Protestant reception of alchemical and Hermetic literatures over the past few centuries. It was this heritage, these techniques of knowing God through perceiving the environment, that Johannes Kelpius adopted and carried with him to Pennsylvania in 1693, a voyage that was motivated in part by the political

"NO WISDOM IN NATURE" 27

consequences of Zimmerman's observance of the Great Comet of 1680 and his ensuing apocalyptic speculations. The prophetic statements that Zimmerman derived from this comet were so consequential, in fact, that almost every event that follows in this book (with the exception of further contextual elaboration in the next chapter) can be traced back, at least in part, to Johann Zimmerman's interpretation of the Great Comet of 1680.

In this chapter I read Kelpius alongside his intellectual precedents and contexts, focusing on the influence of alchemical and Hermetic ideas on seventeenth-century German Pietism. I locate these religious and intellectual movements in their context of climate change and global crisis. In doing so, I argue that the Protestant reception of alchemy and Hermetic philosophy in the sixteenth and seventeenth centuries led to the development of religious practices of intuition and contemplation of the environment, practices that I call Hermetic Protestant environmental knowledge. Seventeenth-century Protestants like Kelpius sought out Hermetic and alchemical literature *because* it offered an environmental knowledge applicable to a changing climate. These concurrent readings offer a theoretical and historical foundation for understanding the intellectual context and heritage of Johannes Kelpius.

The Crises of Early Modernity

Zimmerman's observation of the Great Comet coincided with the peak of the Little Ice Age, a period of sustained cooling in the northern hemisphere that followed the Medieval Warm Period. Although precise estimates vary, ice core and tree ring data suggest that the average temperature in Europe began to drop during the Middle Ages and continued to fall until the decline reached its peak toward the latter half of the seventeenth century.[9] The late seventeenth century in particular was a period of severe cold. Winters during these decades were, Geoffrey Parker writes, "more than 1°C cooler than those of the later twentieth century," and most winters were closer to 2°C cooler than average.[10] While a two-degree average change over a few centuries might not seem like much, it is important to remember that these aggregate climate measurements represented colossal local effects. Climatologists now recognize the period between 1640s to the 1690s as "the longest as well as the most severe episode of global cooling recorded in the entire Holocene era," and the peak of the Little Ice Age.[11]

In addition to the drop in temperature, other environmental phenomena were unusually prominent during this period. Both meteor and comet activity increased dramatically. An analysis of historical reports of meteors and comets throughout the past two millennia in the *Journal of the International Meteor*

Association reserves its strongest language for the late seventeenth century, when it notes a period of "greatly enhanced" activity.[12] Global seismic activity also increased suddenly in the middle of the seventeenth century, including earthquakes and volcanic eruptions. Records from what is now Romania— the place where Johannes Kelpius was born and raised—report forty major earthquakes between 1600 and 1690.[13] Finally, as if all this was not enough, this increase in global seismic and volcanic activity threw enough sulfur dioxide into the stratosphere, where high winds and elevation kept it aloft, to dim the sun in the northern skies for decades. When it did appear, the sun of the late seventeenth-century sky shone through stratospheric sulfur dioxide in pale red, even in broad daylight.[14]

Throughout this period, as the temperature plunged, agricultural practices failed, and food shortages multiplied. Previously stable economies wavered as basic needs failed to be met. A period of sustained conflict ensued throughout Europe. The sociopolitical climate in Europe during and just prior to Kelpius's lifetime was overwhelmingly shaped by the Thirty Years War, a series of catastrophic political and religious conflicts that ravaged the continent from 1618 to 1648. The conflict lasted for a generation and played out on a continental scale, and any attempt to properly sketch the extent of the atrocities and their consequences would quickly escape the scope of this chapter. Writing in 2013, Geoffrey Parker estimated that about 40 percent of the rural population of Germany and about 33 percent of the urban population died between the years 1618 and 1648.[15] We can only imagine the reverberating suffering and social effects of such a genocidal conflict in these regions of Germany.

Of particular importance were the effects of the war in the southwestern German regions of Württemberg. This region was Zimmerman's homeland and the place where radical Pietism would achieve its fullest expression in the ensuing decades of the seventeenth century. The war also devastated the adjacent Palatinate, the border region from which most German immigrants to Pennsylvania would travel in the coming century. The human cost of the war varied throughout Europe, but there was no region of the continent that was more devastated by the effects of the war than these southwestern regions of Germany in which Zimmerman lived and from which the immigrants who appear in later chapters largely traveled. In the Palatinate and Württemberg, the two regions that would burn over repeatedly with the spiritual fire of Pietism in the later decades of the century, any social movement or individual therein must be considered in the context of a war that left behind a sense of "irretrievable disaster" in the course of three decades.[16] As we will see, in his own prophetic statements Zimmerman invoked the memory of the Thirty Years War repeatedly and the extraordinary heavenly phenomena that preceded it.

What did these climatic and geopolitical crises have in common? Historians increasingly acknowledge that the general crisis of the seventeenth century was, in fact, the institutional and cultural result of the changing climate during the period. The ordinary people of the seventeenth century saw the connections between environmental phenomena and geopolitical conflict, too. Early modern Protestants "firmly believed that they fought in response to a direct call from God" during the conflict.[17] The environmental and cultural crisis of the seventeenth century, for those who lived through it, was a *religious* event that demanded *religious* interpretation. This state of ambient, visible crisis was the context for a wave of change that swept through the Christian churches in the seventeenth century.

Following the Reformation, increasingly institutionalized and hierarchical forms of Christianity ignored what we might call the spiritual needs of ordinary people. Brett Grainger sums it up nicely: "Zealous Lutherans had razed the grand houses of Catholic devotion while building nothing to take their place."[18] In an atmosphere of intense doctrinal debate between and within denominations, the spiritual needs of Protestant people were more or less ignored by church authorities.[19] What was missing in the ossifying orthodoxies of the Lutheran and Calvinist churches were the devotional practices that had sustained the inner lives of Christians in Europe for centuries. As religious studies scholars like Robert Orsi have argued, the life-affirming presence of God in the form of the sacraments, the saints, and traditional patterns of devotional life largely evaporated for many Christians during this period.[20] While the importance of such devotional practices might be lost on many of us today, it would be difficult to overestimate their importance for the early modern laity, for whom they provided nothing less than the narrative framework of a coherent and meaningful life on earth. Winnfried Zeller coined the now commonly used term "crisis of piety" to describe this phenomenon, which he identified as beginning in and proceeding through the seventeenth century.[21]

The crisis of piety identified by historians of European Christianity can only be understood within the broader context of the general crisis of the seventeenth century. Climate change placed a severe strain on cultural institutions like the church *while* it transformed the lives of the laity through war, epidemic, and famine. During the late seventeenth century, the people of Europe watched their lives change while they experienced failing crops, a darkened sky full of falling stars, and shaking ground beneath their feet.[22] Given these advances in our understanding of the connections between the crises of early modernity, we can see clearly how the crisis of piety was directly related to the changing climate of Europe during the period.

Enthusiasm, Esotericism, and Ecology

Johann Zimmerman and Johannes Kelpius were both identified with radical Pietism, a Protestant devotional movement that began in Germany in the late seventeenth century. Pietists prioritized a personal, emotional connection with God, and a generally conciliatory attitude of cooperation and pacifism in the wake of the religious polemics that fueled the Thirty Years War. Early Pietists gathered in informal settings of Bible study and fellowship called conventicles, which were often held in private homes. While Pietist principles were gradually incorporated into mainline Lutheranism and Protestant thought generally throughout the eighteenth century, earlier seventeenth-century forms of Pietist Christianity were intensely radical. They were, especially in their earlier iterations that included figures like Zimmerman and Kelpius, often at odds with and occasionally outrightly hostile to the orthodox Lutheran establishment.[23]

Pietist history is a vast and unwieldy field, even as a subfield of church history, dedicated to the study of unbelievably prolific authors like Philipp Jakob Spener (1635–1705) and August Herman Francke (1663–1727), whose writings and ideas were disseminated along informal networks of vernacular transmission rather than official or orthodox sanction. Douglas Shantz lays out the situation rather bluntly: "No one can possibly read all the relevant source material or do justice to the complexity of the movement."[24] Fair enough.

Pietism was a multivalent conglomeration of theologies and practices that spread throughout Europe for the better part of three centuries, intermingling with other radical Christian groups (like the Quakers, Anabaptists, Calvinists, Philadelphians, and even radical dissenting Catholics under the banner of Quietism) and gradually permeated orthodox Protestantism with an emphasis on the inner experience of the individual, an emphasis that persists in the modern evangelical formations of Christianity today.[25] For their religious emphasis on experience, feeling, and an inner emotional life, Pietists were often derided as "enthusiasts," which was a pejorative term, if not an outright accusation of heresy.[26] As we will see in Chapter 3, for many of the Pietists who lived with Johannes Kelpius, this religious enthusiasm (from the Greek *entheos*, meaning "filled with god") often gave way to states of religious ecstasy, trancelike states of paranormal power and knowledge.

In its emphasis on the experience of the individual and what we might describe today as the affective or intuitive quality of human relationship with the divine, Pietism developed a series of beliefs and practices for feeling the presence of God both within the self and in the world. The great eighteenth-century theologian Friedrich Schleiermacher, remembered today as "the father of liberal Protestantism," was given a thoroughly Pietist education as a young man in a Moravian school.[27] Schleiermacher inadvertently provided an elegant articulation of Pietist religious principles in his famous 1799 book *On Religion: Speeches to Its Cultured Despisers*: "Religion's essence is neither thinking nor acting, but intuition and feeling. It wishes to intuit the universe, wishes devoutly to overhear the universe's own manifestations and actions, longs to be grasped and filled by the universe's immediate influences in childlike passivity."[28] Like many liberal scholars of religion who would follow him, Schleiermacher mistakes his own religious background here for something like "religion" itself. But the Pietist religion he describes, this process of knowing by a kind of cosmic environmental *feeling*, of knowing beyond the limits of doctrine, reason, or even words, can be clearly traced back to the early radical Pietist movement, in which both Johann Zimmerman and Johannes Kelpius were directly involved.

During this period of climate change and protracted conflict, "The ordinary faithful needed something simpler and more devotional than the grand theological systems," as W. R. Ward has written.[29] And in the capacious intellectual environment of seventeenth-century Europe, the ordinary faithful had options. Seventeenth-century Germany, like so many other conflict zones, witnessed "a spiritual revival [that] had penetrated to the very roots of society," writes C. V. Wedgwood, "and religion was a reality among those to whom politics were meaningless and public events unknown."[30] This revival was concentrated in the southwestern regions, the aforementioned Württemberg and Palatinate. As Frances Yates pointed out of the same region and period, "The brief reign of Frederick and Elizabeth [1613–1619] in the Palatinate was a Hermetic golden age," in which widespread popular interest in esoteric religious practice briefly coincided with official sanction.[31] Indeed, Yates suggests that "we have found underneath the superficial history of the seventeenth century, just before the outbreak of the Thirty Years War, a whole culture, a whole civilization lost to view," a culture where Christian devotional life was deeply influenced by Hermeticism and alchemy.[32]

Hermeticism and Alchemy

From our position in the twenty-first century, it seems strange that the "ordinary faithful" of the early modern period, in particular the rural poor, sought out and integrated Hermetic and alchemical ideas in their Christianity. A closer look at these ideas themselves and the conditions of their popular reception among seventeenth-century Protestants clarifies the reasoning behind this syncretic practice.

The *Corpus Hermeticum* is a body of literature with origins in the late-antique Mediterranean world (although often believed to be much older), attributed to Hermes Trismegistus, a Hellenized version of the Egyptian god of wisdom.

32   AMERICAN AURORA

For many seventeenth-century readers, Hermes was an ancient Egyptian philosopher and contemporary of Moses.[33] While Hermeticism and its associated practices like alchemy would gradually decline in intellectual acceptance and cultural prestige during the eighteenth and nineteenth centuries, culminating in their modern status as a "cultural wastebasket" (to borrow Wouter Hanegraaff's memorable phrase), the early modern period considered Hermes an ancient philosopher of respectable status and association.[34] As the famous story goes, Marsilio Ficino had already begun the momentous task of translating the works of Plato into Latin when he was interrupted by his patron, Cosimo de' Medici, who had found something more important for his scribe to work on: a manuscript of the *Corpus Hermeticum* I–XIV.[35] In 1462, Hermes was more important than Plato.

This Renaissance prestige enjoyed by Hermes was, in part, the result of a long tradition of European theology and alchemy derived from Islamic and ancient Christian sources, in which the *Hermetica* and their supposed author were well known. As Florian Ebeling has shown, Hermetic ideas persisted throughout the Middle Ages, often entangled with devotional Christian practice and alchemical writings.[36] Hermeticism as a body of philosophical and theological literature did greatly expand through the translation work of Ficino, but this followed a long medieval tradition in its absorption into Christian theology.

What made Hermetic and alchemical ideas so alien to much of early modern Christendom—and, I argue, so appealing to Protestants living through the Little Ice Age—were their description of a cosmos that was thoroughly imbued with divinity. Hermeticism was a cosmotheist theology, as Wouter Hanegraaff writes, that rested on "the fundamental assumption that the divine is at home in the world."[37] Hermetic cosmology, as such, assumed the divinity of matter in practices like alchemy and imbued practices like astrology with immense religious significance. The human body itself, being made of the same matter as this world, was imbued with divinity, and the analogous relationship between the human being, the cosmos, and God was the cornerstone of Hermeticism and the wide range of modern ideas that derived from it. "There are these three, then," declares Hermes in the Tenth Discourse of the *Corpus Hermeticum*, "god the father and the good, the cosmos; and the human. And god holds the cosmos, but the cosmos holds the human."[38] This Hermetic understanding of the analogous relationship between God, the cosmos, and the human would reverberate through the radical Protestant understanding of their changing climate.

Early modern Protestants did not unanimously or overwhelmingly integrate Hermetic ideas into their religion. In fact, the orthodox Protestant churches of the time were quick to reject the *Hermetica* and the popular theologies it influenced. The "logical incompatibility" of Protestant Christianity and Hermeticism, "of monotheism and cosmotheism," writes Wouter Hanegraaff, "has led to an endless series of creative attempts to resolve it."[39] Indeed, a religion founded on the basis of *sola scriptura* was not meant to syncretize other theological systems easily, especially systems that saw the phenomena of the cosmos and the human body to be central sources of divine knowledge. Rather, centuries of conflict and "creative attempts" to resolve the conflict between early modern Protestantism led to the Protestant reception of Hermetic philosophy and alchemical practice.

In the sections that follow, I will explore and demonstrate the ways in which early modern Protestants turned to Hermetic and alchemical literature *because* it offered an environmental knowledge that was applicable to a changing climate. But the skeptical reader does not need to take my word for it: these connections and practices were thoroughly mapped out by the German theologian and heresiologist Ehregott Daniel Colberg (1659–1698) in his 1690–1691 work *Platonic-Hermetic Christianity*.[40]

Colberg was a Lutheran theologian and minister who took it upon himself to attack the rising tide of "enthusiasm" in Germany in the wake of the Thirty Years War. Colberg saw one terrible cause at the root of the problem of enthusiasm in seventeenth-century Europe: "The greatest—I would almost say: the only— danger for theology comes from the scandalous *mixing of philosophical teachings and the Word of God*."[41] Colberg was, first and foremost, diagnosing an epistemological problem: "Although the philosophical arts and sciences are, in and for themselves, a wondrous gift of God from which great profit can be drawn in civil life," he writes, "they create much confusion if they are applied to the divine mysteries of revelation and transcend their natural boundaries of reason."[42] In acknowledging the practical utility of philosophical-scientific knowledge while simultaneously rejecting its potential for religious or ethical insight, Colberg was participating in a dichotomy that would persist long after him. Colberg's writing demonstrates how rapidly the sciences, philosophy, and religions of the seventeenth century were reorganizing into mutually exclusive domains of knowledge.

In a move that anticipated the eighteenth-century Enlightenment and the rise of historical criticism in the nineteenth century, Colberg was resentful of logical or what seem to be proto-historicist readings of scripture: "invented axioms" or "blind intellect" were haphazard and unwieldy blunt instruments that were not to be taken up against the revealed word of God, he argued. Just as deluded were those who attempted to peek behind the curtain of creation, to see those truths that God had declined to reveal in the Bible, as when "one tries to be smarter than Scripture, that is, if with the help of philosophy one tries to fathom the nature of the revealed mysteries about which God's Word keeps silent."[43] Here Colberg was addressing what he understood as the problem with the Protestant reception of Hermetic literature: as Colberg called it, "*magia*," or "knowledge of divine and natural things from the Book of Nature."[44] Deriving knowledge from scripture, Colberg points out, was perfectly fine: But deriving knowledge from the

34   AMERICAN AURORA

interpretation of God's creation? From an orthodox Lutheran perspective, this was several steps too far: in fact, it was *magia*, magic.

But "knowledge of divine and natural things from the Book of Nature" was *exactly* what the ordinary faithful were looking for during the Little Ice Age. A close reading of the texts in which Protestant authors of the period integrated Hermetic and alchemical ideas demonstrates their focus on environmental knowledge. In order to understand the Pietist techniques of environmental knowledge that distressed Colberg, we need to take a detour backward, through the heretical history that Colberg lays out. In the section that follows, I will explore the three major sources of Hermetic Protestant environmental knowledge: Paracelsus, Johann Arndt, and Jacob Böhme.

Hermetic Protestant Environmental Knowledge

During the early part of the Little Ice Age, a Swiss physician and lay Catholic theologian who wrote under the name Paracelsus (born Theophrastus von Hohenheim, 1493/94–1541) laid the groundwork for a new form of piety in which close attention to the natural world was the key to a meaningful Christian life. Although he is best remembered today as the "father of toxicology" for his groundbreaking attention to the operation of poisons, Paracelsus developed a practice in which chemistry, medicine, and theology were part and parcel of a holistic approach to Christian life and knowledge, or *theorica*, as he called it. Paracelsus's scientific writings often sounded devotional, just as his religious writings would veer into chemistry: these disciplines and ways of knowing were thoroughly integrated in his medical and philosophical practice. As Lawrence Principe has written of the history of early modern science, religion, and philosophy, "Moderns tend to make disconnections where early moderns did not."[45]

Alchemical practice was connected with Hermetic philosophy from its origins in ancient Egypt, where Zosimos of Panopolis cited the authority of Hermes in some of the first recognizably alchemical writings.[46] By the early modern period, alchemical ideas had permeated new ideas about medicine and certain corners of Christian theology.[47] Paracelsus's Christian application of Hermetic thought was not the highfalutin philosophy of the Italian Renaissance nor the philosophical Hermeticism of the Cambridge Platonists. For all his theological and philosophical writing, Paracelsus was a medical doctor, and his application of Hermetic philosophy was decidedly practical. Alchemy was useful both because it *worked*, as a worldview for understanding the threefold analogical relationship between God, the cosmos, and the human, and because he believed that alchemical medicines were more effective than the Galenic medicines of the Middle Ages. Divine knowledge permeated creation in the Paracelsian synthesis of alchemy and Christianity, and this knowledge was the basis of all practical endeavors, especially medicine. In this alchemical model of creation, God, cosmos, and the human were abundantly analogous, and events and objects in heaven reflect events and objects on earth.[48]

Paracelsus's focus on the primacy of the relationship between the individual and the divine served as the basis of his natural theology and medical writings. Ancient authorities, modern priesthoods, arrogant university professors: for Paracelsus, these authorities got in the way of a personal relationship with God and, therefore, an ability to understand the world. Paracelsus's thought was thoroughly grounded in scripture, and so his philosophy of nature began with the creation story in Genesis. "From Holy Scripture comes the beginning and guide of all philosophy and natural science," he wrote.[49] Since God created the world, and then created human beings out of the matter of this world, divine will was the root cause of natural bodies and processes. Since the human being (the small world, the microcosm) and their environment (the great world, the macrocosm) were in a process of sympathetic interrelation, understanding the natural world was an integral aspect of not only a reformed theology but a general practice of medicine: "Above all," he writes, "the physician must know . . . the great world, for then the physician has ascertained it in the human being as well."[50]

Paracelsus's writings demonstrated a radical interest in the knowledge and wisdom of common people—the peasantry—whose intimacy with God's creation gave them a familiar wisdom that he deeply valued: "I went not only to doctors, but also to barbers, bathkeepers, learned physicians, women, and magicians who pursue the art of healing. I went to alchemists, to monasteries, to nobles and the common folk . . . to experts and the simple."[51] Paracelsus's interest in the common knowledge of country people is carried through subsequent readers like Jacob Böhme and Johann Arndt. It was also simply good sense. During his systematic study of poisons, heeding the advice of rural people on the medical and toxic potentials of certain plants probably kept Paracelsus alive on a few occasions.

This sympathetic interrelation between the human, heaven, and earth gave astronomy a primary importance in Paracelsus's system. Since philosophy was concerned with earthly nature, astronomy was the practice of attention toward heavenly nature, equally applicable to the practice of medicine and to understanding the world.[52] Of special interest to Paracelsus were certain extraordinary phenomena on earth and in heaven, which Paracelsus interpreted, following Genesis, as portents or signals from God referring to events of the future.

In 1531, Paracelsus produced a work titled *Exegesis of the Comet* in which he interpreted the passage of Halley's comet over Europe as a signal of the imminent "destruction of the monarchies."[53] In the same way that a rainbow might signal God's love and mercy, a comet might signal God's willingness and ability to cleanse the slate of creation. Scripture and cosmos were two sides of one coin: the comet itself, he wrote, was "composed of God's words, and is understood through it."[54] Paracelsus's apocalyptic reading of the comet through the Bible prefigured the extent to which Zimmerman would draw such readings in the next century. Zimmerman suddenly seems less novel in this Paracelsian context: if a comet is "composed of God's words," why should he—or anyone—be prevented from reading?

Following his *Exegesis of the Comet*, Paracelsus produced several writings on extraordinary phenomena, including rainbows and earthquakes. In these works, Paracelsus elaborated on his self-styled role as a theorist of the supernatural, or the manifestations of phenomena on earth that seemed beyond or in defiance of the ordinary course of nature.[55] For Paracelsus, his own philosophy of nature put him in a unique position to unlock the meaning of extraordinary or supernatural events in the physical world. As he wrote in the *Piramirum*: "Strange, new, marvelous, unheard of—so they say—is my *physica*, my *meteorica*, my *theorica*, [and] my *practica*. But how can I not appear strange to those who have never walked in sunlight?[56] In this passage, Paracelsus suggests with some humor that his system unlocks the hidden meaning of miraculous and portentous phenomena to such an extent that he seems "strange" to his peers, benighted as they are in the darkness of the Galenic, Aristotelian, and Ptolemaic models of the cosmos. Paracelsus, unclouded by such delusions, declares that hitherto inexplicable phenomena are his bread and butter, so to speak. Paranormal events are phenomenologically abundant, and their meaning is proportionally greater. This understanding of paranormal phenomena as environmental nodes of meaning would carry through the Protestant imagination for centuries.

Paracelsus's process of environmental knowledge involved careful observation and contemplation rather than a systematic experimentation or dissection. As his biographer writes, for Paracelsus, "It is not hit-or-miss experimentation but rather contemplation of the macrocosm that discloses the secrets of nature."[57] This was a crucial difference between Hermetic Protestant environmental thought and the experimental methods of the sciences.[58] Paracelsus prefigured nearly all of the major features of what I call Hermetic Protestant environmental knowledge: emphasis on the practical knowledge of rural people, resistance toward orthodox and institutional authority, special interest in the paranormal and an essentially alchemical and contemplative approach to environmental knowledge.

Ultimately, Paracelsus advanced an alchemical vision of a Christian cosmos in which the environment was a dynamic, organic whole that was rich with knowledge. Paracelsus "extoll[ed] the divine presence and wisdom in nature" in texts like *De Potentia et Potentia Gratia Dei* (1533), wherein he described the divine power of plants: "God acts in everything, and everything is God and the

"NO WISDOM IN NATURE" 37

Lord, who is everything in everyone."[59] There was wisdom in nature, Paracelsus insisted; the cosmos was not only intelligible but actively *intelligent*. When read alchemically, the biblical texts described a world that was willing to communicate with those who were willing to listen.

Paracelsus's ideas were tremendously influential throughout the modern period across disciplines, but he did not do himself any favors as a communicator: he was "far from a clear and orderly writer"; his works were dense and erudite, and they attacked familiar faces in favor of strange new theories.[60] Ultimately, what made Paracelsus so influential during the centuries following his life was his articulation of a pious Christian perspective on environmental phenomena generally and the kinds of extreme natural phenomena that proliferated during the latter half of the seventeenth century. He just needed the right person to translate his ideas into formats that common Christians would be able to access and be willing to read.

Paracelsus's ideas were integrated into popular Protestant thought most directly by Johann Arndt (1555–1621), a Lutheran author of devotional literature. While Arndt is largely forgotten today beyond historians of Protestantism, his popularity was unsurpassed in seventeenth-century Europe. In contrast to Paracelsus, Johann Arndt's book of popular Christian devotion, *Of True Christianity*, went through twenty print editions before the death of the author and over 125 total printings by the end of the eighteenth century.[61] By 1735 in Württemberg it was reported that there were "more Arndts than Bibles."[62] Simply put, Johann Arndt's books are likely among the most widely read works in the history of Protestantism, excluding only the Bible.[63] But there are only dim echoes of orthodox Lutheranism in Arndt's *True Christianity*. As Douglas Shantz writes, "Arndt appealed rarely to Luther," and the "traditional Lutheran emphasis on word and sacrament is nowhere to be found."[64] More recently, the historian of Christian mysticism Bernard McGinn has noticed the same absence of Luther or much of Lutheranism at all in Arndt's theology.[65] In fact, Arndt was not even a trained theologian: Hans Schneider has demonstrated that Arndt's formal education was in medicine, and his theology was self-taught.[66] In the place of orthodox Lutheran training, Arndt filled in the widening gaps in popular Protestant devotion with Paracelsian Hermeticism.

As a young man, Arndt was a student of medicine at the University of Basel, where Theodore Zwinger first introduced him to the work of Paracelsus. Alchemy exerted a grip on Arndt's mind that never loosened, and later in life he maintained a laboratory near his study for alchemical experiments.[67] Following his formal education, Arndt worked as a schoolteacher, a pastor, and a medical doctor during the plague in Germany at the turn of the seventeenth century. During this period, he committed himself to the study of the German mystics (like Johannes Tauler and Meister Eckhart), alongside further reading

38 AMERICAN AURORA

in Paracelsus. Examples of his preaching from this period show the Paracelsian themes in his thought, as he practiced medicine in plague-ravaged Europe: "The true physician knows that man is a microcosm, a small world, and everything that can be found in nature in the greater world can also be found in man, the small world."[68]

Under simple headings like "Some Beautiful Rules for a Christian Life" and "Concerning True, Proper Worship," Arndt filled in a glaring gap in the center of popular seventeenth-century Protestant thought: he actually gave Protestants *something to do and told them how to do it*. Arndt's writing was clear, it was practical, and it eschewed the intricacies and polemics of Lutheran orthodoxy in favor of simple and precise maxims for the joy and meaning of Christian life. In fact, he *blamed* theologians for the problems of Christendom, for failing to apply their principles to the real world, to imitate Christ in their own lives, and for reducing Christianity to an academic exercise, even worse, an intellectual problem.[69]

While Paracelsus's influence is most pronounced in Book 4 of *True Christianity*, "The Book of Nature," Arndt was inspired and influenced by Paracelsus throughout the work, to the point of simply copying extensive passages of Paracelsus and inserting them into his text directly. As Hans Schneider again has shown, Arndt did not merely quietly excerpt portions of Paracelsus for Book 4 of *True Christianity*, but throughout the text, "There are not only extensive excerpts from Paracelsus, but ideas from Paracelsus play an important role in the whole conception of the work."[70]

Like Paracelsus's attention to the comet and the earthquake, Arndt paid special attention to those environmental phenomena that seemed to *demand* interpretation. Many of Arndt's descriptions of celestial phenomena bear directly on the climatic and environmental conditions of the Little Ice Age. Arndt lived and wrote through a period of severe cooling and seismic activity, in which a series of cataclysmic volcanic events contributed to global cooling by flinging particulate matter into the atmosphere.[71] A recent study by atmospheric chemists of the effects of volcanic activity on the depictions of sunsets in the work of great painters highlights the period immediately preceding and during the writing and publication of *True Christianity*—around 1600 to 1610—as a period of markedly dimmed and reddened skies.[72]

A close reading of *True Christianity* shows the same effect on the works of great theology from the period. "When one now looks at the darkness of the sun and the moon," Arndt writes, "one should think that . . . it is contrary to their nature, and proclaims to us a great wickedness performed on earth."[73] In an era when the sky itself was darkened, Johann Arndt applied Paracelsian and Hermetic ideas to scripture in order to make sense of a cosmos that seemed to be declaring its own decline. Johann Arndt read the climatic conditions of the Little Ice Age as an apocalyptic extortion from the creator:

And when the sky burns like this, and the sun turns blood-red, it is telling us: Behold, one day I will perish in fire. In this way, all the elements speak to us, announcing our wickedness and punishments. What is the terrifying thunder but a mighty voice of the heavens, before which the earth trembles, through which God warns us? What is the earthquake but a terrifying language of the earth, which opens its mouth and proclaims great change?[74]

Throughout *True Christianity*, Arndt portrayed the cosmos as an intelligent and communicative entity, constantly transmitting divine knowledge for anyone who cared to listen. Given what we know now about the needs of the "ordinary faithful" during the Little Ice Age, it is a small wonder that Arndt's book was so excessively popular through the seventeenth century: he gave Protestants *exactly* the kind of religious interpretation of their changing climate that they were looking for, and he did so in accessible and devotional prose.

Above all, Arndt's book interpreted the suffering of the seventeenth century through the fundamental Christian conviction that suffering itself is meaningful:

The suffering of the macrocosm, that is, the great world, is subsequently fulfilled in the microcosm, that is, in humanity. What happens to man, nature and the great world suffer first, for the suffering of all creatures, both good and evil, is directed towards man as a center where all lines of the circle converge. For what man owes, nature must suffer first.[75]

In this deeply Paracelsian passage, Arndt envisions an almost ecological (if admittedly anthropocentric) Hermetic Christianity, in which the suffering of the human being is connected to and shared with a wider suffering of the cosmos.

For all the darkness of the sky and of Arndt's reading of the environmental conditions of the Little Ice Age, Arndt's vision of environmental knowledge implied a deep structure, coherence, and harmony to the world and humanity's place in it. "Consider here the wisdom and goodness of God," he writes, that one can "find special signs on every herb and flower, which is the living handwriting and signature of God, by which each plant is marked according to its hidden power, so artfully, so wondrously, so delicately that no artist can reproduce it exactly." Arndt's interpretation of environmental knowledge did not focus on darkened skies, the quaking earth, or the frigid cold. The deep substance of this cosmos, for Arndt, was *goodness*, knowledge, and an unfathomable vital potency. Herbs drawn in God's own handwriting are "there in front of your eyes everywhere. As soon as you step on a green lawn, you have food and medicine under your feet." Most people, even devout Christians, ignore "the very slightest grass and seed," he wrote, which they "regard very little and uselessly." But in the smallest herb and seed "There is greater wisdom of God, power and effect

40 AMERICAN AURORA

than you can fathom." Humanity had not begun to read the knowledge written into the fabric of the world: "I tell you," he wrote with pious exasperation, "the thousandth part of the herbal power has not yet been fathomed."[76] Finally, the Hermetic emphasis on celestial phenomena informed even the new Protestant reading of herbal power: "And whoever is a good star seer, who understands the stars more than the art of arithmetic, knows when, how and where such a tree will bloom in the sky and give such fruit."[77] The heavens, the earth, and the human body were in constant communicative sympathy.

Without needless exaggeration, there is a salient point here that bears a final emphasis: the most popular theologian in Protestant history was not a trained theologian, and his work owed more to the Hermetic legacies of Paracelsus than it did to Martin Luther.[78] Johann Arndt, who Douglas Shantz acknowledges as "a full-fledged Paracelsist and Hermeticist," accomplished a popular integration of Protestantism and Hermeticism that was *precisely* attuned to the spiritual interests and needs of the common people during the peak of the Little Ice Age. No wonder his book was so popular.[79]

Johann Arndt drew heavily on the Christian mystical tradition as he wrote *True Christianity*, but his writings do not hint at any mystical insights on the part of the author. Arndt's great skill was clear, simplifying communication of religious ideas for a popular audience, not mystical insights of his own. In the writings of Jacob Böhme (1575–1624), on the other hand, the Protestant tradition yielded its first great mystic and its most famously dense and impenetrable author.[80] Indeed, Böhme himself struggled to understand and explain his own immensely abstract and complex mystical insights, which poured from his pen in a staggering lifelong exegetical struggle of auto-analysis that would go unmatched in volume and depth until the *Exegesis* of Philip K. Dick in the later part of the twentieth century.[81]

Jacob Böhme (variously spelled in English as Boehme, Bohme, Behmen) was plagued by existential and essentially ecological anxieties in the years preceding his first vision: "A man of intense and troubled piety, he had come to feel depressed at the very sight of nature. He was oppressed by the heavens, which he took to be an impenetrable blue vault, hundreds or thousands of miles away," his biographer Andrew Weeks writes.[82] Böhme's environmental anxieties reflected a broader European attitude toward the changing cosmologies of the period. Throughout Böhme's lifetime, the neat medieval notion of fixed stars governing a finite life in an ordered cosmos was collapsing into the infinitude of space and time signaled by Copernicus. During this exact same period—roughly the same decades in which Arndt lived and wrote, the turn of the seventeenth century— the climate in Europe continued to cool, while meteoric, seismic, and volcanic activity suddenly increased. Böhme seems to have felt these concurrent philosophical and environmental changes acutely.

It was amid this profound sense of irreconcilable distance from nature and from heaven that Böhme's major visionary episode took place in 1600, as his biographer and follower Abraham von Franckenberg (1593–1652) relates, when he happened to catch a glance of sunlight reflected from a pewter dish.[83] The beam of light catalyzed a visionary experience that his biographer describes as "seeing into the secret heart of nature," or a "concealed divine world."[84] As Franckenberg described it, Böhme, in a visionary daze and trying to shake free from this "phantasy," went outside the city gates of Görlitz and tried to clear his head with a walk in the countryside. "Clear his head" a walk in the countryside did not. In the woods and the fields his fantasy only intensified. Once past the city gates, nature's secret heart unveiled itself even more clearly and acutely to Böhme, who would spend the rest of his life trying to put the next fifteen minutes into words.[85]

Like Paracelsus—an author whom Böhme drew on repeatedly in his own writings—before him, Böhme's writings combined his reading of scripture, esoteric and heterodox philosophies, and a series of insights that he attributed to his mystical episodes. Looking at Paracelsus as the original theorist and Arndt as the popular trailblazer, we can see Böhme as the elaborator of esoteric models of the nonhuman world that he embedded into the core of popular Protestant thought.[86]

True to the legacy of Paracelsus and the Paracelsian Protestants, Böhme's theology, indeed all his learning so far was we can tell, was entirely self-taught. This was a matter of class—as an artisan and peasant, he never had access to such learning—but also as a matter of personal philosophy. Formal learning was unnecessary when cosmic truth could be located in the body and in the world:

> I do not carry in my knowledge letters from many books; rather, I have the letters within me; the whole of heaven and earth, as well as God himself, lies within man: should he then not read the book that he himself is? . . . When I read myself, I read in God's book.[87]

In addition to implicitly justifying the knowledge he derived from his mystical episodes, Böhme's notion of the body itself as part of God's other book, what Paracelsus before him called "the formed word of God," led to new praxes of environmental knowing in the Protestant tradition. Böhme supplemented Paracelsus's abstract, contemplative knowledge of the world with a highly embodied and sensuous model of environmental knowing, in which somatic processes like "seeing, smelling, and tasting" were essential tools for reading God's other book.[88] Later radical Protestants who read Böhme, like George Fox, the English founder of Quakerism, would take up this embodied language of religious experience: "All things were new," wrote Fox of his own conversion experience, "and the creation gave unto me another smell than before, beyond what words can utter."[89] Böhme gave seventeenth-century radicals a sensuous new language for the presence of God.

Despite the density and erudition of his writing, Böhme was careful to ground his practices and ideas in simple scripture and nature, as Paracelsus and Arndt had done before him. One did not need education in Latin or theology to read Nature's Book, since, in the Böhmean synthesis, the world could be read with eyes, tongue, nose, or skin. Furthermore, the incomprehensibly vast macrocosmos of Copernicus was drawn back and scaled down into the microcosmos of the human body through Hermetic and alchemical principles: "If man wants to be in heaven, heaven must be revealed within man." And there was no need to access an alchemical laboratory to do it: "This one can do simply, at home, in one's own place."[90] God's words shaped the heavens as they shaped the earth and the human body, and the process of being "in heaven" was not a matter of location— it was a matter of learning how to read God's words, nature's own language (natursprach), the language of creation in which birds, clouds, and children effortlessly exchanged information.

Böhme would go on to be a tenaciously popular author in the following centuries. As Mike Zuber has recently elaborated, Böhme's alchemical and astrological Christian mysticism would go on to be highly popular among radical Protestants, including Johannes Kelpius.[91] Especially in southeastern Pennsylvania, far from the eyes of Lutheran authorities, Böhme's writings and ideas would flourish to an extent that scholarship has still barely reckoned with.[92] Before we explore the afterlife of the Gorlitz cobbler across the Atlantic, however, we have to return to an astronomer in Württemberg, for whom the meaning of Jacob Böhme's writings were the basis of a conflict that would permanently change his life and the life of his young friend, Johannes Kelpius.

"Nature Is the Interpreter of Scripture"

For all of his contentious theological claims and publications, Böhme generally demurred from open conflict with church authorities. He considered himself to be, more or less, a good Lutheran who wanted to share some special insight. Where Böhme avoided conflict, the provincial Lutheran pastor and astronomer Johann Jacob Zimmerman, whom we met at the beginning of this chapter, was far less conflict-averse. Zimmerman took great pains to spell out and publicize his qualms with Lutheran orthodoxy. This included his opinion of Jacob Böhme, whom he considered a revelator on the order of the biblical prophets.[93]

The first generation of Pietists were mostly concentrated in the Palatinate and Württemberg, areas where generations of war and theological conflict had triggered a sincere desire for an emotional religion of deeply felt piety and a conclusion to the petty theological disputes of Europe. In these regions, the flames of Pietism mingled with the smoldering remnants of what Frances Yates called "the Hermetic golden age" of the seventeenth-century Palatinate. It was in these Pietist conventicles—secret meetings in private homes for devotional reading, prayer, and discussion—that the Protestant laity mingled with some of the most heterodox religious thinkers that Europe had to offer. Before long, Christian Kabbalists like Christian Knorr Von Rosenroth (1636–1689) and esoteric thinkers like Francis Mercurius van Helmont (1614–1698) were intermingling with the Lutheran laity at conventicle meetings.[94]

Johann Jacob Zimmerman was an early participant in the Pietist movement, becoming involved in his native Württemberg in the early 1680s. Zimmerman was a trained theologian and mathematician who took a special interest in the practice of astronomy as a window into the mind of God. This was not unusual for an astronomer in the seventeenth century: Isaac Newton held similar religious convictions beneath his science, though he was less vocal about it than Zimmerman. In fact, Zimmerman was keenly interested in the work of Newton, but he was worried that the young physicist was obscuring what he knew they both understood to be the authorship of God behind the words of the cosmos: "I fear that this highly renowned author wishes his discourse to be understood mathematically only," he once wrote.[95] As a mathematician, Zimmerman was not interested in mathematical practices that ignored the religious implications they brought forth. As his worry with Newton suggests, this approach was becoming unfashionable, even in the late seventeenth century.

As the century drew to a close and Cartesian mechanism was beginning to give way to the full-blown Enlightenment of the eighteenth century, Zimmerman carried on an old-fashioned pattern of philosophical investigation. As Mike Zuber, Zimmerman's exemplary contemporary interpreter, has written, Zimmerman was preoccupied with a metaphysical approach to the natural world that owed more to Paracelsus than to Bacon, and was ultimately concerned with "the invisible being of God" as the object of the study of the natural world.[96] Revising Martin Luther's maxim *sola scriptura*, Zimmerman's mingling of Hermetic and Protestant ideas resulted in techniques he called *scriptura et natura*, "scripture and nature," and even more heretical, *natura scripturae interpres*: "Nature is the interpreter of Scripture."[97] Let's listen to Schleiermacher one more time: "[Religion] wishes to intuit the universe."

Like Paracelsus before him, Zimmerman's science was part and parcel of his theology. He was enthusiastic about the authors and ideas of the Italian Renaissance, but he did not have access to their writings directly, only in summary form by various German authors.[98] He was also deeply interested in the ideas of Giordano Bruno, but again, he had access to his writings only in the form of a summary in the work of the Silesian author Abraham von

44 AMERICAN AURORA

Franckenberg.[99] In his own radical natural theology, he was mainly indebted to the Hermetic lineage that we have traced in this chapter: Paracelsus, Johann Arndt, and Jacob Böhme.[100]

As described in the opening of this chapter, the appearance of the Great Comet of 1680 was nothing less than a revelatory episode for Zimmerman, an event that he explicated as a theologian and measured like an astronomer in the same publication. In the publication of his exegesis, *Cometo-Scopia*, Zimmerman refers extensively to Johann Arndt's *True Christianity*, in which Arndt compared the physical properties of light with the presence of God.[101] In the wake of the Paracelsian establishment of the heavens being equally important to the earth as aspects of God's creation, Zimmerman's apocalyptic science was a century-later culmination of Paracelsus's *theorica*. In Zimmerman's writing, the Protestant reception of Hermetic environmental thought reached a dramatic apotheosis. As outlined at the beginning of this chapter, Zimmerman inscribed Böhmean and Paracelsian notions into the heart of Lutheranism, and with a blunt-force polemical directness that Arndt would have never attempted: *sola scriptura* became *scriptura et natura*, an equivalency between God's two books that Paracelsus, Arndt, and Böhme certainly hinted at, but never declared outright.

In 1684, a second publication appeared, which Zimmerman authored pseudonymously: *Precise Mathematical Determination of the Time of the Two Expected Divine Judgments over the European Babel and the Anti-Christianity of This World*. As this descriptive title suggests, his work was far more direct in its critique of the church and precise in its determination regarding the timing of God's judgment. First, Zimmerman repeats and clarifies the meaning of the Great Comet of 1680, suggesting that it represented a final warning to the people of Europe.[102] The church was not exempt from blame in Zimmerman's prophecy; in fact, Zimmerman blamed the ministry directly for the "Anti-Christianity" of this world.[103] Zimmerman looked to the appearance of other comets in history as he built his argument. The comet of 1618, he pointed out, preceded the Thirty Years War. The comets of 1618 and 1680 were both accompanied by many miracles (*Wunder*) on earth. Doing his math and counting catastrophes, Zimmerman uses the comet of 1618 and the horrors that followed it to deliver a prophecy: that something terrible would happen in 1693.[104] In Zimmerman's writing, we can see how the extraordinary environmental phenomena and the persistent geopolitical conflict of the seventeenth century really did seem interconnected to the people living through them.

Precise Mathematical Determination was quickly determined to be a work of heresy by the local Lutheran authority, and Zimmerman was relieved of his official duties in the church and expelled from the state of Württemberg.[105] After his expulsion, Zimmerman seems to have wandered throughout Germany and Holland, family in tow, for several years before settling in Hamburg and then Frankfurt, where he found work as a private tutor and author.[106] He continued to theorize and publish on his cosmological views. In 1689 and 1690, he published two treatises that leaned even more directly into cosmotheism, deriving their essentially Hermetic insights from Zimmerman's readings of Arndt and Böhme.[107] Mike Zuber summarizes the thought of the apocalyptic sky-watcher: "Astronomical observation and cosmology served the purpose of deeper spiritual insight and the mystical ascent towards God," Zuber writes.[108]

Zimmerman suddenly reappears in the primary sources in 1693, in Hamburg, where he had become involved with a circle of heterodox European dissenters who were colluding with Quaker comrades in London to emigrate to the Atlantic shores of North America.[109] There, English Quakers were busy establishing what they intended to be a utopian safe haven for religious radicals from Europe, including this faction of German Pietists. As one English source put it, "Among these new mystical Men there was one John Jacob Zimmerman." The author, a Quaker historian named Gerardus Croese, described Zimmerman as a devout and brilliant man: "[In] the Temperance of his Life . . . he was inferior to none," and gifted with "all other excellent endowments of mind."[110] Still, even for the early Quakers, Zimmerman's beliefs were strange and outdated, and his brilliance showed through only despite "what he had Contracted of these erroneous opinions."[111]

According to the Quaker histories, Zimmerman's flight from the authorities had taken on a rather urgent turn, and he seemed to be in danger:

> Who when he saw there was nothing but great danger like to hang over himself and his Friends; he invites and stirs up through his own hope about sixteen or seaventeen Families of [Pietists], to prefer also an hope of better things tho it were dubious before the present danger, and forsaking their Country which they through the most precipitous and utmost danger . . . to depart and betake themselves into other parts of the world, even to Pensilvania, the Quakers Country . . . and learn the Languages of that People, and Endeavour to inspire Faith and Piety into the same Inhabitants by their words and examples which they could not do to these Christians here.

The Quaker histories suggest a serious urgency in the Hamburg group's decision to travel to Pennsylvania, although the sources never clarify the situation with precision. Was it Zimmerman's prophetic certainty of the coming disaster of 1693 that motivated the trip?

Almost all later retellings of the story of Kelpius's journey to Pennsylvania have suggested that they were motivated entirely by Zimmerman's prophecy, that the world itself would end in 1693. But if this was true, why did the group wait until the year was nearly over to begin their travels? Kelpius, Zimmerman, and the rest

46 AMERICAN AURORA

of the Hamburg group spent much of 1693 right at home in the Babel of Europe. Instead, it seems more likely that Zimmerman, who had been warned, tried, and even expelled repeatedly by Lutheran authorities, was afraid that he and his colleagues were facing more severe punishments, from the church, rather than God. And indeed, in 1694 the Lutheran church released an edict that took aim at "Boehmist enthusiasm," squarely directed at dissidents like Zimmerman.[112] While the sources are not specific enough to be certain, it seems that Kelpius and company were motivated to flee an earthly rather than divine retribution—but the urgency of their trip and certainty of their decision is clear. They meant "to depart from these Babilonish Coasts, to those American Plantations, being led thereunto by the guidance of the Divine Spirit," according to a letter they sent to their Quaker friends.[113]

Through an anonymous intermediary, they made arrangements with a privileged young Quaker named William Penn, who was busy establishing a new utopian society across the Atlantic.[114] Another German Pietist, Francis Daniel Pastorius, had already made the voyage to Pennsylvania as a first wave of what was widely expected to be mass migration of German Pietists to Penn's new colony. Zimmerman's group included his own family, along with about forty other individuals. One of them, a promising young theologian from Transylvania named Johannes Kelpius, shared Zimmerman's interest in the works of Böhme and a religious affinity for sky-watching.

The apocalypse that Zimmerman foresaw in the sky arrived in 1693, *exactly* when he predicted. But in a deeply Hermetic turn of events, the fate that Zimmerman foresaw in the dome of the macrocosm would play out in the microcosm of his own body.[115] By the late summer of 1693, the Hamburg group had left Germany for Holland, where they arranged for travel to London from the ports of Rotterdam. In Holland, their Quaker benefactor arranged a ship to take them to London, from which they could depart the coasts of Babel for good. Suddenly, in the early autumn of the year for which he had foretold the arrival of the millennium, Zimmerman died.[116] His companions—including his wife and children—went to Pennsylvania without him, but they kept his copy of Newton's *Principia*. Zimmerman's measurements would not appear in the text until a revised edition was published years later, after both Kelpius and Zimmerman were dead. This book of physics and astronomy that Zimmerman carried with him, a book that he would eventually appear in as a source, made its way to Kelpius, who may have kept it both for its detailed celestial information and as a memento of the man who owned it.

Zimmerman's copy of the *Principia Mathematica* sits today in the Library Company of Philadelphia, where it is inscribed by the Pennsylvania bibliophile and statesman James Logan. In his inscription, Logan noted that the book was originally owned by Zimmerman and then Johannes Kelpius, who brought it to

Philadelphia. James Logan, the future mayor of Philadelphia and notorious architect of the "Walking Purchase," apparently purchased Kelpius's library after his death, which Logan noted as taking place in 1707.[117]

"No Wisdom in Nature"

Thus far, I have traced the Protestant reception of Hermetic philosophy through its origins in Paracelsus into its major popularization by Arndt and further elaboration by Böhme and Zimmerman. At this point, I want to step back and widen the lens. If the response to climate change was such a popular subject among Protestants in the seventeenth century, can we not expect to find these notions of "wisdom in nature" appearing in other writings from the period?

Here the history of philosophy can show us how the seventeenth-century intellectuals reacted to what was largely a popular phenomenon among Protestants. As we have seen, the authors who popularized environmental knowledge were not theologians or philosophers: they were, at least the three covered here, two medical doctors and a shoemaker. Orthodox theologians and their university colleagues in philosophy, meanwhile, were focused on entirely different questions and were often hostile toward these vernacular and devotional movements, which they rightly recognized as an implicit critique of their own teachings and authority.

One conversation between a well-known philosopher and theologian shows their resistance toward these popular theological notions. In 1669, the young Gottfried Leibniz wrote a letter to his teacher, the Lutheran theologian and philosopher Jacob Thomasius. Leibniz, who would go on to be remembered as one of the great rationalist philosophers of the seventeenth century, was surprisingly endeared by ancient philosophy and critical of his modern colleagues in the letter: "I don't mind saying that more things please me in Aristotle's book . . . than in the Meditations of Descartes," Leibniz wrote to Thomasius. "That's how Cartesian I am!" He goes on: "Who wouldn't welcome his substantial form? There's nothing more real than prime matter. To me, the view of the reformers seems not only more accurate, but also more in agreement with Aristotle."[118]

Protestant theology was not only a challenge for the uneducated rural laity: it caused occasional headaches for intellectuals, too. Martin Luther's maxim *sola scriptura*—the assertion that biblical text was the only source of religious knowledge—was a serious challenge for early modern Protestant intellectuals negotiating the deep historical connection between Christian theology and ancient philosophy. Christian thought had been steeped in Platonic, Aristotelian, and other non-biblical sources for centuries. Extracting those ideas was not simple, but it was considered essential after the Reformation. This is why, at the end of the seventeenth century, Leibniz expressed his admiration for Aristotle as something edgy, novel—cheeky, even.

Aristotle was of particular interest to Leibniz for his understanding of God as a separate substance that supported, but did not otherwise interact with, the material world. Aristotle put forward a theory of reality in which the material world was composed of what he called "prime matter," an essential substance from which everything took shape. Aristotle's cosmos of prime matter was supported by a theological account of God as a "primary mover," or "uncaused cause." In the *Metaphysics*, Aristotle describes this God: "Our discussion has . . . established that there exists a kind of eternal, unmoved substance that is separate from sensible things."[119] The emphasis, here, is on "separate." In Leibniz's reading of Aristotle's theology, we see a predecessor of what would be called deism by the eighteenth century: a God whose single act in the world was creation. It is not hard to see the appeal of such a God for a figure like Leibniz, a God who is conveniently identifiable as a source of the structure and coherence of the universe but is largely absent from the mechanical and mathematical processes that constitute it.

"Once Aristotle has been reconciled with the reformed philosophy," Leibniz wrote, "what remains, then, is that nothing else exists in the universe but mind, space, matter and motion." Leibniz was trying to get down to brass tacks, and Aristotle helped him get there. Suddenly, Leibniz's letter turns to precisely the kind of wisdom in nature that we have seen in Paracelsus and Arndt. "The better hypotheses are the clearer ones," he wrote to Thomasius. Recognizing the souls of animals and plants would bring one into agreement with Hermeticism, which Leibniz identifies as "Agrippa's occult philosophy" and goes on to describe with an unsubtle distaste: "[These philosophies] assign an angel to each thing as its midwife," Leibniz writes. "Why bother to posit souls of animals and plants?" he asks. As Leibniz goes on, his tone becomes more assertive: "But the fact is that there is no appetite and no wisdom in nature, although a beautiful order emerges from it because it is God's clock."[120]

For Leibniz, to recognize the soul and potency of plants and animals would lead one down a philosophical path that ended with an angelic force within every being and object in the universe. "But the fact," he insists, "is that there is no appetite and no wisdom in nature." Rather, the cosmos was a ticking machine whose beauty and order was just a perceptual artifact of God's original perfection. Why was the denial of the spiritual nature of plants and animals so important? What was so dangerous about finding "wisdom in nature"? I focus on these passages in Leibniz's letter because I think they present important vectors through which we can understand the material covered so far. These were popular, vernacular notions that Leibniz found threatening: the kind of frank admission that we can often only find in a private letter. It is small wonder that Leibniz was so focused on denying the spiritual nature of creation and the wisdom of nature itself: he was writing in a context of climate change and devotional crisis, in which these very ideas were among *the most popular* in Germany.

What happened to these ideas, then? Leibniz provides a clue, here, too: Enlightenment philosophy in the coming centuries was in large part a response to such popular notions of an intelligent, communicative, and living universe. These devotional notions of wisdom in nature were hugely popular among the laity. And yet these ideas are mostly absent from academic writings during the period—except, however, in private places like Leibniz's letter to Thomasius, where he states frankly the kinds of knowledge he means to resist.

Metamorphosis of the Metaphysics

Just a few years after Johann Zimmerman was expelled from Württemberg, a young theology student from Transylvania appeared in Germany, where he produced a work that attempted nothing less than a total reconciliation of modern Protestantism and popular notions of "wisdom in nature."

In his 1689 dissertation *Natural Theology, or, Metamorphosis of the Metaphysics*, a twenty-two-year-old Johannes Kelpius began with one the most glaring philosophical questions facing the early Protestants: With intellectual and religious authority resting solely in the scriptures, why did pagans everywhere seem to have more than a basic awareness of the reality of God? "The fact that God exists has always been a great consensus among all people," he writes, "and that no people were so barbarous nor so untamed, nor so feral, that even though they didn't know how it was fitting to worship God, they knew that he was fit to be honored."[121] How did pagan people, who have never enjoyed access to the scriptures, seem to understand the reality of God? Indeed, how do pagans all over the world and throughout history seem to demonstrate not only awareness of God, but coherent and consistent moral sensibilities? Kelpius goes on:

> Whence indeed was the cognition concerning God appear among the pagans? Did God send them word from above? By no means! But because it would have been possible to more potently mislead them by a word, it happened that, placing his creation in the middle [between humanity and God], so that a wise man from the rude people of Scythia, a barbarous person, by looking at those things that were subjected to eyes, having been taught beauty, might be able to ascend to God.[122]

For Kelpius, there was a simple solution to the Protestant problem of the pagan awareness of God: it was, essentially, the Hermetic and Paracelsian notion of

50 AMERICAN AURORA

"wisdom in nature." Rather than send the pagans "word from above," he writes, which was likely to "potently mislead them," God taught the Pagans by placing something more durable and intelligible before them: creation, the environment, the cosmos, in which a "barbarous" person without access to scripture or even writing could experience some "cognition concerning God."

As Platonic as this might seem, Kelpius was writing a Lutheran dissertation in theology, and he was careful to distinguish himself from ancient philosophical ideas. Ancient philosophers, operating without the benefit of scripture, recognized creation as simply synonymous with God, he writes. The ancient notion that "matter is coeval to God," Kelpius writes, was the "source of this unceasing error . . . the reservoir from which the various modes of Heathen Philosophy appear to flow."[123] Kelpius was neither a Platonist nor an outright pantheist: he was a Lutheran theologian who was deeply influenced by the Hermetic ideas dispersed by alchemists like Paracelsus and popularized by fellow Lutherans like Arndt and Böhme. Kelpius's academic writings show us a young intellectual trying to reconcile his orthodox education with the popular Hermetic ideas of his time.

He supported his claim with abundant reference to scripture. He quoted three passages from 1 Corinthians, where Paul insists that God communicates in ways beyond language: "not with wisdom of words," "came not with excellency of speech or of wisdom," "not with enticing words of man's wisdom."[124] This young theologian was wisely challenging Lutheran orthodoxy not with alchemical or Hermetic ideas directly, but with the words of Paul. Sounding very much like Johann Arndt, Kelpius masked his environmental approach to theology with reference to Paul. Thus, the decidedly un-Lutheran notion that God communicates beyond scripture finds its basis in scripture.

Here Kelpius reaches the same problem that Leibniz addressed in his letter to Thomasius. After a long detour through ancient and scholastic philosophy, Kelpius turns to Aristotle directly, suggesting first that the *Metaphysics* was collated from the *Physics* long after Aristotle's life and that the two must be read together. It is "Only lately therefore," Kelpius writes, that the scholastics "cut the Metaphysical knowledge . . . off from the Pneumatic [knowledge] concerning God and spirits."[125] The following passage might sound nitpicky to us today, but it was tremendously important to the wider intellectual circumstances of the seventeenth century:

[The scholastics] conjoined the creator GOD into one knowledge with the created spirits, so that also today a major part of the "young Turks" [*Recentium*], who would desire to separate particular from universal knowledge, left God with the Angels in the same [category of] knowledge commonly called *Pneumatic* [spiritual], not noticing . . . that there is a greater distance between God and created spirits than between them and natural things; and indeed a finite thing is farther from an infinite one than from another finite thing; again there are more things in common with created spirits and other creatures than with God; and these things are absolutely obvious by which created spirits are separated from God.[126]

Through a reconstitution of the *Physics* and *Metaphysics* of Aristotle, then, Kelpius attempted to correct the philosophical record that has plagued Christianity through the Middle Ages. God *created* the intelligent spirits that share our environment with us, Kelpius writes. It is a mistake, then, to put created things like angels, intelligent spirits, and pneumatic/spiritual forces generally into one category with God, when there is clearly a greater distance between creator and creation than within varying facets of creation. In other words, we have more in common with angels than we have in common with God.

Kelpius concluded his dissertation with a direct critique of the philosophy of his time. The scholastic error of separating the *Metaphysics* form the *Physics* initiated a cascade of mistakes that culminated in contemporary trends in Cartesian mechanism:

The possible resolution of all phenomena into purely mechanical causes (with even the bodies of plants and animals not being excepted) would inflict so great a wound, especially to the essential parts of religion, that the incautious ones [would] persuade themselves that things that may only seemingly be true are actually true and solid . . . exposing the existence of GOD and their own immortal souls to the wickedest derision and contempt.[127]

Again, we see the souls of plants and animals at the core of the early modern negotiations between a living world and a mechanical world, between religion and irreligion, between God and "wicked derision." Kelpius argued that Descartes has built upon this severing of the *Metaphysics* from the *Physics*, and in doing so, he drew the error of the pagans to a logical conclusion: if everything is God, it is not complicated to suggest that nothing is. Although Kelpius and Leibniz never refer to one another, we can see clearly why a philosopher like Leibniz had such an interest in Aristotle's *Metaphysics*, which laid out a modern path for permanently excising the wisdom and spirit in nature.

Kelpius argued precisely the opposite, remaining firmly attached to the popular Hermetic Protestant notion of wisdom in nature, of a creation that was abundantly analogous with both God and the human. He completed his argument with another quotation from Paul. "Let us behave in such a way that, from the visible phenomena of the world, to quote the Apostle, from the creation of the world or from those things done as miracles of God, we understand that his

52 AMERICAN AURORA

power and divinity are forever."[128] Kelpius did not need Plato to advance his critique of Descartes or the scholastics, or to argue in favor of wisdom in nature. Paul backed him up again here, too.

Both Kelpius and Leibniz were writing during a moment that historians like Carolyn Merchant have identified as being of crucial philosophical importance: the transition from traditional models of cosmos as a living, organic whole into images of the cosmos as an utterly material mechanical process: God's ticking clock of Leibniz's letter.[129] Most interesting for our purposes is Merchant's identification of the major outliers in this trend, like Paracelsus, Agrippa, Giordano Bruno, and the later Cambridge Platonists, all of whom were influenced by Hermetic ideas in varying ways.

Kelpius's fierce defense of the souls of plants and animals, the presence of angels, spirit, and intelligence throughout creation, and the scriptural basis for the wisdom in nature shows his clear sympathy for such ideas. Leibniz's assertion that there was "no wisdom in nature" was a direct refutation of Hermetic authors like Agrippa, and of popularizers like Arndt. It was also a kind of prophetic assertion, if we can allow ourselves to imagine Leibniz making one: "no wisdom in nature" was an Enlightenment motto and, we might say, a moment of seventeenth-century climate change denial. We do not have to be seventeenth-century Hermetic Protestants to pay attention as the climate changes before our eyes.

In this chapter, I have argued that seventeenth-century Protestants like Kelpius sought out Hermetic and alchemical literature because it offered an environmental knowledge applicable to a changing climate. Most significantly for our understanding, these authors put forward a *contemplative* rather than experimental or scientific approach to the environment. As Andrew Weeks writes of Paracelsus, "It is not hit-or-miss experimentation but, rather contemplation of the macrocosm that discloses the secrets of nature."[130] The same has been noted of Jacob Böhme: contemplation of nature is not meant to yield scientific fact, but rather moral insight.[131] This contemplative, intuitive posture toward the environment is a challenge for moderns to understand on a basic level. "The watershed that separates us from [Böhme's] vision is that of modern science," Weeks and Andersson write, and the same could be said for the other authors covered in this chapter. Weeks and Andersson go on to explain what exactly separates the sciences from Böhme's worldview: "Natural science instructs us that the universe is not composed of moral or sentient forces."[132] As Zimmerman wrote of Newton, "I fear that [he] wishes his discourse to be understood mathematically only." This anxiety of Zimmerman's cuts to the core of Hermetic Protestant environmental knowledge: for many people living in the seventeenth century, the cosmos was speaking a language that could not be reduced to mathematics.

Vita I

"Strange Things of the Invisible Worlds"

Kelpius in Europe, 1667–1693

Johann Kelp was born in 1667 in a village called Denndorf, known today as Daia, in Transylvania, in what is now part of the modern state of Romania.[1] The Kelp family were members of a long-standing German ethnic group in the region, the Transylvanian Saxons, German-speaking immigrants who had settled the area of Transylvania near the border with Hungary in the twelfth and thirteenth centuries. In the mid-seventeenth century, Johann was born between two tectonic religious and political formations: to his west was the political rubble of Christian Europe following the Treaty of Westphalia and the conclusion of the Thirty Years War; to his east was the Ottoman Empire at its zenith. As one historian put it, "In the second half of the seventeenth century, not for the first time, Transylvania balanced between the powers of Christian Europe and the Ottoman Empire."[2]

It was also a period of persistent drought, cold, and war. Just a few years before Johann was born, a combination of extreme cold and drought brought the Danube River low enough and froze it hard enough that the Ottoman army walked right across it into Romania, where it left "no blade of grass or soul alive anywhere."[3] In 1661, a local official wrote in his journal that "Transylvania never knew such misery as this last year," thanks to the prolonged cold and drought.[4] As Geoffrey Parker has written, "The Little Ice Age seems to have struck the lands around the eastern Mediterranean with particular force," where "winters of the later 1680s were at least 3°C cooler than today."[5] Johann was born into a climate, both environmental and cultural, that was subject to sudden and violent change. The historical circumstances surrounding his youth would not have provided the young man with many reasons to feel fondly toward nation-states, empires, or the churches that served them. It was, by any measure, a bad time and place to be born.

Today, Denndorf is still a country village nestled in the low mountains, reachable only by a gravel road along the Şaeş River. Johann would have been accustomed to the sight of rolling wooded hills, a lonely steeple adorned with a six-pointed star, and the text of Luther's German Bible. He was the youngest child of an evidently accomplished and fairly well-to-do country family among the Transylvanian Saxons.[6] His father, George Kelp, was minister to the small

54 AMERICAN AURORA

Lutheran congregation in Denndorf. The church where Johann's father served as pastor, built in 1447 and subsequently fortified throughout the sixteenth century, still stands over Daia today.[7] His older brother, Martin Kelp, was rector at a school in the neighboring city of Schäßburg (today, the Romanian city of Sighişoara). Another older brother, the junior Georg Kelp, eventually became the mayor of Schäßburg. His mother, Katharina Kelp (née Streitforter), was twenty-nine years old when Johannes was born in 1667, and she died three years later.[8] The sources do not tell us anything else about her.

As a boy, Johann went to the school in Schäßburg where his brother Martin served as rector. The road between Daia and Sighişoara today is a winding country lane that negotiates wooded hills on either side, from an isolated village to the comparatively cosmopolitan Schäßburg. It is a setting that reminds me of Pennsylvania's wooded hills, and perhaps the landscape of southeastern Pennsylvania reminded Kelpius of his home.[9] Johann's father, the senior George Kelp, died in 1685. Johann would have been eighteen at the time. The Kelp family was an established name in the area, and Johann's higher education was immediately sponsored by the mayor of Schäßburg, Michael Deli, and two others: Count Valentin Franck and Johann Zabanius. The youngest Kelp, then, was not a prince or a noble, but he enjoyed enough prestige and connections in his native Transylvania to attend university in Germany. He must have been a precocious student to attract this kind of support.[10]

In 1687, at the age of twenty, Johannes wrote a panegyric for Michael Deli, the mayor and sponsor of his education. This is the earliest surviving document in Johann's ornate Latin, and it is also the earliest appearance of his signature in the Latinized academic fashion of the day: the young man was now "Johannes Kelpius."[11] As a poem in honor of a public official, the document was probably recited by Kelpius in some official setting—no small prestige for the young man from Denndorf. Johannes Kelpius was, it seems, a big fish in the small pond of seventeenth-century Schäßburg.[12]

Kelpius was born and brought up in the Lutheran church, and sincerity of his Christian faith and the primacy of scripture are two facets of this upbringing from which he never once wavers. But sometime between 1687 and 1693, Kelpius underwent a serious shift from orthodox Lutheranism to radical separatist Pietism. During this same period, his signature in matriculation registers at three different universities gives us a scant but nonetheless interpretable itinerary of a young man moving between the major centers of Pietist thought and activity in Europe.

His higher education having been sponsored by the nobles of Schäßburg, Kelpius's name appeared in the matriculation register at the University of Leipzig later that year.[13] Johannes—now twenty—had left Transylvania behind and made the journey to Germany, embarking on a course of study in theology toward the

"STRANGE THINGS OF THE INVISIBLE WORLDS" 55

title of Magister. Kelpius moved from his native Transylvania to the University of Leipzig in 1687, for what must have been a short stint at the university. At this exact time and place, theology students at the university were convening under the early Pietist leader August Herman Francke (1663–1727). Originally, Francke's conventicle was a simple study group, a place for theology students to read and discuss biblical Hebrew and Greek texts together. Eventually, the theologian Philipp Jakob Spener (1635–1705), who would later go on to be known as the founder of Pietism, heard about the group, and he urged Francke to "change the focus from an academic exercise to a devotional one."[14] After a while, the informal study group gave way to ecstatic devotional sessions of biblical interpretation. Under the leadership of Francke, the Leipzig circle eschewed philosophy, technical learning, and academic theology in favor of a devotional and intensely pious approach to biblical interpretation. The Francke group, called the *collegium philobiblicum*, would eventually become one of the core intellectual origins of what became the later Pietist movement, as its members spread across the continent to different European cities and universities.[15]

The possibility of Kelpius's attendance at the *collegium philobiblicum* has not been discussed in scholarship before, but given the timing of his arrival and the facts of his later life trajectory, it must be considered a possibility, if not a likelihood. Kelpius appears to refer to the *collegium* directly in his later correspondence, in which he describes the early circumstances of Pietism in Europe: "The Students in the Universities forsake their former way of Learning and applied themselves wholly to Piety and Godliness, (from whence their name was derived) leaving and some burning their heathenish Logiks, Rhetoriks, Metaphysiks."[16] Later in the very same letter, Kelpius singles out Saxony as an extraordinarily potent area of early Pietism.[17] Since Leipzig was the only city in Saxony in which Kelpius ever lived (according to the sources we have), and since he refers to university students casting off philosophy for devotion, it seems likely that he was referring to the *collegium* of Francke in Leipzig.

Kelpius would have been a latecomer at the *collegium*, arriving in 1687, only months before Francke left for Lüneberg to continue his studies. He would not have been able to attend meetings for very long, but he would have seen the *collegium* just before it ended, meetings where the twenty-year-old would have witnessed deeply radical and prophetic expressions of Christian thought. He also would have been exposed to Böhme and Arndt, if he had not already. After Francke left and the group disbanded, it is not hard to imagine the young theologian looking for a new center of Pietist thought, a place where he could both continue his studies and maintain participation in this new and radical Christianity. Kelpius left Leipzig, but he did not burn his heathenish logics right away.

In December of that very year his name appeared in the matriculation register at the University of Tübingen in Württemberg, at a time when a particularly

56 AMERICAN AURORA

apocalyptic and Böhmian strain of Pietism was sweeping the countryside.[18] It was also the site of some of the most radical articulations of early Pietist thought, suggesting as it did that the Lutheran church itself (in addition to the Catholics and Calvinists) was the Antichrist on earth. Organized Pietist activity in Württemberg began in 1684, when its early leaders were two radical separatists: Ludwig Brunnquell, "a clergyman dismissed for his chiliastic preaching and his affection for the writings of Jacob Boehme," and an apocalyptic astronomer named Johann Jacob Zimmerman.[19] There is no indication that Kelpius interacted with Zimmerman or Brunnquell directly at this point. Zimmerman was probably already lodging with the Pietists in Frankfurt with his family, as he was expelled from the state of Württemberg in 1684 for his prophetic statements about the destruction of the Lutheran church, and reappeared only later in Frankfurt and Hamburg.[20] Kelpius may have been pointed toward the University of Tübingen in Württemberg by his Pietist contacts in Leipzig as another place where he could continue his studies and participate in Pietist conventicle meetings. Kelpius's involvement with the Pietists at Württemberg, like his possible connection with the Leipzig group, would explain much of his later life trajectory.[21]

Kelpius did not leave a memoir or account of this period of his life, and we must try to piece together a narrative from the dates on matriculation registers, historical context, and Kelpius's own oblique references. The details of his study at Tübingen are missing (and the University of Altdorf, which closed in 1809, does not have available records), but there is an intriguing passage from his 1689 dissertation that indicates that he had not left on the best of terms. Here he is addressing his mentor, Johann Fabricius:

> For you are the gracious lord, who have nurtured, cherished, protected me thus (would that I were worthy of such happiness!) under the shadow of your wings when I was shut out through the immense cruelty of the most Christian of Christians from the Grace of Wurtemberg, as you saw.[22]

In this passage, Kelpius discloses that he did not leave Tübingen willingly. Who was "the most Christian of Christians," and why was Kelpius "shut out"? It is not likely that his academic performance was lacking—he found immense success at the University of Altdorf in the next few years, and he was apparently immediately admitted therein under Fabricius's mentorship and protection. But why was he expelled from Tübingen, as he suggests in his dissertation? This reference to *Christianissimi in Christianos* is almost certainly a reference to Louis XIV, who invaded Württemberg and the Palatinate—including Tübingen—in 1688, just after Kelpius arrived. This is a sarcastic reference to the style of the French sovereign, *Rex Christianissimus*, and to Louis, whose invasion likely pushed Kelpius north to Altdorf and Nuremberg. There, the "most Christian of Christians," as he was known, opted for a total-war campaign in the already devastated Palatinate and Württemberg, hoping to deny resources and food to the German army. The site of the "Hermetic Golden Age," as Yates called it, was a horrific war-zone throughout the seventeenth century.

After fleeing Tübingen, Kelpius went on to pursue his degree at the University of Altdorf, in Nuremberg, with Johannes Fabricius (1644–1729).[23] It was a good match for the budding radical. Fabricius's theological focus was an area called "irenics," from the Greek ειρήνη "peace," focused on resolving doctrinal dispute and ameliorating the tensions between different Christian denominations. Fabricius's irenic bent would eventually land him in hot water when, in 1707, he was forced to resign his teaching post after authoring the heretical opinion that a Calvinist and a Catholic might marry without sin, since both religions shared a common root in scripture.[24]

But in 1688, he was the perfect instructor for a brilliant young theologian with an increasingly radical streak. Kelpius's love and admiration for his mentor are evident in his dissertation and in the short correspondence they shared fifteen years later, in 1705.[25] During his time at Altdorf, Kelpius worked as a private instructor and completed his degree, attaining the title of Magister in 1689 at the age of twenty-two.[26] The great Protestant theologian and historian of religions Ernst Benz, reviewing Kelpius's university writings, writes that Kelpius "revealed himself as an opponent of orthodox Lutheran scholasticism and an advocate, like most Pietists, of an irenic theology."[27]

I have already examined Kelpius's 1689 Altdorf dissertation, *Natural Theology, or, Metamorphosis of the Metaphysics* in the previous chapter.[28] More writings from Kelpius's time in Nuremberg at the University of Altdorf quickly followed. In the following year, 1690, he coauthored a major study of the church fathers with his mentor, Fabricius: *Scylla Theology: Some Examples of the Fathers and Doctors of the Church.*[29] In this text, Kelpius and Fabricius analyze early ecclesiastical polemics in the work of several major leaders of the early church, including Tertullian, Saint Dionysius the Great, Arius, Augustine, and Pelagius. This course of study clearly reveals that Kelpius's reading ranged far beyond orthodox Lutheran theology and scripture. Kelpius's future dedication to rigorous asceticism at Wissahickon, perhaps, owed more to the ancient writings of the church fathers than has previously been recognized.

In 1690 another university essay appeared, *Pagan Ethics*, in which Kelpius asked whether Aristotle (and the *Ethics* in particular) was a suitable course of study for "young Christian men." Aristotle is *not* suitable for young Christians, he concluded, because a course of pagan philosophy without sufficient grounding in Christian scripture could lead unwitting young Christians to sin and error.[30] Like Paracelsus before him, Kelpius rejected the mingling of philosophy and theology, which he calls "darkness [philosophy] and light [Christianity]" in the text.

58   AMERICAN AURORA

At this point—around the end of 1690 or early 1691—something changed. Kelpius's prolific pen went silent, and his paper trail in Europe evaporated. He no longer appeared in matriculation registers, and he never accepted a permanent teaching position, at least as far as the primary sources tell us. By the age of twenty-three, the young scholar seems to have walked away from what could have been a prestigious career as a professor, pastor, schoolteacher, or scholar. His next appearance in the primary sources is in 1693, by which point he had joined with a group led by Johann Jacob Zimmerman, with designs to leave Europe for Pennsylvania.

Having reviewed some of the major historical, cultural, and religious trends surrounding Kelpius's life and times in seventeenth-century Europe, we are left with a question: Why would a promising young Lutheran theologian align himself with Johann Jacob Zimmerman in the early 1690s, with Zimmerman's public standing at a nadir, and Kelpius's bright future as a scholar and theologian laid out before him? Why would Kelpius see the author of *scriptura et naturam* as a comrade?[31]

Nearly a decade later, in 1699, Kelpius would write a letter describing the Pietist movement for a Stephen Mumford, an early leader of the Seventh Day Baptists. Here I would like to turn to this source more directly, since it is in this short document, I think, that Kelpius provides some clues of his own experiences in German Pietism and gives some hints at his reason for leaving Europe and the Lutheran church. In the letter, Kelpius describes what happened in Europe when Pietism began to spread in the seventeenth century, going so far as to make Mumford a list. "For when these things begin to ferment everywhere," he writes:

> 1. The Students in the Universities forsake their former way of Learning and applied themselves wholly to Piety and Godliness, (from whence their name was derived) leaving and some burning their heathenish Logiks, Rhetoriks, Metaphysiks. 2. The Laymen or Auditors begun to find fault with the Sermons and Lifes of their Ministers, seeing there was nothing of Ye Power of the Holy Ghost, nor of the Life of Christ and his Apostels. . . . yea some in their tender years came to witness strange things of the Invisible worlds.[32]

In this passage, Kelpius recalls the circumstances of early Pietism from the perspective of university students. I suspect that in this passage in particular, Kelpius is recalling events of his own youth and veering into memoir. The "heathenish Logiks, Rhetoriks, Metaphysiks" are cast aide in favor of "Piety and Godliness," and indeed, this is *precisely* the life trajectory of Kelpius, who abandons his promising academic career in favor of a severe ascetic practice at some point after 1690. The laity, too, he notes, are fed up with overly academic and scholarly preaching, in which they find neither "Ye Power of the Holy Ghost, nor of the Life of Christ and his Apostles." The Pietists, on the other hand, preached an emotional and ecstatic form of Christianity, with feeling, passion, and experience at the root of the religious life.

There is a third and final hidden memoir in that passage: "Yea some in their tender years came to witness strange things of the Invisible worlds." Kelpius is referring here to the ecstatic and outright miraculous episodes attributed to the early Pietists. As Peter Yoder and others have written, supernatural and miraculous phenomena were common and very important among the early Pietists. As Yoder writes, "During the first part of the 1690s there were several reports of visions, prophetic voices, and healings occurring among Pietists during worship services and conventicle meetings." Dramatic events like "miraculous levitation and the sweating and crying of blood" legitimized Pietist practices and "substantiated a Pietist narrative that they were living in a special period of God's presence."[33] As we will see in Chapter 3, many of the Pietists that Kelpius would later travel to Pennsylvania with were known to have ecstatic powers and episodes.

Paranormal phenomena continued to be major factors in later strands of Pietist thought: Ernst Benz has analyzed the paranormal currents in the German theologian Friedrich Christoph Oetinger (1702–1782), which he ultimately traces back to Paracelsus.[34] He has also pointed out the Pietist roots of Swedish seer and prophet Emmanuel Swedenborg (1688–1772).[35] There is clearly more work to be done in understanding the importance of Pietism to the historiography of the paranormal, Kelpius not excluded.

In his letter to Steven Mumford, Kelpius went into great detail about the ecstatic and miraculous phenomena that occurred at conventicle meetings and among the Pietists and related groups during this period. "This Penn is too dull," he wrote, "to express the extraordinary Power the Pietists and Chiliasts among the Protestants in Germany."[36] He goes on:

This only I say, as one who hath read the Histories, that since the days of the Apostles, such Miraculous Powers and operations have not been manifested as in a matter of 3½ years among these. And like as the Miracles wrought by God through the Hand of Moyses was for the main part in the outward Creation or Macrocosm, the Miracles of Jesus the Messia on the Bodys of Man or Microcosm, so these in our days was wrought (much like unto them in the days of the Apostles) on the Soul and more interiour parts by Ectases, Revelations, Inspirations, Illuminations, Inspeakings, Prophesies, Apparitions, Changings of Minds, Transfigurations, Translations of their Bodys, wonderful Fastings for 11, 14, 27, 37 days, Paradysical Representations by Voices, Melodies, and Sensations to the very perceptibility of the Spectators who was about such persons, whose condition as to the inward condition of their Souls, as well as their outward Transactions, yea their very thoughts they could tell during the time of their Exstacies, though they had never seen nor heard of the Persons before.[37]

In this remarkable passage, Kelpius clearly places miraculous, ecstatic, and supernatural phenomena at the *heart* of the narrative of the beginnings of Pietism. These are not auxiliary phenomena or legitimizing events that "substantiated a Pietist narrative," as Peter Yoder suggests. These events and experiences were the *core* of why Pietism was so important to him. Furthermore, they are clearly connected to a Paracelsian cosmology of corresponding macrocosm and microcosm, a cosmotheist worldview derived from Arndt but leading back into Hermeticism.

As we will see in coming chapters, scripture was the ground of Kelpius's thought, and this remains the case in this passage: these phenomena suggested that God is increasingly present in the world at this stage of history, as, Kelpius tells us, in the days of the Apostles. Kelpius refers to the Acts of the Apostles twice in this letter, in what appears to be the closest thing I have found to a joke in his entire written corpus. As he continues to describe the origins of the Pietists and the events and powers they witnessed for Mumford, he opens a parenthetical: "(Excuse me, dear Heart, that I thus run into an Allegoricall Application, for the very same Comedy was played as you read in the Acts of the Apostels, only the time and persons changed.)"[38]

Kelpius is being funny here, and we might just savor that for a moment. But listen to his point: in describing the origins of the Pietists between (up to 1693, when he left Europe), he claims that his experience of Pietism was so analogous to the events of the Acts of the Apostles that "only the time and persons changed." In the same way that Zimmerman's exegesis of the Great Comet drew his reader's attention to the miracles that followed other comets in history, Kelpius puts extraordinary phenomena at the *heart* of his own experience of Pietism.

Reading Kelpius's own explanation of early Pietism in his 1699 letter, we can see a bit more clearly why a promising young theologian walked away from his career: because as a young man (he was still a teenager at Leipzig and Württemberg) in his conventicle and *collegium* meetings in Leipzig, Tübingen, and eventually Nuremberg and elsewhere, Kelpius saw and heard of things that he could only compare to the miracles of Acts of the Apostles: "Yea some in their tender years came to witness strange things of the Invisible worlds," he writes, in an unguarded moment of memoir. When Kelpius responded to a letter asking for information about the early Pietists, his response shows that their extraordinary powers of mind and body were not just part of the story, or legitimizing the story. The paranormal powers and ecstasies of the early Pietists *were* the story.

Personal witness to "strange things of the Invisible worlds" convinced him that he was living through a divine phase of history. So he left his family in Transylvania, he left the church, and he left his promising academic career behind. He was looking for a place where he might dedicate himself "wholly to Piety and Godliness." There were rumors about a British Quaker who was busy establishing just such a place.

2

"Gone into the Ancient Forest"

Hermetic Protestantism and Environmental Knowledge in Early Pennsylvania

> For the lord, who is ungrudging, is seen through the entire cosmos.
> Can you see understanding and hold it in your hands? Can you have
> a vision of the image of god?
>
> —*Hermetica*, Book V[1]

Pastor Schuhmacher's Apocalypse

Sometime in the years just before the American Revolutionary War, an itinerant Lutheran pastor in eastern Pennsylvania named Johan Daniel Schuhmacher produced an untitled illustration depicting a huge stag rearing up in a rolling field, with a quaking church in the background (Figure 2.1). The only text on the document is a quotation from Luther's Genesis: "Naphtali 'ist ein Schneller Hirsch und gibt Schöne Rede,'" "Naphtali is a swift stag and gives beautiful speech."[2] Schuhmacher's illustration was a Pennsylvania *vorschrift*, a handmade manuscript combining illustration, scripture, and elaborate decoration that would serve as illustrated sermons, pedagogical tools, or simply beautiful aesthetic objects. *Vorschriften*, like Schuhmacher's stag, were meant for congregations composed of Palatinate immigrants who colonized southeastern Pennsylvania during the late seventeenth and eighteenth centuries.[3]

The text that Schuhmacher reproduced was an excerpt from Jacob's deathbed poem (often called the "Blessing" or "Testament" of Jacob) to his twelve sons, the originators of Israel's twelve tribes, each of whom he compares with a wild animal. As described in Genesis, Napthali is Jacob's sixth son. In Jacob's verse and in this illustration, Naphtali is likened to a swift stag who speaks beautifully. Schumacher's *vorschrift* displays an autodidactic illustrative technique, and it seems to depict a rather pastoral—simplistic, even—vision of one of the verses in the Blessing of Jacob. Naphtali is rendered simply and literally as a deer rearing up in a meadow, while a creaking steeple leans in the background. But why was the Blessing of Jacob of special interest, and why single out Naphtali?

American Aurora. Timothy Grieve-Carlson, Oxford University Press. © Oxford University Press 2024.
DOI: 10.1093/oso/9780197765562.003.0003

"GONE INTO THE ANCIENT FOREST" 63

Figure 2.1 The Apocalypse of Daniel Schuhmacher. Courtesy of the Pennsylvania German Society.

Why have you gathered us here on Sunday to look at your drawing of a deer, Pastor Schuhmacher?

The artist was a German immigrant to Halifax, Nova Scotia, in 1751. He appears to have taken up the ministry there without ordination and may well have falsified his recommendation from the Lutheran Ministerium in Hamburg. Within a short time of his arrival, an alcohol-related dispute compelled him to flee south to Pennsylvania, where he presented himself again as an ordained Lutheran pastor. He proceeded to preach and baptize widely in southeastern Pennsylvania during the latter half of the eighteenth century. Church records indicate that he baptized at least seventeen hundred children during his lifetime and ordained several other ministers. He was also in perpetual conflict with the Lutheran authorities in the region, who accused him of drunkenness and blasphemy. Henry Melchior Mühlenberg, the eighteenth-century Lutheran mission leader in southeastern Pennsylvania, described Schuhmacher in his diary as "a scandalous vagrant preacher" who brought his congregations to "ruin." Schuhmacher's simultaneous popularity among the laity and fraught relationship with the Lutheran authorities of his day gives us some insight into the influence of Lutheran orthodoxy in southeastern Pennsylvania toward the middle of the eighteenth century.[4]

Schuhmacher also carried a telescope and had a bit of a millennialist streak in his Christianity.[5] I have already described another *vorschrift* piece of Schuhmacher's in the introduction, one that depicts an ornately rendered comet

64 AMERICAN AURORA

blazing through the sky, heralded by a winged angel with trumpet and scripture in hand. The text reads: "Up to the Judgment; up, do not miss it. A comet star of very pale color appeared in Pennsylvania in the year 1769 in August. You people, ask yourselves what this star may mean, whether God wants to punish you. O, do penance while there is still time."[6] Daniel Schuhmacher, as we will see, was steeped in some of the practices of apocalyptic environmental knowledge that proliferated amid the mingling of Hermeticism and Pietism in early modern Germany during the previous century. His will mentioned two books of Johann Arndt's, including *True Christianity*.[7]

Now let's turn back to that weird deer in the meadow.

In 1966, John Stoudt, a historian of early Pennsylvania German material and religious culture, described his reaction to the piece: "At first glance this picture is puzzling. . . . What can that strange-looking stag mean?" The meaning, as Stoudt gradually interprets it, must lie in the allegorical significance "of each one of Jacob's sons" in the Blessing of Jacob. The Naphtali script alongside the other apocalyptic works of Schuhmacher gives a hint, for Stoudt, with which "the full significance of the picture begins to become clear."[8] Stoudt goes on to demonstrate that the piece does not just refer to Genesis itself, but to a particular interpretation of the biblical text: Schuhmacher's illustration, in fact, alludes to the seventeenth-century Protestant mystic Jacob Böhme's 1623 esoteric interpretation of the book of Genesis, *Mysterium Magnum*.[9]

In *Mysterium*, Böhme reads the Blessing of Jacob allegorically, with Jacob's twelve sons representative of twelve stages of history. Böhme guides the reader through the stages, beginning with the creation of the world and culminating in the decline of the church and the end of history. The stage of Naphtali, the tenth mentioned of twelve sons in the Blessing of Jacob, though the sixth born, is a time of complex rhetoric, doctrinal disputes, and "knotty logic."[10] Naphtali is a swift stag who speaks beautifully, *saying nothing*. Babbling his sophisticated but empty words in the sermons and the universities, Naphtali transforms Christian life into a matter of mere academic dispute, bringing on the Antichrist.

Schuhmacher's piece suddenly takes on a dark tone in this analysis: as Stoudt points out, in contrast to his other pieces, Schuhmacher seems to intentionally distort the lines in this illustration. The ground suddenly seems to be trembling rather than gently rolling, and the rearing stag is no longer a gentle pastoral object, but a baleful, menacing presence, with empty eyes and gaping mouth signifying the cacophonous jabbering and moral degradation of the world.[11] Stoudt summarizes his interpretation of the piece in a simple title: "Pastor Schuhmacher's Apocalypse."[12]

In Stoudt's analysis, then, what at first appeared to be a simplistic, if perplexing, example of early Pennsylvania manuscript art turns out to have been a deeply esoteric and subtle apocalypse, composed by one of early Pennsylvania's busiest

"GONE INTO THE ANCIENT FOREST" 65

and most heterodox country pastors. This interpretation, illuminating as it is, is only possible when one acknowledges that Schuhmacher and his audience— rural, German-speaking Lutherans on the fringes of the colonies in the eighteenth century—were engaged in a vernacular tradition that was steeped in the writings and ideas of figures like Jacob Böhme.

Where did these German Lutherans come from? The vast majority of German immigrants to eastern Pennsylvania in the eighteenth century arrived from the *Pfalz*, the Palatinate, that devastated region singled out in the previous chapter, which Frances Yates identified as the site of a brief "Hermetic golden age," and the same place where as many as one-third of the population were killed during the Thirty Years War.[13] The German-speaking population of early Pennsylvania had unique exposure to both the horrors of war and esoteric religion and philosophy. Small wonder, then, that Daniel Schuhmacher drew for them a pastoral apocalypse derived from the works of Böhme.

They came for many of the same reasons that refugees cross dangerous borders today: to escape the indiscriminate violence of geopolitical conflict, in particular the incursions of Louis XIV into the Palatinate and Würtemburg toward the end of the seventeenth century. Many also came to escape the highly discriminate violence of religious persecution, particularly as orthodoxy tightened its grip on the laity amid the repeated waves of Pietistic foment in the region. Ultimately, they came because they believed this other place would afford them a chance to thrive that their homeland did not.[14]

And like many refugees who cross dangerous borders today, the Palatinate Germans were mostly unwelcome in their new home. There were many demagogues awaiting them in Pennsylvania, but the most eloquent xenophobe who greeted the Palatinates in Penn's Woods was Benjamin Franklin, who bemoaned the Palatine incursion into what he hoped would be an English ethnostate:

> Why should the Palatine Boors be suffered to swarm into our Settlements, and by herding together establish their Language and Manners to the Exclusion of ours? Why should Pennsylvania, founded by the English, become a Colony of *Aliens*, who will shortly be so numerous as to Germanize us instead of our Anglifying them, and will never adopt our Language or Customs, any more than they can acquire our Complexion.[15]

Franklin's mobilization of the category of whiteness against Palatine immigrants shows how racial, religious, and linguistic categories blurred as the colony grew into a young state: "In Europe, the Spaniards, Italians, French, Russians and Swedes, are generally of what we call a swarthy Complexion; as are the Germans also," writes Franklin, before going on to ask his reader if they would be better off excluding such undesirables—on the basis of their "complexion"—from what Franklin imaged as a properly English population.

The more things change.

Early American Hermetic Protestantism

This chapter explores how Hermetic Protestant ideas were distributed in seventeenth-century Pennsylvania, in the years leading up to and following the arrival of Johannes Kelpius. Focusing on Francis Daniel Pastorius and Daniel Leeds while exploring the general political and cultural forces at work, this chapter shows how Hermetic Protestant environmental thought flourished in early Pennsylvania.

Writing in 1966, Stoudt's conclusions about Schuhmacher's apocalypse must have seemed far-fetched, but his credentials here are unusually strong. As the author of a still-cited monograph on Böhme and numerous studies of early Pennsylvania material culture, Stoudt was in a unique position to read and interpret the Apocalypse of Daniel Schuhmacher.[16] Still, the notion of such esoteric Christian ideas disseminating through the laity at scale seems to strain our inherited notions of early American religion. Our popular image of early American religion was, and to some extent remains, more Puritan than Pietist, more orthodox than esoteric, and less steeped in Jacob Böhme than in John Calvin. This is by no means a new complaint. The same situation was bemoaned by the nineteenth-century American poet John Greenleaf Whittier in his 1872 book *The Pennsylvania Pilgrim*, an epic retelling of Pennsylvania's religious past that we turn to in more detail in Chapter 6. Explaining the rationale of the poem, Whittier wrote, "The Pilgrims of Plymouth have not lacked historian or poet," in contrast to the comparatively forgotten Quakers, Pietists, and other radicals whom Whittier commemorates in his verse.[17] In John Stoudt's day, these presumptions were just as strong as they were for Whittier.

But nearly half a century later, the historiography is finally beginning to catch up with his interpretation. Matthew Stewart has written of these unexpectedly esoteric forms of rural religion in early America, pointing out that "the remotest regions" of eighteenth-century America were replete with "modes of thought that have almost universally been regarded as too old, too radical, and too continental" for their time and place.[18] But the sources keep telling us their strange and unexpected stories. Indeed, as Alexander Ames has recently demonstrated, early Pennsylvania manuscript arts are often *only* interpretable with a presumption of the immense religious erudition of the artists. In short, these didactic illustrations all over Pennsylvania were not just for nice: they almost always communicated specific and sophisticated religious and philosophical ideas.[19]

"GONE INTO THE ANCIENT FOREST" 67

A number of comprehensive histories of American religion in the past few decades have emerged that have reshaped our understanding of early American religion.[20] Beyond the field of religious studies, historians like Bernard Bailyn and Jill Lepore have noticed the abundant heterodox religious practices in the sources and acknowledged that the religion of early America was more diverse and more frankly occult than has been previously acknowledged.[21] Historians and religious studies scholars have both effectively demonstrated the heterodox, esoteric, and deeply vernacular theology of much early American religious thought. Building upon this foundation, this chapter singles out early Pennsylvania—specifically the Delaware River valley and the environs of seventeenth- and eighteenth-century Philadelphia—as a particularly heterogeneous and radical religious and cultural zone of early America.

Pointing out that early Pennsylvania was marked by religious and cultural pluralism is not exactly a novel scholarly gesture.[22] The founder of the Commonwealth, William Penn, deliberately established the colony as a utopian experiment in religion, ethnicity, and governance, in which—he imagined—persecuted minorities from Europe and Indigenous North Americans could coexist peacefully. Penn's commemoration as the ur-architect of this Pennsylvanian pluralism is persistent. While some of the heterodox religious groups attracted to Penn's Woods would secure and eventually consolidate political power and lasting influence, like the Quakers, other radical and heterodox religious groups, like Pietist separatists, settled the colony in large numbers, largely persisting as vernacular traditions that were denied political influence, institutional power, or public prominence on the basis of attitudes like those of Benjamin Franklin.[23]

In the broader narrative of this book, this chapter serves to contextualize the place where Kelpius and company lived in the Americas, and where they had their most lasting influence: the mid-Atlantic Lenape territory that Europeans claimed as Penn's Woods in the late seventeenth and early eighteenth centuries. Like the first chapter, this chapter builds upon well-trod scholarly foundations and contextualizes each of the chapters that come later while offering its own argument: during the late seventeenth and eighteenth centuries, a vernacular undercurrent of Hermetic Protestantism *flourished* in Pennsylvania beneath the elite cultural constructs of the American Enlightenment.

In the previous chapter, we saw how the German theologian and heresiologist Ehregott Daniel Colberg (1659–1698) called this formation "Platonic-Hermetic Christianity" in Europe. We might follow the historian Catherine Albanese in describing how this new American iteration of Platonic-Hermetic Christianity, in particular its Böhmean current, appeared in America as a decidedly practical and vernacular system of religious knowledge: "The complex theodicy of the Boehmian synthesis, for all its intellectual elements, existed to advance a deeply practical program of spirituality," Albanese writes. Despite the sophistication of

Böhme's theological ideas, in practice, the sensuous and environmental Christian mysticism of Hermetic Protestantism "became a vernacular and nonelite 'path of the heart.'"[24]

As even Colberg recognized, these occultists were, without exception, self-identifying Christians and, more rarely but not insignificantly, sometimes Jews.[25] Popular occultism was always part and parcel of Christian and Jewish life and thought in early America. Following the analysis of Hermetic Protestant environmental thought in the previous chapter, this chapter sketches a brief outline of the place where so many of the European colonists like Kelpius and refugees from the war-ravaged Palatinate found themselves around the turn of the eighteenth century: southeastern Pennsylvania.

In addition to Jacob Böhme, whose writings appear and reappear throughout this chapter, Johann Arndt's *True Christianity* remained enormously popular among German speakers in the colonies and well into the early Republic period.[26] Henry Melchior Mühlenberg, the same Lutheran missionary and ministry leader dispatched to the colonies from the Ministerium in Hamburg (in part to prevent the proliferation of popular clerics like Schuhmacher), mentions Arndt and his writings dozens of times in his journals, often noting with approval that a certain individual kept a copy of "Blessed Arndt" at home as a sign of sincere faith.[27] *True Christianity* was a Protestant mainstay in southeastern Pennsylvania libraries for centuries, and as shown in the last chapter, it served as a vehicle through which essentially Hermetic and alchemical ideas from the Paracelsian corpus could influence the Protestantism of Germans in Pennsylvania (Figure 2.2).

"All of It Is Only Forest"

European colonists, arriving during the seventeenth and eighteenth centuries in the place that would become Pennsylvania, consistently described the area as a "wilderness." As we will see, Kelpius and company would take up the idea of Pennsylvania as wilderness and incorporate it extensively into their theological thought and writings. They were not alone or unique in this regard. William Penn's cousin William Markham declared that Penn's Woods could be "a fine country if it were not so overgrown with woods" when he surveyed the country in 1681. The Germans and the English agreed on this point: "All of it is only forest," complained one early German colonist.[28]

The idea of this mid-Atlantic territory as a vast, forested wilderness was a consistent and pernicious portrayal of early Pennsylvania in the primary literature.[29] The truth of the matter was more complicated. The forested and riparian environment of southeastern Pennsylvania during the seventeenth century was the basis of a comprehensive transportation and economic network that connected

Figure 2.2 Painting and frame, Johann Arndt, unknown maker. Europe or North America, 1750–1800. Oil paint on pine. Bequest of Henry Francis du Pont, Courtesy of Winterthur Museum, Garden & Library.

70   AMERICAN AURORA

the Great Lakes region to the Chesapeake Bay and cut deep into the Allegheny Plateau. Along the Susquehanna, Delaware, Allegheny, and Schuylkill Rivers systems, people, ideas, and commodities drifted from what is now lower Quebec into what is now the coast of Virginia. Recent scholarship on this area suggests that southeastern Pennsylvania was the center of an Indigenous communication and trade network that Bernard Bailyn has described as "certainly more elaborate and efficient than that of eighteenth-century Scotland and probably than those of the rural areas of most of western Europe."[30]

So it was hardly a "wilderness," then, that European colonists and merchants began trickling into throughout the seventeenth century. It was the closely managed and maintained homeland of the Lenape, the Indigenous Algonquin people who inhabited and controlled a territory that ranged from what is now central New Jersey, through the Atlantic plain of southeastern Pennsylvania, and south into the Delaware peninsula. Recent work by the historian Jean R. Soderlund has shown that the Lenape were a decentralized but highly organized tribal group who lived in palisaded towns with an egalitarian social structure, led by sachems who served at the pleasure of "the collective will of the people."[31] This societal structure reflected "their good relations with one another and propensity to avoid war with other nations."[32] The Lenape controlled the coastal openings of one of the most important transportation networks on the continent, and like many cultures who inhabit such crucial interstitial zones, their social structure was determined by a sophisticated practice of diplomacy. Between the Iroquois and the Munsees to the north and the Susquehannock to the west, the Lenape generally maintained a steady and mutually lucrative peace with their neighbors.

This cultural emphasis on diplomacy and conflict resolution among the Lenape is important to bear in mind before we begin a discussion of William Penn's "Holy Experiment" in Lenape country. As David Hackett Fischer has written, Penn's experiment would have been a "disastrous failure" had it been attempted in the homelands of the Wampanoag or the Powhatan. "In the valley of the Delaware, it succeeded splendidly, not only because of the Quakers themselves, but also because of the Indians," Fischer explains.[33] Rather than William Penn and the Quakers bringing peace to the Lenape, as the common story goes, the English Quaker colonization of Lenape territory was an exercise, at first, in conforming to established Indigenous patterns of civic life. The early absence of conflict between the Quaker friends and the Lenape, compared to the extended military campaigns that followed the British colonization of Virginia and New England, were more a Lenape accomplishment than the product of Quaker peacecraft.[34]

And they had been at it for the better part of a century when Penn first arrived in 1681. In fact, as Soderlund's work again has demonstrated, seventeenth-century sources from the Delaware Valley show how the Lenape managed to corral and control European colonial incursions throughout the seventeenth century, as Swedish, Finnish, and Dutch colonists pursued their interests up the Delaware River. With a mixture of sustained, canny diplomacy—and when that failed, controlled bursts of violence—the Lenape established a "model of decentralized authority, preference for peace, and openness toward other cultures and religions."[35] As we will see, William Penn's approach to governance and religion was indeed unique and radical among European colonial leaders, but his "experiment" proceeded in Lenape territory according to cultural terms set by the Lenape themselves.

Seventeenth-century colonists and settlers began their attempts to spread Christianity among the Lenape almost immediately, and with a resounding lack of success. George Fox, the founder of Quakerism, made a journey through Lenape country in the 1670s. He described them as a "loving" people whose leaders had taken pains to learn English, but he had no success at all in talking to the Lenape about Christianity.[36] As it turns out, they had heard it all before. In 1643, Johan Printz, who had been the governor of New Sweden during a short-lived colonial incursion along the Delaware, complained that it would be impossible to make Christians of the Lenape: "When we speak to them about God they pay no attention, but they let it be understood that they are a free people, subject to no one."[37] Printz seems to be identifying what David Graeber and David Wengrow would later call the "Indigenous critique" of seventeenth-century Europeans by Native North Americans, which included staunch resistance to arbitrary hierarchical power and authority, interpersonal subjugation of any kind, and often Christianity itself.[38] And Printz was right: the Lenape rejected Christianity overwhelmingly and repeatedly throughout the seventeenth and eighteenth centuries, as Christian colonists like Johannes Kelpius would witness firsthand.

In the religious cosmos of the Lenape, human beings were one of many intelligent beings coexisting within an animate spiritual landscape. Soderlund writes, "Earth and sky formed a spiritual realm of which they were a part, not the masters."[39] The environment was animated by intelligent spirits, and the numen of a particular rock, plant, river, animal, or sky were interactive presences in the environment. This numinous or sacred aspect of the world, called "manitou" by the Lenape, reflected the divinity and shared community of the cosmos in which humans were one of many participants.[40]

Some Christian colonists tried to integrate the Lenape cosmos into the biblical text in vain attempts at conversion. A Swedish Lutheran priest named Johan Campanius studied Lenape religious belief and learned their language, incorporating Lenape words and ideas into his preaching. Campanius even ventured into some light Lutheran blasphemy in his attempts to meet the Lenape halfway, referring to God, angel, and spirit as "Manetto," explaining the Trinity as "*Manetto Nwk*, God the Father. *Manetto Nissianus*, God the Son. *Chintika Manetto*. God the Holy Ghost."[41] As Jean Soderlund writes, "Campanius translated Luther's catechism into Unami [the Lenape language] trade jargon," the only Indigenous vocabulary he had access to.[42] Some Lenape apparently gamely listened to what must have been an incomprehensible (but perhaps entertaining, since they did listen) mishmash of their own "trade jargon," their word for spirit, and an utterly alien religious cosmology—the book of Genesis and the life of Jesus—all mingled together. However, for all his efforts, Campanius failed to convert a single person. He returned to Sweden after five years on the Delaware.[43]

Holy Experiments

It is hidden right there in the word: "utopia," meaning "nowhere." As his most recent biographer, Andrew Murphy, has pointed out, William Penn is both lionized and caricatured today—he is somehow at once more and less than his historical legend.[44] Penn's shadow falls over Market Street tonight from his perch on top of Philadelphia's city hall; his cartoon stares back at us from the oatmeal box in the pantry. Behind this paradoxically aggrandizing and cartoonish memory was a historical figure who possessed the uniquely potent combination of extreme social privilege and a willingness to use that privilege to apply his wildly radical ideas. Penn's initial utopian ideals would gradually yield during and after his life, as his utopia gradually became what it had always been: one segment of a larger British imperial project, itself one faction in a wider wave of European settler colonialism in the Americas.

William Penn was a sensitive child, more given to inner reverie and Christian devotion than to his studies or his family's wishes.[45] These spiritual impulses led to his conversion to the Quaker faith around 1667. It was a public and intensely consequential confession for the young man and, it would turn out, for future global politics and philosophy of governance. As the immensely well-to-do son of an admiral in the British navy who joined the ranks of an oppressed and highly visible religious minority, Penn was willing and able to apply his father's good name as social leverage against the British government on behalf of his minority religion. Penn became a public force on behalf of Quaker welfare and Quaker principles throughout the next decade, weaponizing his social standing and education in order to protect his new co-congregants against the strong arm of the law. And in so doing, he fundamentally influenced how the law would act upon its subjects in the modern period.

In one highly publicized trial in 1670, Penn managed to convince the jury that the indictment against a group of Quakers for gathering in violation of the "conventicle act" (which forbade private gatherings for religious purposes) was illegal. As Penn later put it in writing, "The Question is not whether I am guilty of this indictment, but whether this Indictment be legal."[46] By turning the eye of the court away from the defendant and toward the inconsistent machinations of the law itself, Penn operationalized what had hitherto been an abstract argument among England's aristocratic reformers and laid it out before a jury. The jury sided with Penn and the Quakers, to which the court responded by imprisoning the entire jury along with Penn.[47] The court won that battle, but in imprisoning Penn alongside the jury, the court lost crucial ground in the war of public opinion and wrote an important chapter in what was becoming Penn's hagiography among the Quakers. This case established the authority and independence of juries in the emerging Anglo-American philosophy of constitutional law.[48]

Penn's first foray into colonial politics was conflict resolution in the English colony of New Jersey, in Lenape territory along the eastern shores of the Delaware River.[49] The territory had been sold to two Quakers in 1674, and the resultant financial dispute between the two Friends had the dangerous potential of a public reckoning within Quakerdom. Penn was a natural choice for a quick and Quaker resolution to the dispute.[50] The result was a reorganization of Quaker territory along the Delaware, most of which would be governed under a new document establishing the law and customs of the inhabitants of "West Jersey." The resulting document, *The Concessions and Agreements of the Proprietors, Freeholders, and Inhabitants of the Province of West Jersey*, essentially codified a colonial agreement with the patterns of governance established by the Lenape in the earlier decades of the seventeenth century: freedom of religion, representative government, and equanimity between Lenape and Europeans.[51] It was not exclusively authored by Penn—other Quakers living in Lenape territory at the time contributed to the document, especially Edward Byllynge—but it bore the mark of his emerging philosophy of governance, and it would eventually form the basis of the frames of government Penn drafted for Pennsylvania.[52]

The political situation in early Pennsylvania would eventually mirror the tension in Quaker religious hierarchy more broadly: the necessity of an organized civil structure and practice of government balanced against an essentially anarchic fundamental right of religious freedom.[53] For Quakers, Pietists, and the countless heterodox sects that followed, submission to civil authority was often an afterthought when one had access to the inner light or the prophetic presence of God. This was perfectly in line with the Lenape civic custom of free religious and cultural expression. Indeed, as Jean Soderlund writes: "The Lenapes and old settlers had created a culture into which the Quaker colonists in West New Jersey and Pennsylvania easily moved. The Friends belief in religious liberty and commitment to friendly relations with Native Americans complemented cultural practices already in place."[54] And for a few decades, the pendulum of early

74 AMERICAN AURORA

Pennsylvania society swung toward this pluralist anarcho-prophetic freedom, until continued colonial aggression toward the Lenape and global geopolitical conflict pulled it back toward consolidated state control.

"Every Plant Praises and Extols God"

Before King Charles signed the deed to Pennsylvania, William Penn visited with a group of Pietists in Saalhof, Germany, in 1677, where he participated in their worship services. The Saalhof Pietists were struggling at the time. Penn later noted that they suffered from "the German sickness," by which he meant that they seemed anxious, fearful of Lutheran orthodox authority and oppression.[55] Penn explained his intention to secure an expansive territory in North America where dissidents like the Pietists could live and practice their religion without fear. He meant to attempt a radical experiment in religion and governance, and he invited the German Pietists to join him. They agreed, and Johann Jakob Shutz, a leader in the Saalhof coventicle, organized and incorporated their agreement in the Frankfurt Land Company, a legal arrangement under which the Saalhof Pietists secured fifteen thousand acres of land in Penn's Woods.[56]

In April 1683, after Penn had secured his land from Charles II and paid the Lenape for its use, the newly organized Frankfurt Land Company departed for the Delaware shores under the administration of a young lawyer and radical Pietist named Francis Daniel Pastorius (1651–1720).[57] Pastorius was successful but profoundly unsatisfied in his chosen vocation, and his attendance at the Saalhof conventicle was a window into an inner life so compelling that he cast everything else aside completely. On his way to Philadelphia, he wrote a letter to his father from England:

> I have suffered myself to be moved by the special direction of the Most High to journey over to Pennsylvania, living in the hope that this my design will work out to my own good and that of my brothers and sisters, but most of all to the advancement of the glory of God (which is my aim above all else), especially as the audacity and sin of the European world are accumulating more and more from day to day, and therefore the just judgment of God cannot be long withheld.[58]

In this letter to his father, Pastorius expressed the same motivations that would eventually compel thousands of heterodox Christians to leave Europe for the North American coast. Europe's descent into sin was unmistakable, and the orthodox mistreatment of sincere Christians was only one sign among many that the time had come to flee what Johann Zimmerman called "the Spiritual Babel of Europe."

Upon his arrival in Philadelphia, Pastorius laid out the Frankfurt Land Company's purchase into a new community just to the west of Philadelphia, called Germantown. Once settled, Pastorius wrote a letter back to Frankfurt in which he sketched his initial impressions of Penn's Woods. Like every other European who made their way up the Delaware shores in the seventeenth century, what really impressed Pastorius about the landscape was the vastness of the forests. Quoting Virgil, he wrote: "Wherever one turns, one may say: *Itur in antiquam sylvam.*"[59] They were "gone into the ancient forest."

In this letter, Pastorius was generally critical of his fellow Christians (with the exception of William Penn, whom he adored) and admiring of the Indigenous inhabitants of the country. He told his friends in Germany: "I cannot classify them better than into the natural and transplanted ones, for if I called the former wild and the latter Christians, I would do many among both a great injustice."[60] His low opinion of Lutheran orthodoxy was also on vivid display: the Lutheran preacher in Philadelphia was, "to put it in one word, a drunkard," he wrote judiciously.[61] Disappointed but not surprised with the failures of the church, Pastorius found a great deal to admire among the Lenape. These "so-called savages," as he called them, put their well-being into the hands of God with a faith that many Christians do not match: "These pagans leave their cares to GOD with a wonderful resignation," he wrote.[62] This is a persistent reaction to Lenape religious perspectives in the early Pennsylvania sources, including the writings of Kelpius, which I will turn to later. Everyone seemed impressed with their relative lack of what we might call anxiety.

As his attitudes toward the local Lutheran authority suggests, Pastorius was suspicious of orthodoxy and generally sympathetic to heterodox and radical religious perspectives. Mennonites and Quakers accompanied him on his 1683 trip to Pennsylvania, and in the early 1680s, Quakers, Mennonites, Lutherans, and radical Pietists like Pastorius still worshiped together in Philadelphia.[63] Pastorius was deeply immersed in the dissenting, heterodox, and esoteric literatures of the Protestant world, and his social milieu at Germantown, an immigrant community that essentially served to select the *most* heterodox and esoteric-inclined people of Europe, was even more radical. While the local Lutheran authority was busy drinking, Pastorius attended Sunday service with Anabaptists and Quakers, which was followed by dinners at the table of William Penn and Lenape leaders. That feeling of "German Sickness" that Penn saw at Saalhof in 1677 could not be farther away.

Pastorius entered this new milieu from the perspective of Hermetic Protestant environmental thought. His library at Germantown included works by Jacob Böhme and the Paracelsian theologian Valentin Weigel, and the primary material is peppered with clues that his esoteric tastes ran even deeper than those of many of his esoteric German contemporaries.[64] Hermes Trismegistus

76   AMERICAN AURORA

himself appears in his commonplace book "The Bee-Hive," in which Pastorius writes: "Mercurius (or Hermes) Trismegistus: a very ancient Ægyptian philosopher, who wrote many books *de sapientia divinâ* [of divine wisdom], whereof some fragments are yet extant."[65] This was the common seventeenth-century understanding of Hermes as a major ancient philosopher, somewhat like Plato, rather than a syncretized divine figure in his own right.

Pastorius's interest in Hermetic philosophy appears again, in a more elaborate and telling fashion, in a manuscript titled *A Few Onomastical Considerations . . .* , which was notably written to William Penn on the occasion of the birth of his son John. Pastorius concluded the piece with a Hermetic flourish:

> But as for Eternity, which Hermes Trismegistus defines to be an intellectual sphere, whose center is illimited no Representation more common than a circle with this inscription:

World Without End

or

Nihil quaesiveris ultra

[Seek nothing further]

. . .

Eternity is Endless, but

these considerations

have

here

an

end[66]

The direct and public nature of Pastorius's interest in Hermetic philosophy is noteworthy here. This is not a Hermetic influence read and rendered via figures like Paracelsus and Arndt, presented as straightforward Christian doctrine. Rather, Pastorius cites Hermes Trismegistus directly and publicly here, in a letter to William Penn himself. Furthermore, he does not refer to Hermes merely as an ancient curiosity, but as a real source of *sapientia divinâ*, of divine wisdom. Pastorius's stylized rendering of the text within a circle and metered out almost like a modernist poem further shows that Hermes was not merely a source of divine wisdom, but that Hermetic thought was *beautiful,* and was rendered as such when reproduced in manuscript. Hermetic philosophy was openly known and valued among the radical Protestants of early Pennsylvania, and, as we will see shortly, Pastorius was not the only reader of Hermes on the Delaware shores.

The precise sources of Pastorius's Hermetic reading are unclear. English translations of Hermetic literature were accessible in England, but Pastorious would not have had to rely on a translator to access the *sapientia divinâ* of Hermes. The Basel edition of Ficino's translation of the *Corpus Hermeticum*, called "Poemander," would not have been inaccessible to the young Latinist, even in the seventeenth century. Indeed, Pastorious's intellectual pursuits were so wide and deep that it would not be hard to imagine his familiarity with Renaissance humanism or the English Neoplatonism that thrived just a few decades earlier at Cambridge.[67]

Pastorius's place in the Hermetic Protestant environmental milieu is evident in his writings, in which a reified concept of "Nature" emerges as the primary teacher of religious truths. An avid horticulturist, Pastorius's religious practice was deeply informed by a Hermetic contemplative posture toward the environment. He enjoyed sharing his homemade beer with local Lenape, and the cross-cultural communion offered by the potency of certain plants was just one dimension of the spiritual world that could be unlocked by literacy in nature's language. "My *hopes* and my *hops* do grow together," he once wrote.[68] Drawing on Böhme's notion of *natursprach*, Pastorius's writings evince a profoundly cosmotheist worldview:

> There is no grass so insignificant, that it does not prove the existence of God.
> In all that grows,
> God's honor flourishes.
> The colorful magnificence of the flowers
> shows God's wonderful power.
> Every plant praises and extols God.
> Every herb and all its seeds
> laud and praise the name of God.[69]

Writing in a 1982 article in *Quaker History*, Shirley Showalter was quick to note the radical cosmotheism in Pastorius's written work. Pastorius's writing "contains the seed of pantheism," she writes, almost apologetically, "but the seed never germinates. Although the poet sees God in the created object, he worships the Creator, not the object."[70] Showalter is right to note the primacy of God in Pastorius's writings, but with our understanding of Pastorius's direct interest in Hermetic philosophy, we might pause before completely absolving Pastorius of something like pantheism. For Paracelsus, Arndt, Böhme, and now Pastorius, the distinction between creator and object remained, but it was essentially a matter of form rather than substance. Creation itself was "God's formed Word," and plants were the "living handwriting" of God, as Arndt called them. The cosmos was already sanctified, to which Pastorius added: "Every herb and all its seeds / laud and praise the name of God." In Pastorius's Christianity, every herb and its seeds actually *were* good little

Christians, singing and praising God's name. If this is not pantheism, it is certainly Hermetic Protestantism.

But Francis Daniel Pastorius was not the only early American reader of Böhme, and his fellow German Pietists were not the only early Americans whose writings "contain the seed of pantheism." The historian John Smolenski has noted that the theology of the English founder of Quakerism, George Fox, "contained traces of the hermetic teachings of Jacob Boehme."[71] Smolenski's suggestion has been backed up by other scholars. In their recent reassessments of previous work in this area, historians Ariel Hessayon and Carole Dale Spencer have concluded that the early Quaker engagement with Böhme, especially in the writings of George Fox and James Nayler, was "more extensive than previously acknowledged."[72] The Quakers were reading Böhme, and the Pietists like Pastorius were busy sharing their tables with Quakers and other radicals.

Simply put, the boundaries between German Pietists, British Quakers, and other radical Christian dissenting groups of the seventeenth century were blurry, *especially* in a setting like Philadelphia. As the life and thought of figures like Francis Daniel Pastorius generally suggest, radical Protestants were often less worried about crossing denominational barriers than their attendant histories and historians have been. Pastorius may well have carried the first copies of Böhme's writing to the Delaware shores in 1683, but it was a British Quaker named Daniel Leeds who was responsible (with help from William Bradford) for the first confirmed printing of Böhme's work in North America.[73] It also happened to be one of the first books printed in the mid-Atlantic coast of North America.[74]

"Moves Nature in a Jumping Fit / According to His Pleasure"

Like William Penn, Daniel Leeds seems to have been a precocious and intensely spiritual child, prone to visions and reveries. Unlike Penn, however, Daniel Leeds was brought up in a poor family of English dissenters. As a boy, Leeds's religious devotion was shaped by his mother, of whom he writes, "[She would,] (being religious), take me aside to pray to God with her upon her knees."[75] This prayerful home life was the setting for a series of childhood visions and ecstasies: "At twelve years of age the God of Heaven visited me," Leeds wrote in a 1699 publication, "and made me sensible of eternity."[76] Leeds went on to describe the vision and his attempt to include his mother in witness to Christ's appearance: "I had a vision of Christ coming down from Heaven, which was wonderful." Leeds cried out to his mother as he watched Christ coming down, hoping that they might "behold the Glory" together, but as he called for his mother, "The vision vanished."[77] Leeds's parents converted to Quakerism while he was still a child, and following the

Quaker doctrine of sincere inner atonement and personal conviction in Christ, they did not take their son to meetings with them.

At the age of twenty, Leeds was "afresh turned to Religion" and "often weeping in secret places because of sin."[78] Leeds's childhood ecstasies continued into adulthood and followed him throughout his life: "I was meditating on a place of Scripture, I was suddenly surrounded with Glory, and with Soul Ravishments of Love and Joy, in so sweet and ravishing a manner as no Pen can or ought to describe, or Tongue declare (with which I have also some time since been visited)."[79] Leeds's narrative of his own life echoes that of the two Protestant mystics he admired most: George Fox and Jacob Böhme. And Leeds would go on to become an avid reader and fierce promoter of Böhme, for which he would pay a steep public price, just like Johann Jacob Zimmerman, who did much the same at the exact same time across the Atlantic.

Leeds's and Böhme's narratives of their early lives are quite similar: both were poor and sensitive young men, retreating to hidden places where they expressed anxious yearnings to know God and nature at once. At the time of his second major ecstasy, Leeds was a parishioner in the Church of England, but he grew increasingly dissatisfied there. Leeds expressed his discontent to his true religious mentors, his parents, and they rejoined him to attend Quaker meetings with them. Leeds found what he was looking for: "Their Ministry had such effect upon me, that I was constrained to believe, what they preached was Infallible, even as the Oracles of God."[80] Even though the sermons were "Infallible," being a Quaker in England in the 1670s carried some disadvantages, including the possibility of being imprisoned (as Daniel's father, Thomas Leeds, was in the Tower of London in 1672) or simply being executed.[81] The Leeds family eagerly anticipated what William Penn was frantically working to establish: a dissenter's paradise, a heterodox utopia in the Lenape territory.

Daniel Leeds traveled to America with his father sometime before 1677, when he arrived in what is now Burlington, New Jersey. His destination was inspired by George Fox's travels up the Delaware shores a few years earlier. Leeds's signature appeared alongside William Penn's on the aforementioned document establishing the law and customs of the inhabitants of "West Jersey," the *West Jersey Concessions*.[82]

Daniel Leeds settled by the Delaware River just outside of Burlington, and within a few years, professional and practical engagements dominated the adult life of the former ecstatic child prodigy: he became a professional farmer and surveyor, constantly assessing and reassessing patterns in the weather, the landscape, and the environment.[83] It is around this time when he must have had his first inklings of the connection between the Hermetic Protestant environmental thought of his beloved Böhme and its practical applications for life

80 AMERICAN AURORA

in America, where agricultural practice was the dominant force in shaping the patterns of daily life.

In 1687, a one-page printed broadsheet appeared for sale in Philadelphia and New Jersey entitled "An Almanack" and attributed to one "Daniel Leeds, *Student in Agriculture.*" Leeds's first almanac was a stripped-down, simple list of the signs of the moon and the stars for every day and month of the year, notable feast days and equinoxes (certain feast days, celestial events, and days of the week were generally considered better for agricultural events like planting, harvesting, even breeding animals), along with lists of natural wonders like eclipses. It was an efficient and economical little document, certainly not designed to make any sort of literary splash, but to help colonial planters better read the letters of nature's book.

The brevity and economy of the first Leeds almanac did not preclude some literary flourishes. Leeds appended a short poem that showed some of the spirit in which he produced the almanac, a novel little remix of Paul's letter to the Romans and Leeds's own original verse:

> No man is born unto himself alone,
> He who lives unto himself lives to none . . .
> Place shews the man, and he whom honour mends,
> He to a worthy, generous spirit tends.[84]

The self and the environment blurred in Leeds's agricultural writings. Leeds's practice of agriculture opened up his sense of self in ways that mere reading or writing did not, and his almanac reflected the practices in which "the man alone" expanded the limits of himself. The practices of carefully observing the movements of the moon, the stars, and the planets along with the times of planting and harvesting became practices of the self as much as practical daily tasks. And in tending to the spirit that "Place shews the man," Leeds tends and mends himself. The primacy of scripture as the counterpart of nature's book remains in Leeds's writing; his own poem spins off from a Pauline verse before landing on the suggestion that the "*Student in Agriculture,*" tending his place, tends and mends his own spirit. Leeds's first almanac rereads the Paracelsian macrocosm and microcosm alongside the letters of Paul, and acts them both out on the cosmic stage of a little farm.

As Leeds developed his practice of agriculture at Burlington, he both leaned on and transformed the Hermetic Protestant environmental tradition that he derived from his reading of Böhme. The stars, planets, and the sun and moon were letters from nature's book, and literacy bred still more literacy: knowledge of the sky led directly to success in cultivating plants. The Lenape were also diligent readers of the night sky, and it does not strain credulity to imagine Leeds drawing on Lenape expertise as he calculated the movements of the moon, sun, stars, and planets from an unfamiliar astronomical position in Burlington. Local Lenape had contributed food and expert advice to the Burlington colonists throughout 1677–78, when Leeds arrived, and Leeds's farming and surveying businesses were probably dependent on Lenape knowledge in their nascent stages.[85] Indeed, an earlier European on the Delaware noted that the Lenape timed their plantings and harvests according to the movements of the moon, and that they "are the most skilful star-gazers . . . [they] can name all the stars, their rising, setting."[86]

Alongside the expertise of local Lenape, Leeds drew upon an extant European genre of practical environmental knowledge. The almanac was a genre with origins in medieval European agricultural practice. With ancient roots and wide practical appeal, almanacs served as a literary hodgepodge of vital information: prophecies, weather patterns, calendars, saint's days and feast days, and the names, dates, and records of extraordinary events.[87] The very same title could contain information on topics ranging from veterinary medicine, planting tables, and medicinal herbs, to reports on the appearance of celestial wonders like comets and eclipses. By the seventeenth century, the genre combined two forms of knowledge that were rapidly falling out of vogue in European intellectual culture: rural knowledge and prophetic and miraculous phenomena. As Phillip Blom has noted, the almanac's content reflects the period in which it was produced: the Little Ice Age, a time when agriculture was disrupted constantly by extreme climatic and weather conditions.[88]

The association between rural life and knowledge of extraordinary, supernatural, or miraculous phenomena was already firm in the Paracelsian corpus. Paracelsus's own writings were critical of physicians whose knowledge and experience were limited to urban areas, and he frequently turned to specialist knowledge of rural and uneducated people in his own rejection of ancient philosophy and medicine. But the American almanac genre, as the Leeds family (Daniel would have a son, Titan, who took on the family business in the eighteenth century) popularized it, gave the Paracelsian *theorica* a starkly practical and popular spin—and as we can see in the pages of the farmers' almanacs in the checkout aisles of many American grocery stores today, this rural-paranormal knowledge complex is so widespread and common today that we might even mistake it for being mundane.

European almanacs and agricultural manuals drew on a deep lineage of meteorological and environmental prognostic thought. Aristotle, Theophrastus (the original, 370–278 BCE, not Paracelsus), Pliny, and Ptolemy were all rich resources for observational techniques and astrological knowledge. These ancient insights appeared alongside and often within the reliable modern information on which the modern working farmer depended: the positions of the stars and the zodiacal signs, certain potent saint's days and feast days that maintained their significance

82 AMERICAN AURORA

for rural Protestants long after the Reformation, and a plethora of other practical insights for rural life.[89] But in Daniel Leeds's writing, it was Hermetic literature (in English translation) that provided the theological structure for his own cosmotheism and practice of astrology.

The almanac, then, was already a fully fleshed out genre when Leeds began publishing his own editions in Philadelphia in the 1680s, but he gave it a certain Hermetic spin that it has retained in Pennsylvania and throughout the United States. His 1695 almanac displays a quotation from Hermes Trismegistus directly on the cover:

> Hermes Trismegistus, *pg 13*, speaking of the nature and composition of man says, if he may lay the cause of evil upon Fate or Destiny, he will never abstain from any evil work. Wherefore we must look warily to such kind of people, that being in ignorance, they may be less evil for fear of that which is hidden and kept secret.[90]

While Leeds does not cite his own Hermetic source directly (beyond the less than helpful "pg 13"), his passage here corresponds exactly with John Everard's 1650 English translation of Francesco Patrizi's 1591 edition of a rearranged *Corpus Hermeticum*.[91]

Reading Hermes in America, Leeds would have found a philosophical scaffolding for his astrology, in which he had probably already incorporated Lenape expertise and his own observations. While the texts translated as *Divine Pymander* by Everard were of a theoretical and philosophical nature, rather than the "technical" *Hermetica* (as Brian Copenhaver has called those texts that contained explicit astrological, alchemical, and magical operations and techniques), the texts that appear in Everard's *Hermetica* would have been recognizably celestial to a practicing astrologer like Leeds:

> 11. For the Lord, void of envie, appeareth thorow the whole world.
> 12. Thou mayest see the intelligence, and take it in thy hands, and contemplate the Image of God. But if that which is in thee, be not known or apparent unto thee, how shall he in thee be seen, and appear unto thee by the eyes?
> 13. But if thou wilt see him, consider and understand the Sun, consider the course of the Moon, consider the order of the Stars.[92]

In this passage, derived from Book V of the *Hermetica*, Leeds would have heard echoes of both Jacob Böhme and George Fox, but from a text with a much deeper weight of ancient authority. The Lord appears "thorow the whole world," and bearing witness to the living presence of God is no more complicated than looking up at the sky.

The *Hermetica* that Leeds was reading went further than asserting cosmotheism in their justifications of astrology as well:

> For the Mind being God, Male and Female, Life and Light, brought forth by his Word; another Mind, the Workman: Which being God of the Fire, and the Spirit, fashioned and formed seven other Governors, which in their Circles contain the Sensible World, whose Government or Disposition is called Fate or Destiny.[93]

In this passage, God creates the seven governors of the world, who would have been recognizable to Leeds as the five planets plus the moon and the sun, whose "Government" is called "Fate."[94] While this might seem to be an alien religious cosmology for a Christian—even a radical like Leeds—it is important to remember that the Hermetic literature was compiled in the cosmopolitan environs of Greek, Egyptian, and Jewish thought, and much of the Hermetic literature seems to incorporate biblical ideas and share a milieu with the origins of Christianity. As Genesis would tell it, "God said, Let there be lights in the firmament of the heavens to divide the day from the night; and let them be for signs."[95] Leeds would have also recognized a few Hermetic features from his background in Böhme: an androgynous God combining elemental forces to form governing structures in heaven would not have been the strangest thing that Leeds read on the Burlington shores. Leeds's Hermetic approach to almanac astrology is demonstrated by his decision to quote Hermes on the cover of his own astrological publications.

As Jon Butler has memorably suggested, the abundant primary evidence that almanacs outsold the Bible in early America is easier for historians to point out than readily interpret. The simultaneous wild popularity of the almanac and the hesitation of scholars to interpret them recalls Peter Brown's description of the status of the antique cult of the saints:

> It is a fact of life which has suffered the fate of many facts of life. Its existence is admitted to with a slight note of embarrassment; and, even when admitted to, it is usual to treat it as "only too natural," and not a subject to linger over for prolonged and circumstantial investigation.[96]

The outlier here is Jon Butler, who argues that the reason for their overwhelming popularity was the practical utility of the information they included. As Butler writes, "Using the Almanac, even semiliterate colonists could plant, bleed, marry, or breed on correct days and, by following its guide to the stars, predict the future."[97] The almanac was a celestial handbook that the laborer, farmer, homeowner, and housewife could use to align themselves with what English

Hermeticists called "the Government of Fate," the movements of lights in the sky. And in doing so, they enlisted the cosmos itself as their collaborator and coworker.

Elite acceptance of the common practice of astrology was already in decline when Daniel Leeds and others began to include newly translated vernacular editions of figures like Hermes Trismegistus in their agricultural writings. As Herbert Leventhal has written, "no learned tracts" on the subject of astrology would appear in America in the eighteenth century. The "primary literature" of early American astrology "was the lowly almanac, the literature of the semi-literate."[98] But this did not mean that it wasn't popular. As we have seen in the previous chapter, this proliferation of Hermetic Protestantism among the rural and less-educated classes was a trend that began in Europe, earlier in the same century in the works of Böhme and Arndt. When considered in the context of the Little Ice Age, a period in which Protestants were motivated by immediate environmental concerns, the popularity of the almanac (and particularly Leeds's Hermetic guides for farmers) is less aberrant than it often appears to scholars today. Rural people in Europe and North America needed practical and religious environmental insights, whether they were sowing crops or interpreting an eclipse. The almanac was there to help.

Indeed, it seems that the content and popularity of almanac literature in American households was difficult for many to understand, even in the eighteenth century. By the time the climate stabilized and Hermetic ideas were less popular, the almanac seemed to be a relic of another era. Writing in 1799, Charles Brockden Brown, an author to whom we will turn directly in Chapter 5, considered the overwhelming popularity of almanac literature despite what seemed (to him) the apparent uselessness of the knowledge it seemed to offer.[99] "There is scarcely a family, however ignorant and indigent," Brown wrote, "without one copy hanging constantly in sight."[100] Even stranger than the popularity of these volumes, for Brown, were their contents:

> A stranger who should meet, in every hovel, with a book, in which the relative positions of the planets, the diurnal progress of the sun in the zodiac, the lunar and solar eclipses, the wanderings of Sirius, Arcturus, and the Pleiades; of Occulus, Tauri, and *Spica-Virginis* were described in a way the most technical imaginable, would be apt to regard us as a very astronomical and learned nation.[101]

Brown does not beat around the bush: he means to suggest that the "ignorant and indigent" residents of "every hovel" were less than the citizens of a "learned nation." We might restate Brown's question more bluntly: Why did poor people require such sophisticated celestial knowledge? Brown did not merely take issue with the interest of the rural poor in stargazing: he was confounded by the complexity and sophistication of almanac data, the "most technical imaginable" sort of astronomical information.

Brown went on to note that the technical detail in these almanacs was often accompanied by what he found to be inscrutable religious and occult information: "these celebrated computations, these mystic symbols, this adjustment of certain days to certain holy names." The saints' days and astrological symbols that seemed to orbit the constellations and planting tables were even more incomprehensible to Brown than the mathematical description of the "wanderings of Sirius." What held all this information together? And why was it so popular among poor people—particularly Palatinate Germans—in Pennsylvania?

In his essay, Brown struggled to make sense of almanac literature, before ultimately attributing it to some distant period of the agricultural past that force of habit compels the most ignorant among us—the rural, the poor—to follow. "One would be naturally led to think," he wrote, "that when almanacks were first invented, mankind were more conversant with the stars than at present, that every cottager was interested in the planetary revolutions, in the places of the moon, in the solar progress, and in the birth days of hermits and confessors." The almanac is a relic, Brown finally concludes, and it must harken back to some time when our conversation with the stars was at some lost climax.

For his part, Brown is halfway right: writing from his own elite, English-speaking standpoint, the almanac does represent a form of knowledge that is completely alien to him, but he locates this strange knowledge in the distant past rather than among the lower classes of people who practice it around him. Brown's exact period was, in fact, perhaps the *zenith* of American reliance on almanac literature, a literature that derived from European traditions of planters guides and household books but took on a decidedly occult dimension as it arose and flourished in Pennsylvania under the authorship of religious radicals like Daniel Leeds. Charles Brockden Brown's frustrated essay further demonstrates the deep esotericism of early American almanac literature, not only to twenty-first century readers, but to many early Americans themselves, particularly the elite social strata of American Quakers, like Charles Brockden Brown.

To return to Daniel Leeds a century earlier: in 1688 another document appeared in Philadelphia under Leeds's name. But this was not an almanac: it was a compilation edition of Jacob Böhme in English for an American audience, with commentary by Leeds, entitled *The Temple of Wisdom for the Little World; in Two Parts*, described by Arthur Versluis as "probably the very first Christian theosophic work in American history."[102] The first part of *Temple of Wisdom* was a compilation of Böhme's writing translated into English. Leeds translates a

86 AMERICAN AURORA

passage from Böhme in the preface, which seems to taunt his readership with an aggressively Hermetic position:

> If you can demonstrate that God is not in the Stars, Elements, Earth, Men, Beasts, Worms, Leaves and Grass, also in Heaven and Earth; also, that all this is not God himself, & that my Spirit is false and wicked, then I will be the first that will burn my Book in the fire, and recall and recant all whatsoever I have written, and will accurse it, and in all obedience willingly submit myself to be instructed by you.[103]

Leeds's preface to Böhme in *Temple of Wisdom* is particularly significant for demonstrating exactly what it was about Böhme's thought that he considered potentially heretical: it was his profound cosmotheism, in which worms and grass could not be meaningfully distinguished from God. Leeds expects and even invites controversy in this preface, and he seems to have succeeded.

Despite the influence of Böhme on the earliest Quakers, Leeds's open cosmotheism was too much for the reading public, even in Philadelphia. Leeds's *Temple of Wisdom* was wholeheartedly rejected by the nascent Quaker intelligentsia in Philadelphia and Burlington, and most copies were eventually destroyed.[104] Leeds continued to maintain a public profile and publish his almanacs, but his posture toward Quakerdom changed dramatically after the censure of *Temple*. Leeds was a Quaker, remember, and his identity as such had been heretofore the most consequential commitment of his life. Leeds seems to have always been something of a heterodox provocateur, but after the Society of Friends rejected his philosophy in print, Leeds finally rejected the church that once seemed infallible to him. Leeds became a staunchly anti-Quaker polemicist, writing and publishing tracts in America and England denouncing the Quaker religion and its founder, George Fox.[105]

For their part, the Quakers returned the favor. One rival almanac published in 1705 mocked Leeds's radical cosmotheism in verse:

> But Leeds exerts a thumping wit
> Above all vulgar measure
> Moves nature in a Jumping fit
> According to his pleasure.[106]

The long public career and sordid controversies of Daniel Leeds, including his role in the Keithian schism (to which we turn in the next chapter) deserve their own book-length study. For the purposes of this chapter, however, we can note his role in introducing both Hermes and Böhme to early Pennsylvania's reading public at a very early date, and the resulting persistence of the originally European

Pietist association between Hermetic Protestantism and rural, working people and their literature.

In this chapter, I have singled out Pastorius and Leeds as two authors and public figures whose writings further elaborated and popularized Hermetic Protestantism in early Pennsylvania. Pennsylvania was a uniquely receptive audience for several reasons. First, the pressures of orthodoxy were nowhere to be found in seventeenth-century Philadelphia (more specifically, as Pastorius noted, they were drunk), and second, the theory and practice of agriculture was gradually becoming a dominant matter of practical concern in early Pennsylvania. Böhme's ecstatic insight into the relationships between the body, the earth, and the heavens was the kind of practical cosmotheism that had been connected with rural people since Paracelsus and the Hermetic literature before him. Pastorius's prayerful plants and Leeds's spiritual agriculture would become part of a general pattern in early Pennsylvania religion, in which the rural arts and esoteric religion were often practiced in tandem if not functionally synonymous.

Catherine Albanese's analysis of the vernacular, practical, and nonelite nature of Böhme's American readership sums it up: "for all its intellectual elements," she writes, Hermetic Protestantism was a "vernacular and nonelite 'path of the heart.'"[107] Albanese's analysis elucidates the individuality and devotional character of Böhme's writings. Furthermore, Böhme's emphasis on the feminine aspect of God as heavenly wisdom, Sophia, made his thought especially appealing to radical Protestant women, who increasingly took on more active and creative roles in the sects that rapidly emerged from Protestantism's slow shattering. As shown in the previous chapter, Böhme's Christianity was meant to be felt and known in ways that people like Charles Brockden Brown considered "ignorant," but only because they often simply failed to recognize it as knowledge.

And it was mostly within the paradoxically occult and wildly popular genre of almanac literature, with its particular attention to celestial phenomena, where Böhme's "path of the heart" made its initial landing in early America. When Johannes Kelpius and company arrived in Philadelphia in 1694, cosmotheist ideas derived from the Protestant Hermeticism of early Pietism, Quakerism, and the vernacular channels of figures like Francis Pastorius and Daniel Leeds had been spreading throughout southeastern Pennsylvania for decades already.

In the sources that I have drawn together in this and the previous chapter, I have tried to give a sense of how this particular lineage—the environmentally attuned Christianity derived from Paracelsian Hermeticism and achieving wide influence among Protestants via the writings of Johan Arndt and Jacob Böhme—appeared and flourished in a colonial environment of Lenape territory and radical Protestant colonists. There is, as always, much more to this story. Daniel Leeds did not invent the almanac, and Jacob Böhme did not invent cosmotheism any more so than the ancient authors of the Hermetic literature originated the idea that the human body is sympathetically connected with the night sky. But these people and texts were the major channels through which cosmotheist ideas flourished in early America.

"The Genius of the Americans Is Bound Another Way"

If the writings of Pastorius and Leeds were the main channels of Protestant Hermeticism in Pennsylvania during the seventeenth century, the Ephrata Cloister of Conrad Beissel would overtake them in the eighteenth century. Beissel was a radical Pietist who came to Pennsylvania in 1720 with the intention of joining with Kelpius in ascetic life on the Wissahickon. Arriving to find Kelpius long dead, Beissel established his own ascetic community deeper in the interior of Pennsylvania at the suggestion of Kelpius's friend and colleague at Wissahickon, the hermit Conrad Matthai. Ephrata was a hugely influential monastic community of radical Pietists who published widely in the eighteenth century. Their successful printing press, whose only regional competitor was Benjamin Franklin himself, spread radical religious literature from Europe (and much written by the Ephrata monastics themselves) throughout the colonies. This intensive printing activity meant that Ephrata material had a deep influence on late eighteenth- and early nineteenth-century radical religious thought in America. As John L. Brooke has written, "Ephrata would have powerful echoes a century later among the Mormons."[108] For a community of such immense influence, Ephrata has largely disappeared from our historical memory. Why? As Pennsylvania was swept up in a broader revolutionary project of proto-American identity, the singularly utopian, pluralist, and pacificist strains of early Pennsylvania history began to drop away.

They did not disappear from history as the result of a conspiracy or even scholarly neglect. By 1771, the Ephrata community recognized that the utopian possibilities that Pennsylvania offered them at the turn of that century were evaporating. Rather than try to stand still in the current of cultural change, Ephrata simply decided to disappear. In 1771, the late leader of the Cloisters, Peter Miller, wrote to Benjamin Franklin: "But [we] shall not propagate the Monastic Life upon the Posterity; since we have no Successors, and the Genius of the Americans is bound another way."[109] After the Seven Years War, as Pennsylvania slipped deeper into intractable geopolitical conflict and commercial interests were increasingly shaping and reshaping the countryside around them, the Ephrata community simply decided to no longer exist. The religious sanctuary into which Kelpius and then his would-be apprentice, Conrad Beissel, had tried to escape was unavoidably becoming what it had always been: a small wave in a larger tide of European colonization, capitalist expansion, and imperial conquest in the Americas.

"GONE INTO THE ANCIENT FOREST" 89

At the beginning of this chapter, the Apocalypse of Daniel Schuhmacher illustrated how the ideas of figures like Jacob Böhme were distributed in Pennsylvania along unofficial, vernacular channels of cultural transmission. In the preceding pages, I have tried to show how the Hermetic Protestant ideas that emerged in Europe throughout the early modern period flourished in the Americas, and in particular, in southeastern Pennsylvania. This brief turn to Ephrata's decline helps us understand how these ideas could have been at once so widespread in their time and so muddled in our historical memory of early American religion. Distributed along channels like the almanac literature launched and popularized in Pennsylvania by Daniel Leeds, the *vorschriften* of Daniel Schuhmacher, and monastic groups who simply decided to embrace oblivion rather than "propagate the Monastic Life upon the Posterity," Hermetic Protestantism was at once so widespread and so inscrutable, that a figure like Charles Brockden Brown, trying to decipher an almanac in 1799, correctly suspected that it *must* mean something, something that connected country people to the stars, the plants, and the presence of God—but he could not understand what.

Vita II

"I Cannot Pass beyond My Homeland"

Kelpius in Rotterdam, London, and the Atlantic, 1693–1694

Their trip was a catastrophe before it even began. They buried Zimmerman in a communal plot near the harbor in Rotterdam, and sent a quick letter home to Germany to inform their network of friends and coreligionists about his sudden death. His wife and children continued on to London and Pennsylvania with the group.[1]

Before Zimmerman died, the group had moved from Frankfurt to Rotterdam. There, an agent of William Penn was going to meet them and front the cost of their passage to London, where they might secure passage on the then-regular shipments from the Thames to the Delaware. They lacked adequate funds before they left Germany, and they knew it: there was a pause in Rotterdam, where they stayed in the Wijnhaven, or Wine Harbor (in what is now the Hague), waiting for their ship to London among the other transients of the city. It seems that things were already going less than swimmingly, then, when suddenly Zimmerman died, but if his death occasioned any hedging on their decision to leave for London en route to Pennsylvania, it does not appear in the sources.[2]

If the group had a coherent plan under Zimmerman, the ad hoc nature of subsequent events seems to indicate that it unraveled quickly. Later secondary sources have suggested that Kelpius was already Zimmerman's "lieutenant," but this is entirely speculative. Only rarely do the sources show Kelpius acting with a position of authority in the group.[3] Indeed, the entire relationship between Kelpius and Zimmerman is a mystery. Were they close friends or simply collaborators in a rather haphazard plan to emigrate to Pennsylvania? They had many religious opinions in common, and we will see that Zimmerman's influence is apparent in Kelpius's later writings. Kelpius also hung on to Zimmerman's copy of Newton, a sentimental indication, perhaps, commemorating a friendship cut short.

There is very little documentation of how the group came together. A single contemporary Quaker chronicle describes their circumstances:

> [Zimmerman], when he saw there was nothing but great danger like to hang over himself and his Friends; he invites and stirs up through his own hope about sixteen or seaventeen Families of these sort of Men, to prefer also an hope

of better things tho it were dubious before the present danger, and forsaking their Country . . . which they through the most precipitous and utmost danger, tho they suffered Death for the same, could not help and relieve as they supposed . . . to depart and betake themselves into other parts of the world, even to Pensilvania, the Quakers Country and there divide all the good and the evil that befall them between themselves, and learn the Languages of that People, and Endeavour to inspire Faith and Piety into the same Inhabitants by their words and examples which they could not do to these Christians here.[4]

The Quaker history suggests that the group faced dangers at home that rivaled the dangers they faced on the journey, which must have been significant, given that they would be traveling through open war zones to reach Pennsylvania. And indeed, there were political winds blowing in 1693 that a radical like Zimmerman would have found particularly threatening.

As scholars like Hans Schneider have shown, seventeenth-century Pietism was divided into two camps with two methods of reform in mind: the first suggested that the church must be reformed from within. Ultimately, these moderate Pietists retained their positions and ended up wielding significant authority. The second, whom Schneider calls the "Radical Pietists" (the milieu that included figures like Zimmerman and Kelpius) argued in "a flood of pamphlets" that the church was beyond reform.[5] At the same time, a wave of "ecstatic, prophetic, and visionary phenomena" accompanied these radical expressions of Pietist belief. More often than not, the content of these visions consisted of "calls to repentance and threats of punishment" against the church authorities themselves.[6] Pamphleteering was one thing, but pious Christians issuing prophetic condemnations of the church in public while they demonstrated the physical signs of ecstasy was another.

Throughout the 1690s, the church responded with waves of sanction, imprisonment, and banishment of radical Pietists, the first of which was a 1694 edict that codified the church's toleration of the activities of moderate Pietists and an implicit signal that the radical segment of the Pietist movement was out of line.[7] According to the Quaker records of their travels, Zimmerman seems to have felt the winds shifting: his own banishment from Württemberg years earlier had prefigured a much wider conflict between radical Pietists and church authorities. Orthodox opinion still held popular sway, and "verbal attacks from the pulpit" even provoked what Schnieder called "a witch-hunt for Pietists in many places."[8] The Quaker chronicle's description of Zimmerman's motivation is borne out in the other sources: "There was nothing but great danger like to hang over himself and his Friends," and so a plan was hatched.

Their group was a mixed assortment of Pietists from Germany: men, women and children drawn from various social strata. Kelpius, Johann Seelig, and probably a few others with ascetic aspirations may have already begun to wear a simple monk's robe or coarse garment. They carried a telescope, musical instruments, and probably many books.[9] They would have stood out, even in the sundry Wijnhaven. Secondary sources claim that the group referred to themselves as "The Chapter of Perfection," or "the Contented of the God-Loving Soul," but these labels do not appear anywhere until the very end of the nineteenth century, casting serious doubt on both. Instead, when they appeared in London in 1693, they simply identified themselves as "Pietists."

For clarity, I refer to them as "the Kelpius group," despite the fact that Kelpius was probably not recognized as their leader.[10] In contrast with the prevailing narrative in most secondary sources, there is not much direct evidence that even Zimmerman held a leadership role, beyond organizing the group in the first place. If Zimmerman was the leader of the group, their decision to simply bury him in Holland and keep moving seems unusual—more likely, the Kelpius group was decentralized in hierarchy, united by circumstance and belief rather than hierarchy or formal organization. They all shared some common need to leave the academy, the church, and Europe behind.

Kelpius names the following companions in his diary: Henry Bernard Köster, Daniel Falkner, Daniel Lutke, Johann Seelig, Ludwig Bidermann, "as well as about 40 other companions."[11] Kelpius names only five of the forty, already giving indication of a kind of group within the group—an arrangement that would later become even clearer when they arrived in Pennsylvania and only a small number of them seem to have adopted the ascetic life.

Most of these close companions had something unusual in common: a history of ecstatic and visionary experiences and capacities to an extent that was unusual even among the radical Pietists. At least one of them, Anna Maria Schuchart, whom Kelpius called "the Prophetess of Erfurt," was well known as such. The unmarried and illiterate daughter of a mason, she woke up one morning and promptly recited two hundred Bible verses from memory, before claiming she could see God's judgment hanging over the city government. Her partner, Daniel Falckner, was the son of a Lutheran minister from Saxony, had participated in one of August Francke's *collegia*, and had been subject to his own ecstatic and visionary episodes. After trying to visit August Francke in prison, Anna was arrested for a time in Halle.[12]

The group that Kelpius traveled with, then, was a hodgepodge of radical religious figures, lapsed academics, and ecstatic college students, probably not a few of whom might have been trying to evade Lutheran authorities in Germany. Emigration to the Atlantic coast of America was a high-risk endeavor in the seventeenth century in any circumstance, even for groups with financial resources and official sanction.[13] The Kelpius group traveled with little money and no official sanction beyond the assurance of a few fellow heretics in England.

Considered together, the circumstances seem to indicate a level of urgency or even desperation the group's own records of the trip do not disclose, and have not yet been recognized in the secondary literature. How many of them were fleeing imprisonment or worse? As we will see, the group left a paper trail of the desperation that their letters and journals describing the journey seem to intentionally omit.

"The Poor People Call'd Pietests"

In late September or early October 1693, the Kelpius group arrived in London, where their paper trail picks up again in the Minutes for the Meetings of Sufferings of the London Quaker Meeting. On October 7, 1693, the Friends wrote:

about Relieving & Imployeing the Pietests

Some mention having been made to this meeting concerning the People called Pietests (who are lately come hether from Germany) of their being pretty Low as to the outward for ffriends to consider them. But They being Strangers to ffriends It's referred to be considered of next Meeting about the Supplyeing and Imployeing of them.[14]

The Kelpius group had apparently landed in London and was referred to the London Society of Friends either by William Penn's agent, Benjamin Furley, or through their own contacts. In any case, they were apparently dependent on charity by the time they crossed the Channel into London. About two weeks later, another entry in the minutes reads, "This Meeting agrees that Twenty pounds be handed forth to the People called Pietests for their Relief."[15] This was a substantial sum in 1693, and it represents a hitherto unrecognized measure of dependence on Quaker charity on the part of the Kelpius group. But it was only a fraction of what the London Friends would provide to the Pietists over the coming months.

Two months later, the Kelpius group was still in London, and the minutes evidence their dependence on Quaker charity: "The Pietests Account of the Ten pounds Given them by ffriends here for their Relief and Assistance have expended. . . . And it's left to Thomas Cox and the other ffriends that handed forth the former money to hand forth Ten pounds more."[16] About a week later, they appear again: "The meeting being acqainted of the poor People call'd Pietests Intention and desire to Transport themselves and ffamilies to America and wanting Assistance." In this entry, however, it seems that the Kelpius group has received some help from their contacts on the continent: "People in Holland in tender Compassion towards them having Remitted one hundred and twenty pounds towards the relief and Transportation of some of them. They being in all about 40. in Number and it falling very short."[17] The minutes of this particular meeting conclude with an agreement to plan for the administration of a fund of another 150 pounds for their transportation.

By January, the Kelpius group was still in London, but they were close to meeting their goal of saving enough money for the trip to Pennsylvania. What did they do for nearly six months in London? A penniless group of foreign dissenters were unlikely to stretch Quaker generosity into comfortable living for forty people. The group fractured at some point in London, according to Kelpius's journal, with one group being excluded from the "spiritual intercourse" of the other due to "wasting their time in brawls and fights."[18] They almost certainly lived in squalorous transient housing, as they did in Rotterdam. Late seventeenth-century London was an urban nightmare of dense and dangerous housing. It was the firsthand experience of cities like London, in fact, that inspired William Penn to actually try to zone Philadelphia into discrete agricultural parcels of land—basically, a capital city of farms—to avoid a similar situation.

The frequency and extent of payments noted in the Quaker meetings underscores just how ad hoc and disorganized the entire effort seems to have been: they arrived in Rotterdam with no money and no plan, and they washed up on the banks of the Thames with nothing, completely dependent on charity from strangers until they were able to secure passage. Even the Quakers found the extent of their own generosity to the group to be unusual, recording that the anonymous Holland donor's contribution was "a very great gift, and so much the more strange, that that same Quaker should be so liberal, and yet would not have his name mentioned, or known in the matter."[19]

A hint to this generosity can be found in movements of William Penn during this period. Penn was desperate for more colonists to start populating and producing on the enormous tracts of land that he had secured, and what everyone hoped would have been a sustained immigration from Germany following Francis Daniel Pastorius's establishment of Germantown had amounted to only a trickle.[20] Though it does not appear in any primary documents, it is certainly possible that Penn, Benjamin Furley, and the London Friends decided to bankroll the Kelpius group from Germany in the hopes that they would provoke more colonists from Germany's most war-torn and religiously dissenting regions, the Palatinate and Württemberg. And eventually, this is precisely what happened, especially after Daniel Falckner's publications promoting the colony in Germany. Regardless of the motivations of the Quaker charity, the fact that the Kelpius group made it anywhere at all is a testament to the tenacious solidarity of Europe's dissenting religious underground, particularly a handful of generous Quakers named and unnamed in the minutes.

"I CANNOT PASS BEYOND MY HOMELAND" 95

In the meantime, Kelpius made long-lasting connections with another heterodox Protestant group. The Philadelphians, or Philadelphian Society, were a group of dissenting English Protestants organized around John Pordage (1607–1681), and later under Jane Lead (1624–1704), with whom Kelpius established extensive contacts during his months in London. Recognized by John in the book of Revelation for its patience, strength, and keeping the promise of God's word, "Philadelphia" was an interdenominational heterodox Protestant ideal that was popular in England at the time. Among seventeenth-century radical Protestants, "Philadelphia" was an apocalyptic shorthand for the *opposite* of Babel and Babylon—it was the place where God would ensconce the faithful while the rest of the world declined. William Penn no doubt had the Philadelphian ideal in mind when he named his city (though he was not connected to Lead's group), and Kelpius certainly did not miss the apocalyptic meanings of the name of his destination.[21]

In particular, Jane Lead—whom Kelpius probably met in London, and whose writings he probably copied and disseminated in America—was a major cultural force in London's radical religious underground. Though her memory sank into obscurity in the nineteenth century, a wave of recent scholarship has begun to reckon with Lead's prolific writing, religious genius, and major role as a religious leader in seventeenth-century England.[22] Kelpius and the Philadelphians would have had a lot to talk about and agree upon. Lead and the Philadelphians were deeply engaged with the thought of Jacob Böhme, which was only just arriving in English translations in the late seventeenth century. Like the Pietists and Kelpius especially, Lead and her followers were given to millennialism and apocalyptic speculations. As we will see in Chapter 4, Kelpius would draw on Lead's reading of Revelation, interpolated through Zimmerman and Böhme's shared tripartite cosmotheism, into his own mystical system, which he called "the Threefold Wilderness State." Kelpius found spiritual comrades for life in London, with whom he maintained contact even after arriving in Pennsylvania.[23]

Throughout the months of December and January, the London Friends organized still more collections on behalf of the Pietists and their transportation to Pennsylvania. By the end of January, the Kelpius group seemed to fully appreciate the extent of their folly. They requested that a "Letter be sent to ffriends in Holland, That any others of the said People where they are may be Cautioned not too hastily to leave Their Native Country."[24] Apparently there were more Pietists on the continent who were ready to make the trip, but the Kelpius group sent word back to hold off for now. But if there was any hedging on their own at this stage, the sources do not show it: they certainly could have made a cheap and easy trip back to the continent at any point during their months in London. Instead, the first line of Kelpius's diary, dated January 7, 1694, simply states: "Having been prompted by God, I undertook a journey to America."[25]

There are two extant accounts of their sea voyage: Kelpius's diary and another letter from the group, anonymously written but almost certainly attributable to Kelpius's companion, Johan Seelig.[26] By early February they had engaged a ship, the *Sarah Mariah Hopewell*, of which Seelig writes, "or, as we called her among ourselves, Faith Love Hope."[27] Kelpius describes paying the cost of their passage to the captain of the ship once on board, one of the few indications in the sources that he held a leadership role.[28] The ship, Seelig writes, was outfitted for war and carried fourteen cannons. They would need them.

On the sixteenth of February, while they sat in the sandbanks of the mouth of the Thames awaiting favorable winds, Kelpius describes a kind of precognitive episode: "My prescient mind," he writes "foresaw misfortunes, leading to an eventual good outcome." He mentioned this episode to Falckner, who shared a similar feeling: "Falckner affirmed the same of himself."[29] The group did not necessarily need two precognitive ecstatics to point out danger: the English Channel was a war zone at the time, and the mouth of the Thames was overcrowded with vessels seeking sanctuary. Suddenly the *Sarah* was struck by a strong wind. The gale was so strong that they were forced to drop anchor to protect the ship from running aground, but the anchor broke, further damaging the ship as they floated helplessly in the storm. "All, saving a few, feared the end was at hand," Kelpius wrote.[30] Seelig also described the scene: "At nightfall, our ship was unexpectedly driven by wind and waves against a hard sand bank . . . the sailors called down [to the Pietists below deck]: Commend your souls to the Lord; we shall go down."[31]

Below deck, the passengers began to pray. Then something extraordinary happened: Kelpius describes watching the "pilot of our ship despairing" when he felt an inner impulse to raise his spirits by "bearing witness concerning the most certain aid of God." But his witness faltered: he was too scared to climb the deck and approach the pilot in the gale. He felt the impulse again, but "seeing [the pilot] intent on other matters and turned away from me, I held my peace in turn." The pilot tried to maintain control as the ship shuddered and veered between the sandbars in the gale.

Just as "all were despairing," Kelpius wrote, he felt a third impulse, which he described as a "divine reprimand" to assure the others of their safety. He finally found the bravery to approach the pilot at the wheel in the storm, and said to him: "Have faith in God, who certainly will save us." Kelpius goes on: "The pilot rejoiced, for he was not so ignorant of divine matters. He pressed my hands and said: 'God alone can help me everywhere, on Him shall I hope.'" As Kelpius describes it, as soon as he and the ship's pilot clasped hands in prayer, the ship veered from the sandbank and into the safety of deeper water, where Kelpius and the pilot quickly cast another anchor before thanking God together again.

"I CANNOT PASS BEYOND MY HOMELAND"   97

Their salvation ensured, Kelpius ran below deck to inform his companions of their safety, only to find that somehow they already knew what had happened:

> Meanwhile Köster, with the rest, had been pouring forth strong supplication to God (and indeed, about that time, when I began to collect my thoughts) as soon as I was reprimanded for the third time, inwardly, and addressed the pilot, he had changed his entreaty to a prayer of thanksgiving, being sure his wish had been granted, though not knowing what just now was being done by us.[32]

The power of his prayer alongside the pilot made more sense to Kelpius now, seeing his forty companions in fervent prayer below deck: "Their prayers had so powerfully aided me," he writes.[33] What at first seemed like a divine impulse from God now seemed, to Kelpius, like a communal act of prayer, in which Köster's supplications seemed to reach Kelpius through "divine reprimand," with the outcome—the turning of the ship to safety—only possible through the sustained prayerful effort of everyone together.

This event made a serious impression on Kelpius. He spends more time describing this moment than any other in his diary, his sole written record of his life. In his own understanding of the events in the channel that evening, Kelpius's "prescient" mind and his divine impulses made him the locus of a prayer so strong that it *steered a ship*. His companions where part of the extraordinary events, too—Falckner admits to a similar precognitive feeling, while Köster claimed a remote witness or uncanny knowledge of the events above deck as they occur. Seelig's record corroborates this event:

> Here Faith . . . proved so strong and heroic in some of the passengers, that they forgot the danger, went to the captain and told him to be of good cheer, the danger was not meant for destruction, but for testing the belief and the love of many. This proved to be true. For when the prayers strove most earnestly against wind and waves, the most powerful waves came, as it were, to the support of the prayers and, at the behest of the Creator, whom they obeyed, lifted the ship and carried it over the bank into a safe depth, contrary to all experience upon sea and to the surprise of the crew.[34]

This is a special moment in Seelig's retelling, too. In the midst of imminent danger, the prayers of the faithful are answered by an anomalous wave that bears them to safety, "contrary to all experience upon sea and to the surprise of the crew."

98 AMERICAN AURORA

After their near wreck, the ship proceeded through the Channel to Plymouth Harbor, in the southwest of England, where they awaited a military escort for five weeks. Seelig and Kelpius agree on how they occupied themselves during this prolonged anchor in Plymouth: "Our exercises on board the ship consisted in discourses of various kinds and interpretations of Scripture," Seelig writes, "in which those who felt inclined took part." They also played music together and sang hymns, for which they put their luggage to use, "several of us accompanying on instruments that we had brought from London."[35]

The English Channel was a war zone in 1694, with England and others arrayed against the French in what is now known as the Nine Years War. After awaiting an English escort for more than a month, the captains of their vessels arranged to follow a passing fleet of Spanish warships. Kelpius and Seelig each mention the prophecy of an unnamed "pious man" in London who told them that they would be born on "Cherub's wings" during the journey.

Their ships were indeed engaged by French vessels shortly after their departure. Seelig writes that the company abstained from combat for religious reasons: "The passengers were given the choice to fight or not," he writes, "We, of course, abstained of carnal weapons and taking the shield of faith sat down between decks behind boxes and cases, prayed and invoked the Lord."[36] They found reason to believe that their prayers were answered here, too: the French vessels were driven off, and one was even taken prisoner. Kelpius in particular took this victory as a sign of divine protection over their journey.

Both Seelig and Kelpius describe their intense interest in various natural phenomena during the journey. After a passing storm, the sea "looked like a beautiful, entirely transparent green emerald," Seelig writes. The group also marveled at the animals around them: "We had frequently occasion to wonder at the works of the Lord, especially at the strange creatures of the deep," writes Seelig. Kelpius seems to record an observation of bioluminescence, writing that the animals alongside them seemed to pass through a "sea of fire."[37] Whales were particularly exciting: "We often saw near our ship fish of monstrous size, spouting water as fire engines do; to watch them in the water keeping us company was wonderful."[38]

Kelpius in particular kept detailed celestial records of their travel. The margins of his journal are covered in astrological symbols, phases of the moon, and measurements of latitude and longitude. Kelpius records stranger things happening at sea, too. "The sailors are frightening themselves," Kelpius records on May 24, because "an upright ship seemed to pass among us not at all distant."[39] This passage is unclear, and it seems that Kelpius is recording a secondhand observation of a strange event described by the sailors. They also paid close attention to celestial anomalies, in particular a solar eclipse on June 10, the same evening they entered what is now called Chesapeake Bay.[40]

On June 19, 1694, Kelpius and company arrived somewhere near New Castle, Delaware. Kelpius's diary reports that they "kissed the earth."[41] Seelig describes the scene of their landing in more detail:

> On the 19th of June, having traversed the sound to its end we stepped on land. The first thing we did was to thank the Lord upon our knees for having carried us, as on eagles' wings such an immense distance through all the gates of death. We hope, in this land also, His mercy will not be wasted on us, especially as we are assured that we have come hither by His will.[42]

George Fox's description of the Lenape country was delivered to his Quaker friends at London, the very same community that would receive Kelpius and company, or as they called them, "those poor people called Pietists," a few decades later. Given the fact that both Fox and Kelpius left from London for port at New Castle, I wonder if their route was inspired by Quaker stories of George Fox's exceedingly "kind" and "loving" reception by the Lenape in the Delaware Valley a few decades earlier. Kelpius does not describe the week between his landfall at New Castle on June 19, 1694, and his arrival in Germantown on June 24, but it is very likely that he entrusted his community to the service of Lenape guides en route to Philadelphia, as George Fox was guided before. Kelpius's diary concludes simply, with the line "[June] 24. Finally, to Germantown."

"I Cannot Pass beyond My Country"

Kelpius's journal and letter book is a pocket-sized leatherbound book with two small clasps, held at the Historical Society of Pennsylvania. The first part of the book is a diary of his journey from London to Pennsylvania, the only extant diary of his life, suggesting perhaps that Kelpius knew that this journey in particular was worth recording for posterity. It is clearly a book that he used and referred to throughout the journey. In addition to the major events of the trip, Kelpius records the movements of the moon and the zodiacal signs for each entry. When their English captain gave them detailed instructions for what to do in the event of a French attack, Kelpius painstakingly recorded his instructions word for word in his unsteady English. Once he arrived in Pennsylvania, the book became a record of letters to friends, which served the handy purpose of preserving his correspondence in the event that letters were lost and needed to be resent. Seelig complained of how often exactly this happened in Pennsylvania, urging his correspondents to make copies of letters. There is a handwritten title page explaining the document: "Copies of letters sent to friends in and outside of Pennsylvania, sent from the wilderness, Johann Kelpio Transylvano."[43] The dating on the document's title page shows that he continued to add to it even after believing it to be complete: "1694–" is quickly followed by "1703–4–5–6–7–," where the dating cuts off.

In the facing front page of the book, Kelpius wrote out a passage he attributes to Seneca. It is, in fact, an excerpt from the *De remediis fortuitorum*, an antique text now attributed to a pseudo-Seneca:

> I cannot pass beyond my homeland, it is a part of everything; no one can cast me out of it. My homeland is not forbidden to me; but in whatsoever land I come, the place I come into is mine. This is in no way an exile; rather it is another homeland. The homeland is everywhere and it is good. Whether the pilgrim is a wise man or a fool, let him exult.[44]

This quotation, and its prominent frontispiece, reflects some of the ambivalence that Kelpius must have felt as he made the tremendously consequential decision to emigrate to Pennsylvania, permanently separating himself from both the church and from the possibility of the ministry or an academic career for which his entire life to this point had been training.

3

"The Woman in the Wilderness"

Kelpius and Company on the Ridge of the Wissahickon, 1694–1707

A certain Philosopher asked St. Anthony: Father, how can you be so happy when you are deprived of the consolation of books?

Anthony replied: My book, O philosopher, is the nature of created things, and any time I want to read the words of God, the book is before me.

—*Vitae Patrum*, CIII (trans. Thomas Merton)

Can a historian of religions read a landscape as a primary source? Does the way that the Jordan River cuts through Palestine help us read the New Testament? Do the caves at Qumran tell us anything about the people who wrote the Dead Sea Scrolls? Timothy Pauketat, an archaeologist specializing in ancient religious sites, has suggested that certain landscapes seem to have an almost innate religious charisma:

> The human history of [such places] is not just human. A place like this, or most other early cities or early religious centers wherever you are, have palpable power already, before people ever get there. There's energy, there's a vitality, there's a particular mix to things, or relationships, that people will arrive and perceive as otherworldly, or special, or as a place to hang around.[1]

Archaeology is rarely a discipline in which one reads such extraordinary or speculative statements, making Pauketat's suggestion all the more compelling. For Pauketat, the archaeology of religion has yielded an environmental phenomenology of the sacred, in which certain places seem to have a nonhuman charisma that different communities of humans will not only notice, but often try to *participate in*—in his words, a nonhuman charisma that compels people to stay there, to "hang around." It is not one feature, or one presence, or one quality of such a landscape. It is in their relations, the way that water plays with rock, the way light plays with them both. Religions, and the people who make them, have places, and the

American Aurora. Timothy Grieve-Carlson, Oxford University Press. © Oxford University Press 2024.
DOI: 10.1093/oso/9780197765562.003.0004

102 AMERICAN AURORA

place of Kelpius and his companions in Pennsylvania would be indelibly connected to their memory in the American mind.[2]

The Wissahickon Creek rises in the Delaware Valley, flowing through what is now Montgomery County, where it negotiates a short route through the land that would become northwest Philadelphia before joining the Schuylkill River on its procession to the Delaware Bay. As it approaches the Schuylkill, the Wissahickon cuts a steep gorge into the otherwise gently rolling hills around it, surrounding itself with high cliff faces to which oaks, maples, and enormous rocks precariously cling. The Wissahickon gorge, with its intermittent glancing sunlight, looming cleaved boulders, and shimmering leaves hovering above a wiggling, incessantly chattering creek has left a consistent impression on its visitors that can be tracked in its appearance in literature. "I have never seen anything so beautiful as the foggy valley of the Wysihicken," wrote the Sussex pamphleteer and politician William Cobbett in his 1821 book *Rural Rides*.[3] The actress Fanny Kemble, another Briton abroad in Philadelphia, commemorated the place in verse in her poem "To the Wissahickon":

> I never shall come back to thee again,
> When once my sail is shadowed on the main,
> Nor ever shall I hear thy laughing voice
> As on their rippling way thy waves rejoice,
> Nor ever see the dark green cedar throw
> Its gloomy shade o'er the clear depths below,
> Never, from stony rifts of granite gray
> Sparkling like diamond rocks in the sun's ray,
> Shall I look down on thee, thou pleasant stream,
> Beneath whose crystal folds the gold sands gleam.[4]

Kemble humanizes the otherwise familiar aspects of the Wissahickon gorge: the river is laughing, the cedar's shade is a welcome sadness. She also points out a more unusual aspect of Wissahickon geology: Wissahickon schist, a metamorphosed shale formation containing large amounts of mica that makes up much of the geology of the area and visibly sparkles and shines when struck by light.[5] The boulders and paths of the Wissahickon have an uncanny shimmer to this day.

The Wissahickon River and the cliffs around it have a certain look that struck the Romantic imagination as richly and darkly beautiful. For all this English attention, however, the Wissahickon would find its most effusive and elegant literary champion in Edgar Allen Poe, who wrote a short piece in 1844 entitled "Morning on the Wissahiccon" for the literary magazine *The Opal*. Poe lavishes the gorge with affectionate hyperbole: "Now the Wissahiccon is of so remarkable a loveliness that, were it flowing in England, it would be the theme of every bard, and the common topic of every tongue," he writes.[6] Poe, like others, finds himself drawn to the effect of the light at midday as it trickles through the gorge and the canopy of trees:

"THE WOMAN IN THE WILDERNESS"   103

The Wissahiccon, however, should be visited, not like "fair Melrose," by moonlight, or even in cloudy weather, but amid the brightest glare of a noonday sun; for the narrowness of the gorge through which it flows, the height of the hills on either hand, and the density of the foliage, conspire to produce a gloominess, if not an absolute dreariness of effect, which, unless relieved by a bright general light, detracts from the mere beauty of the scene.[7]

Poe's warning to avoid the Wissahickon by moonlight seems almost insincere; indeed, a certain gloominess or dreariness never seemed to detract from his sense of beauty elsewhere. Perhaps that is why the Wissahickon under bright light offers only "mere beauty," while a moonlight visit seems to offer something enriched by darkness.

Decades before his reflections on the Wissahickon, Poe composed a short poem to the feelings that overcame him as he stood before a dark body of water, "The Lake":

> In spring of youth it was my lot
> To haunt of the wide world a spot
> The which I could not love the less—
> So lovely was the loneliness
> Of a wild lake, with black rock bound,
> And the tall pines that towered around.
>
> But when the Night had thrown her pall
> Upon that spot, as upon all,
> And the mystic wind went by
> Murmuring in melody—
> Then—ah then I would awake
> To the terror of the lone lake.
>
> Yet that terror was not fright,
> But a tremulous delight—
> A feeling not the jewelled mine
> Could teach or bribe me to define—
> Nor Love—although the Love were thine.
>
> Death was in that poisonous wave,
> And in its gulf a fitting grave
> For him who thence could solace bring
> To his lone imagining—
> Whose solitary soul could make
> An Eden of that dim lake.[8]

104   AMERICAN AURORA

Poe describes a feeling of "mere beauty" transmuted into the full-blown wild terror of the sublime. Standing before a "wild lake, with black rock bound / And the tall pines that towered around," Poe's young narrator finds himself drawn to haunt such a lovely spot; he sees it as a place to "hang around," in Pauketat's parlance. The darkness of night dims this beauty, but it does not simply obscure his vision: the absence of light itself reveals something. A "mystic wind" goes by in this darkness, whispering, bringing up a feeling Poe calls "terror," but this terror is filled with something that he struggles to name. Suddenly Poe sees and hears things beyond the lake and beyond "mere beauty," coalescing into the witness of a nocturnal ecstasy and delight so ineffable that no one could "teach or bribe" him to explain it. The narrator's attitude seems to change: where he once looked at the mere beauty of a dark lake, he now looks out over a "fitting grave." The lake is a place to disappear. The narrator sees the lake as a place of possibility, of transformation, of *holiness*: the "Eden of that dim lake." There is a cryptic death in "The Lake," the disappearance of one whose solitary soul makes an Eden out of a dark body of water.

The Woman in the Wilderness

This chapter is about the life of Johannes Kelpius and his companions at Wissahickon, where they made their home from their arrival in Pennsylvania in 1694 until Kelpius's death in 1707. In the pages that follow, I carve a basic narrative and image of Kelpius and his companions' communal life in Pennsylvania out of the extant primary sources. The chapter is, in a way, the "heart" of this book. Unlike the previous two chapters, this chapter does not present its sources in service of a single argument: rather, this chapter presents a sustained response to several generations of speculative scholarship on the life of Kelpius in Pennsylvania. While the previous two chapters made their own arguments and marshaled their own evidence, they also served as literature reviews, which contextualize the materials that appear later. In the opposite direction, much of the material that follows this chapter depends on my analysis of the materials gathered here, the primary writings of Johannes Kelpius in Pennsylvania (Chapter 4) and the meanings that these people and their place and period would take on in the eighteenth (Chapter 5) and nineteenth centuries (Chapter 6).

There are a few methodological considerations in understanding this period in Kelpius's life. The primary literature from Kelpius and his companions during this period does very little to describe the material conditions of their lives or circumstances. As Oswald Seidensticker wrote in 1885, "Had Kelpius only included some of his everyday life in the letters, the copy of which was preserved by his own hand, we would now be better served than with the extensive theological whims that he spins in them."[9] While one may agree or disagree with Seidensticker regarding the theological import of Kelpius's letters, I share his wish for more insight into the daily life of Kelpius and company.

The primary record is further dimmed by the fact that Kelpius never participated in any of the print conversations that took place in Philadelphia during his life, unlike his contemporaries. For all of his theological training, radical separatist edge, and disdain for church and state, Kelpius never participated in the published polemics that raged in Europe and America during his lifetime. In fact, it seems likely that he did not publish anything at all after his university work. Rather, what writing Kelpius left behind from this period is of a personal and communal nature: letters for friends and hymns written for multiple voices.

There is a hint in the primary sources regarding the paucity of public writings from Kelpius's community at Wissahickon. In 1698, Kelpius's companion Daniel Falckner returned to Germany, where he met with the Pietist leader August Herman Francke. Together, the two prepared a manuscript in which Falkner answered basic questions about life in Pennsylvania for German radicals who were anxious to emigrate. Falkner's manuscript, *Curieuse Nachricht von Pennsylvania* (*Curious News from Pennsylvania*) was published in Germany in 1702, after Falckner had returned to Pennsylvania. In the report, Falckner responds to the question "How to introduce good devout literature . . . for an energetic edification?" Falckner's response reveals the deep importance of what I have called Hermetic Protestant environmental knowledge to the Kelpius community in early Pennsylvania:

> Adam tills his land and tends his cattle, all of which are letters and books, wherein his creator personally instructs him in thanksgiving, and asks him to remember what he has learned. If there is time to spare, then the Holy Bible, next to the church histories and Arndt's works, are enough for those who need guidance.[10]

Like his former companion, Johan Jacob Zimmerman, Falckner seems to subvert the primacy of scripture in favor of a more direct reading of creation itself—of the environment of Pennsylvania. The endless metaphors and analogies employed by Paracelsus and Arndt, as we have seen in previous chapters, seem to finally drop away here: the land and the animals simply *are* the letters and the books. Most telling here is the place of the Bible itself (alongside Arndt), to be read "if there is time to spare." Falckner's attitude toward the proliferation of religious texts in circulation at the time may have been one he shared with his close companion, Kelpius. If so, it would explain the sudden end of Kelpius's public writing after 1690. At this point in their lives and religious development, there were simply more important practices of knowledge than yet more reading and writing.

There were political reasons to avoid public writing, too. After Zimmerman's death, whose public writing activity had brought him and his family so much conflict and misery, Kelpius knew well that the pamphlet itself was the weapon of doctrinal conflict that he saw slowly unraveling the world. The theological battles—and the actual battles—that had shattered Europe for the past century were catalyzed in no small part by a material Christian culture of polemical publishing and doctrinal dispute.

There is a second methodological issue surrounding this period of Kelpius's life. Amid the relative silence of the primary sources on the details of this period, the gaps have been enthusiastically filled in by centuries of speculation. Many of the otherwise worthwhile secondary sources regarding this period rely on the writings of the late nineteenth-century amateur historian Julius Sachse, a topic unto himself, whom I take up in more detail in Chapter 6. At this point, it suffices to say that, at his best, Sachse was overly enthusiastic, playing fast and loose with his source material. At his worst, Sachse manipulated his sources and even invented sources entirely, making certain extreme claims only with reference to "a curious MS in the possession of the author" or "an obscure Ephrata MS." Sachse is not always unreliable, but he was *often* unreliable, and his 1895 book does not serve as a source in this chapter.

To be clear: this legendary material *is* important, but much of it is tangential to our purposes at this phase. Many of these issues in the secondary literature describing Kelpius and company at Wissahickon during this period reinforce a major argument of this book: *that the American Enlightenment would make it difficult for modern and contemporary readers to clearly understand or interpret the worldview and writings of Kelpius and his companions at Wissahickon.* The goal of this chapter is to make the initial reading of the primary sources a foundation against which we might cut back against speculation.

"For Wilderness Signifies Hidden"

Kelpius and his forty companions arrived in Germantown, Pennsylvania, in June 1694, and they seem to have been welcomed into their new community. They would have certainly made early contact with Francis Daniel Pastorius, who had been anxiously awaiting fellow German Pietists in Pennsylvania for nearly a decade. Pastorius still served as the proprietor of the Frankfurt Land Company, under which the Pietists had secured thousands of acres in Pennsylvania. It seems, however, that Kelpius and company declined taking up the lots of the Frankfurt Land Company in Germantown, however, and instead looked up toward the ridges along the sides of the Wissahickon Valley.

"THE WOMAN IN THE WILDERNESS"   107

About one month after their arrival, Johan Seelig reported back in a letter to the Pietists in Europe: "A gentleman of Philadelphia gave us the other day 175 acres of land 3 miles from Germantown; others have promised to give us still more. We are now beginning to build a house there, and the people lend us all possible help."[11] This Philadelphia gentleman was Thomas Fairman, William Penn's surveyor, essentially a confirmation that Penn was aware of and encouraging toward the Kelpius group.[12] Penn was desperately working to promote his new colony in Europe at this moment, and he had good reason to ensure this new batch of radical Germans settled safely.[13] Kelpius's friends were not strangers to Quaker generosity, and this gift of 175 acres was the last in a long succession of extraordinary accommodations made by English and American Quakers to the Kelpius group.

Kelpius and his companions established themselves along the western side of the ridge of the Wissahickon River, just above the confluence of the Wissahickon and the Schuylkill. They were, as Seelig relates, about three miles outside of town. Ensconced on the highest point on the ridge of the Wissahickon, they began to build a house for themselves, and it seems that their new neighbors pitched in. There are other primary references to some sort of communal living arrangement on the ridge. Gerardus Croese, writing in 1696, tells us that he received word in London of the successful establishment of the Kelpius group: "I receive an account, that they arrived at the place they aimed at, and that they all lived in the same house."[14]

Only a few months after their arrival in Pennsylvania, the Kelpius group was able to establish the religious community they had been hoping for. Despite what could have very easily been overwhelming obstacles, like their leader's death, their lack of funds, a near disaster in the English Channel, and dangerous travel through open war-zones, Kelpius and his companions had succeeded in establishing themselves in Pennsylvania, where they again received ample assistance from their community of dissenting comrades in establishing a place to live along the ridge of the Wissahickon gorge. As the journals and letters of Kelpius and Seelig suggest, they understood their unlikely success as a clear indication of the divine sanction of their mission.

Money remained an issue in Pennsylvania, much as it had in Europe, and some scholars have questioned how the group supported themselves financially, however ascetic their lifestyle might have been.[15] One hint comes from an unexpected source: a 1700 letter from Andreas Rudman, the pastor of the Swedish congregation Gloria Dei in what is now Wilmington, Delaware.[16] Kelpius appears very briefly in Rudman's letter as the author turns to the problem of acquiring and binding books in early Pennsylvania:

The present King, Carl XII, whom may God preserve, bless, and counsel, has also, with similar royal grace, sent books over, but as yet they lie unbound, and may well remain so for another year or two. A good, pious, and learned man, Johan Kelpius, has undertaken the work, but in a whole year's time he has succeeded in binding only the Bibles. When will the rest be finished? Binding, here, costs as much as one would pay for the book itself in Sweden.[17]

There was money to be made in early Pennsylvania, even for a monastic society on the edge of Germantown. Kelpius evidently was able to put some of his scholarly skills to use on behalf of himself and his colleagues, and as Rudman complains in the letter, he was unhurried and paid well.[18]

Kelpius did not only bind books at Wissahickon, he read them as well. The Library Company of Philadelphia holds his copy of *The Cherubinic Wanderer*, a 1657 collection of devotional poetry by Angelus Silesius (the pen name of Johann Scheffler [1624–1677]). "Johannes Kelpius of Transylvania, purchased for myself, 1696," he wrote on the title page.[19] Silesius's short, dense noetic verse had a quality that has inspired one recent literary comparison with the Buddhist poetic tradition.[20] Silesius's mystical poetry reflects the popularity of theological ideas derived from Arndt and Böhme, particularly alchemical Christianity and an emphasis on God's creation as a source of divine knowledge, such as the following:

> **Creatures are God's Echo**
> Nothing is without voice: God everywhere can hear
> Arising from creation His praise and echo clear.[21]

Like the Hermetic Protestant poetry of Francis Pastorius, the deep influence of Paracelsus, Arndt, and Böhme on Silesius has led some modern commentators to try to defend this Christian who seems to be "leaning heavily toward pantheistic notions," as one recent edition put it.[22] A clear understanding of the influence of Hermetic and alchemical ideas on popular Protestant thought helps us understand what seems so pantheistic here.

Paracelsian alchemy identified mercury, sulfur, and salt as a trinitarian whole that corresponded directly to spirit, soul, and body, a formation that formed the basis of what Mike Zuber has recently called "spiritual alchemy" in seventeenth-century Lutheranism.[23] There is one verse of Silesius in particular that seems to have had an serious influence on Kelpius's own practice of spiritual alchemy, described in detail in the next chapter:

> **The Threefold in Nature**
> The Godhead is triune, as every plant reveals.
> Sulphur, salt, mercury are all in one concealed.[24]

"THE WOMAN IN THE WILDERNESS" 109

That this particular poem stood out to Kelpius is evident in his own spiritual practice, which he called the "Threefold Wilderness State," and in the copy of Silesius that he bought for himself, where he has marked this particular poem with pen on the page. This notion of a holy threefold quality throughout creation, in the chemical trinity of salt, sulfur, and mercury (and an alchemical means to pursue it spiritually in oneself) was a common idea in Kelpius's milieu. In the following chapter, I will turn to Kelpius's spiritual alchemy directly. For now, it suffices to say that Kelpius's name in this book—which was not an academic or doctrinal work, but rather a book of devotional alchemical Christian poetry— shows us exactly where his interests were turning, now that he was ensconced on the ridge with his companions. His priorities had shifted firmly and permanently from academic theology toward devotional practice and personal spiritual development.

Having glanced at the effects of the Wissahickon Valley on the minds of Poe and others, we can imagine Kelpius looking down into the sparkling gorge from his new home on the ridge. But unlike these other authors, Kelpius did not have Romantic interpretation of his new environment: rather, Kelpius saw his new home in the same way he conceived of everything else: in biblical terms. On the ridge of the Wissahickon, where Poe saw the terrible beauty of the sublime in a later century, Kelpius saw something else: a biblical setting come to life. He addresses his new home in the Wissahickon directly as a subject with the familiar "thou" in a 1706 letter:

Oh everblessed Wilderness! thou rejoyceth and blossometh as a Rose! yea thou blossometh abundantly & rejoyceth even with Joy & Singing! The glory of Lebanon is given unto Thee, the Excellency of Carmel and Sharon! In thee we see the Glory of our Lord, & the Excellency of our God! In thee our weak Hands are Strengthened & our feeble Knees confirmed (Isa. 35, 1). Who would not desire to be a Denison in Thee? Who would not delight to trace they Solitary and lonesom walks?[25]

Europeans in seventeenth-century Pennsylvania consistently remarked on the overwhelming presence of the old-growth forests, and Kelpius's reference here to the "glory of Lebanon," which was known for its ancient groves of cedars, suggests that he was not immune to the charm of that ancient forest. Kelpius and Poe did share one common impression of their environment: they both saw the wilderness as a place where they could retreat, decline, and "become nothing." They both saw this wilderness as a fantasy of their own nonexistence.

Despite the immense religious significance Kelpius found in the idea of wilderness, the actual material circumstances of Kelpius's environment require more clarification. As described in the previous chapter, not only Philadelphia but all of southeastern Pennsylvania was part of an extensive riparian trade and travel network managed by the Lenape.[26] In fact, given that Kelpius and company settled on the confluence of the Wissahickon and the Schuylkill, they were probably surrounded by economic activity. Life on the ridge would have been punctuated by the regular passage of Lenape and European canoes and cargoes from the inland river systems. Kelpius's place on the ridge, as secluded, overgrown, and hidden away as it may have been, was hardly a place without people.

In fact, the town that it sat three miles from could hardly be described as rural or agrarian. When Daniel Falckner reported to the Pietists in Halle in 1699 that "Adam tills his land and tends his cattle," he was not being entirely honest about the economy of Pennsylvania at the time, and certainly not Germantown. One report from 1684 described the people of Germantown as "not too well skilled in the culture of the ground," and as "mostly linen weavers" by occupation.[27] As Stephenie Grauman Wolf points out, the geography of the area simply did not lend itself to agriculture, being too rocky for tilling and too steep and thickly wooded to clear for grazing. The residents mostly took up artisanal trades.[28] The environs of Germantown were so thoroughly urbanized, in fact, that by 1720 even a single sighting of a bear in the vicinity was enough for a major news story.[29]

The wooded, rocky cliffs around the Wissahickon were likely a secluded and peaceful perch from which Kelpius could turn his focus inward, but it was hardly a wilderness. Somewhat like that famous American hermit of centuries later, Henry David Thoreau, Kelpius's wilderness was simply a quiet spot in an otherwise largely suburban setting. Kelpius was not in the "wilderness," then, according to our contemporary understanding. But neither was he in Denndorf, Tübingen, or London. He was, as his new neighbor Pastorius might say, "gone into the ancient forest" of his own ascetic imagination.

Despite having settled in a rapidly urbanizing area, Kelpius's interest in imagining his place in the wilderness lied in his reading of the Bible. Many of the themes of Kelpius's later writing, like wilderness, secrecy, and celestial phenomena, are derived from Revelation 12.[30] Kelpius invoked the apocalyptic and celestial imagery of Revelation 12 repeatedly in his letters and his poetry, locating himself in the wilderness of Revelation and *identifying as* the woman of the passage. "Apoc. 12 . . . for wilderness signifies as much as hidden, or not revealed," he scribbled in a 1704 letter, in which he reads Revelation 12 alongside the events of the seventeenth century, in which persecuted groups of radical Christians fled persecution amid escalating environmental change and societal disruption.[31] As Kelpius himself points out, "wilderness" was more of an apocalyptic and esoteric idea than a description of any real geography: wilderness *meant* hidden, protected, "not apparent"; wilderness meant *secret*. The Hermetic Protestant approach to the environment and scripture is interwoven here into Kelpius's own life and the landscape of Pennsylvania.

The Wissahickon Hermits

Kelpius names a handful of his companions on the first page of his journal, indicating, as I suggested earlier, his most prominent or closest companions within the group of forty Pietists who arrived in Pennsylvania with Kelpius in 1694.[32] Of the forty or so people who traveled to Pennsylvania with Kelpius, it seems that only a small number lived in the communal house on the ridge, and an even smaller number of those left a noticeable mark on the primary sources. Many of the names of this forty are lost, but those whose names are recorded have something unusual in common: a history of ecstatic and visionary experiences and capacities, to an extent that is unusual even among radical Pietists. At least one of them, Anna Maria Schuchart, "the Prophetess of Erfurt," was well known as such, as detailed in Vita II. This shared background of ecstatic experiences and abilities was one thing they had in common, and it suggests another dimension of their shared motivation to leave Europe.

Johann Gottfried Seelig (1668–1745) was one of Kelpius's closest colleagues and friends at Wissahickon. Biographical details on Seelig are scarce. He was born in Lemgo, Germany, in 1668, and he pursued studies in theology before becoming involved in the Pietist movement.[33] Seelig's name appeared in the correspondence of Pietist leaders August Herman Francke and Phillip Jacob Spener. Writing in 1692, from Halle, Francke reported on the ecstatic experiences of some of his students:

> In the past few weeks we have experienced something unusual almost every day, and some of the students, one after the other, have gone into a peculiar state. Some have been overwhelmed with extraordinary and supernatural joy, while others have been filled with sharp contrition and many tears, testifying that their whole hearts seemed to melt in their bodies, or that their hearts felt like they would leap out of their bodies, or when something powerful was spoken from the Word of God, it felt like a lightning bolt running through all their limbs, not to mention other circumstances that cannot be described briefly. Their names, as they came one after the other in such a state, which is always different from one to the other, are as follows: Stophasius, Kohler, Ulrici, Seelig, Kipsch, Schroter.[34]

Seelig was not just another theology student who was swept up in Pietism. He was part of an ecstatic collective of college students who gathered around Francke in Halle in 1692.

Seelig was the author of the 1694 letter that contains the second narrative of the group's journey to Pennsylvania, and he also authored a few extant hymns at Wissahickon.[35] In his 1699 letter to Deichman, Seelig seems to suggest that he and Kelpius were unique in their commitment to the ascetic lifestyle.[36] Like Kelpius, Seelig seems to have committed himself to a severe ascetic regimen. His letters mention the wearing of a course garment (*grob sack*) and a commitment to a celibate lifestyle based on the recommendation of Paul.[37] Kelpius and Seelig's close relationship is frequently indicated in the primary sources, both in the texts and in the arrangements of the texts themselves: Kelpius's collections of hymns include works by Seelig, and one of Seelig's letters appears in Kelpius's own letterbook.[38]

Seelig persisted in his ascetic commitments until his death in 1745, when his will, detailed in the family Bible of the Leverings, gives us a hint of insight into the reading material that Kelpius and company carried with them to Pennsylvania.[39] William Levering notes that Seelig owned "5 bibles, 14 books, 10 of Jacob Boehmen's books, and 120 Latin, Dutch and Greek books."[40] There was evidently a large library at Wissahickon, unsurprisingly dominated by both Jacob Böhme and scholarly works.

Alongside Seelig and Kelpius on the ship that left Rotterdam was Henrich Bernard Köster, a Lutheran minister who was noted by Gerardus Croese as "a famous Man, and of such severe manners that few could equal him."[41] The severity of Köster's manner is apparent throughout the primary literature. Köster himself apparently "excommunicated" Daniel Falckner and his partner, Anna Maria Schuchart, from the group at the end of the trip to Philadelphia, perhaps after learning about their extramarital partnership.[42] Adelung identifies Köster as the leader of the Wissahickon group in his 1789 *History of Human Folly*, where he identifies Köster as "the Chiliast."[43]

Köster had been involved in the ministry in Europe, and he wasted no time in resuming his practice of public speaking in Pennsylvania. According to Seelig's 1694 letter, the group made the early acquaintance of a lapsed Dutch Mennonite named Jacob Isaac in Germantown, who decided to "to acknowledge and abandon the follies, scandals, shortcomings and stains of his former religion."[44] Isaac held a triweekly meeting at his home in Germantown, apparently an interdenominational devotional gathering for similarly questioning individuals, "at which Köster generally speaks publicly to the great edification of those present."[45] Köster also made a weekly trip into the city of Philadelphia, where he preached in English.[46] Köster's severe manner and his surprising (given the company he kept) intolerance for heterodox belief and behavior led to his involvement in the Keithian controversy, a theological rift among the Philadelphia Quakers, described in more detail below.

Less committed to the rigorous asceticism of Seelig and Kelpius and the doctrinal sparring of Köster was Daniel Falckner (1666–1741), the author of the aforementioned *Curious News from Pennsylvania* (1702). Like Kelpius, Falckner was the son of a Lutheran pastor, and like his friends Kelpius, Seelig, and many

"THE WOMAN IN THE WILDERNESS" 113

other early Pietists, Falckner's association with the early Pietist movement began when he was a theology student. Falckner met August Francke at the University of Erfurt in 1690, where he attended Francke's *collegia* meetings—just a few years after Kelpius and Francke likely connected in Leipzig. And again like his friend Kelpius, Falckner seems to have followed his university education not with an academic position, but with deeper engagement with the Pietist movement in Germany. This eventually led him to join Kelpius and Zimmerman's group in Hamburg, from which they departed for Rotterdam in 1693.[47]

Falckner and Anna Maria Schuchart were romantically involved in Europe and during their journey to Pennsylvania, and their extramarital relationship probably led to the episode described by Kelpius in which Köster "excommunicated" them both.[48] And like his partner Anna "the Prophetess," as Kelpius called her, Falckner had his own ecstatic episodes. In a fascinating passage from a letter from Phillip Jacob Spener to August Herman Francke, Spener describes his relief upon learning that Köster had convinced Falckner to control his ecstatic powers: "Mr. Köster has brought Mr. Falckner to the point that he no longer has ecstasies," Spener wrote.[49] With an almost gossiping tone, the leaders of Pietism went on to describe Falckner's account of his ecstatic events: "He also said what brought them about: that by intensely focusing the imagination on Godly things, he could awaken them."[50]

In 1693, the leaders of Pietism were worried about the prominence, meaning, and power of the ecstasies of their followers, and news that one had trained another to control his powers seems welcome to both Spener and Francke. Spener concluded his story with a note of worry: "Were I certain in this matter, concerning *extraordinaria*, on one side or the other, it seems to me, a great deal of concern would be lifted: since in many ways now I do not know how to help."[51] From Schuchart to Seelig, Köster to Falckner, the company Kelpius kept on the ridge had one thing in common: a shared history of ecstatic or paranormal episodes, *extraordinaria*, as Spener called them.

The exceptional nature of these powers is evident in Spener's own handwriting: in the letter, he jumps from a less formal German voice into the Latin *extraordinaria*, reflecting the style among educated German authors to use Latin script for ideas considered foreign.[52] Spener does not refer to the ecstasies of Falkner and company as unambiguous *wunder*, or miracles, which were not at all foreign to the German language or imagination. Rather, Spener's writing shows, both in his own words and in his educated turns of multilingual phrase, that these paranormal powers and ecstasies were beyond the common order, they were alien, they were unknown, they were *extraordinaria*. And while Spener himself may not have known how to help the budding ecstatics among his followers, it seemed the solution for many of them involved leaving Europe for Pennsylvania.

The Keithian Schism

Almost immediately upon their arrival in Pennsylvania, Kelpius and his companions noticed that there was no shortage of doctrinal dispute among the people of Philadelphia. In his 1694 letter to the Pietists in Germany, Johan Seelig describes how, while in London, they heard a Quaker prophet warn of a coming great earthquake—which Seelig interpreted as a schism within Quakerdom.[53] "This has here in America begun to manifest itself among them," he wrote.[54]

Seelig was referring to the schism of George Keith, a Scottish Presbyterian theologian turned Quaker who had lived in Philadelphia and West Jersey since 1685.[55] Between his arrival and 1691, Keith began to notice what he considered to be grievous errors in the religious practice of his fellow Friends. As the Quaker emphasis on the doctrine of the Inward Light, the individual experience of the speaking presence of God, continued to grow in Philadelphia, there was an accompanying lack of emphasis on the Bible or the life and teachings of Jesus.[56] There was also a social dimension of the Keithian schism, which, as Jon Butler has pointed out, reflected the ways in which the Friends were less equal to one another than their doctrines would suggest. Keith "alleged that Friends neglected elemental Christian doctrine in a way that stimulated heresy," Butler writes, "and claimed that the Quakers' hierarchical system of church government placed so much power in the hands of the Public Friends who acted as ministers that it repressed the spiritual vitality of lesser Friends."[57] Even among the Quakers, Keith claimed, "elemental Christian doctrine" was lacking, and power was increasingly concentrated in the hands of the very few.

The Keithian schism ultimately went nowhere. Keith was expelled from the Philadelphia Meeting, and he returned to Europe to defend himself before the London Friends in 1694, only to be expelled there, too. But his criticisms of Quaker theology would prefigure the major intellectual trends in Pennsylvania in the coming century, in which a more clearly secularized entrepreneurial Enlightenment ideology would flourish in the wake of figures like Benjamin Franklin and Thomas Jefferson. Elite Quakers in Philadelphia were gradually shaking off the constraints of biblical theology as they continued to develop a clear religious philosophy of the inner experience of the individual. And as George Keith pointed out, the religious insights of wealthy and powerful individuals tended to be the most important.

In a 1699 tract published in London, Keith laid out his critique: William Penn was, in fact, a deist, who was establishing a colony whose government "contendeth that the Holy Scriptures are not the rule of faith and life, but that the light in the conscience of every man is that rule."[58] The fact that Keith's critique of Penn does not strike our ears today as a serious problem, but rather the obvious

"THE WOMAN IN THE WILDERNESS"   115

basis for any ethical system of governance, demonstrates the extent of William Penn's ideological victory, both at the close of the seventeenth century and today.

With the exception of Kelpius, who never records an opinion on the matter, the entire Wissahickon group involved themselves immediately with the controversy. Seelig's 1694 letter showed him sympathizing with Keith strongly, and the "severe mannered" Köster was so happy to dive in that he personally disrupted a Quaker meeting in Burlington in 1696.[59] This fateful meeting was attended by the great-grandfather of Charles Brockden Brown, the Quaker author who questioned the meaning of the almanac in Chapter 2 and who is the subject of Chapter 5. Since the Wissahickon Pietists left Europe in part to avoid religious conflict, this willingness to immediately embroil themselves in one upon arriving in Pennsylvania is hard to understand. But perhaps it makes more sense given the religious backgrounds of everyone involved. As Brian Ogren has recently demonstrated, George Keith was deeply interested in Jewish Kabbalah and mystical trends in Christianity, having briefly affiliated himself with Anne Conway and Henry More in England.[60] If the Wissahickon group wanted to align themselves with the more radical segment of Pennsylvania religion, Keith was their man.

Keith's other natural ally was Daniel Leeds, the English Quaker author of *Temple of Wisdom*, who was also eager to side with Keith against the Philadelphia Friends who had rejected his book and dogged him with polemical tracts and smears in print. Leeds became a vociferous public partisan for Keith's schismatic claims, in tracts like *A trumpet sounded out of the wilderness of America which may serve as a warning to the government and people of England to beware of Quakerisme* (1697) and *The Great Mistery of Fox-Craft Discovered* (1705), wherein Leeds—in his own didactic way—followed and furthered Keith's theological disputes within Quakerism, ultimately arguing that Quaker belief and practice denied the divinity of Christ.[61]

There is no primary source record of a meeting between the Wissahickon group and Daniel Leeds, but given Leeds's very public championing of the work and thought of Jacob Böhme and the fact that Leeds and the Wissahickon group seem to have chosen the same side of the schismatic controversy that rocked Philadelphia for years after their arrival, such a meeting seems quite likely. Philadelphia was a small town in 1694, with only about two thousand permanent inhabitants, and Leeds was just over the river in Burlington.[62] Leeds and the Wissahickon hermits would have known of each other, and it is not hard to imagine Leeds seeking out and meeting that strange crew of fellow ecstatics, joining the prayer services at the meeting house on the ridge, or using the telescope that the Wissahickon group brought with them to Philadelphia to look up at the stars that he and Kelpius both spent so much time watching and contemplating.[63]

116   AMERICAN AURORA

Another partisan in the Keithian schism was Francis Daniel Pastorius, the German Pietist, polymath, and founder of Germantown. While Daniel Leeds was a Quaker who turned against Quakerism, Pastorius was a radical Pietist who became a Quaker partisan and then a Quaker himself. Pastorius attacked Köster by name as one of "four Boasting Disputers of this World" in a 1697 publication.[64] This particular text was written after Köster had separated from the Kelpius group, and Pastorius does not waste the opportunity to mock Köster's new communal arrangement. Pastorious referred to Köster's new group, "Irenia," as "Erinnia"—a play on "error" as Irenia was a play on peace.[65] Pastorius's tract was a response to Köster's public disruption of the 1696 Quaker meeting in Burlington, an incident that Pastorius witnessed and found intensely offensive.[66]

Kelpius seems to have avoided the Keithian schism completely. Köster, on the other hand, pursued the Keithian argument against the Quakers repeatedly, and apparently he even resorted to some form of violence in his attempt to shut down the Burlington meeting in 1696.[67] This may have been the last straw between Köster and Kelpius. Pointing another away from error toward the word of God was one thing, but physical violence would have been something else entirely. Köster was either dismissed from the ridge or he broke away himself that same year, forming "Irenia," the group that Pastorius mocked in print one year later.

Pastorius would eventually attack the other Wissahickon hermits, too. Seelig's 1694 letter reached Germany and was published in print the following year. In the letter, Seelig reported back to Germany on the Quaker conflict, praising George Keith and noting the sorry state of Pennsylvania Quakerdom. Pastorius heard about the letter through a connection in Amsterdam, and he took it upon himself to defend Quakerism to the German Pietists and, in what Patrick Erben calls "one of the most significant steps of his life," publicly declared his allegiance to William Penn and the Philadelphia Quaker Meeting for an audience of his former Pietist comrades in Europe.[68]

In his letter to the Pietists, "A Missive of Sincere Affection to the so-called Pietists in Germany," Pastorius quoted extensively from Seelig's letter. He derisively called it "a masterpiece" and attacked the Kelpius group directly. "When they were in England and needed money for their passage," Pastorius noted, the Wissahickon group honored and flattered "the so-called Quakers as citizens of Jerusalem . . . [as] a bastion and free city against those collected from the jaws of hell in Babylon."[69] The Wissahickon hermits were hypocritical in their attacks on Quakerdom, Pastorius pointed out, naming the Quakers as comrades during their own time of need, but gleefully jumping on the critique and controversy that consumed the Friends in Philadelphia. Pastorius had a point. The Wissahickon hermits owed everything to transatlantic Quaker solidarity, and some of them had a funny way of showing their appreciation.

He goes on, with a cryptic but apparently severe condemnation of the Wissahickon group's own sins: "They soon revealed openly (and still continue to reveal) through their own discord, quarrelsomeness, and other fruits of the flesh what kind of trees they are and that the bare leaves of the hypocritical testimony of the mouth do not matter."[70] In his typically botanical language, Pastorius appears to point to the conflict with Köster, along with something else: a cryptic reference to the "fruits of the flesh," in which he seems to hint toward a sexual dimension of the problems afflicting the Wissahickon group.

Pastorius went on to defend the Quakers in Philadelphia and Quaker doctrine generally from what he saw as slander. He knew his audience, too: in addressing the Quakers and Pietists each as "so-called," reminding both that each label originated as a pejorative, he reminded his readers of oppression and intolerance faced by the early Pietist movement. He offered a moving memory from his childhood as he wrapped up his missive: "I remember very well that in my youth I heard thousands and thousands of times the name Quaker and Enthusiasts called out"—suggesting, at once, the shared history of oppression of both Quakers and Pietists among orthodox Lutherans.[71] Pastorius knew what kinds of things Pietists liked to hear.

The Keithian schism ended when its leader was shunned from the London Meeting, and orthodox Quaker power was consolidated in Philadelphia. For the Wissahickon hermits, however, having just arrived, there was no "normal" for things to return to. Their disruptive participation in the conflict had burned bridges permanently. Despite what seems to have been a commitment to an irenic philosophy of reconciliation and love between different Christian sects, members of Kelpius's group immediately involved themselves in a doctrinal dispute upon their arrival in Philadelphia. Seelig noted the controversy in print (for subsequent publication) only a few weeks after landing, and Köster went so far as to resort to violence before breaking away from the Wissahickon group, and eventually departing from Pennsylvania altogether. In turning Pastorius against them, the Wissahickon hermits isolated themselves from the nascent German community in Philadelphia and the Quaker elite with whom Pastorius had aligned himself. The ridge of the Wissahickon was only three miles from town, but the space between the inhabitants had widened dramatically.

"Everything Too Spiritual and Too Heavenly"

A commitment to social reform and public welfare programming was a staple of early Pietist thought. In Halle, August Herman Francke would establish a system of schools and housing for orphaned children, alongside sustained medical and publishing programs.[72] Based on the now-established connections between

118   AMERICAN AURORA

Francke and Köster, Falckner, Seelig, and Kelpius, it stands to reason that the Wissahickon group attempted something similar in Philadelphia.

In his 1694 letter, Seelig declares the intention of the group to improve the public welfare of the people of Philadelphia: "For we are resolved, besides giving public instruction to the little children of this country, to take many of them to ourselves and have them day and night with us, so as to lay in them the foundation of a stable permanent character."[73] Seelig's emphasis on the well-being of the children suggests the long-term social goals that the group shared with continental Pietists and their programs of social reform. It seems that the Wissahickon group did commit to running a kind of public school for children in the area, especially during the early period of their time at Wissahickon, in the middle to late 1690s. They would have been suited to it. Kelpius, Köster, Seelig, and Falckner were all university-trained academics who were proficient in English, German, and Latin, in addition to academic areas like mathematics and music.

There is only one extant primary source that describes the school program. In 1742, the Lutheran minister Heinrich Melchior Mühlenberg recorded an encounter with a widowed woman who was dying of cancer. The woman referred to Seelig by name and told Mühlenberg that she had gone to school with the "old, gray" tutors while she was still young, and she "had received tender impressions of the true fear of God through lessons."[74] We can only imagine the circumstances: it would have been a strange experience for children climbing the ridge outside of town where a group of "old, gray" men in robes taught them divinity, language, math, and music in thick German accents. Still, there is a sad beauty in this woman's deathbed recollection for Reverend Mühlenberg: as her life drew to a close, she took some comfort in her decades-old memory of learning "the true fear of God" from the hermits on the ridge.

By 1702, however, something had changed. Kelpius and Seelig in particular, it seems, had continued to withdraw from public life and had ceased their teaching activity. In a letter to Francke, Daniel Falckner wrote to August Herman Francke in Germany: "There are some private individuals here that are quite willing to have their children taught the liberal arts, but there is no teacher here; Mr. Kelpius and Mr. Seelig have withdrawn entirely from all such services."[75] The entire tone of this letter is frustrated. Falckner seems to refer to unfulfilled promises made while in Germany during an earlier visit, and, in what seems like a reference to Kelpius and Seelig, he calls out his companions for being "too godly," "too spiritual," and "too heavenly" to contribute to social reform projects in Pennsylvania:

> People here are altogether too godly, and either put no value upon or prevent the baptism of the dear children, the Holy Supper, the preaching of God's Word, and other doctrines of faith necessary for salvation, or will have everything too spiritual and too heavenly; the consequence is, that some that appear to be and

ought to be our companions are of the above-mentioned sort and, therefore, crawl about in the dark.[76]

It seems that the original core Wissahickon group—Kelpius, Seelig, Falckner, and Köster—did try to establish a program of social welfare at Wissahickon, but by 1702, Kelpius' and Seelig's asceticism had prompted the conclusion of their teaching activities. Letters sent by each man in 1699 make mention of their poor health, and it is possible that chronic illness was a factor in their suspension of teaching activities.[77] Falckner's frustration with his companions notwithstanding, the short-lived school on the ridge fits into the broad theme of Kelpius's life in Pennsylvania: a sustained retreat from every facet of public life as his ascetic practice deepened.

"The Rooms in My Father's House"

Education was not the only public welfare program that Kelpius withdrew from. Like the early Quakers, early Pietist social programs included extensive missionary efforts, particularly among orthodox communities and other dissenting sects of Christians. The Quaker chronicler Croese suggests that missionizing efforts among the colonial Christians were one of the Kelpius group's major goals for their time in Pennsylvania.[78] Seelig's 1694 letter betrays the hermits' view of Germantown as an extensive mission field.[79] The group's disastrous entry into the Keithian schism may have precluded any attempts at extensive missionizing, and Daniel Falckner's 1702 letter to Francke suggests that the Pietists in Philadelphia were yet unable to form even a small congregation beyond the meetings on the ridge.[80] Whatever they had planned, it seems they mostly failed. For his part, Kelpius's irenicism had blossomed into a fully anti-denominational vision of Christian life and practice: "With Peter, I have found out . . . He that feareth Him, and doeth what is right, is agreeable to Him."[81] In so many words (and as always, couched in scripture), Christian life was an inner and individual matter. Kelpius would extend this consideration to non-Christians, too.

Indeed, by 1705 Kelpius was suspicious of any attempts to missionize, convert, or even preach to the Lenape, with whom he apparently spent some time. Even at this early date, Kelpius was critical of colonial treatment of the Lenape people generally. He described his views on the matter in a letter to his old mentor, Johannes Fabricius. "I could report," he writes, of his time "amongst the Indians, and how they are brought to grief now and then by so-called Christians."[82] Kelpius goes on to tell his old mentor a story, apparently based on his firsthand witness: "Yet one instance I will report, as abashed Sir W. Penn, when he was here last, Anno 1701 (if I remember rightly) when he wanted to preach to them

120 AMERICAN AURORA

of faith in the God of Heaven and Earth, at their Kintika (thus they call their festivity)." Here Kelpius describes his own attendance at a *kintika* (a Lenape dance ceremony)[83] in 1701, along with William Penn. During the ceremony, William Penn began to preach to the Lenape in attendance. Kelpius describes the scene that followed: "After having listened to him with great patience;" writes Kelpius, the Lenape responded to Penn:

> You tell us to believe in the Creator and Preserver of Heaven and Earth, though you do not believe in Him yourself, nor trust in Him. For you have now made your own the land we held in common amongst ourselves and our friends. You now take heed, night and day, how you may keep it, so that no one may take it from you. Indeed, you are anxious even beyond your span of life, and divide it among your children. This manor for this child, that manor for that child. But we have faith in God the Creator and Preserver of Heaven and Earth. He preserves the sun, He hath preserved our fathers so many moons (for they count not by years). He preserves us, and we believe and are sure that He will also preserve our children after us, and provide for them, and because we believe this, we bequeath them not a foot of land.[84]

This passage stands out as another example from early Pennsylvania of what David Graeber and David Wengrow have called the "Indigenous critique" of European society and religion.[85] The assembled Lenape could not help themselves when William Penn took it upon himself to preach to them, despite what Kelpius noted as their "great patience." From the Lenape perspective, how could Penn, the representative of a people so obsessed with personal property, capital, inheritance, and private landownership possibly preach faith in God at the *kintika*? It must have been an extraordinarily offensive sermon that Penn delivered to the Lenape, and Kelpius notes that Penn was "abashed" at their response.

In relating this passage to his teacher, Kelpius reveals himself as a strong sympathizer with the Lenape position. This was extremely unusual for a European in Pennsylvania, but not unheard of. As described in the previous chapter, Pastorius deeply admired the Lenape way of life, and especially their "wonderful resignation" to the will and plan of God, *precisely* the same worldview and argument that Kelpius describes above.

Kelpius concludes this letter to his old teacher with a startling statement:

> When we shall be made worthy to see the many and varied dwellings in our Father's house (for who would be so simpleminded, to say they were all the same), I believe we will see that the same Architect cared little about our common formula and systematic architecture.[86]

"THE WOMAN IN THE WILDERNESS"   121

With an elegant and seamless recourse to scripture, Kelpius stakes out one of the most radically pluralist positions that could be found among Christians at the turn of the eighteenth century, and this position is worth parsing for a moment here. Referring to John 14:2, in which Jesus says, "In my father's house are many rooms," before reminding his listeners that a place is prepared for each one of them, Kelpius is suggesting a radical turn against missionary efforts.[87] Human beings were created by God, and they have *differences*, and thus God obviously *approves* of human differences, Kelpius argues.

Kelpius proceeds to his truly radical claim: "It is my belief we shall then see that the same Architect cared little about our common formula and systematic architecture." This is, needless to say, a thoroughly, radically Pietist and unorthodox position; indeed, Kelpius's irenicism pushes against the normative boundaries of what might be called Christian thought generally, not only in 1705, but today. In summary, Kelpius suggests that the Lenape religion is probably perfectly acceptable to God. In any case, God's determinations regarding human decency are probably beyond the capacities of people like the "abashed Sir. W Penn."

For all this radical thought, there is an accompanying political failure in this letter: did Kelpius express these radical ideas to his fellow Christians, other settler-colonists in and around Philadelphia? Where was Kelpius's voice as the Lenape were pushed further inland, as smallpox devastated their families and as their sachems broke apart? Or is this lone surviving letter his only statement on the matter? One is reminded here of Thomas Merton's criticism of monastic life as "the false sweetness of narcissistic seclusion."[88] What is the point of insight, compassion, and love, what is the point of such a radically pluralistic position, if it is held by an otherwise silent hermit? What is compassion without solidarity?

Again, we simply do not know what kind of interactions Kelpius had with the Lenape. Did he attend the *kintika* regularly? And what did the Lenape in turn think about these strange men on the ridge? With so many other questions about Kelpius's life on the ridge, we can only speculate. All we have are a few lines from a letter from student to teacher, in which Kelpius revealed himself to be one of the most radically pluralist religious thinkers in Christendom at the turn of the eighteenth century.

"Contemplation of the Stars"

In his last academic work, his 1690 book on Aristotle, *Pagan Ethics*, Kelpius opens with a beautiful description of an evening that he spent "devoted to the contemplation of the stars," and he relates how he "traveled in thought" throughout the dome of the sky.[89] As we might imagine given his reading material and his affiliation with people like Johann Zimmerman, Kelpius had an intense religious interest in celestial phenomena. His diary of the trip to Pennsylvania is marked up with astrological symbols as he describes the journey, recording the events of the journey and his thoughts and feelings alongside the corresponding patterns in the sky.[90]

And he surrounded himself with fellow sky-watchers. His friend Seelig describes the undesirable effects of "astral Venus" in a 1699 letter, pointing toward a general interest in astrology among the hermits on the ridge.[91] Daniel Falckner recorded a fascinating moment when the Wissahickon companions discussed knowledge of the stars with a Lenape visitor who "came to me and my companions at night in the woods, as we were around the fire. He looked at the polar star, and observed therefrom that it would be cold, as the star was so bright, which came to pass."[92] He also writes that the Lenape both "observe and understand" *extraordinari*, extraordinary or paranormal phenomena, referring again to their knowledge of the stars and their ability to predict storms.[93]

Today, the Library Company of Philadelphia possesses two astronomy books that Kelpius actually owned, Ismael Bouillau's *Astronomica philolaica* (1645) and Isaac Newton *Principia Mathematica* (1688)—texts that came into Kelpius's possession following the death of his friend Zimmerman.[94] In Kelpius's reading of figures like Bouillau and Newton, we can imagine that he would have brought the same religious interpretation to their science that Zimmerman did, a natural theology indistinct from the sciences, harkening back to the *theorica* of Paracelsus, alive and well on the ridge of the Wissahickon at the turn of the eighteenth century. Celestial knowledge, whether it came from Lenape visitors or the works of Newton and Bouillau, was a matter of intense interest among Kelpius and his companions.

In his 1699 letter to Steven Mumford, Kelpius points toward the sky as a text where one might "behold at last an Harbinger," "Gazing upon this Supercaelestial Orb and Sphier from whence with her Children," and contemplating "every new Phoenomena, Meteors, Stars and various Colours of the Skei."[95] In his somewhat nonstandard English, Kelpius nevertheless expresses the central importance of watching the sky at the end of the seventeenth century. And in the same way that he described the biblical precedents of the microcosmic ecstasies of the early Pietists, he describes the macrocosmic wonders of the sky with ample recourse to scripture.

Kelpius's interest in extraordinary heavenly phenomena was derived from the biblical portrayals of miraculous celestial phenomena in the biblical texts themselves. In his letter to Steven Mumford, in which Kelpius detailed the miraculous and paranormal abilities of the early Pietists in their ecstatic states, he makes reference to the biblical theophanies such as the Pillar of Cloud: "Thus partly I have declared how they [the early Pietists] was baptized with such energical drops out

"THE WOMAN IN THE WILDERNESS" 123

of that supercaelestial Pillar of Cloud by Gifts and miraculous Manifestations of the Powers from on high."[96] Kelpius is deliberately cryptic as to whether the manifestation described here is related to the "supercaelestial orb" of earlier in the letter, or *how* exactly the skies and the ecstatic powers of the early Pietists were connected, but their connection is clear.

In another, later letter, the subject of the next chapter, the pillar appears again, as a guiding principle in clearly alchemical language: "But there followeth a night also upon this Day, wherein nevertheless the Pillar of Fire is our Guide, refining us as Gold in the Furnace."[97] The "night" in question here is the dark night that follows mystical achievement. Here the pillar appears as it does in the Exodus narrative, guiding the suffering faithful through their wilderness sojourn. The same pillar of flame appears to the early Pietists in Kelpius's retelling. Kelpius begins describing the challenges of the early Pietists and the persecutions they faced, which he characterizes as a "craggy, uneven yea even dark wilderness" in which God has led them so that they might be purified.[98] Still, God appears here as a pillar of flame to guide them: "Hitherto they have been baptized with the fiery Pillar of many inward and outward Tribulations, Sorrows, Temptations, Refinings, Purifications."[99]

Kelpius's biblical approach to history and the events of his own life make it difficult to see where scriptural reference and memoir begin and end in the text. Indeed, in his remarks on the parallels between the early Pietists and the Acts of the Apostles (see Vita I), he makes it clear that the boundaries between autobiography, history, and scripture are permeable. And as we will see in Chapter 5, anomalous pillars of cloud, light, and flame seemed to follow Kelpius's memory in Philadelphia in the centuries after he died.

The Lamenting Voice of the Hidden Love

In his diary of the trip from London to Pennsylvania, on the second of June, Kelpius describes how the crew of the ship found an animal they called a "dolphin" trapped in the anchor. The crew pulled it onto the deck, where Kelpius describes it as "yellow as gold, spotted with red."[100] He goes on to say that his encounter with the dolphin did not "confirm the credibility of the fable of the ancients concerning the love of music." Apparently, Kelpius and/or some of his companions tried to test the ancient Greek myth of Arion, whose song to Apollo was so beautiful that a crowd of dolphins gathered around him and then saved him from drowning after he was thrown from his ship by pirates. Whether Kelpius sang or played an instrument for the dolphin is unspecified: we have only the brief record of a musical performance for a dolphin somewhere in the Atlantic on June 2, 1694.[101]

124   AMERICAN AURORA

Music is an unfortunately exotic area for many historians, and especially so for histories of American religion. As Richard Crawford has pointed out, otherwise comprehensive surveys of American religious history often devote only a few pages to song and music, despite the primary role of music and performance in American religious life.[102] Sacred music was also an integral part of Christian life and ceremony in seventeenth-century Europe, and Kelpius and his university-trained colleagues would have had some training in sacred music as part of their general university education in theology. Johan Jacob Zimmerman was an instructor of music for a time in Tübingen, and Kelpius and Seelig both had some training in music, as evidenced by their hymnody. They also brought musical instruments with them to America, through the ports of London and New Castle and up the trail into Philadelphia.[103] Their ability to play music must have been very important to them.

Kelpius and Seelig each composed original hymns during their time at Wissahickon, many of which are extant in manuscript form, representing what the musicologist Christopher Herbert has recently called "the first extant compositions in the British Colonies."[104] Still, as Willard Martin points out, Kelpius's role as the first author of an American music manuscript is diminished somewhat in that he probably did not think of himself as a serious composer, and more often than not his hymns and poems are set to older, European melodies.[105] Still, Kelpius certainly took music seriously as a devotional and esoteric form of religious praxis, and being the author of the first extant compositions in the colonies is yet another surprising line on his résumé. The words and music written at Wissahickon were not necessarily meant as stand-alone examples of their author's aesthetic genius: they were community texts, meant to be read and performed in a devotional setting.

Kelpius evidently met some fellow believers in the spiritual power of music in London. His journal records interactions with Frances Lee, the English Philadelphian remembered today in part for the essay "A New Theory of Musick" (1697), in which Lee suggested:

> Musick is an outward Representation of the Harmony of the Divine Powers and Properties in the Nature of God. . . .Thus will the Theory of Musick, duly applied and Spiritualiz'd lead us on to glorious Contemplations, and give us a Key of the great Mysteries of Nature.[106]

Lee's theory was a thoroughly Böhmean exegesis of music composition and performance, in which the metaphysics of sound and the harmony (or discord) between various notes were analogous to God's creation (and the occasional interference of sin), "The six Working Days of the Week ending in the Sabbath, recurring in an Octave."[107] "Theory of Musick" was published a few years after

Kelpius left London for Pennsylvania, but it is likely that Kelpius and Lee had occasion to discuss music at length, and that Kelpius may have read Lee's manuscript in the collections of Philadelphian literature that Heinrich Deichmann sent him throughout the 1690s. Lee's esoteric understanding of the cosmic nature of music performance, thoroughly grounded as it was in scripture and a biblical theology, would have surely resonated with Kelpius.

Most of Kelpius's compositions can be found in a 1705 manuscript entitled "The Lamenting Voice of the Hidden Love" (Figure 3.1), a collection of hymns arranged in a bilingual script with German versions and English translations by his friend Dr. Christopher Witt on the facing pages. "Lamenting Voice" presents us with a deeply mystical, ecstatic, and erotic poetic voice. Kelpius's poetic work strained traditional boundaries of hymnody: like everything else he wrote, they were as much works of theology as they were hymns in the traditional sense. As Lucy Carroll writes of Kelpius's "Lamenting Voice" in her 2008 book *The Hymn Writers of Early Pennsylvania*: "Called a hymn book by history, it is more a collection of Socratic dialogues, theological teachings, and mystic allegories, with perhaps two or three entries that might be more properly called hymns as we

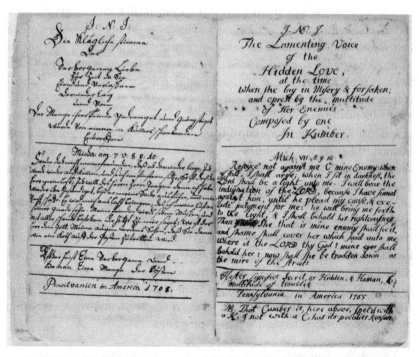

Figure 3.1 "The Lamenting Voice of the Hidden Love," title page. Collection of the Historical Society of Pennsylvania.

126 AMERICAN AURORA

would define them today."[108] As we will see in an excerpt in the following chapter, the texts are severe in their subject matter, focusing on the erotic nature of the soul's longing for reunification with God, personal alchemical development, and outright longing for death.[109] Lucy Carroll sums it up: "They are not suitable for contemporary worship services."[110] As the next chapter suggests, this was community writing. Many of his poems incorporate a dual-voice, dialogic structure suggesting that they were meant for multiple performers. These pieces were not published, they were *sung*.

"An Antient Hermit Who Lives in a Lone House"

The Wissahickon group seemed to intermittently receive new companions on the ridge. In an October 1704 letter, Kelpius describes two new companions, one of whom was Conrad Matthai: "These men came to us about a year ago," Kelpius writes, "& have, in this short time, increased powerfully in the renunciation of the cares of this world & the allurements thereof. May the Lord strengthen & confirm these dear souls furthermore."[111]

Conrad Matthai has the most elusive biography of any of the Wissahickon hermits. His presence on the ridge is well documented, both in Kelpius's letter and in a later document, the *Chronicon Ephratense*, the internal history of the Ephrata community.[112] While primary source documentation of Conrad Matthai's biography and background are scarce, several sources identify him as a Swiss, possibly a noble, who arrived at the ridge in or just before 1704.[113] Matthai is best remembered today as the friend and mentor to Conrad Beissel, the Palatinate Pietist who fled Germany in 1720 to apprentice under Kelpius, only to find Kelpius dead and the group disbanded save for Johann Seelig and Conrad Matthai.[114] Beissel still spent time in Germantown and on the ridge, where his contemporary biographer notes that he "imbibed the views of a few surviving members [of the Kelpius community], such as Conrad Matthai."[115]

Matthai was a latecomer to the Wissahickon group, and he would eventually become the last surviving member after Seelig died in 1745. He was also the crucial connective presence between the Wissahickon group and the two major Pietist groups in eighteenth-century Pennsylvania, the aforementioned Ephrata community and Zizendorf's Moravian church. One of the only primary sources that describes a visit to Matthai comes from Hannah Logan, the daughter of James Logan, the one-time mayor of Philadelphia who seems to have come into the possession of Kelpius's and Seelig's library. She writes:

> After dinner with E. Cathrall, went with me to see Conradus Matthew, an Antient Hermit who lives in a lone house about 7 miles from town on

> Wischickin road, and has done so above 30 years, having taken possession of that house upon the death of Kelpius, a learned man who lived some years there in the same recluse manner. Conrad is a Switzer by birth, but talks English intelligibly. We found him in pretty good health. . . . We had a pretty deal of religious Converse together, but I did not now or when I formerly visited him find that depth of Experience in religion which might be Expected in one that hath so long professed to withdraw his mind from all other objects to be fixed on that alone.[116]

Logan's account is notable for two reasons; first, her description of Matthai's home and her clarification that it was once the home of Kelpius does much to discredit the popular notion that the Kelpius community constructed an enormous facility on the Wissahickon ridge: Seelig's letter and Logan's diary do not specify a size and shape, but the simple description as a "house" in both sources suggest that memories of a great tabernacle hanging from the cliff are exaggerated. The communal house on the ridge was a modest cottage.

Second, Logan's encounter with Matthai gives us a rare sense of what it was like to actually *meet with* a genuine legendary hermit of the Wissahickon: in a word, underwhelming. She seems to have expected more of the "Antient Hermit"; she wanted a "depth of Experience in religion" that Matthai was either unwilling to offer or, more likely, simply unaware that his visitors desired. Logan's account of a pilgrimage to a hermit's hut reminds me of a much more contemporary book by the poet and translator Bill Porter, *Road to Heaven: Encounters with Chinese Hermits* (2009). In this book, Porter describes a 1989 trip to the Zhongnan mountains of central China, trying to ascertain the truth of rumors that the Cultural Revolution had completely extirpated the longtime Chinese Buddhist and Taoist hermit traditions. Porter found many hermits still living and practicing in the mountains around Hubei, and his encounters with them were poignantly similar to Logan's: old men and women who were often simply delighted to see a friendly face, share a cup of tea, and even gossip.[117] Hannah Logan was expecting to meet a severe and profound old sage, and so she was disappointed when she simply met a friendly old man in a run-down cottage. To be honest, Hannah Logan's narrative reminds me of the moment in *The Empire Strikes Back* (1980) when Luke Skywalker realizes that the little green hermit in front of him is, in fact, the legendary Jedi master he is looking for. *Empire* expresses a common reaction when people meet the hermits whose legend precedes them: the disappointing realization that wisdom takes a fragile and unassuming form.

Matthai was also the subject of early Pietist legends concerning his ability to travel beyond his body and even hold conversations with others in his disembodied states. Since these are not primary sources from Matthai or his direct

128   AMERICAN AURORA

companions, they do not belong in this chapter, but we will see more of Matthai in Chapter 6.

The Wissahickon community had another visitor in 1704 who, unlike Matthai, was not remembered as a dedicated ascetic hermit. Christopher Witt (1675–1765) came to Germantown from Wiltshire in England in 1704 at the age of twenty-nine, having already been trained in medicine in his home country.[118] Witt's major association with Kelpius comes to us through the "Lamenting Voice" collection of texts, in which Witt has been credited with the English translations on the facing page.[119] "Lamenting Voice" was a collaborative effort, in which Kelpius and Witt would have had to work together over each page.

Witt is also credited as the artist of a very small oil portrait of Kelpius, which is appended to the "Lamenting Voice" manuscript and preserved in the collections of the Historical Society of Pennsylvania (Figure 3.2).[120] Kelpius is portrayed reclining in the chair of a study, with a book open on the table in front of him with one hand just barely touching the side of his face. He wears a robe and cap, and a clock hangs on the wall behind him. The portrait portrays a scene in which the viewer has intruded on a scholar immersed in study. The viewer stands in Witt's shoes, admiring a mysterious scholar. The presence of the clock in the portrait supports the attribution to Witt, who was a clockmaker.

Witt seems to stand apart from Kelpius's other companions at Wissahickon in that he is the only close companion of Kelpius who did not (so far as we know) originate in a German Pietist milieu, and he may have never lived on the ridge at all.[121] Rather, Witt spent much of his time down the ridge in town, where he lived near Francis Daniel Pastorius and seems to have enjoyed eclectic employment as a doctor, herbalist, and artisan maker of clocks and musical instruments. Witt does not seem to have been a writer himself, but his medical training and botanical knowledge soon led him into the social circle of John Bartram, an early American botanist, author, and traveler, who would later be recognized by none other than Carolus Linnaeus as "the greatest natural botanist of the age."[122]

John Bartram was a correspondent and friend to Peter Collinson, an English businessman and avid gardener who frequently solicited North American specimens from Bartram.[123] Collinson seems to have put Bartram in touch with Dr. Witt, and Bartram's correspondence reveals a transatlantic community of seed and specimen exchange in which Witt was a major participant. Witt is a nearly constant recurring character in their letters, having sent or displayed this seed or that to Collinson or shown them to Bartram.[124] Another source describes Witt's travels in plant-gathering, which apparently carried on into his old age: "When he was 83 years old I did see him ride on his horse like a young man, when he went into the woods to the mountains for seeking plants."[125] John Bartram's son, William Bartram, also a well-known American

"THE WOMAN IN THE WILDERNESS" 129

Figure 3.2 Portrait of Johannes Kelpius by Christopher Witt, 1705. Collection of the Historical Society of Pennsylvania.

botanist and traveler in his own right, might have known Witt himself. His daybook, held in the archives of Bartram's Garden in West Philadelphia today, records an herbal recipe for a special remedy called the "Star Pill," which he attributed to Dr. Witt.[126]

130   AMERICAN AURORA

Bartram and Collinson's correspondence serves as a relatively voluminous record of Dr. Witt's life and thought. In 1743, Bartram describes a visit to
Witt's house:

> I have lately been to visit our friend Doctor wit where I spent 4 or 5 hours very
> agreeable sometimes in his garden where I viewed every kind of plant I be-
> lieve that grew therin which afforded me a Convenient opertunity of asking
> him whether he ever observed any kind of wild roses in this countrie that was
> double—he said he could not remember that he ever did so being satisfied
> with this amusement we went into his study which was furnished with books
> containing different kinds of learning as Phylosophy, natural Magic, Divinity,
> nay even Mystick divinity all of which was the subjects of our discourse within
> doors which alternately gave way to botany every time we walked in the
> garden.[127]

If only John Bartram had taken the time to record some of the titles or authors
of Witt's library of philosophy, natural magic, and "mystick divinity." Witt's religious background is vague, but a contemporaneous letter in memoriam composed just after his death betrays the strong influence of Johannes Kelpius: "A
Separatist was [Witt's] religion, and by his particularly godly life and exemplary
behalf he was loved by all."[128]

There is another passage in the Bartram correspondence that suggests the
connection between Kelpius and Witt, dated "ye 10th of December 1745":

> According to our friend Doctor Witt, we friends that love one another sincerely,
> may, by an extraordinary spirit of sympathy, not only know each other's desires,
> but may have a spiritual conversation at great distances one from another. Now,
> if this be truly so,—if I love thee sincerely—and thy love and friendship be so
> to me—thee must have a spiritual feeling and sense of what particular sorts of
> things will give satisfaction; and doth not thy actions make it manifest?[129]

Bartram and Collinson's correspondence reveals Witt as a believer and propo-
nent, like his friend Kelpius, of a spiritual ability that would not become widely
described or enter the popular imagination until the end of the nineteenth century: remote thought communication, or telepathy. Telepathy, generally understood as a faculty of thought-communication beyond the normal five senses, did
not enter the popular imagination until the very end of the nineteenth century in
the work of psychical researchers like Frederic Myers, the English classicist who
coined the term and codified the concept.

Much like Frederic Myers's, Witt's formulation seems to emphasize the pathos
of telepathic communication, or as he might have called it, "spiritual conversation

at great distances." In other words, the secret requirement for telepathic conversation is love. Bartram's letter does not attribute Witt's spiritual conversation to Kelpius directly, but the association is far too close to be coincidental: the only two proponents of thought communication before the nineteenth century happened to be neighbors, close friends, and creative collaborators. The deep pathos of Witt and Kelpius's spiritual conversation in the "Lamenting Voice" manuscript compels me to look again at that 1705 portrait and the "Lamenting Voice" manuscript, as the work of "friends that love one another sincerely."

Christopher Witt lived until 1765, apparently still riding into the mountains in search of plants only a few years before he died. Collinson and Bartram both noted Witt's gradual physical decline: he went blind in 1759, and Collinson wrote to Bartram, "Pray give my kind love to my worthy old friend Doctor Witt—I am concerned for the loss of his outward sight—may his inward receive a flow of Divine illumination."[130] As he was the last living person who knew Johannes Kelpius well, Witt's death marked the end of Kelpius's direct influence in early Pennsylvania. In 1765, one surviving letter marks the conclusion of this era and the beginning of another: "Now a littel of what hapens Dr. Whit of Jermanton deyed this week."[131] The letter was from Benjamin Franklin of Philadelphia to his wife, Deborah. News of Witt's death also appeared in the journals of the Lutheran missionary Henry Melchior Mühlenberg.[132]

Like his friend Johannes Kelpius, Dr. Witt is a mysterious figure who deserves more sustained scholarly scrutiny. Writing in 1850, John F. Watson noted some of the ambivalence surrounding the memory of Dr. Witt in Philadelphia, particularly his dual standing as an astrologer and generally well-regarded doctor and artisan.[133] As Watson goes to great lengths to point out, the practice of astrology was the task of educated and learned individuals in the early eighteenth century. Watson's recognition of Witt as an astrologer is borne out by a small volume in the collections of the Library Company of Philadelphia, a seventeenth-century astrology handbook that originated in Witt's library.[134] Watson's description also shows how, by the nineteenth century, it was becoming difficult for serious historians to understand the occult interests of the Wissahickon group. Witt is primarily remembered as a "conjuror" or a "fortune teller," despite his status as a physician and a "competent scholar," and the established fact that he was a correspondent and collaborator of the leading American naturalists of the time. Like the Hermetic Protestants who preceded him, Witt's practice of astrology, medicine, and environmental knowledge blurred lines that were much firmer in the latter eighteenth and nineteenth centuries.[135]

Thus far in this book, I have endeavored to understand and explain the social, religious, and political circumstances surrounding the life and thought of Johannes Kelpius. The resulting portrait has been of a precocious young man from provincial Transylvania, who enjoyed success at university while becoming deeply radicalized by German Pietism. In 1693, inspired by the miraculous events of the early Pietist movement and convinced of the failure of the church, he made the enormously consequential decision to travel to Pennsylvania. There, he began a new life along the ridge of the Wissahickon, a life at once ascetic and communal, secluded and cosmopolitan in his association with Pietists, Quakers, and Lenapes, creative and private until its end in 1707. During this period, we have seen a general tension between the personal spiritual life and the material needs of communal living in a growing colony. Kelpius was a bookbinder who wrote hymns and read devotional books in his spare time and enjoyed the company of close friends and colleagues like Seelig, Matthai, and Witt, while he gradually gave up on larger public welfare projects. The next chapter offers a window into the religious thought of Kelpius during this period, as his ascetic labors deepened and his religious thought developed.

4

The Threefold Wilderness State

Ascetic Alchemy and the Technology of Self-Negation

And as they departed, Jesus began to say unto the multitudes concerning John,

>What went ye out into the wilderness to see?
>A reed shaken with the wind?

>—Matthew 11:7

There is a passage in Kelpius's hymn "The Paradox and Strange Pleasure of the Divine Lovers," a particular verse, that has consistently stood out to the handful of scholars who have read the manuscript. Toward the end of the poem, he writes:

>When will I finally witness and feel this!
>When will I dissolve and disappear completely into it!
>When will my tiny spark merge into his light-fire!
>When will my spirit be but a single flame with him.[1]

Kelpius's yearning for a closer and deeper connection with God throughout the hymn approaches a climax in this verse that can only be called erotic. This form of erotic devotion is common throughout Kelpius's later writings, to use Jeffrey Kripal's meaning of the term as "the specifically religious potentialities of human sexuality."[2] In Kripal's analysis, the erotic in the history of religions is not merely a psychoanalytic reading of sublimated sexuality finding religious expression— although there is that, too. Rather, what Kripal calls "the erotic" is a recognition that sexuality itself has some frankly "religious potentialities," or ontological capacities that are generally expressed symbolically through images of death, annihilation, and ecstatic sensuality, comparative patterns that are borne out repeatedly in the history of religions.

Kelpius's verse highlights some of these religious or ontological potentials. His desire to be closer to the divine is rendered in entirely sensuous and embodied language: he wants to literally "feel" God (*Empfiden*). Kelpius's urge to be submerged, dissolved (*Zerfliessen*) and disappeared (*Verschwinden*) in the flame of God is also expressed explicitly: he wants to be the kindling in God's bonfire,

American Aurora. Timothy Grieve-Carlson, Oxford University Press. © Oxford University Press 2024.
DOI: 10.1093/oso/9780197765562.003.0005

134 AMERICAN AURORA

and after that, he wants to be indistinguishable from that fire itself. Kelpius's desire to "become one," to join fully, to dissolve, disappear and finally self-negate, expresses this erotic dimension in Christian mysticism.

Encountering this passage in 1870, Oswald Seidensticker wrote: "While [Kelpius] usually dresses his conception of the ultimate things in biblical images, a pantheistic conception breaks through which is more reminiscent of Plotinus than Christianity."[3] Indeed, Seidensticker deserves some credit here for recognizing the frankly pantheistic qualities of Kelpius's verse, and he did so without the advantage of decades of scholarship on the history of esoteric philosophy to confirm the Platonic and Hermetic influence on Pietists like Kelpius.

In an introductory note, Kelpius wrote that this hymn was "an answer to a letter so full of love, trust, and humility."[4] The poem was meant for someone, then, an anonymous correspondent whose words filled Kelpius's heart to the point that he could only respond in poetry. "Paradox" was a dialectical hymn, with several different parts meant to be sung by several people. The poem is part of a conversation, even as it takes the form of a conversation itself. This was the nature of almost all of Kelpius's writing toward the end of his life: conversational, practical, often widely referential to concurrent and previous discussions and meetings as he moves the conversation forward. This was community writing, rather than the academic prose of his life in Europe.

Another example of Kelpius's community writing is a 1706 letter to Esther Palmer, a Quaker missionary from Flushing, Long Island. Palmer was a "Public Friend," a minister who traveled through the North American colonies, working to establish networks among different groups of American Quakers and to hold meetings in communities where there were too few friends to maintain a consistent meeting.[5] Palmer traveled through the Philadelphia area in 1705 and 1706, attending Friends meetings throughout southeastern Pennsylvania. And although she did not leave us a record of their meeting from her perspective, she also visited with Johannes Kelpius.[6]

The community-based nature of the text is clear in its opening lines, which reference several concurrent conversations: "Beeing presented lately with a letter of yours, directed to our beloved Friend M.B. I found in the P.S. that the Remembrance of Mine, was not yet slipt out of your Minde, insomuch that you desired to see a few lines from my Hand," Kelpius writes.[7] Evidently, Kelpius made an impression on Palmer, who in turn shared her feelings with the unknown "M.B." (likely Mary Bannister, one of Palmer's traveling Quaker companions), who in turn shared them again with Kelpius.[8] This research continuously reminds me just how closely the transatlantic community of radical Protestants kept in touch and just how *small a town* Philadelphia was in 1706. The contents and print history of this letter, and the several conversations it connects, represent an excellent example of the extent of these networks. More importantly for

THE THREEFOLD WILDERNESS STATE   135

our historical purposes, these extensive private networks often became public—
the existence of the Ashbridge memoir indicates that Palmer's copy of Kelpius's
letter was shared and copied as well. Not only did everyone seem to know each
other, but they freely copied and distributed each others' letters.

I am not the first or only reader of Kelpius's letter to Palmer to suggest its
importance. As Patrick Erben has written, "The letter seems to have struck
a nerve among American Quakers."[9] The letter's significance for Kelpius's
American legacy is further indicated by its appearance in Quaker publications
in Philadelphia throughout the eighteenth and nineteenth centuries.[10] The same
letter appears excerpted in an 1886 edition of the spiritual autobiography of
Elizabeth Ashbridge, an eighteenth-century Quaker minister. This printing was
based, apparently, on an earlier lost manuscript that anthologized Kelpius's letter
and Ashbridge's memoirs.[11] Either copied by Esther Palmer herself or sought
out in manuscript by an anonymous Quaker publisher in the nineteenth century, Kelpius's correspondence lived on as another form of community writing in
eighteenth- and nineteenth-century Quaker manuscripts and print publications
of the devotional lives of the Christians who came before them.

Kelpius's letter to Palmer, one of his few written in English, makes reference
to an earlier conversation the two shared: "And since our discourse broke of[f]
just as we was about this matter," he writes, picking up a conversation abruptly
left off, Kelpius names the matter about which they spoke: "Viz. *The Threefold
Wilderness State*: I'll venture upon your patience a few lines concerning this subject."[12] This was an important subject to Kelpius, so much so that he took the time
to make a clear statement on it for his friend in writing after their conversation
had been cut short. Kelpius goes on, alluding to some of the difficulty in putting the subject into words despite their mutual interests: "Assure yourself that
it is with no less Fervency on my side," he writes, acknowledging his own desire
to pick up the conversation. He then alludes to some sort of obstacle in their
communication: "I finde as yet a double wall between us, which indeed seems to
stop the Current of this Firy Love-Stream," he writes. A "double wall" obstructed
the mutual understanding of Kelpius and Palmer, a mutual understanding of
divine things that Kelpius describes in prose as a "Firy Love-Stream." Kelpius
acknowledges that from their humble human position, there are things that will
continue to surpass their understanding—at least for the time being, "least we
should embolden ourselves to break through before the time appointed by him,
who nourisheth the Woman in the Wilderness (Rev. 12,14)." Our mutual understanding is hindered by our position in time, Kelpius writes, and certain barriers
will only be lifted when creation is restored, when the great wonder appears in
heaven, the woman clothed with the sun of Revelation 12. Here we find a clear
example of why the phrase "Woman in the Wilderness" has been so closely associated with Kelpius through the centuries. The Woman of Revelation 12 was of

136 AMERICAN AURORA

such deep personal significance to him that she appears in his writing unbidden and without explanation.

As mentioned in the previous chapter, Kelpius's letters are full of what Oswald Seidensticker called "extensive theological whims." We might sympathize with this good nineteenth-century literary scholar facing a scribbled archive of dense theology that continues to thwart clear scholarly understanding.[13] But there are no whims in his 1706 letter to Palmer. Instead, Kelpius describes a complete tripartite system of spiritual development that he calls "The Threefold Wilderness State," Kelpius's own personal practice of alchemical asceticism, a practice in which Kelpius applied contemporary ideas of spiritual alchemy to his own reading of scripture and his own ascetic experience. Throughout the letter, Kelpius reads and interprets the biblical theme of wilderness as a site of spiritual labor and, eventually, the medium of that final disappearance into God that he yearns for in "Paradox." He is as explicit in his meaning here as he is in his verse: "To be nothing," he writes to Palmer, "is to be deified."[14]

In the previous three chapters, I worked to understand Kelpius's religious thought by understanding the wider intellectual and historical circumstances surrounding him, reading Kelpius alongside his wider social and religious milieu. In this chapter, I focus on Kelpius's religious writing exclusively, in particular this 1706 letter and the Threefold Wilderness State that it describes. There are a number of reasons I choose to focus on this letter, the relic of an interrupted conversation between a Pietist hermit and an itinerant Quaker public Friend. This letter is the only extant complete theological statement that Johannes Kelpius produced during his time in Pennsylvania, and apparently since his time as an academic more than a decade earlier. Furthermore, written only one year before his death, it also likely reflects Kelpius's final religious thought. The letter *feels* final: unlike his academic works, which showcased a verbose tenacity riddled with self-doubt that characterizes the writing of many young scholars, Kelpius's thought in this letter is mature, confident, replete with clear reference to scripture and the personal experience of a short lifetime of Christian devotion. Indeed, by 1706 he was writing with more than a decade of ascetic labor behind him. Gone are the doctrinal and philosophical concerns of his academic work. There is no parsing of Aristotle, very little critique of modernity, or references to major contemporary Lutheran theological disputes. Instead, there is a simple Christian technique of personal development, what Michel Foucault might call "the care for the self," refracted through a Hermetic Protestant understanding of the cosmos as a site of divine knowledge and an alchemical method of self-transformation.

Kelpius's Threefold Wilderness State consists of three stages of spiritual development that he derived from his close reading of scripture. The first stage, the Barren Wilderness, is characterized by suffering and doubt, analogized with the wilderness period of the Hebrews following Exodus. The second stage, the Fruitful Wilderness, is a spiritual rebirth of the faithful that follows the death and failure at the end of the first stage. This stage is characterized by environmental confirmations of spiritual progress, miracles, and paranormal phenomena like the pillars of cloud and fire that appear to guide the Hebrews in the biblical narrative. The third and final stage, the Wilderness of the Elect of God, is an ultimate perfection of the body and soul in which the human becomes a living instrument of God's will on earth.

Kelpius's Threefold Wilderness State is a clear example of what Mike Zuber has called "spiritual alchemy," which developed in the wake of Paracelsus and was elaborated most influentially by Jacob Böhme and popularized in Kelpius's immediate milieu of seventeenth-century German Lutheran radical circles. Zuber defines spiritual alchemy as "the practical pursuit of inward but real bodily transmutation."[15] This was a transformation of the body that could, in theory, actually undo the effects of the Fall and restore human beings to a state of spiritual perfection on earth.

It is important to understand that there was nothing metaphorical about the transformations that spiritual alchemists pursued. As Zuber writes, "Boehme and his later disciples believed that actual bodily changes—albeit not subject to the ordinary laws of physics or conventionally measurable—were taking place within them" as they applied these techniques.[16] The techniques in question were not laboratory based or actually chemical; rather, they consisted of "prayer, penitence, ascetic deeds, or other rituals, which may also be purely internal or contemplative," precisely the kinds of techniques that Kelpius practiced in Pennsylvania.[17] The idea that techniques like these could actually bring about *physical* changes in the body strikes our contemporary sensibilities as strange, and, indeed, we will see that nineteenth-century readers of Kelpius had a very hard time understanding why such an educated individual would commit to such a practice. We have to remember that for Kelpius and his immediate milieu, spirit was a subtle but very real physical force that permeated and animated the cosmos. Changes in the soul would be spiritually imprinted on the body, just as changes in the macrocosm, the environment, found their mirror in the microcosm of the human.

Despite the similarities with other spiritual alchemists from the period, Kelpius's Threefold Wilderness State is unique in a few important ways, most notably the severity of his asceticism, his conceptual focus on "wilderness," and his biblical theology. As the previous chapters have shown, Kelpius lived in a radical milieu of ecstatic, Hermetic, and mystical forms of Christian life and practice. But even with neighbors like Francis Pastorius and Daniel Leeds, Kelpius seemed to stand out. Henry Melchior Mühlenberg, the German Lutheran missionary sent to Pennsylvania a few decades after Kelpius's death, once described

Kelpius as "the strange one among those strange ones."[18] And indeed, withdrawn from public life, absconded up the ridge of the Wissahickon, practicing his strict celibacy, wearing a coarse garment and abstaining from the public and printed disputes that characterized religious life among his neighbors and colleagues, Kelpius adopted a form of Christian practice that seems more suited to the ancient world than the modern. Throughout his writings during his life in Pennsylvania, Kelpius can sometimes sound less like a Lutheran theologian than one of the desert monks of late antique Egypt.

As Richard Valantasis has defined it, ascetic behaviors are "performances within a dominant social environment intended to inaugurate a new subjectivity, different social relations, and an alternative symbolic universe."[19] Valantasis emphasizes the social nature of asceticism at the expense of its meaning for the individual practitioner, but his definition can help us understand how ascetic practice shaped Kelpius's public profile and his memory in history and legend. While I cannot imagine that Kelpius ever thought of his practice as a performance, there is no doubt that the highly visible and countercultural nature of his ascetic behaviors led to an escalating level of public religious interest throughout Philadelphia, during and long after his own life. Kelpius's ascetic practice, his focus on inner cultivation, and his willingness to explain himself to people like Palmer all contributed to this public and historical profile that would escalate throughout the following centuries.

Such a practice, however ancient its origins or out of place it feels, has deep relevance for our current moment. As Niki Kasumi Clements has written of another Iohannes, the fourth-century monk John Cassian, "Attention to concrete, daily practices . . . allows us to take seriously the potential for late ancient Christian asceticism to involve not just the renunciatory practices but also a transformative ethos. Cassian's pragmatism articulated at the edge of empire . . . speaks directly to contemporary interest in the possibility of transforming selves in uncertain times."[20] Clements attends carefully to the spaces that Valantasis neglects: for the practitioner, asceticism is never a mere performance, nor is it merely renunciation for its own sake. Asceticism is a concrete, daily method of self-transformation. Kelpius's ascetic Christian life, at the edge of the British Empire, attentive to environmental signs amid a declining world, speaks to the same possibility of transformation that Clements locates in Cassian.

With his greetings and preemptive explanations out of the way, Kelpius dives in. But before we join him, it is worth pausing for a moment to better understand the most important word in the letter and the word that would be most closely tied to Kelpius's religious legacy: the English "wilderness." As we will see, Kelpius found a rich symbolism in this word that defies any simple etymology, but a few points on its use by a German Christian writing in eighteenth-century English are in order.

The American environmental historian William Cronin once wrote that "far from being the one place on earth that stands apart from humanity, [wilderness] is quite profoundly a human creation—indeed, the creation of very particular human cultures at very particular moments in history."[21] We might take Cronin's main point well: wilderness is an idea rather than a thing, and it is an idea that appears exclusively in the imagination of human beings. Bearing this in mind, it is important to note that the actual places and communities labeled "wilderness" are not mere conceptual constructs. As we saw in Chapter 2, the Indigenous communities of southeastern Pennsylvania in the seventeenth century were more economically active and organized than much of Europe, but dehumanizing attitudes toward the Lenape and the overwhelming presence of the old-growth forest collapsed this complex community into one word in the European imagination: wilderness. How did one little word take on such semantic heft?

As Roderick Nash has shown, the English word "wilderness" has a fairly simple and recent pedigree. It seems to derive from a root in the old Norse *wil*, the same root that gives us "willful," meaning headstrong or uncontrollable. From *wil*, Nash tells us, we get the adjective "wild," which carries a range of meanings, from lost and/or confused to unruly, violent, and ungoverned. Then came the Old English word *dēor*, applied to any animal that was not under human control such as pets or livestock, such as game animals, hence our modern word "deer." *Wil* and *dēor* became attached to the root sometime before the eighth century, when we find *wildēor* appearing in the early English of *Beowulf* as "wild animals." Over the centuries, *wildēor* contracts to "wilder," and eventually the noun "wilderness," which Nash defines lexically as "a place of wild beasts."[22]

The modern word and idea of wilderness, then, is not original to the Hebrew Bible or Christian New Testament: it was placed there in early modern English translations. "Wilderness" was originally a northern European word and concept for an ungoverned place of animals until the fourteenth century, when it began to appear in translations of the Bible in vernacular European languages. "Wilderness" stood in for both the Hebrew מִדְבָּר (*midbar*) and the Greek ἐρήμῳ or ἔρημος (*erēmos*) in the Hebrew Bible and the New Testament. Suddenly, the word "wilderness" was (re)introduced to the English-speaking world as the arid environs of the Middle East, especially the deserts of Sinai and Palestine, in the areas around the Jordan River, the setting of many of the events of the Gospels— lands that Jesus, John the Baptist, and countless others unambiguously refer to as "wilderness" in your English editions of the biblical text. Kelpius was well aware of this quality of modern Bibles in vernacular languages, and throughout the letter to Esther Palmer, he occasionally criticized the "common translation" of certain passages, reflecting his own expertise in scripture and knowledge of biblical Greek and Hebrew.

140   AMERICAN AURORA

This biblical tradition of uncultivated, arid, harsh and dangerous land blended with the old European "place of wild beasts" meaning throughout the early modern period, so much so that Samuel Johnson's 1755 *Dictionary of the English Language* defined wilderness as "a desert; a tract of solitude and savageness."[23] In the same way that the German *himmel* signifies both the physical dimension of the sky and religious meaning(s) of heaven, the word "wilderness" slipped into modern English with multiple meanings. It was a synonym for desolation, solitude, or the homes of people that English-speakers would consider somehow less than fully human. But through its frequent appearance in the King James Bible, it also became the site of the most significant spiritual labors and miraculous theophanies described in scripture. The deep biblical roots of our contemporary English word and idea of wilderness, then, were firmly established by these translations long before John Muir made such connections even more abundantly clear in the late nineteenth century.

The multiple meanings of *midbar* and *erēmos* can be found in the original texts, well before the superimposition of modern meanings. In his major study of the meaning of wilderness in the Christian tradition, George H. Williams stresses at once the foundational and multiple role(s) of wilderness in scripture:

> It is indeed so basic a concept in Christian history that the wilderness motif might be said to exceed in significance the frontier as a category in the interpretation of not only American history but of Church history in general; for, like the frontier, the wilderness is not only geographical but psychological. It can be a state of mind as well as a state of nature. It can betoken alternatively either a state of bewilderment or a place of protective refuge and disciplined contemplation, as well as literally the wilds.[24]

These multiple meanings—wilderness as suffering, wilderness as the site of spiritual labor, and wilderness as a simple description of a place—occur and recur throughout Kelpius's letter. To these three basic Christian meanings, Kelpius reads Revelation through the rest of scripture to add a fourth, that we might call wilderness as apocalypse. In the letter to Palmer, wilderness—the environment itself—is both the site and the medium of divine knowledge, miraculous phenomena, and spiritual disclosure. As quoted in the previous chapter, in one 1704 letter, Kelpius states this outright: "Wilderness means hidden." This is the special meaning of wilderness as the site of Revelation 12 for Kelpius, and as the site of the wondrous, miraculous, and paranormal expressions of God's waxing presence on earth as creation declines. As he suggested more than a decade earlier in *Natural Theology, or, Metamorphosis of the Metaphysics*, Kelpius saw creation itself, his environment, as the primary text of religious knowledge. In his 1706 letter to Palmer, he advances a practical technique of this original insight.

The Threefold Wilderness State

Kelpius picks up the conversation in media res with "no better subject," he writes, "then to begin where we left it." "Of the First [state]," he writes, "we did discourse somewhat, viz, of the *Barren Wilderness* & as we were beginning the second viz: *Of the Fruitfull Wilderness*: we was interrupted." The first two states have already been elaborated in person, but Kelpius has ink to spare for redundancy.

The first state, he writes, is marked by hesitation, doubt, and failure: "The First seeth indeed the stretched out Arm of God in Egypt as well as in the Wild[ernes]s, but murmurs, provoks & tempts God & limiteth the Holy one in Israel, alwais turning back with its Heart lusting after Egypt," he writes.[25] The journey of the Hebrews in the Pentateuch is the central allegory of the soul in the first two states. The soul in the Barren Wilderness sees the signs of God's presence, but wavers, hesitates, and retreats. "The first is in continual Fear of Death, and what he feareth cometh upon him." Kelpius cites Numbers 14:38, in which all but two of Moses's scouts into the wilderness die after forty days, and Proverbs 10:24, "The fear of the wicked, it shall come upon him." Every developing spirit must pass through this stage of doubt and failure.

The first wilderness state, the Barren Wilderness, culminates in death: "The first is begotten in Egypt, & then arriveth to its manhood, & being led out of Egypt falls and Dieth in the Wilderness." This is a necessary passage through suffering and spiritual death, in Kelpius's understanding. It leads to the second stage, the Fruitful Wilderness. Where the soul in the first stage wavered, fell, and died, the soul in the second stage is resolute.[26] "The Second is also begotten in Egypt but is educated, & arriveth to its manhood in the Wilderness, & after the death of the First enters Caanan." And as the label "Fruitful" suggests, the soul in the second stage develops through this effort: "The Second seeth God & its life is preserved," he writes, before returning to the book of Numbers: "Its Heart with Joshua & Caleb (Joshua signifieth Aid, Salvation, Conservation; Caleb, full of heart, courageous, undaunted, faithfull) stands faithfull and seeth Ye Salvation of God, being filled with the fervent & only desire of attaining the same."[27] Kelpius returns here to Numbers 14: of all the scouts that Moses dispatched into the wilderness for forty days, only Joshua and Caleb returned. Their return makes them emblematic of the second wilderness state, in which the soul passes through the station of "Spiritual Egypt" and reaps the rewards of resolution, courage, and faith.

Why does Kelpius continually refer to Exodus and Numbers in illustrating his first and second stages? Throughout the Hebrew Bible, wilderness was a place of pain, of homelessness, and of destitution. Indeed, in writings throughout the history of Judaism, "wilderness" is more often than not simply a euphemism for suffering, often in reference to the events of Exodus and Numbers.[28] Paradoxically, this suffering is mirrored by an intensification of the presence of

142   AMERICAN AURORA

God. God is inescapably and abundantly present in the wilderness like nowhere else in scripture—often speaking clearly and rendered literally as a pillar of cloud or flame in the sky—actively guiding, sustaining, and teaching the Hebrews. In the Hebrew Bible, wilderness is both a location of existential pain and a place of heightened intimate contact between human beings and divinity, in which faithful persistence leads to progress.[29]

The visible presence of God is a main feature of the second wilderness state. "Let us insist a little upon the mystery of the second," he writes, "in which fruitfull wilds we enjoy the leading Cloud by day, out of which so many gracious drops of the heavenly dew . . . as a Baptism of Grace upon us do fall."[30] Where the soul in the first stage was unguided and retreated in fear, the soul in the second stage is sustained by environmental signs of God's attention and presence. The same baptism of grace from the cloud appears elsewhere in Kelpius's writings: "Thus partly I have declared how they was baptized with such energical drops out of that Supercaelestial Pillar of Cloud by Gifts and miraculous Manifestations of the Powers from on high," he writes of the miraculous abilities of the early Pietists.[31] The Pillar of Cloud is an extended reference in Kelpius's writing for such "miraculous Manifestations of the Powers," for paranormal phenomena as a signal of God's attention for those who progress along the spiritual path.

Paranormal phenomena maintain their importance for Kelpius in his late theology. There is no Calvinist ambiguity or hunting for hints of grace in this system. Spiritual development will be apparent to you and everyone around you, he suggests. Later in the letter, Kelpius refers to the necessity of "Commission and Credentials (viz. Miracles & Signs)" for the soul's development. For Kelpius, there was no tension between Paracelsian attention to extraordinary phenomena and the way miracles are portrayed in scripture: God's attention and presence causes ripples in creation itself. In Kelpius's early Pietist Christianity, paranormal phenomena were "Credentials" from God; whether they serve as personal encouragement or as outward indications of an example for others to follow, these ripples in the cosmos command attention and interpretation.

The second wilderness state is a pinnacle in the soul's development, an intimacy with the presence of God that represents the highest goal for the majority of people. As he will describe, only a very small number (he will name six) in history have ever passed beyond it. "This is a day of Joy & Triumph," Kelpius writes, "when the Holy Ghost moves & Stirreth the waters in our Hearts so that this living Spring diffuseth itself through the Eyes in a sweet & joyfull Gush of Tears."[32] This arrival in the second stage after the death of the first is a moment for rejoicing, Kelpius writes—but just a moment.

"There followeth a Night also upon this day," Kelpius writes, "wherein nevertheless the Pillar of Fire is our Guide, refining us as Gold in the Furnace, which is the Baptism of Fire of ye Son."[33] There is where the influence of spiritual alchemy on Kelpius's system becomes clear: human souls are refined and smelted in a furnace of trial and tribulation. This refinement never ends: the soul in the second wilderness state is immediately given over to even further ascetic demands, which Kelpius describes as an alchemical process of inner transformation. This inner alchemical power, the cultivation of the soul and the ability to refine every challenge into further spiritual fortitude and sustenance, is the ultimate reward of the second state.

Kelpius waxes like an Egyptian desert ascetic on these progressive inner refinements, with abundant reference to scripture:

> The darkest sorrow contains in herself the most inward Joy & Gladness (2 Cor. 6,10). Darkness is like the Light (Psal. 139,12). To dye is in this pleasan[t] Wilderness is to grow lively. Poverty maketh rich. Hunger is the most desirable Meat, & Thirst the most refreshing Nectar (Matt. 5,6). To be nothing is to be deified (2 Pet. 1,4). To have nothing is to enjoy all 2 Cor. 12,10. To become weak is the greatest strength.[34]

The limits of the body and the spirit are gradually pushed away and cast off in this second state, as the soul develops into a furnace of refinement in which every torment becomes a blessing. Physical pain, poverty, weakness, death: spiritual alchemy transforms them all into gifts.

In this passage and others like it, Kelpius extols an ascetic process with inner cultivation, and ultimately, alchemical self-transformation as its goal. Spiritual alchemy is central to Kelpius's religious thought at this stage of his life. When he describes the end times as a "Restitution of all things" in a 1699 letter, he characterizes this final transformation of the cosmos as an essentially alchemical refinement: "Night is swallowed up in ye Day, Darkness into Light, Death into Life, Judgment into Victory, Justice into Mercy, all imperfect Metals into Gold, and Gold itself is refined seven times," he wrote in 1699.[35] The inner transformations of the body that result from ascetic practice mirror the regular cycles of nature (like night into day), while the spiritual transformations of the regular cycles of nature mirror the final refinement of the cosmos at the end of time. The analogy of the human, cosmos, and God that appears in Paracelsus and Hermetic literature recurs here: "As the Miracles wrought by God through the Hand of Moyses was for the main part in the outward Creation or Macrocosm, the Miracles of Jesus the Messia on the Bodys of Man or Microcosm," Kelpius writes.[36] Kelpius reads scripture, in part, as a history of the alchemy of the cosmos and the body.

As ancient as Kelpius sounds here, this is a thoroughly modern ascetic alchemy, steeped in seventeenth-century spiritual alchemy and modern understandings of experiment: "No work no Pain doth tire ... for the more we work the stronger

144   AMERICAN AURORA

we grow and yet we do experimentally find that the greatest weakness hath the greatest strength hid in herself," Kelpius writes.[37] This is an entirely modern notion of the "experiment" in its earliest form: the content of *experience*, of the personal insight that can only follow firsthand knowledge. For everything that made him "the strange one among strange ones," Kelpius remained a highly educated German of the early modern period, and his ascetic devotions on the edge of the British Empire were carried out with this modern notion of experiment in mind. Use of words like "experiment" reminds us that this practice of inner alchemy was not as ancient as might seem.

Kelpius returns to his own setting here in the letter, indicating that the allegorical meanings of wilderness in the first and second stage are underwritten by a real environment: "Oh everblessed Wilderness!" he exults. "The glory of Lebanon is given unto Thee, the Excellency of Carmel and Sharon! In thee we see the Glory of our Lord, & the Excellency of our God! In thee our weak Hands are Strengthened & our feeble Knees confirmed (Isa. 35, 1)." Kelpius refers again to biblical Lebanon, seeing some of this setting in the old growth around Wissahickon, and something of the fertile plain of Sharon at the foot of wild Mount Carmel. These settings from the Bible came alive for Kelpius in Pennsylvania, where the cliffs of the Wissahickon became a place to "see the Glory of our Lord."

This wilderness was more than a setting and more than a symbol: it was a living imaginal construct wherein Kelpius could live inside the world of the scriptures. Kelpius's environment was both an allegory and living subject that he addresses directly:

> Who would not desire to be a Denison in Thee? Who would not delight to trace thy Solitary and lonesom walks? Oh ye Inhabitants of this happy desolation, bless & kiss that gentle hand of that Divine Sophia who at the first did so wittily allure you, when she intended to bring you into this Wilderness, for to speak to your Heart, in order to search & trie the same![38]

This exultation and rejoicing in the guiding presence of "that Divine Sophia" remind us again that Kelpius's attempt to live an ancient lifestyle was conducted within a richly modern religious imagination in which the Divine Wisdom, personified as Sophia, popularized in the works of Jacob Böhme, became another divine presence in his life.

At the edge of this exulting, too, Kelpius turns to the third stage, "a Wild[ernes]s yet of a *higher* degree than the second, which it exceeds by so much as the second does the first." This third stage cannot be explained in the same way that the first and second were. Kelpius can only show examples, "Two out of ye Old and Two out of the New Test[ament]." This third and final stage represents the culmination of the Threefold Wilderness State, a station occupied by only a very small handful of God's chosen vessels: "We may call it the *Wilderness of the Elect of God*, as being traced by few & non but peculiarly chosen Vessels of Honour & Glory."[39]

These examples pass through the second stage and become a living instrument of God's will. His first example is Moses: Kelpius recounts his "Revelation that He should deliver Isräel out of Egypt" and his initial failure in this attempt, "whereupon he fled into the wild[erness], where he remained 40 years." The wilderness sojourns of the major figures of the Bible are of great interest to Kelpius, who points out that "what He [Moses] did there is nowhere described." But the forty years come to an end, after which Moses arises following the hierophany of the burning bush, empowered to demand his people's freedom. Kelpius sees clear cause and effect in Moses's life story: Moses is inspired to liberate his people to the point of acting impulsively, as he does when he kills the Egyptian who was beating a Hebrew slave. In acting this way, Kelpius writes, "He had got only an . . . Impulse . . . of what he was to do, without any express Commission and Credentials (viz. Miracles & Signs)."[40] Moses acts on his divine impulse to liberate others without first developing himself in the wilderness to the point where his credentials were clear, and this attempt ends in a disastrous flight into the desert.

Exodus may not state plainly what Moses did in the forty years in the wilderness, but Kelpius is able to infer it by considering the state of Moses at the beginning and end of his life. We meet Moses, he writes, full of "Presumptions & fervent at first in which he killed the Egytian," and at the end, when "his great humility & meekness" was the result of his labors. With this development in mind, "We may easily find what he had done during the 40. Years in the wild[ernes]s," Kelpius writes. We meet Moses "with a firy Quality," Kelpius writes, but his long life in the wilderness and the ascetic lifestyle such a setting enforced "thourowly tinctured & metamorphosed" him, slowly transforming his very self "into the Lamlike Nature" that we find at the end of Exodus. Kelpius's use of "tincture" here is a clear indication his alchemical understanding of spiritual development: in the writings of alchemical spirituality by Böhme, the "tincture" is "an agent of transformation, an essence that imparted its qualities to the object into which it was introduced."[41] In Kelpius's retelling, Moses's life story is a process of alchemical refinement, as God "thourowly tinctured & metamorphosed" him, leading to his final state, "the Lamlike Nature."

Kelpius's second example is Elijah, whose life, he notes, "runs in many things parallel tw. [with] the First Wittness," or the life of his precursor, Moses. Elijah's early life is certainly marked by the same wild zeal as Moses: "He was very zealous & had slain the Priests of Baal, as Moses had the Egyptian," after which is forced to flee into the wilderness.[42] But his sojourn takes only forty days rather than

146 AMERICAN AURORA

years, in which "God appeared unto him," first as "the great & strong Winde & the Earthquake & the Fire," before finally speaking to him in the "still aethereall breat[h]ing voice."[43] Kelpius sees the similarity of these biblical narratives: Moses and Elijah each act on their commitment to God with zealous, violent intensity before being humbled in the wilderness, where God ministers to them with extraordinary environmental phenomena. Elijah baptizes "with fire," and so God's ministry takes the form of a burning tempest before speaking in the small, still voice. Elijah is then taken up into paradise "by the same Elements wherein he had ministered," Kelpius notes, the burning whirlwind: the same media that God used to speak with him in the first place.

Kelpius's reading of the winds and earthquakes and flames in which God speaks in 2 Kings 19 draws on the legacy of Hermetic Protestant environmental thought. God's will is only rarely expressed in words, Kelpius wrote in *Metamorphosis of the Metaphysics*, because words can be misunderstood. His medium is more often creation itself, in earth, wind, and fire. The meaning of God's ministry in quaking earth and burning wind is completely clear to Kelpius at the end of the Little Ice Age.

Kelpius was not the first or last biblical scholar to point out the parallels between Elijah and Moses: in the books of Kings, Elijah is portrayed to recall Moses deliberately, and it has been noted that these parallels are especially clear in wilderness settings.[44] Both Moses and Elijah found themselves in the wilderness and an intensified state of contact with God following a time of conflict. In 2 Kings, Elijah is easily identified by his garments, a hair shirt and a leather girdle. Following this wilderness theophany, God guides Elijah clearly, and Elijah is able to work miracles like his precursor. Kelpius's ascetic behavior is an attempt to model himself after this pattern of spiritual development that he sees throughout the Bible. His pattern repeats itself. The Hebrew prophets (Jonah, Hosea, and others) consistently come into contact with God in wilderness settings.[45] For all his radicalism, Kelpius approaches his own alchemical asceticism with the training of a Lutheran theologian. He reads closely and follows the text where it takes him.

These themes and patterns lead him to his third example of a soul who reached the third wilderness state, "the old John, the Precursor of the Messiah," John the Baptist.[46] John the Baptist is the first character we encounter in the Gospels, and his portrayal recalls someone we have seen before: "Now John was clothed with camel's hair, and had a leather girdle around his waist, and ate locusts and wild honey."[47] John's depiction, consistent throughout the gospels, is a direct allusion to 2 Kings 1:8, which depicts Elijah wearing the exact same clothes.[48] John is written to recall Elijah even as Elijah is written to recall Moses. Kelpius sees these literary similarities as clear facts of history and a model for him to follow. John baptizes "in the Spirit & Power of Eleijah," recalling the prophet even as he revises the medium, "baptizing with water to Repentance, as the first Eleijah had baptized with Fire for destruction." This shift in the element of baptism reflects the alchemical developments coursing through history. As the ages shift, the medium and alchemical element of the baptism shifts with it. The cosmos is being refined, too.

Kelpius notes again the absence of clear textual detail but the clear indication of John's ascetic labor in the wilderness: "What he did in the Wilderness is not described, but by that what hath been said we may safely conclude, that he was qualified there for his so great a Ministry." And even without much detail, Kelpius found in John and Elijah models for his own form of life. Kelpius's companion Seelig mentions the wearing of a rough sack (*grob sack*) in a 1699 letter, and it is very likely Kelpius wore the same.[49] In Christopher Witt's small oil portrait of Kelpius, he is pictured wearing a long robe.[50] This unique garment is mentioned in an 1847 *Germantown Telegraph* article about the hermits, which recalls that both Seelig and Kelpius wore a coarse robe.[51] In his attempt to model his own life after the clear examples of the great figures of the Bible, we can see clearer still what made Kelpius stand out as "the strange one among those strange ones."

John brings Kelpius to his fourth example of a soul in the third wilderness state, "the last & greatest Wittness I am to produce," he writes, "*jesus* the Messiah of God, our God & Saviour, the Center of all." Kelpius first draws our attention to the parallels with previous figures, "in likeness of the first Lawgiver Moses was 40 days (the 40. Years of Moses being thus abridged) in the Wilderness & tempted there with all manner of Temptations," and to the continuous biblical theme of the obscure nature of their precise activity in the wilderness: "The Scripture indeed maketh mention of his fiery Trials . . . But nowhere saith what they was or are."[52] In comparing these biblical figures, Kelpius does not see the development of a literary tradition: he sees four clear historical examples of human perfection, whose similarity reflects their distinction as the "Elect of God."

Kelpius finally lands on an eighteenth-century explanation for this lack of textual clarity regarding the nature of ascetic labor: ascetic development and the alchemical process of inner refinement "cannot be described," he writes, because "it is only Experience which can teach them best."[53] Kelpius's use of modern notions of experience and experiment persists, this time connected with one of the arguments of *Metamorphosis of the Metaphysics*. Words can "profoundly mislead," and so scripture remains vague regarding the details of ascetic cultivation. What cannot be described simply is not described.

The major spiritual events of Jesus's life all take place in the wilderness, theophanies and "Commissions & Credentials" that he seems to trigger at will. In the Gospels' depiction of the Transfiguration, the apostles see Moses and Elijah appear and speak with Jesus on the mountain. Suddenly God appears in the form he traditionally has taken in desolate places—a great cloud, well known to

Moses and Elijah. And as it said when it tore open the sky and came down as a bird during Jesus's baptism, this voice declares: "This is my beloved Son."[54] This bodily transformation recalls the change that overcame Moses's body after he descended from Mount Sinai—Jesus's shining body is clearly meant to show his analogy with the shining face of Moses following the Sinai theophany.[55] In these similarities, Kelpius sees a common practice of spiritual alchemical progression, a tradition of celestial phenomena indicating spiritual progress followed by very real bodily transformation, shared by the great spiritual leaders of scripture.

In placing Jesus himself at the heights of the Threefold Wilderness State, Kelpius at once makes God a participant in his system while seeming to set a clearly unachievable goal for Christian life. This paradox—the humanity of God, the central mystery of Christianity—is not fully resolved but acknowledged in his own alchemical understanding. This process by which God can take a human form is "a Mystery surpassing all humane & angelicall understanding," Kelpius writes, "nor is it to be found out by the same." That is, such a mystery will thwart mere human understanding. It depends on a different form of knowledge, "solely from the Revelation of the Father, like as that of the Father depends from the Revelation of the Son."[56] Kelpius sees the Incarnation as the central meaning of Christian life, the "very Ground of the Christian Religion." The Incarnation, the life of Jesus, was itself an alchemical demonstration of the correspondence between the divine, the cosmos, and the human.[57]

We can see how Kelpius's alchemical and ascetic Christianity adapts itself to such a mystery. In the Hermetic and Paracelsian cosmic analogy of human, cosmos, and God, the three mirror each other to such an extent that their borders become indeterminate.[58] The body is a gate between the human and the cosmos, just as the sky is the gate between the cosmos and the divine. These three forms are not merely an analogy: their mutual resonance and harmony constitute the entire system. God ripples through creation in the pillar of fire and the small, still voice, and even these miracles pale in comparison to the Incarnation itself, the presence of God in a human body, the person of Jesus. God, cosmos, human—in the same way that God progresses through these three forms, ascetic behavior refines the body and soul, transforming the human, until the "little spark falls completely into his Light-Fire," until the individual and creation are disappeared and dissolved, indistinguishable from that Light-Fire of God. The alchemical meaning of Kelpius's yearning for dissolution becomes clear: "To be nothing," he writes, "is to be deified."

The "Mystery surpassing all humane & angelicall understanding" is not necessarily just the Incarnation; it is the *process and possibility of inner alchemy itself*, the tincture that saved Moses from pride and refined him into the "Lamlike Nature" that saved his people. It is Elijah's passage through fire and wind and quaking earth and into humility, and it is Christ's passage through a human body

THE THREEFOLD WILDERNESS STATE   149

only to be "humbled himself unto the death, even the death of the Cross, styling himself at this side of the Grave only the son of man (or mankind, the Greek word denoting both the sexes) though He was the Son of God."[59] The Incarnation, in the Threefold Wilderness State, was as much a model for alchemical development as it was the salvation of human sins.

Kelpius acknowledges that there are more examples than he has space to describe, citing the Letter to the Hebrews: "They wandered in deserts, and in mountains, and in dens and caves of the earth."[60] Kelpius sees a common pattern of spiritual development throughout all of scripture: prolonged ascetic labors in wilderness settings. Kelpius digresses to two more brief examples: "The First is DAVID that man after Gods own Heart, who was 10. years in the Wild[erness] & exercised in continual Sufferings & Sorrows," Kelpius writes, as evidenced by his Psalms. "The second is that great Apostle of the Gentiles, *Paul*, who abided seven years in the deserts of Arabia (Gal. 1,17. & as the antient Church Records bear Wittness) before he went out for the Conversion of the Gentiles."[61] From the four major examples to these brief mentions of David and Paul, Kelpius starts to press his interpretive point: examples are numerous and consistent. "I could produce a whole Cloud," he writes,

> of such chosen Vessels out of the Antient Records of the first Christians, who being prepared in the Wild[erness] some for 10. some for 20. Some for 40. years after their coming forth converted whole Cities, wrought signs & miracles, was to their disciples as living Oracles, as the Mouth of God, through whom he fed & guided them.[62]

Kelpius is referring here to antique desert monasticism of the early Christians, whom he was evidently familiar with through his theological training. Kelpius is describing something to his reader that is obvious to him: once this pattern of inner cultivation in wilderness settings is noticed, it is *everywhere* in the Bible and in the church histories. Their numbers are almost countless, Kelpius writes, and though the nature of these labors is rarely described, the result is always the same: ascetic development in the wilderness brings on spiritual transformation, and paranormal phenomena serve as outward signs of God's presence. Thus credentialed, they become "living Oracles, as the Mouth of God," and God actively guides and sustains them.

Having made his point and pressed it, Kelpius offers something like a thesis: "I hope what hath been said manifested to the full, that God hath prepared alwaiis his most eminent instruments in the Wilderness." Their numbers are countless, their similarities undeniable, their labors the same: God prepares Himself and his instruments in the wilderness, the environment itself is the medium, and inner alchemy is the goal of Christian life and biblical religion.

150 AMERICAN AURORA

The nature of the path is clear, but he cautions his reader that the decision to begin walking it cannot be made lightly. To begin the work of alchemical self-refinement is to become "a spectacle to the world & to Angels & to Men," he writes.[63] Undertaking such a transformation is like painting a cosmic target on your forehead, Kelpius suggests. Spiritual alchemy requires one to take a deliberate step into the furnace. There is nothing of the demonic trials that found Jesus or Saint Antony in the wilderness in Kelpius's writing, but the trials and tribulations of the ascetic path are well known to him. Even Moses, he notes, resisted when God first pushed him down the path. "And what good reason Moses had," Kelpius notes with compassion. The first state ends unavoidably in death and failure.

On the other hand, Kelpius notes the danger of setting out without caution: "And what great Presumption it is on the other Hand to go forth without being thus duly prepared beforehand." Both Moses's and Elijah's early lives are marked by this zealous setting out and subsequent humbling. Even the very wise can misstep in the wilderness: "For though such may have inspirations, Revelations, motions & the like extraordinary Favours; yea may have arrived to the very Manhood in Christ (which truly is a high attainment) yet they will effect & build nothing," Kelpius writes.[64] The inner furnace that smelts the soul into gold can also burn: "Yea there is no small danger of loosing themselfs, & to bruse & grind that good seed, which was not designed for meal but for increase, not for to be sent forth but to be kept in an honest & good Heart."[65] These passages show that even as Kelpius sees this process of biblical inner alchemy as the only sure path of spiritual cultivation, the dangers are real, and the death and failure that await the soul at the first stage is not an allegory.

As he finally concludes, Kelpius paints a tantalizing picture of the extent of his thought on the meaning of wilderness for inner transformation: "I had many Considerations more to add, as also what the wilderness it self is in each of these States, having spoken only of some of the Inhabitants thereof & of some of their Qualities & Circumstances," he writes, reinforcing the understanding that the environment is not mere setting, but the medium of the refinement of the body and soul. "Nor have I counted the Number of the Wilderness-Time but touched only the Root thereof, which is 40 Sun-days for the New Birth & 42 Moons or Nights for the Old: (which last I have not so much as mentioned)," he goes on, suggesting a mathematic or numerological understanding of the ways that time is measured in scripture and in the cosmos.

The manuscript abruptly reminds us that we are listening to a personal conversation between friends: "But my beloved & esteemed Friend! This was to write a volume & not a Letter. And I beginn almost to fear, that I have ventured to much upon your Patience this first time, not considering also the Wall between us." With this apology, Kelpius concludes the letter, and so we read the final extant words written by Johannes Kelpius: "I remain your sincere though unworthy Friend—J.K."[66]

The Sources of the Threefold Wilderness State

Throughout the letter to Esther Palmer, we can see that even long after Kelpius separated from the church and surrounded himself with other religious radicals, his identity as a Christian and his training as a Lutheran theologian remained the core of his religious thought. Unlike some of his colleagues and neighbors, who turned directly to more esoteric sources in their thought and writing, Kelpius kept his religious attention trained squarely on the understanding and interpretation of the Bible. And yet familiarity with his contemporary colleagues and their writings shows that the Threefold Wilderness State, like any other biblical interpretation, was very much a product of its wider historical and philosophical circumstance. We have already seen how both the specific language and general sense of spiritual alchemy and Paracelsian cosmology seem to anchor Kelpius's entire notion of spiritual development. But the influence of closer colleagues that Kelpius knew personally, like Jane Lead and Johann Zimmerman, can be found throughout the document as well.

As studies like George H. Williams's *Wilderness and Paradise in Christian Thought* have shown, the biblical notion of wilderness is "so basic a concept in Christian history" as to almost be useless as a stand-alone category of analysis.[67] Indeed, as Williams writes, "The *wilderness state* has indeed become almost a technical term in certain theological traditions."[68] Even the apparently novel notion of a "wilderness state" into which the woman of Revelation 12 enters is not unique to Kelpius. It would appear later that century in the English theologian John Gill's *Exposition of the New Testament* (1746–48).[69] It occurs across the Atlantic around the same time, in the writings of John Wesley, in which it appears without the apocalyptic meaning of Revelation 12. Rather, for Wesley, the wilderness state is simply a state of separation from God, or "that state of doubt . . . which so many go through . . . after they have received remission of sin."[70] But these examples occur decades after Kelpius wrote to Esther Palmer.

Other examples, which Kelpius likely read, came earlier. As I have already noted, Kelpius met and came under the influence of the Philadelphian Society during his time in London. He kept in regular contact with the secretary of the Society, Johann Deichman, and he certainly read the works of its leader, Jane Lead. Lead's visionary and prophetic writings would have been a familiar genre to Kelpius after reading Jacob Böhme. Like Böhme's, much of Lead's writings were descriptions and interpretations of her own visionary and prophetic experiences. Indeed, as Arthur Versluis has noted, the visionary nature

152   AMERICAN AURORA

of her thought and writing is occasionally "much more explicit" than even in Böhme himself.[71]

Jane Lead may be more explicit than Böhme, but much of her visionary grammar derived from her own close reading of the Gorlitz shoemaker. Lead and the Philadelphians were deeply engaged with Böhme's writing, which arrived in English translation on the island toward the middle of the seventeenth century. And like some of the early Pietists, Lead and her followers were given to millennialism and apocalyptic speculations. Sophia personified the divine spirit of a new apocalyptic age, Lead wrote, as signified by both the "ancient prophecy" of the book of Revelation *and* by the "latter day prophecies" of figures like herself and Böhme.[72] Lead's writing on the book of Revelation seems to have deeply influenced Kelpius's later thought, in particular, their shared focus on the prophetic meaning of Revelation 12. Lead writes in *The Ascent to the Mount of Vision*:

> concerning the great Wonder seen in Heaven, (mentioned by St. John) of the Woman Cloathed with the Sun, and the Moon under her feet. . . . Now as to this, it is made manifest that her coming forth out of the Wilderness. . . . Now this Wilderness-State, (according to the Spiritual and Mystical sense thereof) is to be understood of a quiet Retirement, Shelter and Defense from the Fury of the Dragon, where she is fed and nourished with the true Manna and Eternal Word of Life.[73]

This text was written by Lead in 1698 and published the following year, and it very likely passed on to Kelpius. Kelpius mentions Lead's apocalyptic writing in letters to Deichman, and their transatlantic correspondence likely included exchanges of Lead's writings. And as we can see, many of the basic elements of Kelpius's Threefold Wilderness State are here: the apocalyptic reading of the wonder in heaven, the woman clothed with the sun, is the scriptural basis for a "Spiritual and Mystical" wilderness state of "quiet Retirement, Shelter and Defense from the Fury of the Dragon." Kelpius does not cite Lead directly (he cites the Bible almost exclusively in all of his later writing), but their close connection and the similarity of their thought here evidence her influence on Kelpius's understanding of Revelation 12 and his general understanding of the meaning of spiritual development. Jane Lead's *The Ascent to the Mount of Vision* seems to provide the symbolic and scriptural inspiration for Kelpius's system: the wilderness condition of the woman of Revelation 12, as an allegory for personal spiritual development, represents the core of his religious self-understanding.

Somewhat like the theme of wilderness, the notion of spiritual development as a tripartite system—often akin to childhood, adolescence, and maturity—is such a widespread notion in Christian history that it appears rather untraceable at first. But as was the case in Chapter 1, here the seventeenth-century heresiologist

THE THREEFOLD WILDERNESS STATE   153

Ehregott Daniel Colberg has already beaten us to the punch on this particular question. As already described in the first chapter, Colberg was the author of the 1690 book *Platonic-Hermetic Christianity*, in which he identifies ancient Platonic and Hermetic literature in translation as the source for everything wrong—in his orthodox opinion—in the popular Christianity of his day.[74] In doing so, as Wouter Hanegraaff has noted, Colberg is the earliest scholar to offer a comprehensive (as of 1690) analysis of what is now called "Western esotericism."

Writing about fifteen years before Kelpius would meet with Esther Palmer, Colberg singled out the *Mystical Theology* of pseudo-Dionysius the Areopagite, a sixth-century Syrian Christian theologian and Neoplatonic philosopher, as the source of "erroneous and Platonic teachings."[75] The "main flaw" of the *Mystical Theology* is its adherence to the "three Platonic ways," Colberg writes, "For there they teach / one must through purification to enlightenment / and through this to come to union / which purpose the deification [*Vergötterung*] and Christification [*Verchristung*] is."[76] Colberg's summary of pseudo-Dionysius will sound familiar to the reader of Kelpius's letter to Palmer: "Concerning the *summa* or content of this hidden teaching or wisdom / the old fathers divided it into the 3 parts, namely: In the 1st the Purification / 2. Illumination / 3. Unification."[77] Here we have a threefold mystical theology whose ultimate goal is the dissolution of the practitioner into the being of God, which was especially influential in the formation of Christian mysticism in the Middle Ages: Gallus, Tauler, Eckhart, and the anonymous author of *The Cloud of Unknowing* each rely in part on pseudo-Dionysius.[78] Christian mysticism had a Platonic and Hermetic pulse long before anything was translated in the Renaissance.

The threefold mysticism of pseudo-Dionysius erupts again in the writings of modern Protestants under the influence of Hermetic literature. Thus, the *Mystical Theology* of pseudo-Dionysius came to the attention of a heresiologist like Colberg, who writes: "We should touch on the erroneous and Platonic teachings / which are hidden in the *Theologia Mystica* / pull them out / and present them properly."[79] But even within this wider trend of Platonic-Hermetic Christianity, there was tremendous variation. Kelpius's reading in particular is unusual. The emphasis on wilderness, the exclusive nature of his third stage, and the overall emphasis on unyielding ascetic endeavor show that his system remained unique even as it superficially resembled other models of spiritual development.

Kelpius's own tripartite system, in particular his emphasis on the environment of the ascetic subject, reflects the pseudo-Dionysian tripartite theologies of two figures he undoubtedly read: Johann Zimmerman and Jacob Böhme. As we have seen in Chapter 1, Johann Zimmerman was an apocalyptic astronomer and Lutheran theologian from Nuremberg who was repeatedly sanctioned by the Lutheran authorities for his stance on the millennial significance of comets and the writings of Böhme. He also seems to have been the central figure in

154   AMERICAN AURORA

organizing the group with which Kelpius would travel to Pennsylvania. The letter to Esther Palmer shows, not unexpectedly, that Kelpius was familiar with the contours of Zimmerman's theology.

Kelpius would not go as far as his radical friend in his identification of God with the environment, but like Kelpius, Zimmerman elaborated a threefold spiritual system in which contemplation of the environment led to spiritual insight. As described in Chapter 1 of this book, Johann Zimmerman represents the culmination of what I have called Hermetic Protestant environmental thought. Zimmerman's reading of Copernican astronomy into Protestantism pushed the analogies and boundaries of figures like Böhme and Arndt farther than these authors went in the radical identification of God and the cosmos. Mike Zuber puts it more succinctly: "Zimmermann aligned God and the sun rather too closely."[80]

Zimmerman's influence on the Threefold Wilderness State is perhaps most evident in his 1688 poem *Tergemina lucis mysticae mysteria*, "The threefold mysteries of mystical light."[81] In this work, Zimmerman took a Böhme-derived position on the spiritual meaning of physical sensation—of the perception of light, in particular:

> There are, among the hearts trusted by Sophia, those
>> whom it pleased to establish *light* at the center of nature
> Thus, in varied senses, the Crowd of the Wise cuts itself off
>> and they attend to the rational souls that will have to be convinced.
> But although the *nature* of shining *light may lie hid*
>> A *function* in this mass is nevertheless not *hid* in every respect
> while *nature hides, it lays open* by a triple *virtue*
>> this etherial radiance which cannot lie hid
> There are, I say, *three* established *functions* in which LIGHT rejoices:
>> radiant RADIANCE and WARMTH along with MOTION.[82]

Zimmerman's poem expresses the radical cosmotheism that we have come to expect from him. The nature of the cosmos—of God—is at once abundantly manifest in the light of the sun and subtly hidden from those "rational souls" whom the wise waste their time in convincing. Light itself is a perfect yet subtle form that divinity takes on earth, and the understanding of light's true place at the center of creation is a level of wisdom found only among those trusted by Wisdom herself: Sophia. In particular, he is suggesting that three qualities of sunlight—motion, radiance, and warmth—are not just metaphors for God's love, but the actual form that God takes on earth, and the sensory experience of these qualities is a kind of perfect knowledge of God.

Mike Zuber characterizes Zimmerman's system in *Tergemina lucis* as a contemplative mystical system in a sequence of stages: "Through the contemplation of nature, particularly of light and the sun, it was possible to move from the visible and intelligible light to the superintelligible, which was God's domain."[83] Here we can see a clear precedent for what, at first, seemed like a novel aspect of Kelpius's Threefold Wilderness State, what I have called his apocalyptic meaning of wilderness: the environment serves as the *medium* of revelation and divine knowledge, alongside and perhaps superseding other intermediaries. In the shadow of a radical like Zimmerman, who posited an almost one-to-one identification of God and the sun, Kelpius's own cosmotheism in works like *Metamorphosis* and the letter to Esther Palmer seems almost pedestrian. And his emphasis on the Bible, an emphasis that Zimmerman does not share, seems conservative. But this was the milieu in which Kelpius lived, practiced, and wrote. Zimmerman's threefold light mysticism has other important differences from that of Kelpius. His system derives more from Copernican astronomy than from the Bible, and he uses few references to scripture or direct descriptions of what the initiate might undergo at each stage. What remains the same, however, is a threefold mystical system in which contemplation of (and identification with) the environment yields increasing stages of human interface with divinity.

Both Kelpius and Zimmerman found inspiration for their threefold mysticisms in the threefold anthropology and theology of Jacob Böhme. In texts like *Description of the Three Principles of Divine Being* (1618) and *On the Threefold Life of Man* (1620), Böhme elaborated the threefold nature of God, cosmos, and the human: an alchemical theology that is never directly cited but obviously influenced Kelpius's Threefold Wilderness State. In *On the Threefold Life of Man* in particular, Böhme outlines the alchemical process that runs through Kelpius's letter. Andrew Weeks interprets Böhme's three stages of human spiritual development as beginning with "an unredeemed human existence in nature," a verbiage that strongly recalls Kelpius's Barren Wilderness. Stage 2, for Böhme, is "the soul that stems from God," which culminates in a final third stage, "the God who is reborn as a human."[84] Finally, even Kelpius's alchemical reading of the Incarnation might find an origin in Böhme's writing, wherein "the eucharistic miracle of Christ's locally present flesh and blood" is understood as an alchemical demonstration of the perfectibility of matter.[85]

A close reading of Kelpius's immediate milieu has yielded some clear inspirations for many of the basic features of the Threefold Wilderness State as he describes it to Esther Palmer. There is a final component, however, the same component that makes Kelpius yet "the strange one among strange ones."

The Technology of Self-Negation

My focus on the novelty of Kelpius's asceticism in this chapter might give the erroneous impression that he was the only modern Protestant with an interest

156   AMERICAN AURORA

in ascetic behavior, and this is far from the case. Indeed, beyond the institutions of Christian monasticism, direct exposure to Neoplatonic thought has led to more than a few "Christian ascetics who, following in the footsteps of Plotinus, have sought salvation in flight and union with God in solitude," as Paul Henry has written.[86] Closer to our period, scholars like Timothy Wright have pointed out that "the Reformers likewise curtailed what had been for centuries the typical means by which many Christians expressed intensified spirituality" in "suppressing what they considered the corrupt, institutionalized medieval markers of the holy, 'religious' life—chastity, poverty, and physical withdrawal from the world."[87] White connects this suppression of chastity, poverty, and unworldliness with the devotional crisis in Protestantism, a local manifestation of the wider seventeenth-century "crisis of piety" covered in the first chapter.

Kelpius's novel adoptions of biblically derived ascetic behaviors can be seen within this larger "devotional crisis," as Wright understands it. In fact, Wright's emphasis on the asceticism of the Ephrata community—which was established in the wake of Conrad Beissel's search for an ascetic mentor in Kelpius—suggests Kelpius's unrecognized significance in the early modern Protestant development of ascetic practices. Another slightly later German Pietist, Gottfried Arnold, would publish a German translation of the *Vitae Patrium*, or the *Sayings of the Desert Fathers*, in 1700.[88] Kelpius was a few years too early to meet this later generation of Pietists with a clear interest in asceticism, in part, because he was actually factor in its development.

We have seen how Kelpius incorporated essentially modern notions of alchemy and experiment into his asceticism, but his basic models for ascetic behavior were undoubtedly ancient. The letter to Esther Palmer shows only a single source for Kelpius's interest in asceticism: the Bible. Kelpius's ascetic practice was part of his general attempt to recover the religion of the earliest Christians. In the same way that his interest in paranormal phenomena reflected his own belief that the events of the seventeenth century mirrored the events of the Acts of the Apostles, Kelpius's ascetic practice reflected a sincere desire to *act out the spiritual labors of the Bible*—right up to dressing like John and Elijah. The "Antient Records of the first Christians" were his models for self-cultivation and right living as the world declined around him.

And those models were plentiful. "Early Christian ascetics assumed that humans were transformable," writes Elizabeth Clark in her 1999 book *Reading Renunciation: Asceticism and Scripture in Early Christianity*. "The human person could be improved by ascetic practice."[89] As Niki Clements has shown, early Christian ascetic practice was a much richer field of knowledge and practice than it has typically been regarded in the reductive readings of Nietzsche and Weber. Rather, following Michel Foucault's turn toward the study of ancient asceticism, Clements reads early Christian ascetic practice as a form of self-cultivation: "Ascetic formation is arduous, communally rooted, and never complete," Clements writes.[90] Kelpius would have agreed: as we have seen, the soul's reward in the second wilderness state is an even hotter furnace of spiritual refinement.

In his analysis of the ascetic practices of the early Christians, Michel Foucault characterized ascetic development as a kind of self-regulation. The "art of existence," the *techne tou biou*, was the practice and care for the self as a kind of substance that can be modified—Kelpius might say "refined"—with a spiritual goal in mind.[91] Foucault would call these regimental practices in early Christianity "technologies of the self,"

> which permit individuals to effect by their own means, or with the help of others, a certain number of operations on their own bodies and souls, thoughts, conduct, and way of being, so as to transform themselves in order to attain a certain state of happiness, purity, wisdom, perfection, or immortality.[92]

With Foucault's understanding in mind, we can see how the ascetic practice outlined in the letter to Esther Palmer shows precisely this kind of understanding of the self as an object of transformation, refinement, and perfection.

Beyond cultivation, ancient asceticism presented a model of resistance to authority and the mechanisms of power. Ascetic mastery of the self was a practice that "denies access to an external power," as Foucault writes. Wilderness practices of spiritual labor brought the self under such total mastery and regulation that these mastered selves were beyond the reach of empire.[93] What power can threaten an individual for whom "Poverty maketh rich," "Hunger is the most desirable Meat, & Thirst the most refreshing Nectar," as Kelpius writes?[94] These practices clarify the limits of institutional power on the individual. It might be easy to overlook this element in Kelpius's asceticism based on a reading of the letter to Esther Palmer, which makes no mention of resistance to institutional power. But resistance to institutional power was the *defining characteristic* of Kelpius's entire historical circumstance.

Kelpius's educated Pietist milieu was a religious movement of resistance to an overwhelming institutional force: the unified Lutheran church and nascent nation-states of Europe. Particularly, the early form of Pietism practiced by Kelpius and Zimmerman was characterized by a fierce anti-institutionalism, emphasis on personal commitment to religious development, and what William G. McLoughlin describes as "hostility to worldliness and the kinds of compromise which the established church-type systems have to make with the state."[95] Kelpius's decision to migrate to Pennsylvania can only be understood as an attempt to further separate himself from the institutions of church and state power. His ascetic practice at Wissahickon rendered this separation complete.

158   AMERICAN AURORA

Kelpius's "definite spiritual objective" in the letter to Esther Palmer resonates strongly with the desert ascetics in whom Foucault would develop his notion of technologies of the self. But Kelpius's writings demonstrate a spiritual goal that ultimately runs counter Foucault's notion of a perfected self: "When will I completely *dissolve* and *disappear*," he asks. Johannes Kelpius's spiritual alchemy worked toward a "tinctured," "Lamlike" self, a self that declines and hides before it eventually disappears: the very opposite, a photo-negative of Foucault's augmented, perfected selves.

This desire for personal decline and dissolution is so common in Kelpius's writing that it is easy to gloss over. Assessing the entire corpus of Kelpius's hymns written in Pennsylvania, Willard Martin makes a glancing yet profound observation: "Kelpius seems to have conquered his apprehension about physical death," he writes. "He yearned for it in almost all of his hymns."[96] I think this is worth some final emphasis: the desire for disappearance was not a minor theme or poetic image in Kelpius's writings. It was the objective of all his spiritual activity, the "concrete daily practices" that shape the life of the ascetic.[97] These practices reflected a notion of spiritual perfection that was synonymous disappearance. Kelpius's Threefold Wilderness State can only be described as an alchemical technology of self-negation.

This kind of spirituality—particularly a phrase like "self-negation"—might strike the reader as an overly pessimistic reading of Kelpius's religious life. Here our heresiologist helps us again: as Colberg shows, this urge toward reunification with God, Kelpius's desire for *unio mystica*, was an essentially Platonic and Hermetic religious impulse, especially in Kelpius's richly cosmotheist readings of the biblical meanings of wilderness. Self-negation, for Kelpius, meant finally becoming what he has always been: one part of God's whole, a "little spark" in God's Light-Fire, a microcosm within a macrocosm.

To conclude this chapter as I started, a return to Kelpius's poetry can unlock—or at least elucidate—the meanings of his theology. His "Lamenting Voice" manuscript includes one long poem that touches on many of the same themes as the letter to Esther Palmer. In his poem "Of the Wilderness, The Hidden Virgin Cross-Love," a narrator named Johannes is found despairing in the wilderness that his spiritual labors have come to naught. He is met by a friend who encourages him, painting a series of wilderness scenes in verse meant to revive Johannes's flagging spirit:

Think, he said, how the current flows pushes itself onward,
how / by being very still, the river demonstrates its depth:
One cannot see the depths / nor the reason of love
Until her Sun's radiance / comes to stand over her.

THE THREEFOLD WILDERNESS STATE   159

> Think how Gold so deep in the bowels of the Earth
> Lying hidden growing; and it should be useful
> So it must shine glowing, like lightning-weather,
> That it can sit on hand and brow, like Crown and Scepter.
>
> Thinking of the spreading roots, the seeds in the earth
> Which are hidden, yet growing full of strength,
> So grows the Hidden Love, as it bears its fruit
> That winter's fury and storm should never kill its growth.[98]

In these verses, Johannes's friend demonstrates that development is not always outwardly visible, that the "fruit" of "Hidden Love" is not borne in spectacle, but in quiet resilience. A stream only babbles when it runs shallow, its currents pushed over the rocks. But the deeper passages of a river are slow, silent, in fact, "their stillness shows their depth," the friend says. It bears mentioning here that the site of the Wissahickon hermitage, walking straight to the east along the ridge, stands over a place in the river where quiet, still depth gives way to sudden chattering as the river makes a steep turn through shallow bedrock.

In the same way that silence begets depth, the wilderness metaphors of the poem show how the soul develops quietly, subtly, and invisibly: the flourishing roots are immune to frost and storm; gold must grow underground before it can shine like lightning. This silence and depth are not something to be ashamed of, Johannes's friend suggests. Precious things are worth protecting:

> Think of sensitive herbs, when they would be touched
> They turn inwards in mourning, showing their seeds lost;
> It is from Heaven alone you would be touched,
> Shined on only by pure sunshine.[99]

Kelpius paints himself here as a sensitive sapling, recoiling from the world's touch. Throughout "Of the Wilderness," Kelpius portrays his doubts and suffering along the ascetic path, as the voice of his friend likens his quiet development to the environmental phenomena that surround him: the river flowing by, the rocks and minerals underground, and the herb that recoils to protect itself. In fact, throughout the poem, "Johannes" gradually disappears. Looking toward him, we see a river, a small sapling, the roots and minerals beneath the earth.

160 AMERICAN AURORA

This pain he feels, the poem shows, this despair in which his friend finds him is in fact the evidence of his soul's slow blossoming:

> The hidden Jesus-love is like a deep wound,
> Your inner bleeding only felt in the heart,
> Nothing heals her, nothing makes her pain sweeter,
> Until the heart of her loved one erupts.[100]

This is the reward of the second state rendered in verse; the fruits of these trials are yet more trials. Ascetic development is "never complete," as Niki Clements writes. Here Kelpius's poem reaches an erotic climax in which he openly delights in the trials before him, begging God for still more pain and injury on the ascetic path:

> Wound me more and more, by the force of your love,
> that I would only notice this strength and its effect on me,
> to kill my strengths! Until I cross the Red Sea
> to penetrate you, so wound me more and more

If wounds are the fruit of Jesus's hidden love, then wound me, Kelpius exclaims, until I feel nothing but the force of these inflicted wounds. Kelpius's frantic erotic expression gives way to a final ascetic determination:

> Make me as living Gold, after I come out of the Earth,
> awakened to vanity, to be purified by the Cross,
> Yet the last thunder-strike is missing, the final wage of Sins,
> So fire the furnace yet longer, and make me as living Gold.

In the letter to Esther Palmer, Kelpius wrote, "We do experimentally find that the greatest weakness hath the greatest strength hid in herself."[101] The challenges that face the ascetic are the sources of her strength. Her soul is the refining furnace that transmutes them, and final negation is her ultimate reward. Facing his own ascetic challenges, Kelpius's self gradually disintegrates throughout the poem: there is a river, there are rocks, and there are delicate saplings—there is pain refined into gold. Here the ascetic alchemy of the Threefold Wilderness State is expressed clearly in verse: recognizing pain as the fruit of his spiritual labor, Kelpius cries out in alchemical ecstasy: "Make me as living Gold," *wound me more and more.*

Kelpius's interest in the biblical theme of wilderness can elucidate his religious practice as a technology of self-negation. God, cosmos, human—by the end of the poem, the three are increasingly indistinct.

Vita III

"Delay Not Longer the Blessed Day"

Kelpius in Germantown, 1694–1703–4–5–6–7

> Tormenting love, Oh sweetest pain,
> Delay not longer the blessed day!
> —Johannes Kelpius, *Ein verliebtes Girren der trostlosen*
> *Seele in der Morgendämmerung* (A lovestruck coo of
> the desolate soul in the dawn)

In 1706, Kelpius appended a "Lamenting Voice" hymn with a note describing the circumstance of its writing: "As I lay in Christian Warmers House very weak, in a small bed, not unlike a Coffin."[1] Kelpius's fragile health was a matter he referred to repeatedly in his letters. On the front page of his letter book there is a hint of when his decline began. He wrote "1694–1703," before tacking on more years as he added more copies of letters: "1694–1703–4–5–6–7," indicating four years of borrowed time, four sequential years that he did not anticipate living through as his condition worsened and he looked ahead into future that he did not expect to see. (Figure V3.1).

The little portrait that Christopher Witt made seems to suggest his unwellness: his elbow and hand on the chair support his head with his legs stretched out in front, stiff with the exhaustion of simply sitting upright for a while. Witt seemed to go out of his way to remember Kelpius toward the end of his life: the "Lamenting Voice" collaboration and the portrait both suggest a friend who watched his decline and struggled to preserve some piece of him.

His last good year was 1706, in which he wrote poems and letters and seemed to even keep up with visitors. The last year he dashed in the letterbook was 1707 (despite not sending any letters), and it was the year when James Logan recorded his death on the inside of his copy of *Principia Mathematica*, which he bought, along with the rest of the books that Seelig did not keep, shortly after Kelpius died.

Neither Kelpius nor Zimmerman could have known that Zimmerman's measurements of the comet of 1680 would appear in the third edition of Newton's book. That edition would not come until 1726, long after they were both dead. By then, Kelpius and Zimmerman would have noted that comets were well on their way to being meaningless celestial ice, reduced entirely and finally to the

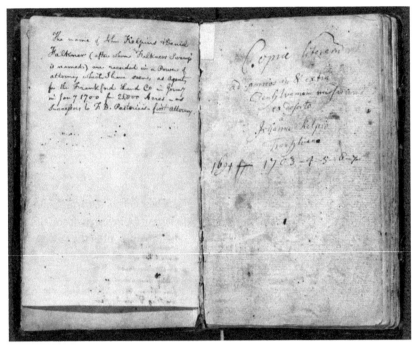

Figure V3.1 Johannes Kelpius's journal, title page. Collection of the Historical Society of Pennsylvania.

quantities and measurements that Newton extracted from Zimmerman's apocalyptic writings.

Someone must have helped walk down the ridge into Germantown, across the river and down the narrow rocky path into town, where he lay in a small bed not unlike a coffin. He was in pain, but those dashes between the years on the cover of the letterbook show that he was used to it. Anyway, I suspect that by then Kelpius had learned how to turn physical pain into something else.

5

The Long Shadow of the Enlightenment

Memories of Kelpius in Charles Brockden Brown's *Wieland* (1798)

And I will shew wonders in the heavens and in the earth, blood, and fire, and pillars of smoke.

—Joel 2:30

The Long Shadow Falls

On March 9, 1814, the *Providence Gazette and Country Journal* ran a strange obituary. The deceased was Major Richard Elliot, a veteran of the Seventh Connecticut Regiment of the Continental Line. As the *Gazette* related it, Elliot was walking home one Sunday night when "he observed two lights coming towards him in the shape of a half moon." The two lights surrounded him before he heard a voice say: "Are you prepared to die?" Elliot responded, "If it is God's will, I think I am." The two lights proceeded to follow him as he walked home before they stopped at a cemetery, where, according to Elliot, "They made a stand, and he could observe them on looking back for half a mile." Elliot made it home, where he told his wife and children about what had happened to him, adding that he indeed believed that "he was soon to die, and made preparations accordingly, with manifest resignation to the will of Providence." Three days later, Elliot succumbed to what the *Gazette* called "the prevailing epidemic" in the area.[1]

As bizarre as it may seem to us today, Elliot's obituary was not terribly unusual among early American letters. The death of Johannes Kelpius and his colleagues by no means concluded the appearance of such phenomena in early American literature, which abounded with descriptions of wonders, signs, and miraculous phenomena, like strange lights in the sky, telepathic communication, and clairvoyant knowledge of distant events. The prevalence of what we recognize today as paranormal phenomena in early American sources is a feature across archives, as historians like Adam Jortner are just beginning to lay out. "The subject matter," as Jortner writes of such phenomena in early American archives, "is voluminous."[2]

American Aurora. Timothy Grieve-Carlson, Oxford University Press. © Oxford University Press 2024.
DOI: 10.1093/oso/9780197765562.003.0006

164   AMERICAN AURORA

This is also the subject matter of the Philadelphia author Charles Brockden Brown's (1771–1810) novel *Wieland, or, The Transformation: An American Tale* (1798). At the center of the novel is the Wieland family, a group of immigrants to Pennsylvania from Germany whose particular form of Christianity might strike us as familiar. As Jon Butler has written of the family at the center of the novel, "The religion of the Wielands was not evangelical Christianity or even Quakerism, however. It was an ecstatic, highly individualized, personal spirituality whose followers were obsessed with manifestations of divine intervention."[3] These similarities between the characters and events in *Wieland* and the life and writings of Johannes Kelpius are indeed much more than circumstantial, as scholars of Charles Brockden Brown have confirmed.[4]

This chapter marks a shift in this book: as my temporal focus turns to the years after Kelpius's death in 1707, I turn now to the legacy and memory of Johannes Kelpius, the texts in which both his name and a more ambient memory of the man appear in American history and literature. In this chapter, I explore early American attention to the miraculous by examining *Wieland*, an eighteenth-century American novel in which the challenge of interpreting paranormal phenomena was placed at the center of early American life—a novel based, in large part, on the memory of Johannes Kelpius.

We first met Charles Brockden Brown earlier in Chapter 2, where he was trying to make heads or tails of the almanac genre in eighteenth-century Pennsylvania. His opinions on almanacs and the people who used them will remain relevant in his fiction. In this chapter, I focus on *Wieland* as I begin to excavate the memory of Johannes Kelpius as it appears in history and literature following his death in 1707. In the next and final chapter of the book I will examine a more varied body of American history and literature in which the memory of Kelpius appears. For now, I want to focus on Charles Brockden Brown and his novel, which is by far the most influential, robust, and fascinating posthumous appearance of Johannes Kelpius.

Charles Brockden Brown was a prolific intellectual by any standard, which makes his context in eighteenth-century Pennsylvania—a place that produced little literature, let alone professional novelists—all the more extraordinary. Brown was born into a family of English Quakers in Philadelphia in 1771. He was educated at the Friends' Latin School in the city and went on to apprentice himself in a law office. The law was less intellectually stimulating than Brown seems to have hoped, and he would go on to join a series of informal reading and discussion groups as a young man in Philadelphia. He eventually took a job at a grammar school, leaving the practice of law to more fully dedicate himself to intellectual exploration, before moving to New York in 1797. Just after this move, Brown lost a close friend to yellow fever before he nearly succumbed himself—an intense personal mixture of the tragic loss of a dear friend and a close brush with his own mortality.[5]

During a period of intense writing that followed between 1798 and 1801, Brown suddenly produced the four novels for which he is remembered today: *Wieland* (1798), *Ormond* (1799), *Edgar Huntly* (1799), and *Arthur Merwyn* (1801). Something shifted again in Brown shortly after this period, and he returned to Philadelphia, claiming his intention to give up publishing. He joined the family business, married, and went on to gradually shift his opinions again, this time from "an Enlightenment-influenced religious questioner and political progressive to a more conservative orthodox Christian."[6] He died of tuberculosis in 1810 at the age of thirty-nine.[7]

The complex ideological makeup suggested by this biography is evidenced throughout his novels. Despite his position as one of the very first American authors who produced exciting novels in a decidedly popular style—they are usually identified as something like early Gothic adventures—Brown is rarely read or even generally known today beyond American literature classrooms. Brown's writing is "difficult," his critics write, both in content and style. From my perspective, Brown's novels often read more like dreams than simple narratives. Plot lines open and suddenly close, characters behave inexplicably, irresistible motivations and paralyzing anxieties appear and evaporate without explanation, and terrible plagues of yellow fever, animal attacks, apparitions, and menacing ventriloquists beset the good people of urban and rural Pennsylvania throughout Brown's corpus. To be completely achronological, Brown's novels often feel more viscerally surrealist than properly Gothic to me, a bit like reading an eighteenth-century David Lynch. Small wonder that many American literature surveys begin with Washington Irving or James Fenimore Cooper, despite their place as latecomers to the American literary scene relative to Brown.

Brown's novels tend to strain the confines of genre in critical analysis, even as "Gothic" is as close as we are likely to get in labeling them. As Jay Fliegelmen has written, "For all its Gothic trappings, *Wieland* subverts the demystifying and secularizing agenda of the Gothic novels. . . . If the Faustian agenda of enlightenment science sought to demystify the world, Brown sought to remystify it."[8] Brown certainly subverts a wholly secularizing agenda in his novel, but his project in *Wieland* was not simply re-enchantment or a return to Christian virtue. Nor was it simply a revision of the Gothic novel, which had not yet been clearly established as a literary phenomenon at the time of Brown's writing. Rather, *Wieland* was Brown's thorny, "difficult" answer to his specific intellectual climate.[9] Bill Christopherson capably summarizes the eighteenth-century cultural climate that Brown so fiercely critiqued: "an overconfidence in reason" and an "unappreciativeness of Enlightenment paradox" had led to an intellectual atmosphere "unwilling to scrutinize dark corners of the self."[10] Suspicion of the Enlightenment *and* an interest in scrutinous examination of the self? The closer we look at Brown, the less surprising his interest in Kelpius seems.

166   AMERICAN AURORA

Brown's ideology is as complex and equivocating as his genre. Brown's revolutionary sympathies and scientific interest give way to severe critiques of Enlightenment rationalism and empirical knowledge in his writing, while sincere expressions of religious longing and devotional impulses lead to harmless ignorance at best and ecstatic frenzies of violence at worst. Brown—like so many of the other figures we have studied so far—just does not seem to fit very well in any of the neat boxes historians or critics have prepared for him.

Brown established his general critique of Enlightenment hubris by setting his novel within a time and a place he knew well, a setting in which religion was not so easily reduced to moral philosophy, and apparitions were not so easily revealed to be people in sheets. This is the exception to Brown's evasion of critical and historical understanding, an area where we might make some clear interpretive passes at Brown's difficult novels and patchwork ideology. The overwhelming source of Brown's fiction was his hometown and his personal familial background, what Peter Kafer calls his "underworld of tribal knowledge," the tribe in question being the Philadelphia Quakers, an institution more than a century old by the time of Brown's birth.[11] This area in particular—his family background and the novel's setting along the Schuylkill River just outside of Philadelphia—lead to some of the clearest critical insights on *Wieland* and its author.

According to family history, the first Brown to convert to Quakerism was a Northamptonshire farmer in the mid-seventeenth century. At some point between 1677 and 1684, the farmer's two sons traveled with other English Quakers to Pennsylvania. Here the elder Brown brothers made contact with the Kelpius group when they attended the 1696 yearly meeting of the Society of Friends in Burlington, where Heinrich Bernard Köster stood up and told the Burlington Friends that the inner light had failed them, before the meeting descended into chaos. Like almost everyone else at the meeting, the Brown brothers were not persuaded, and their great-grandson Charles was brought up with the inner light of Quakerdom.[12]

The place of Kelpius in Charles Brockden Brown's novel is best understood as a function of one theme that continues throughout this book: even in the late eighteenth century, Philadelphia remained, in many ways, a small town. The young Brown would have wandered past the ruins of the Wissahickon hermitage, and his father probably told him about those strange men who sided with George Keith against the truth of Quaker religion. As we will see, Brown makes extensive use of the small town he called home and the areas of its history that inspired his critique. *Wieland* is not a novel in which Kelpius and company are portrayed neutrally or simply: rather, Brown used certain dimensions of the *memory* of Kelpius to show how overconfidence in traditional religion and Enlightened reason could fail.

THE LONG SHADOW OF THE ENLIGHTENMENT   167

In order to clearly describe this posthumous portrayal of Kelpius, I will sketch a summary of *Wieland* before exploring the specific connections between Brown, his novel, and the broader themes of this book. In the second section, I dive more deeply into the themes of the novel, exploring how these themes played out in the imagination of a Quaker author in Philadelphia at the turn of the nineteenth century. While the connections between *Wieland* and the broader religious landscape of the region and period have been well mapped, scholars continue to superimpose political and specifically revolutionary themes onto the text—perhaps telling us more about the contemporary interests of scholars of eighteenth-century American literature than about the intentions and meanings of Brown's novel. This analysis culminates in a rereading of Brown's novel based on the themes of this book, in which the interstitial zone that Kelpius seems to inhabit—between Enlightenment rationalism and traditional religion—takes center stage in Brown's twofold critique.

An American Tale

Wieland takes the form of a series of sketches from the perspective of the protagonist, Clara Wieland. "You are a stranger to the depths of my distresses," she writes by way of introduction: "Hence your efforts at consolation must necessarily fail." Despite the hopelessness of consolation, there might yet be some value in a record of her experiences: "I acknowledge your right to be informed of the events that have lately happened in my family," she writes, adding, "Make what use of the tale you shall think proper."[13] We meet Clara, then, as a wounded narrator of events that have led to her destruction—events that she records only in grudging acknowledgment of others' right to be informed.

Immediately, the reader has the sense of being let in on a private tragedy, a devastating family secret. She goes on to fill in the background of her family: her father, she writes, was "a native of Saxony" who experienced a profound conversion to deep Christian devotion after chancing upon some radical Protestant writings, and as he devoted himself to the study of scripture, he developed a singular and individual interpretation of both the biblical text and Christian practice.[14] Eventually, her father "embarked for Philadelphia" after he "imbibed an opinion that it was his duty to disseminate the truths of the gospel among the unbelieving nations," as Clara records.[15] Having read several historical accounts of other radical Protestants who make such a journey in this book, the next part of Clara's narrative is unsurprising: once ensconced in William Penn's incubator for religious radicals, her father's religious commitments deepened further.

Her father settled on the banks of the Schuylkill, in a hamlet called Mettingen, the setting of much of the novel. Mettingen is set "five miles" beyond the city

168 AMERICAN AURORA

along the Schuylkill River—a fictional setting that is easily located in the real world. As Peter Kafer notes of this locale, "[Brown] *literally* locates his fictional Wieland family estate, and their 'temple,' in the very place near Germantown where in the 1690's a renowned group of 'Saxon' radical pietists had set up their own little 'Philadelphia.'"[16]

We have, then, in "Mettingen" a rough fictionalization of Germantown—and Brown's description of the location of the Wieland family home "turns out to be where the Schuylkill meets the Wissahickon, and this is where the Kelpius community lived."[17] For readers today, Brown's associative and referential setting in *Wieland* requires detailed understanding of early Pennsylvania, and in particular the religious history of Philadelphia. But for many of his readers in 1798, particularly those in Philadelphia, Brown's references and setting were perfectly clear—probably a bit like a New Englander today feels while reading Stephen King.

Clara Wieland describes the setting as an almost Edenic refuge from the city in a few lines that recall the descriptions of the area shown in Chapter 3:

> Schuylkill was here a pure and translucid current, broken into wild and cease-less music by rocky points, murmuring on a sandy margin, and reflecting on its surface, banks of all varieties of height and degrees of declivity. These banks were chequered by patches of dark verdure and shapeless masses of white marble, and crowned by copses of cedar, or by the regular magnificence of orchards, which, at this season, were in blossom, and were prodigal of odours.[18]

The cedar groves along the cliffs that Kelpius described so lovingly as "the glory of Lebanon" were evidently still standing, at least in part, when Charles Brockden Brown visited the site of his community a few decades later.

Here, Clara records, her father passed his time industriously, where "new objects, new employments, and new associates appeared to have nearly obliterated the devout impressions of his youth."[19] The elder Wieland's religious zeal relaxed at first in the face of the daily toil and regular society. He married, had two children, and after a long period of "thrifty and laborious" living, her father retired. During this period of retirement, Wieland's religious zeal rekindled, whereupon the "reading of the scriptures, and other religious books, became once more his favorite employment."[20] With his religious devotions suddenly renewed in idleness, her father settled back into the deep personal Christianity of his youth:

> He allied himself with no sect, because he perfectly agreed with none. Social worship is that by which they are all distinguished; but this article found no place in his creed. He rigidly interpreted that precept which enjoins us, when we

THE LONG SHADOW OF THE ENLIGHTENMENT   169

worship, to retire into solitude, and shut out every species of society. According to him devotion was not only a silent office, but must be performed alone.[21]

Clara's father was a separatist, then, and a bit of an ascetic, whose religious commitments eschewed institutional and social settings of devotion to focus on a more intimate and solitary religious labor. "The character of my mother was no less devout," Clara writes: "She was punctual in the offices of prayer, and in the performance of hymns to her Saviour, after the manner of the disciples of Zinzendorf."[22] The picture becomes clearer still: Nicolaus Zinzendorf (1700–1760) was a Lutheran Pietist who attended August Herman Francke's school as a boy before going on to lead the Moravian missions in Pennsylvania during the eighteenth century. Brown, an English Quaker, clearly goes out of his way to stress the German and Pietist origins and milieu of the Wieland family. Kafer notes that the novel, "in its broadest aspect . . . is grounded in the radical pietist origins of William Penn's colony," a context that Brown "invokes in various ways."[23] The elder Wieland is a "separatist," an epithet likely to recall the seventeenth-century radical strain of Pietism in which figures like Kelpius grew up, and his wife was a Moravian. The chronology is warped, but Brown's message is clear: the Wielands are radical German Pietists.

My own reading of the primary sources of Kelpius's community bears out Kafer's conclusions. Clara's description of her father seems to pick out many of the themes of Kelpius's life and writing outlined in previous chapters: "His own system was embraced not, accurately speaking, because it was the best, but because it had been expressly prescribed to him. Other modes, if practised by other persons, might be equally acceptable," she writes.[24] The alignment here between the elder Wieland and the ecumenism of Kelpius and his colleagues is clear enough, and it also recalls Kelpius's views on the religious beliefs of the Lenape.[25] She goes on to illustrate her father's overall demeanor:

> His deportment to others was full of charity and mildness. A sadness perpetually overspread his features, but was unmingled with sternness or discontent. The tones of his voice, his gestures, his steps were all in tranquil unison. His conduct was characterised by a certain forbearance and humility, which secured the esteem of those to whom his tenets were most obnoxious. They might call him a fanatic and a dreamer, but they could not deny their veneration to his invincible candour and invariable integrity.[26]

The extant primary record contains no description of Kelpius's demeanor, or his character, or his "deportment to others." Unlike his later colleagues Conrad Matthai and Christopher Witt, there is no source that records a personal meeting with Kelpius. While such a reading is admittedly speculative, I hear in Clara's words the popular memory of Kelpius around Germantown in the decades after his death: mild, sad, forbearing, and humble, a reputed fanatic and a dreamer who was nevertheless generally held in esteem even by those who found his beliefs "obnoxious."

Her father's preference for solitude led to the construction of a tabernacle on a cliffside overlooking the river as a site for his devotions. As Clara writes:

> At the distance of three hundred yards from his house, on the top of a rock whose sides were steep, rugged, and encumbered with dwarf cedars and stony asperities, he built what to a common eye would have seemed a summer-house. The eastern verge of this precipice was sixty feet above the river which flowed at its foot. The view before it consisted of a transparent current, fluctuating and rippling in a rocky channel, and bounded by a rising scene of cornfields and orchards.[27]

Clara's father's tabernacle was the site of his daily and nightly meditations and prayers—in a manner recalling the eighteenth-century Ephrata monks and nuns, Wieland would climb the ridge at midnight to pray under the night sky. "This was the temple of his Deity. Twice in twenty-four hours he repaired hither, unaccompanied by any human being. Nothing but physical inability to move was allowed to obstruct or postpone this visit," Clara writes.[28]

The possibility that the coincidence of the fictional Mettingen and the Kelpius site could be simple chance is further reduced in Kafer's research. Kafer points out that the country home of a lawyer Brown studied with was within walking distance of the hermitage—and that the adjacent property along the ridge of the Wissahickon belonged to the family of one of Brown's closest friends. Brown's description of the tabernacle as appearing like a "summer-house" is also in line with what we know about the Wissahickon hermitage: contrary to what later authors would write, Kelpius and company lived in a modest cottage.

Kafer's connection of Wieland's temple to the site of the Kelpius community is clear enough to surprise even Brown's readers today. As Caleb Crain writes of Kafer's findings regarding Brown and Kelpius, "To a Brown fan, this is heady. It is equivalent to telling a Melville fan that the *Pequod* has been located and raised from the deep. Wieland's temple is crucial to Brown's first novel."[29] Far from forgotten or being "of necessarily limited influence," as Leigh Eric Schmidt has written, Peter Kafer has shown that Kelpius, his community, and his strange style of Christian life were profoundly influential at the very beginning of American literature.

The Schuylkill tabernacle is the setting for one of the most profound and paranormal events in the novel, an event that the characters recall and contemplate repeatedly throughout the text. As Clara remembers it, one day her father's spirit seemed suddenly troubled: "Sighs, and even tears, sometimes escaped him. To the expostulations of his wife he seldom answered any thing. When he designed to be communicative, he hinted that his peace of mind was flown, in consequence of deviation from his duty."[30] His agitation seemed to grow as the clock approached the midnight hour. "He had predicted evils," Clara writes of her father, "but professed himself ignorant of what nature they were."[31] The clock struck midnight, the appointed hour of his prayers: "The clock tolled. The sound appeared to communicate a shock to every part of my father's frame. He rose immediately, and threw over himself a loose gown. Even this office was performed with difficulty, for his joints trembled, and his teeth chattered with dismay."[32]

Wieland's wife, children, and uncle were all understandably anxious about this particular trip up the cliff: "My mother's anxiety would not allow her to remain where she was. She rose, and seated herself at the window."[33] The family sat together in darkness. "An half hour passed away in this state of suspence," Clara writes, her mother sitting by the window, "Her eyes were fixed upon the rock." Clara records what happened next:

Suddenly [the rock] was illuminated. A light proceeding from the edifice, made every part of the scene visible. A gleam diffused itself over the intermediate space, and instantly a loud report, like the explosion of a mine, followed. She uttered an involuntary shriek, but the new sounds that greeted her ear, quickly conquered her surprise. They were piercing shrieks, and uttered without intermission. The gleams which had diffused themselves far and wide were in a moment withdrawn, but the interior of the edifice was filled with rays.[34]

Clara's uncle is immediately roused by this scene, and proceeds to fly up the ridge toward the tabernacle. "He also imagined what he saw to be fire," Clara writes. "The shrieks were no longer to be heard; but a blazing light was clearly discernible between the columns of the temple."[35] Clara's uncle "speedily gained this spot . . . for a moment exhausted by his haste."[36] What he saw as he looked into the tabernacle is worth quoting at length:

Within the columns he beheld what he could no better describe, than by saying that it resembled a cloud impregnated with light. It had the brightness of flame, but was without its upward motion. It did not occupy the whole area, and rose but a few feet above the floor. No part of the building was on fire. This appearance was astonishing. He approached the temple. As he went forward the light retired, and, when he put his feet within the apartment, utterly vanished. The suddenness of this transition increased the darkness that succeeded in a tenfold degree. Fear and wonder rendered him powerless. An occurrence like this, in a place assigned to devotion, was adapted to intimidate the stoutest heart.

172 AMERICAN AURORA

His wandering thoughts were recalled by the groans of one near him. His sight gradually recovered its power, and he was able to discern my father stretched on the floor. At that moment, my mother and servants arrived with a lanthorn, and enabled my uncle to examine more closely this scene. My father, when he left the house, besides a loose upper vest and slippers, wore a shirt and drawers. Now he was naked, his skin throughout the greater part of his body was scorched and bruised. His right arm exhibited marks as of having been struck by some heavy body. His clothes had been removed, and it was not immediately perceived that they were reduced to ashes. His slippers and his hair were untouched.[37]

Clara's uncle describes a luminous object hovering over Wieland's body before it suddenly disappears. His clothes have been burned away—except for his slippers—and he seems to be severely injured. "What is the inference to be drawn from these facts?" Clara asks. Brown rejects the possibility of unreliability of the narrator in the text: "Their truth cannot be doubted. My uncle's testimony is peculiarly worthy of credit, because no man's temper is more sceptical, and his belief is unalterably attached to natural causes."[38] Clara's uncle brings her father to the house, where he shortly dies of his wounds.

As Clara concludes this narrative, she offers two unsatisfactory explanations: First, the interpretation of her father's religion—that her father's death was a clear punishment from God: "Is it a fresh proof that the Divine Ruler interferes in human affairs, meditates an end, selects, and commissions his agents, and enforces, by unequivocal sanctions, submission to his will?" she asks.[39] Second, she offers a speculative naturalistic interpretation: "Or, was it merely the irregular expansion of the fluid that imparts warmth to our heart and our blood, caused by the fatigue of the preceding day, or flowing, by established laws, from the condition of his thoughts?"[40] Clara never reaches a firm conclusion for herself, and neither does Brown explain the cause to his readers.

Brown does, however, offer a footnote in the text to assure his readers of the reality of the phenomenon he describes, suggesting that he favors the naturalistic explanation: "A case, in its symptoms exactly parallel to this, is published in one of the Journals of Florence," he writes, referring us to the text in question, a 1792 article from the *American Museum* titled "Letter Respecting an Italian Priest, Killed by an Electric Commotion, the Cause of Which Resided in His Own Body." The case as described in the article clearly mirrors the death of the elder Wieland: a priest entered a private room where a loud noise was heard; his cries alerted others, who found him "extended on the floor" while "a faint flame" gradually retreated "as it was approached, and at length disappeared entirely." The priest, like Wieland, died of his wounds. The cause of death? It seemed that "lightning is sometimes kindled within the human body," the authors of the article suggest, "and destroys it."[41]

THE LONG SHADOW OF THE ENLIGHTENMENT   173

The death of the elder Wieland has been almost universally described by later critics of the novel as a case of "spontaneous human combustion," and indeed, there are parallels between the events described and the literature of spontaneous combustion. This description, while helpful in allowing critics to describe such a prolonged and mysterious event simply and quickly, suppresses a great deal of ambiguity in the novel and Brown's cited source material.[42] As Bernard Rosenthal has noted, nowhere in the book is the phrase "spontaneous human combustion" used to describe what happened to the elder Wieland. And yet "The label," he writes, "has stuck to the event from the earliest writings to the present."[43] Brown repeatedly suggests that the object or substance that killed Wieland was *like* a flame, but something else: Clara's uncle "imagined what he saw to be fire"; the object that he comes upon "he could no better describe, than by saying that it resembled a cloud impregnated with light. It had the brightness of flame, but was without its upward motion." Again and again, Brown warns the reader against simply assuming that the mysterious object was a fire or even the cause of a fire: "No part of the building was on fire," he writes, as though to drive the point home: please do not mistake my description for something as mundane as fire.

Peter Kafer leans into these ambiguities in comparing the luminous death of the elder Wieland with the common local religious understandings of the presence of God as an object of light or fire. "The Word of the Lord was like a fire in me," reads a typical passage of George Fox, an author that a young Quaker like Brown would have known well.[44] We have already seen how Brown's novel reflects his local and familial awareness of the Kelpius community. And while there is no direct evidence that Brown read any of the contemporary Quaker printings of the letter to Esther Palmer that circulated during his lifetime, it is certainly possible that he read lines like "There followeth a Night also upon this day," as Kelpius writes in the letter, "wherein nevertheless the Pillar of Fire is our Guide, refining us as Gold in the Furnace, which is the Baptism of Fire of ye Son."[45] If Brown had read the Palmer letter, which, as Patrick Erben notes, "struck a nerve among American Quakers," his local awareness of the Kelpius community and site on the Wissahickon combined with these provocative lines on personal religious devotion and the guidance of nocturnal luminous pillars could have been the inspiration for this entire scene.[46]

Following Kelpius's death in 1707, a variety of legends about celestial phenomena would swirl around the memory of the Wissahickon hermits—and perhaps this is unsurprising for a figure who urged fellow Christians to "observe every new Phoenomena, Meteors, Stars and various Colours of the Skei" for signs of God's will.[47] One example comes from the amateur antiquarian Julius Sachse's 1895 *German Pietists of Provincial Pennsylvania*. "One of the most curious legends in connection with the Tabernacle in the forest is the following tale," Sachse wrote, "recorded in the Ephrata manuscripts, which partakes

174 AMERICAN AURORA

somewhat of the supernatural." During a midnight ceremony in commemoration of the seventh anniversary of their arrival in Wissahickon—this would make the date St. John's Eve, June 24, 1701—a white object from the sky descended on the group and transformed into an angel before retreating:

> Whilst engaged in their accustomed services or ceremonies in commemoration of their arrival, which they observed with solemnity, a white, obscure, moving body in the air attracted their attention, which, as it approached, assumed the form and mien of an angel. It receded into the shadows of the forest, and appeared again immediately before them as the fairest of the lovely.[48]

As we will explore more fully in the following chapter, Sachse's history cannot be relied upon as a scholarly source. If there is an extant Ephrata manuscript that describes such an event, it is unknown. What is far more likely is that Sachse was describing a local legend surrounding the Wissahickon community, legitimized through the claim of its basis in an Ephrata manuscript source—a citational practice that Sachse employed elsewhere. We only have textual fragments of the body of legends that sprang up around Kelpius's memory in the centuries that followed his death—but these fragments are resonant enough to suggest the outline of a consistent local tradition, an oral practice of telling strange stories about the old men who used to live on the ridge and look toward the sky.

Strange as it may sound, there were so many adjacent local sources of such encounters that Brown was practically swimming in source material for his own luminous divine presences. A more local Quaker, John Woolman, described an encounter with a luminous nocturnal divinity in his journal, published in 1774 in the *Works of John Woolman*, a Philadelphia Quaker classic that the young Brown would have certainly read:

> I awoke; it was yet dark, and no appearance of day or moonshine, and as I opened mine eyes I saw a light in my chamber, at the apparent distance of five feet, about nine inches in diameter, of a clear, easy brightness, and near its centre the most radiant. As I lay still looking upon it without any surprise, words were spoken to my inward ear, which filled my whole inward man. They were not the effect of thought, nor any conclusion in relation to the appearance, but as the language of the Holy One spoken in my mind. The words were, CERTAIN EVIDENCE OF DIVINE TRUTH. They were again repeated exactly in the same manner, and then the light disappeared.[49]

While the direct influence of the writings of Kelpius and Woolman on Brown is admittedly speculative, the author was clearly working within and portraying a religious milieu in which such phenomena were regularly described in writing.

In local religious sources, the American Pillar of Fire burned brightly in contemporary local Quaker and Pietist writings available to Brown.

Brown's own dark spin on these sources was the suggestion of a possible *natural* cause of these apparitions. As Clara speculates, "Is it a fresh proof that the Divine Ruler interferes in human affairs.... Or, was it merely the irregular expansion of the fluid that imparts warmth to our heart and our blood, caused by the fatigue of the preceding day, or flowing, by established laws, from the condition of his thoughts?"[50] Brown's own Enlightenment skepticism of religious experience has none of the optimism or reverence for reason that we find in someone like Thomas Jefferson: perhaps a violent God is watching us, Clara wonders, or perhaps the human mind and body can unwittingly produce a lethal, luminous, and ambient substance. In Brown's novel and Clara's imagination, the final outcome is so terrible that the difference is almost unimportant.

Effects without Cause

The death of the elder Wieland serves as an almost Freudian primal trauma of the death of the father for the Wieland children: a scene-setting and shared memory for our protagonists. The novel goes on to introduce the children, now grown, and still living in Mettingen during the years between the Seven Years War and the American Revolution. Clara Wieland, our narrator, is joined by her brother Theodore, his wife Catherine, and their mutual friend, the affable Henry Pleyel. The four of them enjoy a close friendship, meeting regularly in the ruins of their father's tabernacle along the Schuylkill for conversation. Theodore is as devoutly religious as his father, "But the mind of the son was enriched by science, and embellished with literature."[51] As an illustration of this embellishment, Theodore arranges for a bust of Cicero to be placed in the ruins of his father's temple—no longer a site of solitary nocturnal devotions, but of educated conversations between friends.

The engine of this Enlightenment influence is their friend Pleyel, a young man who "had been some years in Europe" and whose "conversation abounded with novelty."[52] Pleyel was worldly, he was trendy, and Kelpius might say he had that "Athenian curiosity," which is how he described the Enlightenment interest in novelty for novelty's sake.[53] Pleyel and Theodore were dear friends, "and Pleyel was not behind his friend in his knowledge of the history and metaphysics of religion."[54] Their approaches to this subject, however, were opposite: where Theodore "discovered only confirmations of his faith" in the history of religions, Pleyel "could find nothing but reasons for doubt."[55] Brown portrays Theodore Wieland and Henry Pleyel as the two poles of an ideological spectrum: traditional religious belief and Enlightenment rationalism. Where

176 AMERICAN AURORA

the young Wieland awaits signs and signals from God, Pleyel, the rationalist, "rejected all guidance but that of his reason."[56] Between them Brown places our narrator, Clara.

This pleasant scene is challenged by a series of anomalous events. Theodore hears the voice of his wife whisper in his ear one evening as he climbs the ridge toward the tabernacle, while she is sitting in the house far below. Pleyel attributes the entire episode to a "deception of the senses," while Clara is reminded of the mysterious events leading up to her father's death at the same location. For her brother, she writes, the incident "was always regarded by him as flowing from a direct and supernatural decree."[57] He remembered it often, she says, and the effects on his mind were "more gloomy and permanent" than on her own.[58] One night, as brother and sister discuss the event together in light of recent events in the tabernacle, Theodore equivocates: "Here is an effect, but the cause is utterly inscrutable."[59] Charles Brockden Brown's theory of the miraculous comes into closer view.

The anomalous events continue. A voice speaks to Theodore and Pleyel in the tabernacle together, bringing Pleyel dismal news of the death of a woman he was courting in Europe. "You are now convinced that my ears were well-informed," Theodore says to his friend. "Yes," Pleyel responds, "this, it is plain, is no fiction of the fancy."[60] Faced with an undeniably anomalous series of phenomena, Brown portrays Henry Pleyel as a thwarted mind: he "sunk into an anxious silence" after explaining the events to Clara.[61] When the senses fail, reason fails with them, and so fails a person like Pleyel.

Clara ruminates on the events so far, from somewhere between the ideological poles of her brother and Pleyel. "I am not fearful of shadows," she writes, and "tales of apparitions and enchantments did not possess that power over my belief which could even render them interesting." She has no personal interest in what we might call the paranormal, no religious or aesthetic urge to seek out the wondrous: "I saw nothing in them but ignorance and folly, and was a stranger even to that terror which is pleasing." And yet the events that her companions have experienced are an undeniable challenge to her perspective. "But this incident was different from any that I had ever before known," she admits. "Here were proofs of a sensible and intelligent existence, which could not be denied. Here was information obtained and imparted by means unquestionably super-human."[62] Clara is somewhere between the religious devotions of her brother and the reason of Pleyel, neither accepting strange phenomena as signs from God nor rejecting them outright.

To understand Clara's perspective and the subtle philosophical position that Brown is expressing with her voice, we might look forward to another American author of the impossible. Charles Fort (1874–1932) was a New York author who specialized in anomalous phenomena that prevailing philosophical modalities

THE LONG SHADOW OF THE ENLIGHTENMENT 177

of science and religion could not account for. Fort's writing held both science and religion in tense critical distance (more often, he held them both in contempt) as forms of knowledge. These "twin dominants" of thought, as Fort called them, distort reality by shaping our perception of phenomena. Between these two dominants, writes the historian of religions Jeffrey Kripal, Fort developed another register of experience and knowledge called "Intermediatism." "Both *belief* and *explanation*, or faith and reason," Kripal writes of Fort's Intermediatism, "are now replaced by a more humble *acceptance*."[63] Faced with undeniably anomalous events, with intelligent communication that imparts "by means unquestionably super-human," Clara does not collapse into either religious faith or rationalistic reduction. Rather, she adapts, taking on the Fortean stance of Intermediatism.

Brown further portrays this proto-Fortean quality of our hero, Clara, in this monologue: "That there are conscious beings, beside ourselves, in existence, whose modes of activity and information surpass our own, can scarcely be denied," she admits. "Is there a glimpse afforded us into a world of these superior beings? My heart was scarcely large enough to give admittance to so swelling a thought."[64] Even after traditional religion gives way to Enlightenment rationalism, human beings are at the mercy of discarnate or otherwise invisible intelligences whose knowledge, motives, and "modes of activity" can scarcely be denied any better than they can be explained. Again, Brown suggests that sensebased reason itself as a method or criterion of knowledge is inadequate, if not dangerous.

Brown's critique of the prevailing intellectual atmosphere of his time and place was severe. In Brown's portrayal, the rationalists were not assuming the dominant position in the cosmos as they imagined: in their flippant dismissal of traditional religious belief and practice, they were simply choosing to ignore the animate intelligences that surrounded them. Ideologies fail when effect precedes cause, Brown suggests. The American Enlightenment called for Fortean heroes.

"Hermes Never Taught Thee"

This sequence of anomalous events is interrupted by the appearance of a singular individual in Mettingen. "One sunny afternoon," Clara writes, "I was standing in the door of my house, when I marked a person passing close to the edge of the bank that was in front." Brown's class consciousness suddenly comes right to the fore in Clara's description of an encounter with a country person. "His gait," she goes on, "was rustic and aukward." His shabby shoes, "deeply discoloured by dust, which brush had never disturbed," as Clara notes, matched the status of the man and confirmed his "rustic" origins. Clara admits that there "was nothing

178   AMERICAN AURORA

remarkable in these appearances; they were frequently to be met with on the road, and in the harvest field."[65] And yet something about this passing stranger compels Clara's attention, though she cannot explain why. She lingers by the doorway long after he passes, "contemplating the image of this wanderer, and drawing, from outward appearances, those inferences with respect to the intellectual history of this person, which experience affords us." This is Clara's polite way of saying what she eventually states simply: "I reflected on the alliance which commonly subsists between ignorance and the practice of agriculture," she says, acknowledging that this passing stranger was clearly a working farmer.

The appearance of this country person must be read through Brown's eighteenth-century elite, urban, Quaker perspective. This scene is not meant to condemn Clara's frank disdain for country people, or even to suggest her elitism. She is merely expressing the opinions of Brown himself. Recall Brown's editorial on almanacs, discussed in Chapter 2, and the author's incredulity that country people could understand, much less actually *use* the detailed astronomical information he found therein. In painting a scene of this character's rustic origins and Clara's reaction within a novel that is "grounded in the radical pietist origins of William Penn's colony," Brown is expressing a tangle of class relations—rural versus urban, working versus leisured, and superstitious versus Enlightened—that his contemporary audience would have recognized well.[66]

As Clara goes on about her day, she overhears a knock on the door, which her servant girl opens. Clara hears snatches of a conversation: a polite request for a glass of buttermilk, a quick answer that the house has no one, and a strange reply: "Aye, but there is some in the dairy yonder. Thou knowest as well as I, though Hermes never taught thee, that though every dairy be an house, every house is not a dairy." Clara's serving girl does not precisely follow the stranger's meaning. Most of Brown's readers today probably find themselves in the same position of understanding as Clara's servant in interpreting this scene: here comes a dusty farmer, whose country accent mingles with references to Hermes. This character, and his exchange with the servant, almost meaningless to us today, would have been immediately recognizable to a Philadelphia audience aware of the almanacs of Daniel Leeds in which the philosophy of Hermes Trismegistus blended seamlessly with the local theory and practice of agriculture in a context of radical Protestantism.[67]

And so a Hermetic farmer suddenly intrudes on the Enlightened sanctum of the Wieland children, and a character who is utterly mysterious to today's readers (but likely appeared as a walking stereotype to Brown's immediate audience) enters the novel. Clara eventually formally meets the man, named Carwin, through Pleyel, who had met him in Spain during his travels in Europe.[68] Carwin joins their little group, and when he is asked for his perspective on the anomalous events that have troubled them, Clara is impressed with his response: "If he did not persuade us, that human beings are, sometimes, admitted into a sensible intercourse with the author of nature, he, at least, won over our inclination to the cause."[69] Not only is Carwin a Hermetic farmer in the familiar early Pennsylvania mold, his understanding of miracles seems to harken back to Hermetic Christian authors covered in Chapter 1, like Johann Arndt and Paracelsus: God is nature's author, and paranormal phenomena may be understood as artifacts of God's handwriting in nature's book.[70] Pleyel and Theodore listen politely while holding their philosophical positions: Theodore "maintained the probability of celestial interference," while "Pleyel was by no means equally credulous."[71]

After Carwin's introduction, the anomalies that plague the Wieland family and Pleyel escalate. Clara hears threatening voices not only on the ridge of the Schuylkill, but in her own home. Strange lights are seen in the woods around Mettingen. After Clara hears the voices of two strange men in her closet conspiring to murder her, Pleyel, "who treated my fears with ridicule," moves into the room next door to assuage her fears.[72] Her fears are discovered to be well founded one night when she discovers Carwin hiding in her closet, who seems to threaten her with rape before he complains of being thwarted by some power "beyond the compass of human organs."[73] Carwin flees, his mysterious powers and ill intent revealed if not fully explained.

With Carwin's villainy exposed, the central tragedy of the novel begins to unfold. The very next day, Pleyel accuses Clara of some kind of sexual impropriety with Carwin. She is devastated and dishonored by the false accusation. Returning home to Mettingen after traveling into the city to explain herself to Pleyel, Clara arrives to see strange lights and a terrifying apparition at the foot of her stairs, with "lips were stretched as in the act of shrieking, and the eyes emitted sparks, which, no doubt, if I had been unattended by a light, would have illuminated like the coruscations of a meteor."[74] She goes on to speculate on the nature of the sparks that flew from the eyes of the apparition, and the lights that she has seen in the woods of Mettingen. "Now, for the first time, suspicions were suggested as to the nature of the light which I had seen," she writes. "Was it possible to have been the companion of that supernatural visage; a meteorous refulgence producible at the will of him to whom that visage belonged, and partaking of the nature of that which accompanied my father's death?"[75] The meteor-eyed apparition, the lights in the woods, the luminous column that killed her father: all of these events seem connected and remain unexplained.[76]

After seeing the apparition, Clara finds the body of her sister-in-law, Theodore's wife, Catherine. Clara is struck numb and is unable or unwilling to leave Catherine's body, when eventually her brother appears. "What could I say?" she asks. "I was mute, and poured forth those tears on his account, which my own unhappiness had been unable to extort." Her sorrow is overcome with a recognition that all is not well with her brother: "After a silence and a conflict which I could not interpret, he lifted his eyes to heaven, and in broken accents exclaimed, 'This is too much! Any victim but this, and thy will be done.'" Clara realizes, at length, that her brother is speaking with a presence invisible to her, and that the victim under threat is not Catherine, but herself.

The lives of the Wieland children unravel. Theodore resists the divine command to murder his sister. Eventually, Clara is found by a distant relative of her mother, who informs her that all four of Theodore and his wife Catherine's children have been found dead. Clara succumbs to a delirium-induced illness, and falls under the care of her distant relation. Eventually she learns that the killer has been captured and has confessed to the murder of the Wieland family. Her uncle is hesitant to give her news of the details of the case, but when he assures her that Carwin is not the murderer, Clara becomes incensed and demands information. Her relative places news of the confession in her hand and walks out of the room.

Clara opens the papers and reads her brother's confession: "It is needless to say that God is the object of my supreme passion," he writes. "I have cherished, in his presence, a single and upright heart. I have thirsted for the knowledge of his will. I have burnt with ardour to approve my faith and my obedience."[77] Theodore's confession describes his religious zeal and overpowering urge for divine approval. Even in his mania, the reader can clearly hear the voice of a young boy deprived of a father in his accounting of himself. He describes an afternoon in which he slipped into a state of religious reverie while walking to his sister's house. He arrived to find her missing, and as he was leaving the house, he beheld an apparition: "I opened my eyes and found all about me luminous and glowing," Theodore writes. "It was the element of heaven that flowed around. Nothing but a fiery stream was at first visible; but, anon, a shrill voice from behind called upon me to attend." Theodore Wieland's luminous vision recalls some of the Quaker testimonies described earlier—and his use of the words "fiery stream" mirrors exactly the use of the phrase in Kelpius's letter to Esther Palmer and the King James book of Daniel.[78] He goes on: "I turned: It is forbidden to describe what I saw: Words, indeed, would be wanting to the task. The lineaments of that being, whose veil was now lifted, and whose visage beamed upon my sight, no hues of pencil or of language can pourtray."[79] The apparition began to speak to Wieland, apparently aware of the content of his prayers: "Thy prayers are heard. In proof of thy faith, render me thy wife." Wieland proceeds to lure his wife to Clara's home, where he kills her, before returning to his own home after being commanded by the voice of the apparition to kill his children.

Brown based this murder, like the death of the elder Wieland, on a contemporary incident that made its way into American newspapers. The Yates family murders took place in Tomhannock, New York, in 1781, and were recorded in testimony given to a magazine reporter. Mr. James Yates, a young husband and father of five, described relaxing with his wife by the fire when "a new light shown into the room, and upon looking up I beheld two Spirits, one at my right hand and one at my left." So far, these events sound like the Quaker testimonies of the luminous presence of God. Brown would have noticed these similarities as well. Yates reported that the spirits commanded him to "destroy all my *idols*," at which point Yates threw his Bible into the fire. Mrs. Yates, who apparently saw neither the light nor the spirits, was trying to recover the Bible when her husband fled the house, took up an ax, killed his own horse, and destroyed his sleigh. Mrs. Yates begged him to calm down, when the spirits again whispered to Yates: "You have still more idols (said he), look at your wife and children."[80]

Both the fictional Theodore Wieland and historical James Yates understood the appearance of luminous beings as a proof of God's existence and their own special status as revelators—a situation that, in both cases, carries obvious allusions to the binding of Isaac by his father in Genesis. The Yates family murders were a nationally known sensation, coming from a part of the country that would spend the better part of the following century repeatedly "burning over" with waves of religious zeal.[81] Brown's depiction of a fictionalized version of the Yates family murders suggests an implicit critique not only of the religious environment of the early Republic, but of the mechanism of revelation itself. Specifically, Brown is suggesting a moral condemnation of the willingness of the revelator to act on *any* divine command, no matter how atrocious. The only difference, Brown implies, between a respected Quaker like John Woolman and a murderer like James Yates is what their respective beings of light commanded them to do.

As Clara begins to realize that the machinations of Carwin are behind strange voices and the lights in the sky at Mettingen, she speculates on how a human being might use paranormal or religious knowledge against others: "Where is the proof, said I, that daemons may not be subjected to the controul of men?" Catching herself slipping into the kinds of speculation that she ridicules in country people, she pauses: "The dogmas of the vulgar, with regard to this subject, are glaringly absurd; but though these may justly be neglected by the wise, we are scarcely justified in totally rejecting the possibility that men may obtain supernatural aid." We must remember that in Brown's eighteenth-century use of the Latin word "vulgar," he is not referring to coarse speech, but *coarse people*— country people. The opinions of such people might "justly be neglected by the wise," Clara posits, but how can we doubt "the possibility that men may obtain supernatural aid"? She goes on, carefully distinguishing her own elite perspective from what she considers base superstitions: "The dreams of superstition are worthy of contempt," she writes. "Witchcraft, its instruments and miracles, the compact ratified by a bloody signature, the apparatus of sulpherous smells and thundering explosions, are monstrous and chimerical. These have no part in the scene over which the genius of Carwin presides."

182   AMERICAN AURORA

Brown continues to use Clara's voice for his own opinions, distinguishing between the believable events recorded in the journals of Florence and New York and the contemptible beliefs of the stargazing country people. There are no devils, no talking goats, nothing from the *Malleus Maleficarum* to be found in the countryside of Pennsylvania, Brown writes. But how can we doubt the animate, intelligent presences on which these superstitions find belief? Clara seems to speak for Brown again, from that Fortean position between Theodore and Pleyel, between Cotton Mather and Thomas Jefferson: "That conscious beings, dissimilar from human, but moral and voluntary agents as we are, some where exist, can scarcely be denied. That their aid may be employed to benign or malignant purposes, cannot be disproved."[82] This is not your grandmother's superstition, he practically shouts at the reader. Brown paints a world in which Enlightenment hubris leaves us vulnerable to a subtle, animate, intelligent cosmos.

The novel climaxes as Carwin confronts Clara and confesses his role in the heinous killings and visions of the people of Mettingen. The reader is finally shown the mechanism of Carwin's power: "You are not apprized of the existence of a power which I possess," Carwin says. "I know not by what name to call it. It enables me to mimic exactly the voice of another, and to modify the sound so that it shall appear to come from what quarter, and be uttered at what distance I please."[83] Carwin goes on to explain his central role in many of the important events of the novel: whispering to the Wieland children as they made their way around the cliffs and hills of Mettingen, and convincing Pleyel that he and Clara were having an affair.

Brown explains the powers of Carwin in a footnoted reference:

> BILOQUIUM, or ventrilocution. Sound is varied according to the variations of direction and distance. The art of the ventriloquist consists in modifying his voice according to all these variations, without changing his place. See the work of the Abbe de la Chappelle, in which are accurately recorded the performances of one of these artists, and some ingenious, though unsatisfactory speculations are given on the means by which the effects are produced.[84]

Brown is referring here to the work of Joannes Baptista de La Chapelle (1710–1792), a French mathematician and acoustician whose 1772 book *Le Ventriloque, ou l'engastrimthye* has been noted by Leigh Eric Schmidt as "peculiarly influential," despite its exclusion from "the standard genealogies of the Enlightenment's production of a critical study of religion."[85] La Chapelle's original contribution, writes Schmidt, was a reinvention of "ventriloquism as a generalized category for the rationalistic explanations of religion's most puzzling vocal phenomena."[86]

In La Chapelle's analysis, *all* auditory religious phenomena could be attributed to this strange talent, whose limitations were understood to be essentially boundless. The range of the voice could be extended, the sound of the voice itself could be modified to imitate another, and perhaps most importantly, the voice of a skilled ventriloquist could be "duplicated and disjoined from the body of the speaker."[87] The Witch of Endor, the Oracle at Delphi, and the Inuit shaman could all now be recognized not as technicians of the supernatural, but as curiously endowed performers. We do not need to wonder why La Chappelle's popular book has escaped the standard genealogies the Enlightenment's critical study of religion: as a work of acoustics and religious history, *Le Ventriloque* is almost farcical in its reduction of its source material and its overestimation of the abilities of the voice. For his part, Brown cites La Chappelle's popular book even as he notes that "unsatisfactory speculations are given on the means by which the effects are produced."[88]

Brown's portrayal of Carwin is somewhat hobbled by his simultaneous insistence that Carwin's powers "can scarcely be denied to be real," and that they are natural human faculties requiring nothing but vocal cords—an explanation that he openly finds wanting. In his fictionalized portrayal of La Chapelle's critique of the aural history of religion, Brown developed Carwin into a possessor of *all* superhuman aural faculties. Carwin is portrayed as a Hermetic farmer, a rustic and villainous Charles Xavier, wandering the banks of the Schuylkill River in Brown's novel. By relying on the still-nascent science of acoustics, La Chapelle both provided the source material for Carwin and undercut Brown's ability to fully understand the character he had created, an amalgam of the strange aural powers described throughout the history of religions.

Having explained his powers and his willingness to use them, Carwin's ventriloquy is revealed as a mechanism for many of the mysterious events of the novel: he denies, however, any complicity in the death of the Wieland family or in the revelations of Theodore, a denial that Clara rejects. Theodore bursts into the house, apparently escaped from prison and intent on making his sister another sacrifice to God. Clara, in her terror, accuses Carwin of being the source of the strange voices, although in her internal monologue, she still suspects that he may be innocent of being the voice of God that her brother hears. Theodore moves to kill his sister when a voice from the ceiling commands him to stop. Theodore asks the voice if he has been led by delusions all along, and the voice affirms it. Theodore, despairing, stabs himself in the neck.

As the novel reaches its denouement, Clara writes from three years after the incidents. Her house in Mettingen has burned down, and she has moved to Europe with Pleyel, her new husband. Carwin, filled with remorse, has moved deeper into the countryside, presumably near his brother toward the mouth of the Lehigh River, and has again taken up farming. Although Carwin's ventriloquy explains many of the events of the novel, a great deal remains unresolved. At the very end, Clara writes, "I leave you to moralize on this tale. . . . If [Theodore]

184   AMERICAN AURORA

Wieland had framed juster notions of moral duty, and of the divine attributes; or if I had been gifted with ordinary equanimity or foresight, the double-tongued deceiver would have been baffled and repelled."[89] Brown does not leave much room for ambiguity in his invitation to the reader: the novel is meant to deliver an ultimately moral message on personal responsibility for the interpretation of paranormal phenomena within a twofold critique of Enlightenment hubris and traditional religious belief.

The Great Derangement

In an introductory essay to *Wieland*, Jay Fliegelman summarizes the essential meaning of the novel to most scholars who examine it: "*Wieland* reminds us— from the vantage point of the earliest years of American fiction—that our national literature is, inescapably, a political literature."[90] While it might come as a surprise after reading the above summary, *Wieland* has indeed been interpreted as a novel whose central concerns are political: most often, with the contestation of authority in a young republic. Shirley Samuels, for instance, has suggested that the orphaning of Clara and Theodore following the death of their father is meant to be read as analogous to the young United States, suddenly freed from the authority of the British Empire.[91] Even Peter Kafer, whose research established that Brown's novel was "grounded in the radical pietist origins of William Penn's colony," interprets many of the events therein as revolutionary allegories. Brown's depiction of the death of the elder Wieland, Kafer argues, is meant to recall the opening battles of the American Revolution. Kafer's argument rests on the sound of the light on the hill, which Brown describes as "a loud report, like the explosion of a mine." Of this scene, Kafer writes, "There are unquestionably echoes here of 1777 Philadelphia."[92]

Echoes of 1777 or not, it must be acknowledged that these political interpretations of the novel are unavoidably subtextual. Nowhere in the text do Brown's characters discuss or even express an interest in government or politics, despite the abundant space that Brown devotes to their discussions and inner thoughts. What is *not* subtextual is the subject of these discussions and ruminations: the philosophical tension between religion, rationality, and the religious landscape of early Pennsylvania. While the scholarly interest in revolutionary politics and nascent statehood is a valuable frame of reference for interpreting a text from eighteenth-century America, it is also possible that such a reading can overestimate the importance of such themes in the text, if indeed those themes are present in *Wieland* at all.

In the analysis that follows, I interpret Brown's novel on the basis suggested in his conclusion: as a twofold moralizing narrative that attacks overconfidence and hubris in what Charles Fort would call the twin dominants: in the sense-based Enlightenment rationality portrayed by Pleyel, who ultimately retreats from any phenomenon that defies his philosophy; and in the faith-based submission to traditional religion portrayed by Theodore Wieland, who hears in every voice a personal message to him from God. Between these two ideologies is our hero, Clara, who hears in the anomalous lights and voices neither error of the senses nor a personal message from God—but confirmation of her place in a world that she ultimately does not understand. As stated in the introduction, Brown's novel is entirely based on the challenge of interpreting paranormal phenomena.

Despite the early date of 1798, the use of the supernatural in fiction was still relatively new when Brown must have imagined the story of *Wieland*—and reading the novel today, he is clearly operating beyond the boundaries of genre as he sketches the trials of the Wieland family. Indeed, there was not much of a "genre" for him to lean on at the time. As scholars like E. J. Clery have shown, the first instances of English supernatural fiction, works like Horace Walpole's *The Castle of Otranto* (1764) and Anne Radcliffe's *The Mysteries of Udolpho* (1794), are "today identified and dealt with by literary critics as examples of the Gothic novel, as if that label were already securely in place by the time of their writing."[93] Rather, Clery suggests, these early works must be seen as "breakthroughs" in their own right, of the "barriers to the fictional use of the marvellous."[94] Even before the genre was established, Brown himself was certainly aware of these novels as new and unusual literary products: "The Castle of Otranto laid the foundation of a style of novel writing, which was carried to perfection by Mrs. Radcliff, and which may be called the *terrific style*," Brown wrote in a magazine in 1805.[95]

The fact of the "breakthrough" that Clery describes is evidenced in Walpole's apology for even including the supernatural in *Otranto*, which was initially published as a lost Italian manuscript from the Middle Ages rather than the product of Walpole's imagination. "Miracles, visions, necromancy, dreams, and other preternatural events, are exploded now even from romances," Walpole writes in his preface. Respectable authors in *any* genre today (today being 1762) simply cannot portray such events, Walpole acknowledges. And yet, "That was not the case when our author wrote; much less when the story itself is supposed to have happened," he writes. "Belief in every kind of prodigy was so established in those dark ages, that an author would not be faithful to the manners of the times, who should omit all mention of them." An author cannot faithfully present the premodern without a few miracles, visions, necromancy, or dreams, Walpole tentatively suggests. He continues to reinforce his own apology: "He is not bound to believe them himself, but he must represent his actors as believing them." This is not a matter of my own belief, Walpole writes, feigning analytical distance like the social scientists studying the supernatural who would appear after him in the century that followed. Walpole appends a final request for

186   AMERICAN AURORA

excuse: "If this air of the miraculous is excused, the reader will find nothing else unworthy of his perusal."

Walpole's preface shows that during the late eighteenth century, the time of Brown's writing, the paranormal itself was subject to a kind of temporal orientalism. Such wonders can appear in Europe's darkened past, but not today. This temporal orientalism shaped the nature of the fantastic itself by reshaping the stories that could be told about it, especially as various genres of "weird" and "fantastic" fiction emerged to carry such stories in the later centuries. Literature demands paranormal phenomena, and yet paranormal phenomena can happen in the distant past, or the distant future, but never *here*, never *now*, never *us*.

Brown's writing turns this temporal orientalism on its head by putting the "air of the miraculous" on vivid display in the here, now, us. In deliberately situating his novel in the radical Protestant origins of the colony, with abundant reference to the Quaker revelations, the Wissahickon hermitage, and Hermetic agriculture, Brown hoped to show that the "past is never dead. It's not even past," to quote William Faulkner. In Charles Brockden Brown's intellectual context, John Locke's theory of mind had privileged sight among the modes of perception to the exclusion of largely invisible forces of traditional religion, to the extent that, as Clery notes, sight simply "became a metaphor for knowledge."[96] In frontloading the *sensory* aspects of traditional religion in early Pennsylvania (things like voices, visions, apparitions, and intelligent beings of light), *Wieland* shows that the Enlightenment's reliance on sensory knowledge, and sight in particular, will not necessarily lead to a great decline in religious belief or rational behavior. What about the Yates murders, Brown asks? What about skilled manipulators like Carwin? Just *how far* should we follow our senses?

In this light, Brown's novel can be read as a long-form exercise in a philosophical problem that the poet John Greenleaf Whittier would state simply in the following century any account of an "apparition of a disembodied spirit" is a "subversion of all known laws of matter and mind," Whittier writes. But "What will that avail the man who has actually seen a ghost? Facts before philosophy always."[97] Whittier could be addressing Pleyel directly: all the reason in the world cannot prepare us for the moment when the senses fail, or effect precedes cause. "If a man is *certain* he has seen a thing," Whittier writes, "that is the end of the matter."[98] What does it mean to reject paranormal phenomena in favor of sensory reason when our senses perceive paranormal phenomena?

But Brown's critique is more comprehensive than Whittier's. *Wieland* opens with a prefatory statement cautioning his readers against being too quick to reject the portrayal of extraordinary events in the novel:

The incidents related are extraordinary and rare. Some of them, perhaps, approach as nearly to the nature of miracles as can be done by that which is not truly miraculous. It is hoped that intelligent readers will not disapprove of the manner in which appearances are solved, but that the solution will be found to correspond with the known principles of human nature. The power which the principal person is said to possess can scarcely be denied to be real. It must be acknowledged to be extremely rare; but no fact, equally uncommon, is supported by the same strength of historical evidence.[99]

Just as he concluded his novel with his own moralizing interpretation, Brown frontloads the primary role of paranormal phenomena in the narrative, almost offering to hold readers' hands as they approach what he knows will be a "difficult" text.

Brown is performing a significant literary move in this prefatory statement. In his 2007 book *Ecology without Nature*, Timothy Morton describes a technique in environmental writing that they calls "ecomimesis," in which the author addresses the reader directly beyond the frame of the narrative concerning the environment of the writing. Morton uses the example of Thoreau at the beginning of *Walden*: "When I wrote the following pages . . . I lived alone, in the woods, a mile from any neighbor." Morton shows us how nature writers use ecomimesis to "break out of the normative aesthetic frame, go beyond art."[100] What is the purpose of ecomimesis in fiction? It is a direct statement from author to audience, setting the stage, stepping outside the constraints of narration in order to reach a mutual understanding on terms. "Ecomimesis is an authenticating device."[101]

To use Morton's term, Brown's prefatory statement at the opening of Wieland might be viewed as another form of ecomimesis. Brown steps beyond the frame of the narrative to address the reader on the validity of the phenomena therein: an eighteenth-century version of the "based on a true story" marketing technique. Brown wanted his readers to understand his text and his sources clearly. Brown anticipates here what would become, and still is, the most common criticism leveled against his work: his use of fantastic events and powers as plot devices. These events and powers are not fantastic or impossible, he writes. They are merely uncommon and poorly understood. Rejecting such events is putting philosophy *before* fact, Brown suggests. His novel demonstrates two polarities of this common mistake, the attempt to overwrite lived experience with prefabricated ideology: Are you a Pleyel or a Theodore?

Brown's ecomimetic preface and his moralizing conclusion reinforce the central themes and challenges of the novel: the interpretation of paranormal phenomena and what he saw as the dangers of overconfidence in the powers of Enlightenment reason *and* traditional religion. Why, then, are these themes, so clearly signposted, often placed on the backburner of critical response to the novel? In his 2016 book *The Great Derangement: Climate Change and the Unthinkable*, Amitav Ghosh puts forward a satisfying explanation. The modern

188 AMERICAN AURORA

novel is overwhelmingly a product of an Enlightenment ideology, Ghosh argues. "Probability and the modern novel are in fact twins," Ghosh writes, "born at about the same time, among the same people, under a shared star that destined them to work as vessels for the containment of the same kind of experience."[102] This experience was, above all, one of bourgeois regularity: quoting the literary theorist Franco Moretti, Ghosh writes that most important to this portrayal in eighteenth-century novels was "a world of few surprises, fewer adventures, and no miracles at all."[103]

The same argument that Ghosh makes for the novel can be made for the discipline of history, which was developing around the same time. As Robert Carroll and Stephen Prickett write, the intellectual discipline that we call history today arose from the Enlightenment trend of suppressing and denying anything that escaped the boundaries of their hastily defined and inconsistent category "nature":

> If twentieth-century historians have accepted the premises of Hume and Niebuhr that "miracles do not happen," they have learned, after Schleiermacher, to read that statement, too, hermeneutically. The century that discovered quantum mechanics, quarks, charms, and black holes has much less certainty about precisely what are the "laws of nature" than the eighteenth or the nineteenth. Einstein's famous statement that not merely have we learned to think that the universe is very queer, but that it is "much queerer than we think," has found many echoes. The modern historian excludes miracles not because "they do not happen" but because that is the way in which we have cautiously learned to define "history."[104]

As Carroll and Pricket note, our approach to historical material often simply recapitulates the philosophical trends and attitudes of the eighteenth century, in which the rules of history developed and the world we inhabit seemed much simpler. Indeed, reading people like Hume, one gets the sense that the eighteenth century saw itself on the precipice of a total understanding of the cosmos. The Enlightenment cast a long shadow that the humanities and the sciences have taken centuries to become aware of, much less to take a step into some brighter light. The magnitude of Brown's critique becomes clearer in Carroll and Pricket's analysis.

With this perspective in mind, we can better understand the need for the prefatory statements that open novels like *Otranto* and *Wieland*. Walpole used a kind of temporal orientalism as an excuse for portraying the miraculous. Brown, on the other hand, begs his reader to understand that his novel portrays phenomena that "approach as nearly to the nature of miracles as can be done by that which is not truly miraculous." Both novels open with an apology for portraying an

THE LONG SHADOW OF THE ENLIGHTENMENT   189

animate and intelligent cosmos because they are the products of a period that insisted that the cosmos was inert, the exact ideology that Amitav Ghosh predicts "will come to be known as the time of the Great Derangement."[105]

As Ghosh points out, *literary* fiction—the kind of fiction that draws serious intellectual attention—has failed almost entirely to attend adequately to non-human beings, forces, and events. Despite the overwhelming popularity of su-pernatural themes in popular fiction, the notion of barriers to the appearance of the supernatural in literary fiction today persists, and such themes have become a matter of almost literary classism. This includes environmental phenomena, as Ghosh notes, but more significantly for our purposes, Ghosh sees the exclu-sion of nonhumans and the exclusion of the paranormal as part and parcel of one another.[106] In excluding the uncanny, the nonhuman, and anything beyond the "moral adventure" of the individual, Ghosh highlights the ways in which the development of English literature, following the Enlightenment context of its de-velopment, drew increasingly tight borders around the acceptable contents of the novel. The persistent theme of the challenge of interpreting paranormal phe-nomena was the central meaning of *Wieland*, and with Amitav Ghosh's analysis in mind, we can see more clearly why literary scholars seem to look right past the text itself in their haste to connect the story of the Wieland family with 1776.

Long Shadow Fallen

Charles Brockden Brown's *Wieland* shows us a late eighteenth-century Quaker perspective on one of the central themes of the life and legacy of Johannes Kelpius: challenge of interpreting paranormal phenomena. Through the writings of Paracelsus and Johann Arndt, miraculous phenomena were recognized just as Carwin describes them: as a kind of "intercourse" with "the author of nature," as legible artifacts of God's mind in the phenomenal landscape of creation. For this reason, miracles were a matter of central concern in early Pietist theology and communal life. As Kelpius and his colleagues described repeatedly, "Ectases, Revelations, Inspirations, Illuminations, Inspeakings, Prophesies, Apparitions" were at the very heart of religious life for the early Pietists: they were nothing less than the fingerprints of God on the "Bodys of Man or Microcosm."[107]

In the following chapter, we will see the memory of Kelpius persist through the eighteenth, nineteenth, and twentieth centuries. In many of these cases, we will find only a vague distortion, a legendary hermit on the cliffside who serves as a poetic image or voice for various authors' theological warnings, romantic speculations, and personal claims to occult power. In other cases, we see authors who seem to understand the memory of Kelpius as Brown does: as a challenge to the hubris of the Enlightenment, as a paradoxical reminder of a period in history

190   AMERICAN AURORA

whose curtain was rapidly falling, in which the world was a living thing inviting communication and interpretation rather than an inert machine.

Charles Brockden Brown's *Wieland* was and remains the single most substantial and influential posthumous appearance of Johannes Kelpius, despite the fact that the novel and its inspiration are only glancingly recognized as such today. And for all his authorial liberties taken in the portrayal of the elder Wieland, Brown's novel really does manage to point the overconfident eyes of the eighteenth century toward a place and a period that, he imagined, refuted their overconfidence in reason: a ruined little cottage among the cedars on the edge of the cliff over the Wissahickon.

6

"Weird as a Wizard"

History and Literature in the Emergence of the American Kelpius Legend

A hermit's hut. What a subject for an engraving!
—Gaston Bachelard, *The Poetics of Space*

All folk songs are true.

—Jean Ritchie

Shortly after I started to work on the project that eventually became this book, I mentioned my research on Kelpius to a friend of mine who had grown up in Philadelphia. My friend is an avid cyclist, and he was very familiar with the Wissahickon Valley and the little network of urban parks that enclose it today. I watched a flicker of recognition flash across his face as I described Kelpius and the Wissahickon hermitage, and he began to describe a dim memory of a legend of a hermit in Wissahickon Valley Park. But as he went on with his description, he couldn't remember if it was supposed to be a ghost story, if there was a real hermit, or just something he was simply struggling to remember clearly. Despite having never heard the name "Johannes Kelpius," the hermit of the Wissahickon was an ambient, spectral presence in Philadelphia and in my friend's imagination.

Michel Foucault has written that "the great obsession of the nineteenth century was, as we know, history: with its themes of development and of suspension, of crisis, and cycle, themes of the ever-accumulating past, with its great preponderance of dead men and the menacing glaciation of the world."[1] As we saw in the previous chapter, if the intellectual obsessions of the eighteenth century were revolution and Enlightenment, with a new kind of utopian faith in the endless possibilities waiting in the future, the nineteenth century began to take stock, take an anxious look backward, and, in some places, this gaze locked and dwelled on figures that the Enlightenment had rendered *weird*.

In this final chapter, I will look at the afterlives of Johannes Kelpius, reaching through their earliest stage in the eighteenth century, before fully blossoming and overtaking the memory of the man in the nineteenth and twentieth, as they continue to do today. In the previous chapter, I considered Charles Brockden

American Aurora. Timothy Grieve-Carlson, Oxford University Press. © Oxford University Press 2024.
DOI: 10.1093/oso/9780197765562.003.0007

192   AMERICAN AURORA

Brown's 1798 novel *Wieland* as the earliest robust appearance of Johannes Kelpius in American literature. Here I arrange and interrogate a more varied array of literature. These literatures fall into two basic categories: the "legendary Kelpius," the distinct literary figure who emerges from the collision between Kelpius and the nineteenth century's "obsession" with history, and the "historical Kelpius," roughly, the figure who emerges from primary sources rather than the literary and historical imagination. As we will see, over the eighteenth and nineteenth centuries, these literatures collide, merge, and blur, transforming Kelpius into a better-known and more comprehensively misunderstood shared memory: the ambient, spectral presence not only in my friend's imagination, but in the modern historiography of American religion.

Mühlenberg's Report

The earliest contribution to the legendary Kelpius in the primary literature comes from journals of Henry Melchior Mühlenberg, a Lutheran minister dispatched to the colonies by the church authorities in Halle to compete with Nicolaus Zinzendorf's (1700–1760) major missionary successes in Pennsylvania.[2] The early form of German Pietism we engaged in Chapter 1 was a nascent, radical, and easily oppressed novel religious group: by 1740, Pietist thought was an ascendent force in mainstream Lutheran theology, and the orthodox ministry found itself in active competition for congregants with figures like Zinzendorf.[3]

Mühlenberg's writings during his time in the colony have become some of the most widely cited primary sources of German life in Pennsylvania during the eighteenth century. I have already leaned on Mühlenberg's journal for his mention of an old woman's deathbed description of learning "delicate impressions of true fear of God" during her childhood lessons from Seelig and Kelpius on the ridge in Chapter 3.[4] Mühlenberg's descriptions, compiled from his journals for regular reports back to the Lutheran leadership in Germany, make abundant references to the variety and veracity of the informants he relies on. While the woman's deathbed description of the school on the ridge can be considered accurate because she describes Seelig by name, and because the hermits' brief foray into public education is confirmed in a letter from Daniel Falckner, Mühlenberg goes on to relate a series of stories from informants who seem to be drawing on something other than firsthand experience.

Mühlenberg's descriptions of Kelpius and Seelig must be treated with care for several reasons: first, he is relaying information on Kelpius and company more than thirty years after Kelpius died, and at no point does he describe any meeting between himself and Johan Seelig or Conrad Matthai, the Wissahickon hermits who were still living in 1742. Second, Mühlenberg found himself in Philadelphia *in the first place* as a competitor with a later form of Pietistic thought that was enjoying wide popularity, Zinzendorf's Moravian church. While it seems that Zinzendorf recognized the hermits as predecessors, and perhaps even went out of his way to meet with Matthai, Mühlenberg would not have seen allies or folk heroes in the elderly hermits or the memory of Kelpius. Indeed, the competition between orthodoxy and Pietistic forms of Lutheranism seems to color his description of the Wissahickon hermits:

> Several years ago I was asked from Germany about certain *Canditatis theologia*, which came to the country a long time before me.... As much as I can get news from one or another impartial old acquaintance, it seems to me that most of the former candidates have kept little or nothing of the sacred sacraments ordained by Christ, the baptism and the Lord's Supper, which were inspired by the Spirit of God, and the word of God written down by the prophets, evangelists and apostles respected as dead letters, and on the other hand had much to do with the heavenly Sophia, with contemplation, and at the same time with alchemy.[5]

If we rely on the primary evidence covered in Chapter 3, Mühlenberg's "impartial old acquaintance" seemed to have the facts about halfway right. Kelpius's overwhelming emphasis on scripture and his biblical theology is either ignored, suppressed, or simply unknown. Mühlenberg was also misinformed on Kelpius's position regarding the sacraments and baptism. Kelpius writes effusively about the ritual of water baptism in the letter to Esther Palmer.[6] Finally, Mühlenberg makes a somewhat heresiological reference to three different beliefs and practices: to devotion to Sophia, to contemplation, and to alchemy.

Mühlenberg's informant is accurate on all three counts. Devotion to Sophia, as an apotheosis of divine wisdom and the feminine aspect of an androgyne God, was popularized throughout the seventeenth century, in particular through the writings of Jacob Böhme, and it was a major component of early Pietist devotional life. Kelpius makes reference to Sophia in the "Lamenting Voice" hymns and twice in his correspondence: in the letter to Esther Palmer and the letter to Steven Momfort. In fact, he does so specifically as an antithesis to orthodox Lutheran life and learning: "The Sophia from on high should be adored and instead of Temples or Universities, the Hearts of men should be consecrated."[7] Contemplation (*Beschaulichkeiten*) might refer to Kelpius's ascetic practice. As indicated below, Kelpius was interested in contemporary trends of "inner prayer," a form of meditative Christian practice that could well be described as contemplations. Finally, Mühlenberg's source is well informed on the alchemical focus of Kelpius and his colleagues, as we have seen repeatedly. Spiritual alchemy, contemplation and ecstasy, and Sophianic devotion were all quite common in seventeenth-century Pietism, but these esoteric practices were fading by the

194   AMERICAN AURORA

middle of the eighteenth century. Mühlenberg saw all three as only a cautionary tale of Pietistic excess and sin.

From his own orthodox perspective, Mühlenberg was right to be suspicious of and hostile to these practices, since these practices were innately suspicious and hostile of orthodoxy. Within less then a few decades, then, the memory of Kelpius's Christian devotion, biblical theology, and ascetic practice was declining in favor of an escalating interest in the more esoteric aspects of his religious life at Wissahickon. Mühlenberg either distorts the facts here he was misinformed: in either case, it did not take long at all for Kelpius's memory to begin to warp when left out in the rain.

Mühlenberg's reporting seems to decline in accuracy as it goes on. He turns to a figure called "Mr. G.," whom he refers to as "the oldest and most distinguished" of the Wissahickon group, described by a new informant, who was "eight and twenty years ago a credible man who was over sixty years old, who had also been with Mr. G. for various years, and had been a trusted friend."[8] At this stage, Mühlenberg's reporting turns into a complex mixture of factual information and demonstrable distortion. It is not precisely clear if "Mr. G" is Kelpius. Kelpius was not the oldest of the Wissahickon group, nor was he necessarily the most distinguished. It is unclear why a pseudonym would be necessary at all: Kelpius was a secluded figure, but his identity and presence on the Wissahickon was not a secret. The use of a pseudonym here, especially the mistaken first initial, seems to indicate the informant's confusion, rather than firsthand insight.

Mühlenberg's informant goes on: "Among other things, Mr. G had firmly believed that he would not die, that his body would not rot, but would be transformed, transfigured, . . . and that he, like Elijah, should be accepted."[9] This passage seems to derive from some genuine familiarity with Kelpius's theological ideas. In the letter to Esther Palmer, Kelpius describes a similar process for those entering "The Wilderness of the Elect of God," the final stage of the Threefold Wilderness State of which Elijah was one example. But nowhere in the letter does Kelpius presume that he himself had reached the third stage—indeed, his examples of those who have done so are extremely limited. For an almost chronically humble person like Kelpius, it is difficult to imagine him telling anyone that he considered himself alongside the spiritual stature of major biblical figures, or that he expected to be assumed into heaven like Elijah. This informant may have been connected with Kelpius's ideas from reading the extant letter to Esther Palmer or one of the copies that circulated later, or it may represent a half-remembered and mistaken conflation of the details of Kelpius's religious ideas and his own biography on the part of Mühlenberg's informant.

The final passage in Mühlenberg's report has become one of the best-known incidents from the life of Kelpius, and one of the most easily discredited. Earlier in his account, Mühlenberg refers to Kelpius being visited by distinguished

English and Scottish men who were interested in finding the *Lapidem*, the Latin alchemical technical term for what later occultists have called "the philosopher's stone," a fabled alchemical substance capable of turning base metals into gold and perfecting the human soul. Mühlenberg goes on:

> A few days before his death, Mr G. handed a tightly sealed box to his friend Daniel and seriously ordered him to throw it into the river called Schuylkill without delay. Daniel went to the water with it. But because he thought that this hidden treasure might still be useful to him and his fellow men; he hid the box on the bank and didn't throw it into [the river]. When he came back, Mr. G. looked at him sharply, and said: You did not throw the box into the water, but hid it on the bank, which frightened the honest Daniel, and believing that his friend's mind must be omniscient, he ran back to the water, and he really threw the box into it, and he saw and heard with astonishment, that the *Arcanum* in the water, as he put it, flashed [with lightning] and thunder. After he came back, Mr. G. called out to me: Now it is done, what I have told you to do.[10]

Most readers of this passage have associated this *Lapidem* with the box given to Mr. G's friend Daniel: the result being the legend that Johannes Kelpius, possessing the philosopher's stone in Philadelphia in 1707, commanded his friend to throw it into the Schuylkill River, where it rests to this day. The association between Kelpius and the philosopher's stone would continue unabated through the centuries: in 1909, the Philadelphia *Evening Star* ran a story with the headline "Philadelphia Girl Owns Stone of Wisdom" (Figure 6.1). in which the girl in question attributes her knowledge of the philosopher's stone to Kelpius, whom she described as originally acquiring the stone on the floor of a cave in India. By 1909, it seems, Kelpius was even getting swept up in a bit of occult orientalism.[11]

This final passage of Mühlenberg's report is, of course, a retelling and embellishment of Thomas Mallory's *Le Morte d'Arthur* for an audience in eighteenth-century Philadelphia. In *Morte d'Arthur*, King Arthur lies on his deathbed, mortally wounded from his final battle with Mordred. He commands his knight, Sir Bedivere, to throw Excalibur back into the lake where it came from, but Bedivere wavers at the last moment. As Tennyson puts it: "In act to throw: but at the last it seem'd / Better to leave Excalibur conceal'd." Bedivere returns and lies shamefully, which Arthur immediately sees through. Bedivere and Arthur enjoy the same song and dance that the legendary "Mr. G" and Daniel execute, before Bedivere finally gets up his nerve and throws Excalibur back into the lake, watching in wonder as the Lady of the Lake reaches out to claim the sword, symbolically concluding the supernatural sanction of Arthur's reign.

In the Mühlenberg variation, it is Kelpius rather than Arthur on his deathbed, but their roles are bizarrely analogous: Kelpius and Arthur both represent a

Figure 6.1 "Philadelphia Girl Owns Stone of Wisdom," *Philadelphia Evening Star*, August 14, 1900, 6. The image is captioned "The Sacred Stone of the Hermit Kelpius."

mythic past of the place where their stories are told: early England and early Philadelphia, respectively. But how did Mühlenberg come up with this fantastic story? Some of the basic details are right: Daniel Geissler was a real person who knew Kelpius, Kelpius really was interested in alchemy (but of a very specific Christian devotional alchemy), and he did live near the Schuylkill River—but everything else is clearly derived from *Morte d'Arthur*. It's not likely that Mühlenberg, who had little in the way of sympathy for Kelpius, would have contrived the story himself or reported it if he knew it to be false. Rather, it seems like one of Mühlenberg's various informants offered a genuine emergent folktale surrounding the death of Kelpius, absurdly but vividly told by and through the legend of King Arthur. A later variation of the legend appears in 1858, recorded by Horatio Jones, but Mr G. has been replaced by Johann Seelig, "who had a divining rod, which he directed should be cast into the water at his death. This was done, and the rod exploded with a loud noise," Jones records.[12] The legend evolved through the decades, with the divining rod replacing the *Lapidem* as a physical instrument of occult power.

Considered as a whole, Mühlenberg's report seems to include a strange mixture of firsthand information, second- and thirdhand accounts, and straight-up fantastic conflations of Johannes Kelpius with a figure no less a legend than King Arthur. All this is contained within just a little over a page in a Lutheran minister's notebook, gathered over chats with various informants in a backwater colony on the edges of the Lutheran world. Even just a few decades after his death, Kelpius's legendary profile had already swelled enormously. With this passage, Mühlenberg inaugurated what would become a permanent tendency in the secondary literature to distort and expand the person and powers of Kelpius.

The Philosopher of the Forest

The primary record does not maintain a consistent or coherent picture of Kelpius throughout the eighteenth century. Mühlenberg's report provides a valuable ethnographic snapshot of the popular image of Kelpius as of the middle of the century that, as we have seen, was an idiosyncratic mixture of accurate personal and theological information, quickly spinning out into a full-fledged mythos.

Instead, the sources from the period offer only scattered hints toward some level of public interest in Kelpius. One major indication of Kelpius's posthumous public profile occurred with the Germantown printer Peter Leibert's 1788 publication of *Several Lovely and Edifying Songs*, an anthology of early American hymnody in German, which included three of Kelpius's hymns. The title page of Leibert's pamphlet emphasizes the inclusion of "several, never before printed, and very edifying hymns by Joh. Kelpius, who already passed away 80 years ago in his blessed savior."[13] Leibert's front-page advertisement for rare Kelpius hymns in print includes the explanation: "At the request of many admirers, in the hope of edification, by Peter Leibert."[14] Who these "many admirers" were, exactly, goes unfortunately unexplained: all we have for certain is a brief textual indication that demand for Kelpius hymns was strong enough in 1788 for Peter Leibert to go to print with them. Leibert would also go on to append two of Kelpius's hymns to an 1800 Germantown edition of the *Confession of Faith*, a well-known Pietist text by Ernst Christoph Hochmanns von Hochenau.[15] In the printing activities of Peter Leibert, it seems there was sufficient growing interest in Kelpius to begin including his writings in standard editions of German Pietist devotional literature.

Beyond the world of radical Protestant devotional literature, there are hints of Kelpius's swelling public profile at the end of the eighteenth century. The first and most significant remains Charles Brockden Brown's portrayal of the elder Wieland in his 1798 novel *Wieland; or, The Transformation: An American Tale*. For reasons first suggested by scholars like Peter Kafer and Jon Butler, which were fully explored and elaborated upon in the previous chapter, Brown's depiction of the elder Wieland presents the most important appearance of Johannes Kelpius in early American literature. And as Kafer in particular has established, there is strong evidence to suggest that Brown was aware of and interested in the history of Kelpius and the Wissahickon group.[16]

198   AMERICAN AURORA

The nascent literary scene in Philadelphia at the turn of the nineteenth century was small by anyone's standards, and Charles Brockden Brown's awareness of the Wissahickon group may indicate a more generalized regional recollection, however distorted, of the Wissahickon hermits. The Philadelphia poet Phillip Freneau, writing mostly in the decades just before Brown was active, demonstrated more than a passing interest in the hermit as a literary trope. In his 1788 poem "On Retirement," Freneau portrays the hermit as a countercultural Romantic ideal:

> A hermit's house beside a stream,
> With forests planted round,
> Whatever it to you may seem
> More real happiness I deem
> Than if I were a monarch crown'd.[17]

It is tempting to read Freneau's portrayal of the "hermit's house beside a stream" and imagine the poet standing beside the ruin of the Wissahickon hermitage, looking over the river below, and imagining the life and legend of Johannes Kelpius.

In addition to his poetic depictions of the hermit life in works like "On Retirement" and "The Hermit of Saba," Freneau penned a series of essays entitled "The Philosopher of the Forest," published throughout the 1780s, in which he develops a character called "The Pilgrim" or "Philosopher," who seems to suggest the inspiration of a local occult hermit. The Philosopher was an immigrant who, after traveling the world, took up his residence "in the midst of a forest of considerable extent on the western side of the Delaware, not many miles from the beautiful and populous city of Philadelphia," from which he observes and critiques the world and its inhabitants.[18] As he does so, he works on a philosophical tract called *De Anima Mundi*—the subject of which, according to the Philosopher, is "the divine and incomprehensible intelligence which pervades and enlivens the immensity of matter, in the same manner as the body of man is put in motion by the actuating spring within it."[19] Freneau's Philosopher, then, was a hermit living in the forest just beyond Philadelphia who espoused an essentially Platonic-Hermetic philosophy while he criticized and rejected society at large. The resemblances between Freneau's Philosopher and Kelpius, while nowhere near as direct as the connections between Kelpius and Brown's elder Wieland, are intriguing, and merit consideration within our general analysis of Kelpius's appearance in history and literature.

Like Charles Brockden Brown, Freneau was at once a product and critic of the Enlightenment. His education led him to a rejection of what he considered traditional Christianity, and his deep reading in the classics of the ancient world shows through his poetry with a metaphysical posture that sounds almost modernist to the contemporary ear: Apollo shares a verse with Newton, and Christ is nowhere to be found. Like many of his Enlightenment contemporaries (and many of the modernist poets, for that matter), Freneau found a form of religious inspiration that was compatible with his fierce scientism in the esoteric literatures of Europe.[20] His poem "On the Honorable Emmanuel Swedenborg's Universal Theology" makes this clear:

> HERE truths divine in heavenly visions grow
> From the vast influx on our world below.
> Here, like the blaze of our material sun,
> Enlighten'd Reason proves that GOD IS ONE.[21]

In one particularly memorable passage of "The Philosopher of the Forest," Freneau portrays his hermit-Philosopher as an Enlightenment visionary on the order of Swedenborg. In this passage, Freneau's philosopher—deep in a visionary state—converses with an omniscient spirit referred to as "Superintendent of the Temple of Oblivion."[22] Here is a sample of their conversation, in which the hermit asks the Superintendent why human beings are subject to desires that cannot be fulfilled:

> Tell me, kind spirit, for what wise purpose could man have been . . . actuated by desires which [are] [n]ever meant to be . . . gratified, and tormented with expectations which, in the end, are answered only by delusions?
>
> THE miseries of your species, replied the spirit, are principally owing to the suggestions of the spirit of pride. What is the race of man, that they should be panting for habitations beyond the stars! You imagine yourselves the most curious work of the Deity because you possess five distinct senses—Believe me, there are beings in the universe that possess as many thousands.[23]

The Superintendent spirit's metaphysics displays a vision of spiritual reality deeply conditioned by a scientific understanding of the human perception, and the rapidly growing number of demonstrable physical phenomena that escaped direct sensory perception. Freneau's literary occultism was an attempted reconciliation of Enlightenment rationalism and the belief in a transcendent dimension of reality and a spiritual dimension of human life. Emerson suddenly seems late to his own party.

Freneau's writings represented an early American occult vision of the Enlightenment. Transcendent realities and omniscient spirits coexist with cutting-edge developments in natural philosophy and science. Unlike their contemporaries across the Atlantic, Charles Brockden Brown and Phillip

200 AMERICAN AURORA

Freneau's occult Enlightenment acknowledged esoteric knowledge and miraculous phenomena as harbingers of new horizons in the field of human knowledge, rather than troubling anomalies to be identified, isolated, and denied. In the early American literature of Brown and Freneau, miracles were poked and prodded by their characters and were central events of primary narrative and philosophical import, and such phenomena were *central* to the political and cultural critiques leveled in each author's work.

As scholars like Leigh Eric Schmidt have pointed out, popular American interest in solitude, self-reliance, and the simplicity of a solitary life in the natural world emerged as a major literary theme in the late eighteenth century and persists in the work of relatively ignored authors, like Freneau, into the titanic forces of American literature represented by Thoreau, Dickinson, and Muir.[24] While Freneau's interest in hermits and proximity to Kelpius is intriguing, it is important to remember that Freneau's work appeared during a period of general American interest in hermits.[25] Freneau's poetic and philosophical hermits coincided with best-selling contemporary hermit literature like James Buckland's 1786 *A Wonderful Discovery of a Hermit* and Samuel Brake's 1787 *An Account of the Wonderful Old Hermits Death, and Burial.*[26] Freneau's hermits cannot be directly tied to Kelpius with the same level of confidence with which Brown's elder Wieland character can, even if the similarities are clear and proximate. Freneau may have also been drawing on the local memory of Benjamin Lay, the Quaker radical who took to living in caves outside of Philadelphia later in the eighteenth century. Even in the local lore of Philadelphia, there were plenty of radical religious hermits to go around.

Chronicon Ephratense

Another important appearance of Kelpius in eighteenth-century literature comes to us through the chronicles of the Ephrata community, the monastic community established on the banks of the Cocalico River in Pennsylvania in the eighteenth century by Georg Conrad Beissel (1691–1768).[27] Beissel, who immigrated to Pennsylvania from Germany in 1720, would later claim that he emigrated in order to join the Kelpius community on the banks of the Wissahickon.[28] Arriving to find Kelpius dead and many of the Wissahickon hermits disbanded, Beissel revised his plans—but Beissel did have the chance to connect with Kelpius's friend and colleague Conrad Matthai.

The Ephrata community viewed Kelpius and the Wissahickon hermits as important predecessors, and their internal history, the 1786 *Chronicon Ephratense*, provides a clear and worthwhile snapshot of the perspective of a group who saw themselves as coreligionists and descendants of the Wissahickon hermits.

The Ephrata chroniclers saw Kelpius in particular as a kind of sainted forebear. The Wissahickon hermits "for a time were a peculiar light among men because of their holy living," the authors wrote. Kelpius's origin in Transylvania, some details of his education, and the date and company of his travel to Pennsylvania are accurately recorded.[29] The compilers of the *Chronicon* (Peter Miller, using the pseudonym "Brother Agrippa," edited a manuscript attributed to Jacob Gaas, "Brother Lamech") were clearly aware of the basic facts of Kelpius's life and religious thought. The *Chronicon* is also the first source to mention that "The Woman in the Wilderness" was something the Wissahickon hermits actually called themselves, in reference to Revelation 12.

If there is one area in which the influence of Kelpius on American religion must be clearly noted, it is in the history of the Ephrata community. Submitting to rigorous ascetic principles that Beissel learned, in part, from Conrad Matthai, the Ephrata monastics present a clear religious legacy that can, in part, be traced to Kelpius's own religious thought. Their literary output and printing operation were formidable, competing with Benjamin Franklin and distributing heterodox and Hermetic Christian literature to figures as significant as Joseph Smith.[30]

In the eighteenth century, we have thus far seen what can only be called literary and religious approaches to Kelpius and company in the primary record: the glimpse in Mühlenberg's report, a few hymns published in Germantown, the *Chronicon Ephratense*, and the literary work of figures like Brown and Freneau. By the turn of the nineteenth century, Kelpius and company began to appear in a new kind of literature: what might properly be called history, or something like it. Before turning to the emergence of Kelpius in the historical record proper, however, we have to contend with a particularly unusual appearance—or more accurately, attribution—of the Wissahickon group in a European source.

The Spiritual Travel of Conrad Matthai

As the eighteenth century passed and the religious climate in Europe continued to shift, German Pietism underwent continuous transformations based on social and intellectual pressures around it: by the dawn of the nineteenth century, Pietism was no longer threatened by an overzealous and oppressive Lutheran orthodoxy. Rather, German Pietists found themselves increasingly marginalized in Europe by an ascendance of Enlightenment thought and what would later be called the historical-critical approach within liberal theology. As we have seen in the previous chapter, the European Enlightenment was particularly hostile to paranormal phenomena. These events in which early German Pietists like Kelpius found such deep wells of meaning, the "strange things of the Invisible

202 AMERICAN AURORA

world," as Kelpius called them, were precisely the events that Enlightenment thought still struggled to deny.

It is no surprise, then, that some prolific late Pietist thinkers found themselves working to rehabilitate the miraculous for the European intelligentsia. Johann Heinrich Jung-Stilling (1740–1817) was a German Pietist author and medical doctor who defended popular religious thought from the rising tide of Enlightenment philosophy and German idealism. Jung-Stilling took the religious and miraculous meanings of Pietist life and thought seriously, and his training as a doctor gave him the capacity to study and publish his thoughts on these areas. As one recent scholar put it:

> The basic difference between Jung-Stilling's life and those of the "Stillen im Lande" [the "Silent in the Land," a common epithet for Pietists that reflected their perception as a largely rural and excessively pious group] is that he actively pursued a variety of careers that led him out of an introspective rural existence into the public professions of doctor, professor, and writer.[31]

What kind of scholarly insights emerged from the "introspective rural existence" of this Pietist-turned-doctor? Jung-Stilling's major work was his 1808 book *Theory of Pneumatology*, a work that remains widely unknown despite its critical role in the history of the paranormal.[32] *Theory of Pneumatology*, which deserves a much deeper treatment than I can offer here, was an attempt to reconcile extraordinary phenomena like spirits, apparitions, and visionary experiences with both scientific *and* Christian worldviews.

For our purposes, however, I am interested in one passage from the book, which has been connected consistently with the memory of Conrad Matthai. Jung-Stilling described receiving from a friend of a friend "upon whose veracity I can depend," the following account: "In the neighbourhood of Philadelphia ["about sixty or seventy years ago"], not far from the mills above-mentioned, there dwelt a solitary man in a lonely house. He was very benevolent, but extremely retired and reserved, and strange things were related of him, amongst which were his being able to tell a person things that were unknown to every one else."[33] Jung-Stilling went on to narrate a story in which a Philadelphia man, the captain of a ship, set sail from Philadelphia for Africa and Europe. "He promised his wife that he would return again in a certain time," wrote Jung-Stilling, "and also that he would write to her frequently." No letters arrived, and the appointed time came and passed. The woman was despondent.[34]

At the advice of a friend, the woman went to visit the hermit, since he was able "able to tell a person things that were unknown to every one else." After sharing her worries with the hermit, he asked her to wait for one moment, "until he returned and brought her an answer." The hermit got up and went into a small closet. After waiting for a while, the woman's curiosity got the better of her and she "rose up, went to the window in the door, lifted up the little curtain, and looking in, saw him lying on the couch or sofa like a corpse." "At length," writes Jung-Stilling, "he came and told her that her husband was in London, in a coffee-house which he named, and that he would return very soon.'[35]

Jung-Stilling goes on to relate how "what the solitary had told her was minutely fulfilled, her husband returned, and the reasons of his delay and his not writing were just the same as the man had stated." Understandably curious about how exactly the hermit knew where her husband was and what he was doing, she decided to take her husband to see him.

> The visit was arranged, but when the captain saw the man, he was struck with amazement; he afterwards told his wife that he had seen this very man, on such a day; (it was the very day that the woman had been with him), in a coffee-house in London; and that he had told him that his wife was much distressed about him; that he had then stated the reason why his return was delayed, and of his not writing, and that he would shortly come back, on which he lost sight of the man among the company.[36]

In Jung-Stilling's *Pneumatology*, we have a thirdhand account from an early nineteenth-century Pietist author of a "pious solitary" near Philadelphia who is "able to tell a person things that were unknown to every one else." The hermit in the story was able to bilocate or travel in spirit beyond his body, and even communicate with others in this state of spiritual travel, as he does with the captain in the London coffee shop, apparently in some sort of apparitional state, since the captain was later able to recognize him. In the nineteenth century, belief in this ability would develop under several different rubrics: as astral projection by Theosophists, and as clairvoyance in the burgeoning field of psychical research, both of which drew on earlier theoretical works like Jung-Stilling's *Pneumatology*.

Why, then, are we reading this story here? In 1895, the very same story is retold in the amateur Philadelphia historian Julian Sachse's 1895 book *The German Pietists of Provincial Pennsylvania*, but in Sachse's book the pious solitary is recognized as Conrad Matthai, the last surviving member of Kelpius's monastic community on the Wissahickon. Sachse's source for the story is vague: "The following well-authenticated account has come down to us," he writes.[37] As we will see later in this chapter, Sachse's book is unreliable as a historical source, but it continues to be widely read and cited. Sachse's version of Jung-Stilling's narrative appears in another widely cited 1941 article in the *German-American Review* by the historian Andrew Steinmetz entitled "Kelpius: Mystic on the Wissahickon."[38] In this article, Steinmetz writes that he "had known this story for many years, and it has been related by at least one American historian as well-authenticated."

204 AMERICAN AURORA

This American historian was, presumably, Julius Sachse, whose authentication, as we will see, is less than ironclad as a measure of historical accuracy. Steinmetz goes on: "Recently I came upon an old booklet which proves that the story just related was generally known and believed in in Philadelphia two hundred years ago. This booklet is one of the Jung Stilling works of 1759 [sic] . . . it is an almost verbal repetition of the story we know, except that there are no names given."[39] While we might take issue with Steinmetz's claim that the story itself is "well-authenticated," Steinmetz does provide the valuable service of triangulating this Philadelphia tradition of Matthai's clairvoyance, the appearance of the story in Sachse's *Pietists*, and the earliest source, a thirdhand Pietist account that comes to us from Philadelphia by way of Jung-Stilling in 1808.[40]

Where does this mess of sources and attribution leave us? Jung-Stilling's account preserves a Pietist oral tradition of a pious Philadelphia hermit with extraordinary spiritual powers, an account that would be directly tied to Matthai by Sachse and, later, Steinmetz. While this is hardly a reliable primary document on a Wissahickon hermit (which is why it appears in this chapter rather than Chapter 3), there are deep parallels here with the sources describing Kelpius's and Witt's interest in thought-communication and other extraordinary phenomena, and the Pietist sources describing the ecstatic powers and experiences of Daniel Falckner, Johann Seelig, and Heinrich Bernard Koster.[41] Whatever the provenance of Jung-Stilling's source, he was a well-connected Pietist long before Sachse went about distorting the primary record, and he may have been exposed to some of the oral traditions regarding the Wissahickon hermit's interest in extraordinary phenomena. Indeed, Jung-Stilling's *Pneumatology* is precisely the kind of source in which we would expect such oral traditions of the ecstatic and miraculous experiences of the early radical Pietists to resurface in later Pietist literature.

Once the repeated claims of the narrative being "well-attested" have been replaced with a frank understanding that these narratives represent oral traditions rather than primary documents, we can see these sources for what they are: fascinating artifacts of oral traditions with clear resonances with the primary Wissahickon material covered in Chapter 3 and the broader historiography of Pietism.

The Method of Prayer

Current bibliographies of Kelpius list a publication usually titled *A Short and Easy Method of Prayer* as one of his works produced in Philadelphia. A translation and commentary on this text by Gordon Alderfer, a scholar of early Pennsylvania religion, appeared in 1951, and more recent editions continue to appear every few years.[42] A brief tour through the publication history of this mysterious little text shows how convoluted the historical and literary legacy of the Kelpius community can be.

In the middle of the eighteenth century, a publication appeared in Philadelphia entitled *A Short and Easy Method of Prayer or Speaking with God*. The first publication was in 1756, and has been attributed to the German printer Christopher Sauer, although none of the extant print copies of that edition contain a cover page with any authorial or printing information.[43] This edition was followed up by two English editions of the text, printed in 1761 by Henry Miller and in 1763 by Christopher Sauer Jr.[44] None of these editions contain any clue of the provenance or authorship of the text, other than indicating authorship "by a lover of internal devotion." In fact, the very first authorial attribution of this text appears more than a century later in 1878, in an article by Oswald Seidensticker on German print history in the Cincinnati publication *The German Pioneer*. After noting the publication information about the second edition of *Method of Prayer*, Seidensticker suggested that John Watson makes the following remark in *Annals of Philadelphia*: "I have seen a second edition of a small book on Prayer by Kelpius, which had been printed in Germantown in 1763 by C. Sower. It had been translated into English by Dr. C. Witt."[45] Seidensticker makes an identical claim in his 1893 book *The First Century of German Printing in America, 1728–1830*.[46]

Here is where things begin to get interesting: Watson makes no such claim at all in any of the print editions of *Annals of Philadelphia*. It is possible that Seidensticker meant "manuscript" in the sense that he had reviewed an actual manuscript edition of *Annals* in which this claim was made, though this seems unlikely. But the claim was made, and it held: *Method of Prayer* has since been attributed exclusively to Johannes Kelpius, and various suggestions of earlier printings and confirmations of his authorship have been made. In a pocket-sized popular paperback edition of the text published by Harper's in 1951, Gordon Alderfer called the book "a little masterpiece which has been reliably attributed to Johannes Kelpius."[47]

The real key to the mystery of the *Method of Prayer* might lie in a manuscript at the Free Library of Philadelphia under the title "The Hymnal of the Pietists of the Wissahickon." This leather-bound manuscript contains 175 hymns, some of which appear to have been composed by Kelpius but many of which can be found in other, earlier sources.[48] This same manuscript also contains a handwritten translation of the French Quietist Jeanne-Marie Bouvier de la Motte-Guyon's (1648–1717) 1685 booklet titled *A Short and Easy Method of Prayer*.[49] This handwritten edition clearly indicates Guyon's authorship, and, if the Free Library hymnal did originate with the Kelpius group (and I am inclined to accept that it did, with Willard Martin, since one of the hymns is attributed to "Transylvanus"), it is an exciting confirmation that Kelpius or his colleagues were

206 AMERICAN AURORA

interested in current Catholic contemplative practice, of which Guyon's *Method* is a classic example.

At first glance, Guyon's *Method* appearing in a Kelpius hymnbook is not the slam-dunk attribution that it might seem: the text of the *Method* attributed to Kelpius and Guyon seem to differ. That is, until one looks at publications of Guyon's book in German during the early part of the eighteenth century, in which we can clearly see the origins of the early American text attributed to "a lover of internal devotion."

Here is the first sentence in German of the American edition of *Method of Prayer*, attributed to Kelpius: "Demnach das innere Gebet ein so wichtiger Punct ist, daß man dasselbe das einßige Mittel nennen kan, zu Der Vollskommenheit in diesem Leben zu gelangen" (Accordingly, inner prayer is such an important point that it can be called the one and only means of attaining perfection in this life). For comparison, here is an excerpt from a German edition of Guyon's writings published in Leipzig in 1730: "Das innere Gebet ist ein so wichtiger Punkt, dass man sagen kann, es sei das einzige Mittel, um in diesem Leben zur Vollkommenheit und zu einer lauteren, selbstlosen Liebe des Herzens zu gelangen" (Inner prayer is such an important point that it can be said to be the only means of attaining perfection and pure, selfless love of heart in this life).[50] The differences between these two passages are minor, but their consistency is clear. The origins of the text that appears in so many archives as the work of Johannes Kelpius is clearly derived directly from early eighteenth-century German editions of the work of Guyon, warped gradually over the course of decades and then centuries as Guyon's work was subjected to a three-way translation between French, English, and German and then anthologized and digested in print publications distributed in Europe and North America, like the two cited here.

How, then, did this relatively well-known text come to be attributed to Kelpius? Again, the manuscript sources leave enough breadcrumbs to tell a clear story. The Free Library manuscript hymnal in which we find a handwritten English translation of Guyon's *Method* is signed "Benjamin Lehman," in one corner, the signature of an owner rather than author. On the 1761 Miller printing of *Method of Prayer*, a text with no authorial attribution, there is a handwritten note confirming "Christian Lehman's endorsement as to the authorship."[51] Without knowing what happened for certain, it seems safe to assume that the Lehman family, who possessed Kelpius's handwritten copy of Guyon's *Method* in manuscript on the reverse face of a collection of hymns, erroneously asserted at some point before 1873 that the German and English editions of Guyon's *Method* held in Philadelphia archives were, in fact, the work of Kelpius himself. The differences in the various editions, and various translations, of Guyon's popular works were enough to keep the attribution going through the centuries, even under the nose of scholars.[52]

The History of Human Folly

Kelpius and his colleagues appear in a number of other eighteenth-century sources. The most notable of these is Johann Christoph Adelung's seven-volume *History of Human Folly* (1785–1789), in which Kelpius appears as a colleague of Heinrich Bernard Köster. Wouter Hanegraaff has called Adelung's work "the most famous example" of a "new genre of Enlightenment literature intended for 'learning and entertainment': that of 'histories of stupidity.'"[53] Rather than a general history of mistakes and intellectual failure, Adelung was specifically interested in attacking Platonic, Hermetic, and magical ideas throughout the modern period. Adelung's history shows how "stupidity" had "come to be identified with adherence to quite specific beliefs and historical traditions," as Hanegraaff writes.[54] Kelpius was now firmly in the same lineage of stupidity alongside Giordano Bruno, John Dee, and Jacob Böhme, all of whom are recognized now as paradigmatic figures in the history of human foolishness. The philosophical tide had now turned, and Kelpius's memory was warping permanently.[55]

Another important eighteenth-century source is the Transylvanian-Saxon Johann Seivert's 1785 *Report on Transylvanian Scholars and Their Writings*, which includes a short passage on Kelpius and the Kelp family: he describes the death of Kelpius's father in 1685 and Kelpius's matriculation at Tübingen and Altdorf. Seivert goes on to record Kelpius's three academic publications, including a short description of their contributions in German. Finally, he adds this poignant detail: "Afterwards [referring to his academic career], he traveled to Pennsylvania, and his homeland never heard from him again."[56] Like many other details of Kelpius's biography from this period, we are simply left to wonder if Kelpius's decision to leave the continent and apparently never send a letter home to Transylvania (while managing to correspond with his university colleagues and his new friends in the Philadelphian Society in London) reflects some hidden detail or trauma in his biography.

Meanwhile, back in Pennsylvania, a series of historians would turn their attention to Kelpius throughout the nineteenth century. In 1829, Thomas F. Gordon, a prolific author of local and popular historical works, published his formidable *History of Pennsylvania*.[57] Describing Kelpius and his companions, he wrote: "They were principally men of education, whose peculiar and wild views of religion drove them from the universities of Germany, to seek among the American wilds some immediate and strange revelations."[58] Given the extensive evaluation of the primary literature surrounding the Wissahickon hermits in Chapter 3, Gordon's quick summary of the Wissahickon hermits is essentially accurate—the core Wissahickon group were all lapsed academics who shared a background in radical Pietism and ecstatic experiences.[59] At the early date of 1829, Gordon provided a clear and level understanding of the historical

208   AMERICAN AURORA

Kelpius, even as he refused to mask his disdain for the radical Pietism of the Wissahickon group.

Gordon goes on to refer to and quote some of Kelpius's writings from Wissahickon, including his letter to Esther Palmer and his diary. Kelpius was "well versed in the Hebrew, Greek, Latin, German, and English languages, in the last of which he wrote with a freedom and purity of style rarely attained by foreigners," Gordon writes. These early citations are important because they substantiate that the primary Kelpius literature, including the letters and the diary, were all clearly connected with Kelpius in the early nineteenth century. Especially when compared to some of the histories that would follow in his wake, Gordon's accuracy and clarity as Kelpius's earliest American historian demonstrate the relatively late development of the legendary Kelpius in the historical record.

Accurate as it generally is, Gordon's text demonstrates the ways in which subsequent historians would eventually try but fail to understand Kelpius. Quoting a passage from the letter to Esther Palmer in which Kelpius refers to "signs and wonders," Gordon finds Kelpius to be an author "with more good sense than usually accompanies such vagaries."[60] Gordon's *History of Pennsylvania* is the first history to treat Kelpius after what Wouter Hanegraaff has called "the epistemic rupture of the Enlightenment," and his writing shows how this rupture affected his ability to understand a figure like Kelpius. "On all topics," Gordon writes, "save his peculiar religious opinions, he reasoned acutely and soberly."[61] There is a new, deep dissonance in this nineteenth-century historian trying to parse the simultaneous immense erudition and profound apocalypticism of Kelpius's life and thought. Indeed, I think that it speaks to Gordon's capacity as a historian that this dissonance and ambiguity is preserved, rather than smoothed over or manipulated out of print. Gordon's book demonstrates that the primary literature and basic facts of Kelpius's biography were accessible in nineteenth-century Philadelphia, even as it shows how the process of the Enlightenment distorted the historian's ability to look at a figure like Kelpius clearly and understand him.

Another major Philadelphia historian produced a reliable sketch of Kelpius in the middle of the nineteenth century. John F. Watson's 1833 *Historic Tales of Olden Time, Concerning the Early Settlement and Progress of Philadelphia and Pennsylvania* includes a useful passage confirming much of the primary Kelpius literature: "Several of the MS. books of Kelpius are still in existence, and are preserved as curiosities; his journal and diary I have seen in Latin." While offering little unique information in its own right, Watson's early work does the valuable service of confirming the existence of Kelpius's journal and probably his letterbook, "preserved as curiosities" by the early nineteenth century, as suggested by Gordon's familiarity with the material before 1829.[62]

By 1850, Watson's antiquarian work on Philadelphia had expanded dramatically, and a new, two-volume edition of *Annals* was published with extensive material on Kelpius.[63] Much of this material clearly derives directly from the *Chronicon Ephratense* and Gordon's 1829 *History of Pennsylvania*. Watson declares the style of Kelpius's written English to be "free" and "pure," precisely the same two adjectives that Gordon used decades earlier. Watson quotes directly from Kelpius's letterbook and diary, further cementing his access to those sources. He also goes a step further than Gordon did in 1829, describing and quoting from Kelpius and Witt's "Lamenting Voice of the Hidden Love," drawing together what is still the core of the primary Kelpius corpus from his time in Pennsylvania: the diary, the letters, and the hymns.

"Weird as a Wizard"

Many of the historical sources described so far would not have been widely read or well known to any segment of the American or European public. But Kelpius, or versions of him, continued to appear with surprising regularity in American literature. In fact, he appeared in some of the most widely read novels and poems of the nineteenth century.

His first major nineteenth-century literary appearance was in the Philadelphia Quaker George Lippard's 1848 novel *Paul Ardenheim, the Monk of the Wissahikon*.[64] Lippard is more or less forgotten today, but between 1844 and 1854, he was among the most widely published and read authors in the United States.[65] *Paul Ardenheim* is an almost unbelievably strange novel in which a secret Christian fraternity known as the "Congress of Brotherhood" conspires to restore peace to the world by selectively intervening in history. Lippard's novel, too, selectively intervenes in this history, describing historical figures like William Penn as "an Apostle of Peace" sent by God "to plant the Olive Branch of Brotherhood on the shores of the New World."[66] Lippard's own words recall Charles Brockden Brown's theory of the romance as the only true history: "These are certain truths that cannot be told, unless linked with the charm of fiction."[67]

In the novel, the titular figure of Paul Ardenheim and his father are loosely based on Kelpius, as scholars like Carsten Seecamp have argued, but only insofar as it served the needs of Lippard's novel. Paul is born of noble lineage in the Wissahickon Valley, through the dense and millennia-old machinations of the Congress. As the novel approaches its climax, Paul's father tells him that the final Deliverer of the New World into peace has been called by mysterious forces to the Wissahickon Valley. The mysterious stranger approaches their cabin, where he is initiated by Paul's father in an alchemical ceremony in which the Congress of Brotherhood anoints him and describes his mission as Deliverer. This mysterious stranger, Deliverer of the New World, it turns out, is none other than George Washington, and the founding of the United States is the culmination of the Congress's millennia-old mystical conspiracy to usher in an age of global peace. *Paul Ardenheim* is a strange read, whose wild success is both hard to imagine and yet easy to see in light of contemporary fictions concerning secret societies and national origins, like *National Treasure* or *The Da Vinci Code*. In 1848, it might be said, Lippard was the Dan Brown of Philadelphia.

Paul Ardenheim shows us how the Kelpius legend continued to develop in the nineteenth century, as public awareness of and interest in secret societies like the Freemasons and the Rosicrucians grew. There is very little historical information in Lippard's text. Indeed, Lippard was vocal about not only his willingness but his insistence on subverting historical accuracy to the deeper needs of unspeakable "certain truth." Refracted in the characters of Paul and his father, the legendary Wissahickon monks were a blank slate on which Lippard could spin his occult narrative of millennia of spiritual labor and development culminating in the historical person of George Washington and the creation of the United States. Lippard's novel seems to be the first to connect the memory of Kelpius with the notion of secret occult fraternities, a fictional notion that would become a standard feature of Kelpius's biography by the end of the nineteenth century.

Another enormously popular nineteenth-century American literary figure who turned to Kelpius directly was the poet John Greenleaf Whittier. While the memories of literary scholars have justifiably circled and lingered on more incandescent American poets of the period like Whitman and Dickinson, in terms of poetry as popular song, as folk literature, Whittier's reputation in his own lifetime was unmatched. As Michael Cohen has suggested, "No American poet was more celebrated in the late nineteenth century than John Greenleaf Whittier."[68]

Whittier's career began in the 1820s and 1830s alongside that of the anti-slavery author William Lloyd Garrison. In the decades leading up to the Civil War and abolition, Whittier was a staunch public opponent of the institution of slavery, and his anti-slavery verses and songs were published in a variety of popular media. In the decades following the Civil War, however, as Whittier's public profile grew, he became known for a more bucolic, pastoral, and supernatural quality to his verse.[69] As a poet of New England folklife and folklore, supernatural and occult topics loomed large in Whittier's writing. This feature was recognized approvingly by critics of his own time. Writing in 1885, the critic Edmund Stedman declared that "Whittier's successes probably have been scored most often through ballads of craft, our eastward [New England] tradition and supernaturalism."[70] Underscoring the historiographies of scholars Jon Butler and Catherine Albanese, who have convincingly argued for the overwhelming popularity of occult and supernatural beliefs and practices in American religious history, literary critics of the time contended that it was Whittier's frank approach to supernatural and occult topics that earned him his popularity.

It was in this poetic mode of popular occult regionalism that Whittier produced his 1872 poem "The Pennsylvania Pilgrim," a long ballad describing the life and legacy of Francis Daniel Pastorius, the Pietist turned Quaker polymath covered in detail in Chapter 2. "Pilgrim" is an unabashedly epic retelling of early Pennsylvania's radical religious history from a poet who does not preserve a lick of ambiguity regarding his fondness for the subject. As we have seen, Pastorius's role in the first legal challenge to the institution of slavery in the American colonies—not to mention his emergence in a historical context saturated with the occult regionalism to which Whittier's later poetic imagination clung—made him a perfect subject for a song.

Kelpius appeared in the middle of the poem, in the midst of a kind of roll call of the radical and noteworthy figures from Pennsylvania's radical past:

> Or painful Kelpius from his hermit den
> By Wissahickon, maddest of good men,
> Dreamed o'er the Chiliast dreams of Petersen.

> Deep in the woods, where the small river slid
> Snake-like in shade, the Helmstadt Mystic hid,
> Weird as a wizard, over arts forbid,[71]

Writing in 1872, Whittier appears to possess a solid biographical background in his approach to Kelpius. His piercing adjective "painful" seems to recognize the radical asceticism which set Kelpius apart, even among the radical religious community of seventeenth-century Philadelphia. Wearing his coarse robe in his modest monastic cottage, transforming himself according to the model of the early Christians, "painful Kelpius" was a descriptor that demanded little in the way of poetic license.

Whittier does, however, manage to engage the legendary Kelpius even as he remains tethered to history: Kelpius is "weird as a wizard"; indeed, as the "maddest of good men," he is portrayed as strange as one can be without crossing some imaginary moral horizon in Whittier's mind. He goes on:

> Reading the books of Daniel and of John,
> And Behmen's Morning-Redness, through the Stone
> Of Wisdom, vouchsafed to his eyes alone,

> Whereby he read what man ne'er read before,
> And saw the visions man shall see no more,
> Till the great angel, striding sea and shore,

212   AMERICAN AURORA

> Shall bid all flesh await, on land or ships,
> The warning trump of the Apocalypse,
> Shattering the heavens before the dread eclipse.

Here the legends and history simply accumulate and intermingle: references to Daniel, John and "Behmen" (the common English spelling of Jacob Böhme's last name) show Whittier's familiarity with Kelpius's apocalyptic Christianity, while the reference to the Stone of Wisdom clearly builds on the *Morte d'Arthur* legend, first collected by Mühlenberg in Philadelphia around a century earlier. Alongside this bit of legend-mongering, however, Whittier lands many of the basic facts, and his sudden shift into an apocalyptic register provides a fitting frame to this brief poetic portrayal of Johannes Kelpius in "Pennsylvania Pilgrim." Whittier cites Oswald Seidensticker's historical writing as the source for his historical information, which explains how he managed to hew close enough to history in "Pilgrim," even as he flirted with legend.

Whittier's work is worth exploring not only for his mention of Kelpius, but for his clear attention to what I have called Hermetic Protestant environmental knowledge. Whittier's interest in occult and supernatural beliefs and practices belied a deep resistance to Enlightenment materialism and rationalism from the perspective of a poet. Whittier was not a practicing occultist or even necessarily a believer in the supernatural practices of rural America. As he wrote in his 1847 book *Supernaturalism of New England*: "I have been informed by the comparatively innocent nature and simple poetic beauty of the traditions in question; yet, not even for the sake of poetry and romance would I confirm in any mind a pernicious credulity, or seek to absolve myself from that stern duty to which the true man owes to his generation, to expose error, whenever and wherever he finds it."[72] Beneath this skepticism, however, Whittier recognized something profound in the supernatural folklore of America: "For the supernaturalism of New England and of all other countries is but the exaggeration and distortion of actual fact—a great truth underlies it. It is Nature herself repelling the slander of the materialist," he wrote.[73]

The puritanical quality of Whittier's claim (he was a Quaker) of the "stern duty" to "expose error" shows us another example of the nineteenth century's anxious backward gaze, a simultaneous obsession with and rejection of the occult and supernatural. While we have thus far seen this anxious gaze appear in the historical work of Thomas Gordon, Whittier demonstrates the same hand-wringing rejection of occultism from the poet's perspective. Like Phillip Freneau a century earlier, Whittier scanned the world for wonders, the supernatural, and the occult as sources of spiritual meaning; indeed, he seems to have seen these things as the *substance* of the meaning of poetry. Unlike Freneau, however, Whittier was careful to remind his readers—and perhaps he is reminding himself, too—that beneath the "simple poetic beauty of the traditions in question" there lay merely "error."

Whittier was not merely inconsistent on his Enlightenment principles—he was sincerely conflicted, particularly in how such rationalism seemed to evacuate the meaning from the world itself. While reading Whittier today, one encounters several compelling intellectual, spiritual, and poetic positions: the fierce Quaker activism and profound moral certitude with which he protested the institution of slavery, his abiding love for the knowledge and lifeways of rural people, and finally, the deep spiritual yearning with which he turns to local legends of ghosts, witches, and wizards as fossilized representations of meaning itself in a world whose meaning he saw slowly bleeding away.[74]

This poetic attention to the meaning of the world portrayed through occult and supernatural themes was on vivid display in Whittier's "Snow-Bound: A Winter Idyll," a long poem that depicts the inhabitants of a New England home settling into each other's company and into the warm embrace of cozy domesticity. Returning home as the snowstorm increases, the residents of the home, based on Whittier's own family in his childhood home, take turns telling stories and warming themselves by the fire. Published in 1866, just after the end of the Civil War, "Snow-Bound" proved extremely successful, apparently appealing directly to a reading audience desperate for sustained depiction of nostalgic familial warmth. This domesticity of the poem was not simply a return to normalcy. It was a deliberate invocation and re-instantiation of rural lifeways and knowledge that were rapidly declining in an increasingly industrialized nation.[75] Even as "Snow-Bound" portrayed a return to normalcy in American domestic life, it harkened back to a rapidly dissolving preindustrial American landscape.

For our purposes, however, it is Whittier's explicit attention to the esoteric dimension of early American rural life that makes the poem worth pausing over here. The poem begins with an epigraph from the Renaissance philosopher Heinrich Cornelius Agrippa's 1531 book *Occult Philosophy*:

As the Spirits of Darkness be stronger in the dark, so Good Spirits, which be Angels of Light, are augmented not only by the Divine light of the Sun, but also by our common Wood Fire: and as the Celestial Fire drives away dark spirits, so also this our Fire of Wood doth the same.
—Cor. Agrippa, Occult Philosophy, Book I.ch. v.[76]

The choice of Agrippa for the opening epigraph of "Snow-Bound" not only suggests Whittier's occult interests and literacy (Agrippa was an author whom Whittier read throughout his life) but it signals the occult significance of the apparently mundane and domestic events to follow. The warmth of the hearth is not just warmth. Rather, Whittier wants the reader to know that the fireside is a well of spiritual power. In 1866, the knowing reader would see the name "Agrippa" on

214   AMERICAN AURORA

the frontispiece and recognize that they were in for more than a simple depiction of domestic bliss.[77]

While a full analysis of the occult themes of "Snow-Bound" would quickly escape the scope of this chapter, most important for our purposes is what appears to be an outright depiction of Hermetic Protestant environmental knowledge. Whittier's uncle is portrayed as an illiterate woodsman who is nonetheless profoundly well read in God's other Book:

> Our uncle, innocent of books,
> Was rich in lore of fields and brooks,
> The ancient teachers never dumb
> Of Nature's unhoused lyceum.[78]

The uncle's "innocence of books" directly recalls Kelpius's companion Daniel Falckner's suggestion in 1702, when asked if there were good books to read in Pennsylvania, that "Adam tills his land and tends his cattle, all of which are letters and books. . . . If there is time to spare, then the Holy Bible, next to the church histories and Arndt's works, are enough for those who need guidance."[79] Falckner would have heartily approved of Whittier's uncle's syllabus.

Whittier goes on to demonstrate the immense practical utility and the clear occult heritage of his uncle's deep literacy in God's other Book:

> In moons and tides and weather wise,
> He read the clouds as prophecies,
> And foul or fair could well divine,
> By many an occult hint and sign,
>
> Holding the cunning-warded keys
> To all the woodcraft mysteries;
> Himself to Nature's heart so near
> That all her voices in his ear
> Of beast or bird had meanings clear,
>
> Like Apollonius of old,
> Who knew the tales the sparrows told,
> Or Hermes, who interpreted
> What the sage cranes of Nilus said.[80]

Whittier's uncle—a mystifying character, an invocation of a disappearing art and technique of rural life and occult literacy—seems to be able to conjure the elemental forces by reading the world itself, as the literate preacher might stir up her congregation with a turn to scripture. Whittier is not being subtle in his references to Agrippa,

Hermes, or "occult hint and sign." His uncle is reading God's other book, like Paracelsus, Arndt, or Böhme. As he goes on, creation seems to read him in return:

> Till, warming with the tales he told,
> Forgotten was the outside cold,
> The bitter wind unheeded blew,
> From ripening corn the pigeons flew
>
> The partridge drummed i' the wood, the mink
> Went fishing down the river-brink

As Whittier's uncle speaks, the wind blows "unheeded," the house warms, and the animals stir outside. The environment rustles and pulses in response to the uncle's stories, the cosmos itself seems suddenly to turn and look into Whittier's cozy home.

Whitter's language throughout the poem demonstrates that the uncle's special literacy was not mundane down-home country wisdom—he "divines," he "read the clouds as prophecies," interprets the "occult signs" of the environment. If the Hermetic Protestant Book of Nature has been rendered completely illegible to generations of intervening scholars, it is because Whittier, writing in 1866, was referring to an occult technique that was obscure even as of 1702, when Daniel Falckner rejoined his fellow Pietists to let go of the written word, even the Bible, in favor of more subtle literature. Whittier's "Snow-Bound" "describes scenes and manners which the rapid changes of our national habits will soon have made as remote from us as if they were foreign or ancient," wrote Whittier's contemporary, James Russell Lowell.[81] Lowell was exactly right: these ideas were already foreign enough to seem ancient in 1866, but Johannes Kelpius would have known *exactly* what Whittier's uncle was reading.

Both Whittier and Lippard, it bears repeating, are rarely read today, even as they were among the most widely read authors of the nineteenth century. Their portrayals of Kelpius, divergent as they were, suggest the emergence of a historical use of the legendary Kelpius that has continued unbroken right up through the present. Kelpius appears as a seventeenth-century ur-occultist, the tabula rasa over which generations of post-Enlightenment American occultists would write their own legitimating narratives even as they completely disengaged with the historical figure who still appears—dimly, but discernibly—in the literature and history of the early nineteenth century.

"Rosicrucian Vestiges"

By the latter half of the nineteenth century, a second generation of historians would turn to the memory of Kelpius and the Wissahickon hermits. Some of these

216   AMERICAN AURORA

historians, like Horatio Jones and Oswald Seidensticker, can be credited with preserving much of the historical record on which we rely today, and ensuring its safekeeping in the nascent archival and historical institutions of Philadelphia.

Horatio Gates Jones (1822–1893), a pastor and Pennsylvania state senator, released a valuable genealogy of his mother's family, the Leverings, in 1858, which included an appended note on Kelpius as notable contemporaries of the first generation of Leverings in the Germantown area. Jones's work relies on John Watson's work in *Annals* volume 2, with the useful addition of confirming the location and ownership of each primary Kelpius document, enabling the contemporary historian to clearly trace the diary, letterbook, and "Lamenting Voice" hymns from Kelpius to their place in the Pennsylvania Historical Society today. If it were not for the work of Jones, it would be difficult to directly authenticate these sources with the certainty we have today.[82]

Oswald Seidensticker (1825–1894), professor of German language and literature at the University of Pennsylvania, was among the first professional scholars to look carefully at the history of the German community in Pennsylvania, and his work provides an invaluable coda to the contributions of the historians who came before him. Kelpius was the very first subject on which Seidensticker published.[83] In his 1870 article "Johann Kelpius, der Einfiedler am Wissahickon" (Johann Kelpius, the Hermit on the Wissahickon), Seidensticker firmly connects Kelpius's American memory to his scholarly legacy in Europe via the *Gelehrten-Lexicon* of Heinrich Wilhelm Rotermund, sketching some of his academic publications and clearly identifying Kelpius and his companions as heterodox European academics. Seidensticker's contribution also included an excellent (if likely misattributed—he suggested it was Daniel Falckner) translation of Johann Seelig's letter from Pennsylvania to the Halle Pietists.[84]

By the end of the nineteenth century, then, a series of enthusiastic antiquarians and professional historians in Philadelphia had done an admirable job in identifying the primary source archive and sketching a basically reliable portrait of Kelpius and his companions. Many of the details were still missing—indeed, many are *still* missing—but the image of Kelpius that appears in the work of these figures was reliably drawn from a combination of oral traditions and primary sources. Alongside their work, literary images of Kelpius were flourishing, from Brown's and Freneau's visions of an occult Enlightenment and Whittier's hermit, as "weird as a wizard," to George Lippard's mystic harbinger of an American golden age. On the one hand, historians offered a modest but accurate assessment of Kelpius as a radical Pietist, an apocalyptic and ascetic Christian who was out of place even in a setting as radical as seventeenth-century Philadelphia. To the American literary imagination, however, Kelpius was "weird as a wizard," a leader of ancient secret societies, nothing less than the keeper of the philosopher's stone.

"WEIRD AS A WIZARD"   217

These two images, historical and literary, had, for the most part, remained clearly separated. This changed permanently in 1895, when Julius Sachse (1842–1919), a Philadelphia antiquarian with a deep interest in the fin de siècle occult topics of the day, published *The German Pietists of Provincial Pennsylvania.* Sachse's biography itself is an illuminating illustration of how the discipline of history was often practiced in the nineteenth century. Sachse enjoyed success as an investor and merchant of men's clothing throughout his life, which allowed him to retire comfortably in the 1880s, at which point he began to pursue his two passions as full-time hobbies: photography and antiquarian local history. Despite having no training as a scholar, Sachse diligently pursued his antiquarian interests and published extensively in his retirement.[85]

Sachse was deeply interested in the esoteric histories of Philadelphia and southeastern Pennsylvania generally. In addition to his work on German religious minorities, he researched and published on the history of American Freemasonry, especially the Masonic backgrounds of George Washington and Benjamin Franklin, a combination of interests that suggests some familiarity with the works of George Lippard, whom he cites approvingly in *German Pietists.*[86] Sachse spent freely and traveled widely to accumulate manuscripts and relics of interest in his later years, and as his efforts continued, he eventually produced a series of monographs on Pennsylvania history: *German Pietists,* the first, focused on Kelpius and company.[87]

German Pietists is a sprawling and lavishly illustrated tome that marshals a confusing combination of painstakingly acquired primary material and outright falsified sources. Legendary material with literary origins intermingles freely with Sachse's generally reliable translations of primary source documents. Compelling depictions based on solid research stand alongside frequent citations of "an ancient Rosicrucian MSS in possession of the author" or "a curious Ephrata MSS." Speaking as a scholar who would hope to understand Kelpius, I have, at times, thought of Julius Sachse as a kind of perfect storm for the historian trying to grapple with his material: reliable and valuable preservations of primary documents coexist with outright frauds, and there is often no easy way to tell the two apart.

Jeff Bach's estimation of Sachse's impact on Ephrata scholarship is accurate and can be applied to his effect on the Wissahickon community: "For reasons already demonstrated, [Sachse's] work is not reliable, although it is valuable for its preservation of much source material. Sachse was not above altering material to suit his purposes. All work that depends primarily on Sachse must be approached cautiously."[88] A full accounting of Sachse's sources would be impossible, given his citation practices. In one clear example of what makes Sachse so difficult to work with, he rewrites Mühlenberg's report so "Herr G." is simply "Kelpius," erasing all ambiguity, and ignoring the clear connection to *Le Morte d'Arthur.*[89] In Sachse's writing, the boundary between the legendary Kelpius and the historical Kelpius finally dissolves, and we are met with a figure who would become standard in the historiography of the twentieth century. The philosopher's stone legend is presented as unambiguous history, and Kelpius and company are represented as "True Rosicrucian Mystics," representatives of an ancient occult fraternity in the New World.[90] Given the continued reliance on Sachse's work, it is easy to see how contemporary scholarship has struggled with Kelpius.

As frustrating as Sachse's work is for a contemporary historian hoping to engage with his subjects, it must be acknowledged that rewriting and inventing sources was not a terribly unusual practice for the period, even among trained professionals, which Sachse was not. Take, for example, James Frazer's *The Golden Bough* (1890), a monumental opus on myth and religion by anyone's standards, which had more to do with the author's own fantasy than the primary sources. J. Z. Smith has estimated that only 10 percent of Frazer's material really came from his sources. The rest, in Smith's estimation, was "the product of the author's literary imagination."[91] As much as I have struggled with Sachse, I have to acknowledge that his methods were not wildly divergent from the standards of his day. Sachse was hardly the first or the only nineteenth-century historian to give way to his imagination or fantasy, then, but he has also not had the benefit of a J. Z. Smith to set his record straight.

Sachse's 1895 book is *easily* the most widely cited secondary source on Kelpius, and its influence can be felt everywhere from the leading introductory textbook on American religions to the area around the Kelpius hermitage itself, where a commemorative monolithic plaque has been raised outside of an old root cellar (popularly known as the "Cave of Kelpius") describing the journey of the first Rosicrucians in the New World (Figure 6.2). Due to the widespread influence of Sachse's book in this area, identifications of Kelpius and his companions as Rosicrucians are very common in popular and scholarly writing on the subject.[92]

Before assessing Sachse's claim of a Rosicrucian identity for Kelpius, we must take a moment to describe what such an identification would mean. The complex of cultural phenomena called Rosicrucianism can be traced back to the 1614 publication of three philosophical texts in Germany, quickly followed by *Confessio Fraternitatis* (Confession of the Fraternity) and the *Chymische Hochzeit Christiani Rosenkreutz Anno 1459* (The Chemical Wedding of Christian Rosenkreuz in the Year 1459) in 1615 and 1616.[93] The Rosicrucian manifestos and *Chemical Wedding*, a novel, demonstrate a largely Paracelsian religious philosophy of analogy between the human and the cosmos.[94] Despite their anonymous attribution and veneer of an ancient and mysterious origin, these texts were in all likelihood authored by a group of Christian philosophers gathered by Johann Valentin Andrae in Tübingen in 1610.[95]

Figure 6.2 The overgrown root cellar with commemorative monolith known today as the "Cave of Kelpius," in Wissahickon Valley Park. Author's photo. See the introduction for a close-up photo of the monolith.

The early Rosicrucian texts recast Hermetic and Paracelsian Christianity within a decidedly mysterious, literary, and fashionable aura, and they were immediately popular in Europe. This wide seventeenth-century influence remained, however, a largely literary phenomenon—the books were exciting, intriguing, and they carried a weight of ancient wisdom. Unlike the hefty Paracelsian works on which their philosophy was based, the Rosicrucian manifestos were *fun*. They were also fiction masquerading as history. As Roland Edighoffer writes: "There is no proof that the Brotherhood of the Rose Cross described in the *Fama Fraternitatis* ever existed, and it is only in the 18th century that actual organizations calling themselves 'rosicrucian' first come into existence."[96]

In the following centuries, a number of occult groups would take up the label "Rosicrucian" and claim the ancient lineage outlined in the manifestos of the early seventeenth century. It is from the perspective of these modern esoteric groups calling themselves Rosicrucian that Julius Sachse applies the label to Kelpius and company. As Frances Yates writes in *The Rosicrucian Enlightenment*, these fully modern occult groups calling themselves Rosicrucian are simply "a different subject" than the seventeenth-century literary and religious phenomena she identifies as Rosicrucian. Edighoffer is more direct: "No Rosicrucian Orders in the 19th and 20th century could rightly claim a direct connection to 17th-century counterparts," he writes.[97]

220 AMERICAN AURORA

Sachse appears to be the very first author to describe Kelpius and his companions as Rosicrucian, but his own understanding of the term is unclear.[98] The label itself is evidently very important to Sachse, who uses it constantly, but in his writing, it seems to signify a general occult meaning rather than a specific set of beliefs, texts, or even a specific lineage. As he writes of the group: "They were a company of Theosophical Enthusiasts—call them Pietists, Mystics, Chiliasts, Rosicrucians, Illuminati, Cathari, Puritans, or what you may."[99] Indeed, Sachse makes no mention of *any* specific Rosicrucian doctrines, authors, or texts. As Frances Yates writes, the word "Rosicrucian" takes on such "strange vagarites" in the nineteenth century that it becomes impossible to cut a historiography through the dense network of ideas, texts, and people called Rosicrucian.[100] And indeed, Sachse applies the label in a manner unique to those forms of nineteenth-century esotericism to which Yates refers. In Sachse's work, "Rosicrucian Theosophy" is a general term for ancient wisdom carried along hidden, fraternal channels, nurturing a secret, universal religion.

The association between Kelpius and hidden societies of ancient knowledge is a hallmark of the legendary Kelpius material, dating back to the claim of his knowledge of the philosopher's stone in Mühlenberg's journal, but only achieving sustained popularity in George Lippard's *Paul Ardenheim*. By the end of the nineteenth century, Sachse fused these disparate areas of knowledge together into one narrative in one very popular book, permanently cementing the historical Kelpius clearly recognizable to figures like Gordon, Watson, Jones, and Seidensticker to a wider body of legend and a fin de siècle fascination with occultism, secret societies, ancient wisdom, and perennial philosophy. Kelpius's place in history was permanently transformed as centuries of legend and popular occult philosophy were suddenly superimposed over him.

Still, Sachse's identification of the group as Rosicrucian was almost immediately questioned by several twentieth-century literary occultists with an interest in Rosicrucianism. Arthur E. Waite, the British occultist and author of *The Brotherhood of the Rosy Cross*, while being open to the possibility that Kelpius and company were "in some way integrated into the Order," admitted that he "had searched in vain for traces of . . . any Rosicrucian vestiges in the letters of Kelpius."[101] Another leader of a modern Rosicrucian group, R. Swineburne Clymer, memorably noted in a 1931 magazine article that the Kelpius group was "diametrically the opposite" of a Rosicrucian group based on the fact that Kelpius "watched for and expected the Millenium," a decidedly non-Rosicrucian belief in Clymer's estimation.[102] For twentieth-century occultists who were willing and able to read primary documents, the legend of the "True Rosicrucian" order on the Wissahickon seemed inconsistent with the facts.

Despite the skepticism in certain corners, the identification with Kelpius persists among modern Rosicrucian groups, most notably the Ancient and

Mystical Order Rosae Crucis (AMORC), founded in 1915 by the New York psychical researcher Harvey Spencer Lewis (1883–1939). Lewis was particularly enthusiastic about the Rosicrucian identity of Kelpius and company, calling it "the first American Rosicrucian experiment," and even claiming direct descent from members of the group, cementing his own ancient Rosicrucian bona fides.[103] Lewis's identification rests entirely on the work of Sachse, but he expands the scope of the Rosicrucian Wissahickon group to involve such figures as Benjamin Franklin and Thomas Jefferson as major figures in this "national headquarters of the Rosicrucians in America."[104]

In Lewis's work, we rehearse the fictional speculations of George Lippard on the occult origins of the American national identity a century later, with the veneer of fiction thoroughly removed. Kelpius's role as the primordial American Rosicrucian is further cemented for the twentieth-century reading public. Somewhat like the transformation of Rosicrucianism from a literary phenomenon to religious practice in the previous century, Lewis's reading of Sachse and Lippard shows us how the right kind of literature only takes a generation or so to become a religion. The Johannes Kelpius Lodge of AMORC currently operates in Allston, Massachusetts.

Scholarship on Kelpius has also struggled with the Rosicrucian label, although it has been met with some skepticism. The biggest issue, as Frances Yates warns us, is the multiple meanings that the label "Rosicrucian" takes on in the nineteenth century. Even for scholars with training in this area, it is never precisely clear what it *means* to be a Rosicrucian. Writing in 1973, Willard Martin concurred with Waite that there is no documentary evidence of any kind for a Rosicrucian association with the group.[105] Donald E. Durnbaugh had written the same three years earlier in *Church History*.[106] Ernst Benz identifies Kelpius as a Rosicrucian without clarifying the term or citing a source.[107] Elizabeth Fisher claimed the same on the basis of Kelpius's possible proximity to adjacent figures in European occultism, but her identification is entirely based on Sachse.[108] To her credit, Fisher does acknowledge that the similarities between Kelpius's writings and the Rosicrucian *Confessio* are similarities that both texts share with a familiar figure: Jacob Böhme.

To summarize again in the words of Jeff Bach, "Most of the literature depends too uncritically on Julius F. Sachse."[109] Sachse did preserve a great deal of primary literature on the Wissahickon group, and his translation of Kelpius's diary and letters is reliable enough that it can still be used by scholars today. But there is simply no documentary or scholarly evidence to identify Kelpius as a Rosicrucian or anything but a radical Pietist. Indeed, as generations of scholarship in Western esotericism has shown, there were simply no Rosicrucian groups for him—or anyone—to join in the late seventeenth century. Kelpius was a radical Protestant of a decidedly esoteric bent, but there is no evidence that he was a member of a fraternal group of any kind.

222 AMERICAN AURORA

All Folk Songs Are True

This undifferentiated complex of literatures, historical, literary, esoteric, and legendary, has constituted the Kelpius archive in American religious history for the past century. In this chapter, I have tried to place these literatures in their cultural and chronological context to show how the authors build on one another, in some cases circling back to primary documents but more often simply repeating each other's unfounded claims. Very much like the facts of Kelpius's biography, the posthumous literatures appear mysterious at a distance but follow a clear trajectory when placed in a row: Gordon relies on oral tradition and the *Chronicon Ephratense*, while Watson relies on Gordon. Seidensticker credits Jones, while Jones was simply citing Watson and confirming his sources. Alongside these historians, the Kelpius legend is periodically injected with literary material: Whittier offers an occult reinscription of Mühlenberg's report on the philosopher's stone. Lippard relies on his own imagination, like Charles Brockden Brown and Freneau before him, who used Kelpius as an inspiration for their philosophical fictions. All the while, Johannes Kelpius himself became less and less recognizable. Thomas Gordon's clear image of a radical Pietist academic with apocalyptic beliefs transforms into the legend of Johannes Kelpius, the wizard on the Wissahickon.

Both the historical and the legendary Kelpius are known and loved by the people of Philadelphia today. There is no better example of this than the Kelpius Society, a group of like-minded local antiquarians "whose goal is to research the community, restore the site, and spread the original group's message of peace and brotherhood to all."[110] In 2004, the group successfully petitioned the state of Pennsylvania to erect a historical marker near the site of the hermitage, which was installed after a series of presentations by Kelpius Society members, historians, and park and city officials. Lucy Carroll directed the Monastery Choir in her transcription of Kelpius's hymn "Upon Rest" during the commemoration of the plaque.[111]

I met with Alvin Holm, the former head of the Kelpius Society and one of the organizers of the historical marker campaign, in his Philadelphia studio in the summer of 2018. Al greeted me beneath a sign decorated with a Rosicrucian rosette and welcomed me into his workshop. I have not had the chance to spend much time in professional architecture studios, but I would imagine that there are few very like Holm's. Strewn with books, paintings, his own objets d'art, Al's studio seemed more like a Renaissance workshop than a contemporary design firm. Manila folders filled with photocopies of material he had gathered on the legend of Kelpius sat on a table. While I sat at his desk and examined his collection, Al bounced around his studio, producing arcane manuscripts and occult photocopies from hidden compartments like a twenty-first-century Cornelius Agrippa.

After a period of going over sources together, Al took me out to lunch before driving me to Wissahickon Valley Park, where we investigated the site of the Wissahickon hermitage together. Approaching the approximate site of the Hermitage today, along what is now Hermit Lane and the Yellow Trail in Wissahickon Valley Park, the evidence of a thriving legend is all around: a small park bench along the trail features an enormous carving of the words "The Hermit is Watching," as though Kelpius was now a strangely surveillant ghost.

Al's love for the place and for the legend was palpable as we explored together. He invited me to stretch out my hands as I passed directly through what he told me was the fortieth parallel, not only a measurement of latitude, but an occult circuit of energy girding the planet that guided the Wissahickon hermits to this exact location in Philadelphia. And to be completely honest, I clearly felt the energies of the fortieth parallel pulse through my hands as Al and I walked along the ridge together.

I had a train to catch, and Al drove me to Thirtieth Street Station after a stop at the Philadelphia Museum of Art, where he explained the electromagnetic powers of stone columns as receivers of spiritual energy. He dropped me at the station and I thanked him profusely. We both enjoyed connecting with someone else who shared the same obsessive interest in Kelpius. After being dropped off at the station, I found myself lingering over the memory of one model he had shown me in his studio, a proposal to the city of Philadelphia for an architectural project. It would have involved a redesign of J.J. Anderes Park at the end of the Benjamin Franklin Parkway, just at the foot of the museum of art, one of the best-known and photogenic parts of the city. Holm's proposal would have turned the park into an immense *theatron* in the style of ancient Greece, only more ornate, with columns, terraces, and esplanades arrayed within and around the Schuylkill River and the museum. Imagine Rocky Balboa pumping his fists over the Acropolis. It was, he told me, the monument that his city deserved: a fitting and classical architectural tribute to his home, a truly great city home to great people which, as he told me, deserved better than another statue of "Benjamin fucking Franklin."

I sat beneath the statues of angels in Thirtieth Street Station and I thought of the *theatron* of Alvin Holm, finally reaching something like an understanding of the Kelpius legend. Beginning with Mühlenberg's report that Kelpius held the philosopher's stone, the legendary Kelpius has been a self-perpetuating folk song, an anonymous vernacular body of knowledge in Philadelphia that fulfills a deeper need than historiography. The ancient wizard of literature was not the Kelpius of history, but it was the Kelpius that Philadelphia wanted: an occult origin story of deeper consequence and value to a segment of the public imagination than the vacuous nationalism and entrepreneurial Enlightenment that every public inch of Philadelphia commemorates. The legend imbues the history of the city with a spiritual meaning, rather than a simply national one, and a hidden meaning, rather than one of relentless public commemoration. From his death in 1707 to the twenty-first century, the sources have transformed Kelpius repeatedly, writing and rewriting him to suit the needs of the age and the needs of the city in which he died.

In his 1957 book *The Poetics of Space*, Gaston Bachelard singles out the image of the hut of a hermit as a structure of immense imaginal potency. "The hermit's hut is a theme which needs no variations," he writes, "for at the simplest mention of it, 'phenomenological reverberation' obliterates all mediocre resonances."[112] For Bachelard, the hermit's hut is that rare phenomenological image with a meaning we might call *innate*—it requires no elaboration, no explication, and certainly no citation: it speaks directly to the imagination of the witness. "The hermit's hut is an engraving that would suffer from any exaggeration of picturesqueness," he writes. It is already fully embellished, ornately illustrated for the sensory organ of the human imagination. He goes on:

> The hermit is *alone* before God. His hut, therefore, is just the opposite of the monastery. And there radiates about this centralized solitude a universe of meditation and prayer, a universe outside the universe. The hut can receive none of the riches "of this world." It possesses the felicity of intense poverty; it is one of the glories of poverty; as destitution increases it gives access to absolute refuge.[113]

As much time as this chapter has devoted to the details of the historiography and literary history, I think Bachelard's elaboration of the poetic power of the hermit's hut is the real explanation for the proliferation of the Kelpius legend. Bachelard's is the same impulse which Freneau engaged in his Philosopher-Hermit of the forest, an image of "absolute refuge" that is inherently legible to the imagination. Leigh Eric Schmidt, writing in 2005, made this very point about the memory of the Wissahickon hermits: "Mining this vein, lovers of solitude found their gold."[114] The image of solitude, and the juxtaposition of this romantic solitude with the silhouetted city in the distance, has always been the poetic core of popular interest in Kelpius and company.

There is an indelible potency in looking up onto the ridge and imagining Kelpius in his hut. Bachelard describes the feeling: "We are hypnotized by solitude, hypnotized by the gaze of the solitary house; and the tie that binds us to it is so strong that we begin to dream of nothing but a solitary house in the night."[115] Bachelard seems almost to have Kelpius in mind as he elaborates the poetic and phenomenological meaning of the hermit's hut: "Great images have both a history and prehistory," he writes. "They are always a blend of memory and legend, with the result that we never experience an image directly."[116]

And indeed, there was something of a block in the experience of that image for my friend, the cyclist, as he tried to dredge up his memory of the hermit on the Wissahickon ridge. Images blurred and failed to materialize clearly beneath the dense layers of history, memory, legend. The case has been the same for centuries of history, literature, and religious writing on Kelpius and his companions. The city of Philadelphia and generations of occultists, scholars, and antiquarians have been "hypnotized by the gaze of the solitary house" up the ridge on the Wissahickon, where an ambient, spectral presence can still be felt today, on the pages of the archive and in the air over the ridge.

Conclusion

An Unmute Gospel

In 2018, Philadelphia 6abc Action News ran a segment about Kelpius on local television. On location at the site of the hermitage, reporter Jeanette Reyes spoke into the mic and declared for the camera: "Now it's time to unravel the mystery of Johannes Kelpius." The camera cut to Kris Soffa, then the trail ambassador for the Friends of the Wissahickon, the local nonprofit organization that conserves Wissahickon Valley Park. "Kelpius was a man who brought a doomsday cult to Philadelphia," said Soffa by way of introduction, as though that was the most important thing to know about him.[1] Mystery unraveled, indeed.

We shouldn't blame Soffa or 6abc Action News for running a bit of a sensational segment about Kelpius. A cursory web search shows that perceptions of the Kelpius group as a "doomsday cult" became very popular throughout the twentieth century, all of which derive from Sachse's reading of Zimmerman's apocalyptic speculations about the year 1693 based on his observation of the Great Comet of 1680. This understanding of Kelpius as the leader of a doomsday group is the most common popular understanding of Kelpius today, an emphasis that has much more to do with our contemporary interest in doomsday, I think, than anything about the life or religion of Johannes Kelpius.

By now, this book has hopefully made very clear that Kelpius was not the leader of a doomsday cult (Zimmerman predicted a vague cataclysm on the scale of the Thirty Years War in 1693, and the Kelpius group did not arrive in Pennsylvania until 1694), although the historical and environmental circumstances that shaped his life are deeply relevant, I think, to our own in the twenty-first century.

In this book, I have used the word "apocalyptic" to describe the basic religious orientation of Kelpius and his immediate milieu. As described in the introduction, I do so thinking with the ancient genre of apocalyptic writing alongside the historian and scholar of mysticism Eliot Wolfson, who defines "apocalyptic" as "the revelation of divine mysteries through the agency of visions, dreams, and other paranormal states of consciousness."[2] Apocalypticism has less to do with the immanent conclusion of this world than with special techniques and powers to derive deeper knowledge, understanding, and insight of the divine *in this world*. Apocalypse, in this sense, can simply mean listening to the world when it speaks.

American Aurora. Timothy Grieve-Carlson, Oxford University Press. © Oxford University Press 2024.
DOI: 10.1093/oso/9780197765562.003.0008

CONCLUSION 227

This does not mean there are no political valences to this apocalyptic perspective. Indeed, the political meanings of apocalypse are exactly that which makes contemporary doomsday enthusiasts continue to read apocalyptic literature. Revelatory literature is almost *always* a religious genre in which certain rhetorical aims are enacted: the singular importance of a group of people, the failure of their enemies, their ultimate success through the establishment of a righted world order. This is made clear in the Greek meaning of the word from which apocalypse is derived, which translates to "revelation," "unveiling," we might even say "clarification." We might translate it, then, as a conclusion to some kind of epistemic hiddenness, the telling of a truth, seeing something clearly.

The impact of global climate change in the seventeenth century is something that historians now see very clearly. Religious studies scholars are also starting to pick up this thread and run with it: as Philip Jenkins points out in his 2021 book *Climate, Catastrophe, and Faith: How Changes in Climate Drive Religious Upheaval*: "Climate remains the missing dimension in the history of religions."[3] My own research trajectory here in this book has been much more limited than Jenkins's, but for my part I am inclined to agree, with a twist. The agency of nonhumans and our techniques for living alongside them—techniques of interpretation, negotiation, and mediation—is indeed the missing dimension in the history of religions.

Like my use of the word "apocalyptic," scholars of esotericism might find my use of "Hermeticism" to be somewhat idiosyncratic. Frankly, this is because my sources use Hermetic ideas in varied ways that reflect their own personal interpretations and contexts. As recent decades of scholarship on Hermeticism and esotericism have clarified, the narrative of a single unbroken "Hermetic tradition" that arises in the Renaissance has been complicated by a much more nuanced understanding of medieval Christianity's deeply Neoplatonic influences.[4] The complexity of these religious and philosophical ideas and their movements throughout history and geography are rendered even more complicated in a setting like early America, where the linguistic and institutional boundaries that might otherwise clarify transmission histories are largely replaced by vernacular methods of distribution. Stephen J. Fleming, Egil Asprem, and Ann Taves have recently problematized the historian John L. Brooke's attribution of many novel ideas in the history of Mormonism to a "Hermetic tradition," largely through the work of Frances Yates. Recognizing the impact of Hermetic and esoteric ideas on Mormonism "was a great advance in contextualizing Smith's radical ideas," as they write, but Yates's understanding of Hermeticism as an unbroken tradition has now been largely rejected by scholars. Fleming, Asperem, and Taves point out that a clearer understanding of the esoteric sources Smith was working with (which, I hasten to add, largely came from Ephrata writings, Kelpius's only real American institutional legacy) can help us

228 CONCLUSION

to situate Smith and Mormonism within "a richer understanding of the history of Christianity."[5] This does not mean there was no Hermetic influence on Joseph Smith (or Kelpius, for that matter). It means that Hermetic literature, since the Middle Ages, has always appeared within an already densely tangled association with a major tradition.

This is why I call this religious perspective, focused here on Kelpius and his immediate influences and colleagues, "Hermetic Protestantism." At the risk of overgeneralizing about early modern sources, Hermetic material *always* appears as an adaptable religious perspective within a wider traditional religious framework: Hermeticism is not alien to Christianity any more than it is alien to the early modern forms of Judaism or Islam that have engaged these ideas. And this is where we find the Hermetic Protestants: clearly within the history of Christianity.

In my reconstruction of Hermetic Protestant environmental knowledge, I run the risk of reinscribing an imagined Hermetic "tradition" into my Christian sources, like Yates. Indeed, Yates's depiction of early modern Hermetic writings sounds quite a bit like the environmental knowledge I have described in this book. Yates sees a world in which "every thing, every being, every force is like a voice yet to be understood . . . where the stars are looking, listening, and exchanging signs amongst themselves the way we do ourselves. A universe, finally, that is an immense dialogue."[6] But Yates was not wrong in her readings of the sources, she was wrong in assuming that their collective marginalization must mean that they formed a coherent and self-containing tradition, as scholars like Brian Copenhaver and Wouter Hanegraaff again have shown.

Indeed, how could one read an author like Paracelsus (or Arndt or Böhme) and come away with anything less than a sense of the cosmos as an "immense dialogue"? In *The Order of Things*, Michel Foucault arrives at a similar conclusion while reading Paracelsus, which he mistakenly attributes to a universal Renaissance episteme of knowledge derived from "sympathy." Foucault offers his own interpretation of a form of knowledge that we are now familiar with, in which contemplation of the environment yielded personal and moral insight. "A knowledge of similitudes is founded upon the unearthing and decipherment of these signatures," he writes, sounding very much like Arndt's *Book of Nature*: "It is useless to go no further than the skin or bark of plants if you wish to know their nature, you must go straight to their marks."[7] Foucault describes a worldview in which "wisdom" and "knowledge" of a person "resemble the order of the world," before turning to quote Paracelsus directly: "Man will discover that he contains 'the stars within himself . . . and that he is thus the bearer of the firmament with all its influences.'"[8]

To repeat a point from the introduction: environmental historians and others have been reading the same sources as scholars of esotericism for decades, often

CONCLUSION 229

noting their immense significance and influence, particularly in environmental history. Writing in 2021, Amitav Ghosh pointed out that "vitalist modes of thought were pushed to the margins of Western culture, but they did not disappear; they were kept alive on the one hand by those who lived close to the European continent's soils, forest, and seas; and on the other hand by celebrated intellectuals like Paracelsus."[9] Reading Ghosh here, I am reminded again of the immense popularity of the almanac, the Hermetic sources almanacs relied on in early America, the poverty of the people who used them, and the scorn of elite Quakers like Charles Brockden Brown who tried to understand them.

In his 2022 book *Hermetic Spirituality and the Historical Imagination*, Wouter J. Hanegraaff performs an immense excavation beneath centuries of speculative scholarship on Hermetic literature to reveal an ancient spiritual method for healing the human soul through experiential practices. This adaptable and experiential understanding of Hermeticism, as an ancient spirituality rather than a philosophical system or religious tradition, shows us that the ancient authors of Hermetic literature were much more concerned with practice than belief.[10] And alongside these techniques there was an unyielding religious perspective: "The Hermetica never stop praising the astonishing beauty of creation," Hanegraaff writes, "while lamenting the irreverence of those who have lost their sense of wonder and admiration."[11] This unflinching sense of wonder, of *reverence for the beauty of this world*, of *eusebia*, "is absolutely central to Hermetic spirituality," Hanegraaff notes.[12] Everard's Hermetica, which Daniel Leeds excerpted in a Philadelphia almanac, rejoins the reader that the Lord "appeareth thorow the whole world . . . if thou wilt see him, consider and understand the Sun, consider the course of the Moon, consider the order of the Stars."[13]

This is why the historian Jan Assman calls the theological perspective of these texts a kind of cosmotheism, a divine that is at home in the world. This highly adaptable religious perspective, filtered through the Christian imaginations of Paracelsus, Arndt, and Böhme, was expressed beautifully by Kelpius in the Wissahickon forest, which he addresses directly as a living presence with the familiar "thee":

> Who would not desire to be a Denison in Thee? Who would not delight to trace thy Solitary and lonesom walks? Oh ye Inhabitants of this happy desolation, bless & kiss that gentle hand of that Divine Sophia who at the first did so wittily allure you, when she intended to bring you into this Wilderness, for to speak to your Heart, in order to search & trie the same![14]

Throughout the seventeenth century, the historical sources are filled with hints of what Amitav Ghosh has called "a vitalist politics," a sense of nonhumans as living and communicative agents with a kind of moral status during a period of

230 CONCLUSION

severe climate change and social upheaval, what Leibniz mocked and denied as "wisdom in nature." As Ghosh notes, the primary source of such a politics is and has always been Indigenous and traditional peoples around the world. Hints of such a politics are also found elsewhere among the peoples pushed to the edges of the world by the colonial powers and institutions during the period, and "those who lived close to the soils," as Ghosh calls them.

The agency and vitality of nonhumans often forces itself into our perspective through phenomena that we tend to dismiss as paranormal. The presence of nonhumans is "the frontier where colonial power meets a limit beyond which lies something unfathomable," Ghosh writes. The vitality of the landscape is always uncanny to the modern imagination, which has repressed nonhuman agency into a box, labeled it "paranormal," and tried to set it aside. "Here were proofs of a sensible and intelligent existence, which could not be denied," Clara Wieland reminds us. Mechanistic determinism and Enlightenment hubris not only subject the living world to horrific, immense cruelty—they leave all of us ignorant of a subtle, animate, and intelligent cosmos.

A vitalist politics, like the one hidden and hinted at in these sources, one that takes the moral status of nonhumans and the challenge of climate change seriously, might be a form of "magical thinking," as Ghosh acknowledges. But the difference between a vision of terraforming Mars and actually *loving* and *taking care* of this planet is that "a vitalist mass movement, because it depends not on billionaires or technology, but on the proven resources of the human spirit, may actually be magical enough to change hearts and minds across the world."[15]

American Aurora

I am putting the finishing touches on this conclusion in August 2023, likely the hottest recorded period in our planet's history, as the US Congress is being publicly briefed about anomalous, intelligent celestial phenomena that seem intent on communicating and interacting with human beings. The more things change.

Writing in his journal in 1839, Ralph Waldo Emerson wistfully recorded a spectacular celestial event: "Here came the other night an Aurora so wonderful, a curtain of red and blue and silver glory that in any other age or nation it would have moved the awe and wonder of men." It was only ten years after *Hazard's* recorded that "meteor of rather singular character" in 1829.

But Emerson too felt something other than awe and wonder. "In any other age or nation," he writes, it would have *moved* us, we would have *felt* it. But something had changed permanently by 1839. "We all saw it with cold, arithmetical eyes, we know how many colors shone, how many degrees it extended, how many hours it lasted, and of this heavenly flower we beheld nothing more: a primrose by the

CONCLUSION 231

brim of the river of time."[16] By 1839, Emerson recognized that there had been an acute change in the relationship between human beings and their environment. It was a change that went beyond aesthetics: Emerson was not claiming that people simply failed to see beauty in the world. There had been something like a hermeneutic transformation, a permanent change in how we exchanged information with the world around us. By 1839, the phenomena of the cosmos no longer reflected the inner world and inner life of the human subject. Instead, Emerson laments, we look at the night sky with "cold, arithmetical eyes." I am reminded again of Johann Zimmerman's concern over the work of the young Isaac Newton: "I fear that [he] wishes his discourse to be understood mathematically only."[17]

Emerson hammers this point home with a note of irony: "Shall we not wish back again the Seven Whistlers," he asks, the seven seabirds of folklore whose cries warned sailors of danger, or "the Flying Dutchman," the seventeenth-century legend of a ghostly ship that glowed on the horizon as a portent of doom, "the lucky and unlucky days," those auspicious times and places for business and planting and marriage recorded in almanacs, "and the terrors of the Day of Doom?"[18] Emerson purposefully chooses those folkloric stories that sound the silliest to our modern ears, sounding the same note that John Greenleaf Whittier would a few years later. In denying these superstitions, as silly as they sound to us now, we have somehow amputated our shared capacity to share in and interpret the meaning of the world. Something had been permanently lost.

It might not surprise us to learn, then, that Emerson was a close reader of Jacob Böhme, according to his biographer Robert D. Richardson.[19] Emerson turned to Böhme repeatedly throughout his life, reading him alongside "Swedenborg, Guyon, Fox, Luther," he writes, attributing to these authors the "discovery that God lies within" and the "worthlessness of all institutions."[20] Once Emerson's lifelong appreciation for Böhme's thought is noted, it is hard to miss in his writing: "Moral law lies at the center of nature. . . . All things with which we deal, preach to us," Emerson wrote in *Nature*. "What is a farm but a mute gospel?"[21]

Emerson never had the chance to read Daniel Falckner's 1702 pamphlet for German immigrants, but this passage would have moved him: "Adam tills his land and tends his cattle, all of which are letters and books." Emerson's "mute gospel" is an unwitting paraphrase of Falckner's "land and cattle, letters and books," written more than a century apart by two authors who had much in common in their American receptions of Böhme's *Aurora*. But for Falckner, a century earlier, a farm was a gospel anything but mute.

In this book, I have tried to understand the transformation of early modern environmental knowledge in microcosm: through the context, writings, and legacy of Johannes Kelpius. In doing so, I have explored the role of the Little Ice Age in the Protestant reading of Hermetic literature in the seventeenth century,

232 CONCLUSION

the persistence of Hermetic Protestantism in Pennsylvania, and the legacies of Hermetic Protestantism in the eighteenth and nineteenth centuries. Throughout this tangled history there proceeded the life of Johannes Kelpius, who seems so much stranger to me now than he did when I started. The precocious student from Denndorf became the ascetic spiritual alchemist of the Wissahickon, whose legendary afterlife was warped by the intellectual transformation that he foresaw with trepidation in his 1689 dissertation.

The watershed barrier that makes Böhme so challenging for modern readers is modern science, as Andrew Weeks and Bo Andersson noted. That same threshold, modern science and Enlightenment philosophy, permanently reshaped the memory of Johannes Kelpius. "Natural science instructs us that the universe is not composed of moral or sentient forces," Weeks and Andersson write[22]—not "composed of moral forces" in the sense of being always and utterly *good* or *peaceful*. A world that communicates in burning sky and quaking earth is hardly simply docile. Rather, this was a cosmos of moral status, of moral significance, of moral intent and meanings that existed alongside *and beyond* human beings.

"Natural science instructs us that the universe is not composed of moral or sentient forces": the life and thought of Johannes Kelpius instruct us in the opposite: an entirely moral and sentient universe.

Notes

Introduction

1. *Hazard's Register of Pennsylvania*, vol. 4, no. 3 (Philadelphia, July 18, 1829), 48. See also Jacques Vallee and Chris Aubeck, *Wonders in the Sky: Unexplained Aerial Objects from Antiquity to Modern Times* (New York: Tarcher/Penguin, 2009), 302.
2. *Hazard's Register of Pennsylvania*, vol. 4, no. 3 (Philadelphia, July 18, 1829), 48.
3. *Hazard's Register of Pennsylvania*, vol. 4, no. 3 (Philadelphia, July 18, 1829), 48.
4. *Hazard's Register of Pennsylvania*, vol 3, no. 4 (Philadelphia, January 24, 1829), 49.
5. *Hazard's Register of Pennsylvania*, vol 3, no. 4 (Philadelphia, January 24, 1829), 49–51.
6. Simon Schaffer, "Late Enlightenment Crises of Facts: Mesmerism and Meteorites," *Configurations* 26, no. 2 (Spring 2018): 142.
7. Schaffer, "Late Enlightenment Crises," 147.
8. Schaffer, "Late Enlightenment Crises," 119.
9. Daniel Schumacher (ca. 1729–1787), Scrivener (ca. 1769), Drawing (Up to the Judgment [Auf zum Gericht]), Free Library of Philadelphia, Manuscripts. Retrieved from https://libwww.freelibrary.org/digital/item/6372. "Ein Comet Stern sehr Blasser farb, in Pensylvanien, erschienen im Jahr 1769 im August \ Ihr Menschen fragt euch doch, waß dieser Stern thut deuten Ob Gott euch straffen will \ ach thut doch Buß bey Zeiten."
10. Johannes Kelpius, Letter to Steven Momfort in Rhode Island, December 11, 1699, in Journal, 1694–1708, , Historical Society of Pennsylvania, Ferdinand J. Dreer Autograph Collection (#0175), 42.
11. Leigh Eric Schmidt, *Restless Souls: The Making of American Spirituality* (San Francisco: HarperSanFrancisco, 2005), 79–80.
12. Schmidt, *Restless Souls*, 80.
13. Julius Sachse, *The German Pietists of Provincial Pennsylvania* (1895; University Park, PA: Metalmark Books, 2012).
14. Arthur Versluis, *Wisdom's Children: A Christian Esoteric Tradition* (Albany: State University of New York Press, 1999), 335. Versluis capably demonstrated Kelpius's intellectual connection to Jacob Böhme's theosophical Christianity rather than Rosicrucianism.
15. Jeff Bach, *Voices of the Turtledoves: The Sacred World of Ephrata* (University Park: Pennsylvania State University Press, 2003), 186.
16. Catherine Albanese, *America: Religions and Religion*, 5th ed. (Belmont: Thomson/Wadsworth, 2013), 188. See also the first edition of the same text (Belmont: Thomson/Wadsworth, 1981), 170–171.
17. Wouter J. Hanegraaff, *Esotericism and the Academy: Rejected Knowledge in Western Culture* (Cambridge: Cambridge University Press, 2012).
18. Personal communication with Erin Prophet in 2017.

234 NOTES

19. "Historical Pageant, Friday, October 9, 1908," in folder "Oberholtzer, Ellis Paxson," Box 3, Marion Dexter Learned Collection, Archives and Special Collections, Boyd Lee Spahr Library, Dickinson College, Carlisle, Pennsylvania. See Russell A. Kazal's article "The Lost World of Pennsylvania Pluralism: Immigrants, Regions, and the Early Origins of Pluralist Ideologies in America," *Journal of American Ethnic History* 27, no. 3 (Spring, 2008): 13.
20. See W. R. Ward, *Early Evangelicalism: A Global Intellectual History, 1670–1789* (Cambridge: Cambridge University Press, 2006), 6–23.
21. See Vitae I and II, where Kelpius identifies himself and his community as Pietist in the 1699 letter to Steven Momfort and in the 1693 Quaker Minutes at the London Meeting.
22. Geoffrey Parker, *Global Crisis: War, Climate Change and Catastrophe in the Seventeenth Century* (New Haven: Yale University Press, 2013), 1.
23. Parker, *Global Crisis*, 10–11, 13.
24. Hanegraaff, *Esotericism and the Academy*, 370.
25. Hanegraaff, *Esotericism and the Academy*, 370.
26. Hanegraaff, *Esotericism and the Academy*, 371.
27. Frances Yates, *Giordano Bruno and the Hermetic Tradition* (Chicago: University of Chicago Press, 1964), 176.
28. Philipp Blom, *Nature's Mutiny: How the Little Ice Age of the Long Seventeenth Century Transformed the West and Shaped the Present*, trans. by the author (New York: Liverwright, 2017); Carolyn Merchant, *The Death of Nature: Women, Ecology, and the Scientific Revolution* (New York: HarperCollins: 1980).
29. See Paul Warde, Libby Robin, and Sverker Sörlin's *The Environment: A History of the Idea* (Baltimore: Johns Hopkins University Press, 2021), for a detailed conceptual history.
30. Kelpius, Letter to Steven Momfort.
31. Robert Bartlett, *The Natural and the Supernatural in the Middle Ages* (Cambridge: Cambridge University Press, 2008).
32. Kelpius, Letter to Steven Momfort.
33. C. V. Wedgwood, *The Thirty Years War* (1938; New York: New York Review of Books, 2005), 20.
34. Bernard Bailyn, *The Barbarous Years: The Peopling of British North America: The Conflict of Civilizations, 1600–1675* (New York: Vintage, 2012), 40–41.
35. Jill Lepore, *The Name of War: King Phillip's War and the Origins of American Identity* (New York: Vintage, 1999), 99–101.
36. Amitav Ghosh, *Gun Island* (New York: Straus and Giroux, 2019), 137.
37. Lorraine Daston and Katharine Park are capable guides in their *Wonders and the Order of Nature, 1150–1750* (New York: Zone Books, 2001).
38. Ármann Jakobsson, *The Troll inside You: Paranormal Activity in the Medieval North* (Brooklyn, NY: Punctum Books, 2017), 22.
39. Revelation 1:9–10 KJV.
40. Elliot R. Wolfson, *Through a Speculum That Shines: Vision and Imagination in Medieval Jewish Mysticism* (Princeton: Princeton University Press, 1994), 29.

NOTES   235

41. Parker, *Global Crisis*.
42. Kelpius, Letter to Steven Momfort, 48.
43. Kyle Harper, *The Fate of Rome: Climate, Disease, and the End of an Empire* (Princeton: Princeton University Press, 2017), 293.
44. Andreas Malm, *Corona, Climate, Chronic Emergency: War Communism in the Twenty-First Century* (London: Verso, 2020), 117.
45. Wedgewood, *The Thirty Years War*, 7. Wedgwood's use of the male pronoun as default for the historian sticks out here since she was, at the time of writing those words, a leading historian in her field and a woman.
46. Brett Grainger, *Church in the Wild: Evangelicals in Antebellum America* (Cambridge, MA: Harvard University Press, 2019).
47. Jan Assman, foreword to Florian Ebling's *The Secret History of Hermes Trismegistus: Hermeticism From Modern to Ancient Times*, trans. David Lorton (Ithaca, NY: Cornell University Press, 2007), xiii.

Chapter 1

1. "Den 23sten Nov. nach der 17den Stund / Astronomischer rechnung; oder den 24sten Nov morgens nach 5. Uhr, gemeiner Rechnung gienger etwas spater / als gestern auss; . . . Die distance des Cometen von dem hellen mittnachtigen Sternen in der Waag nahme / und sie besande 1184 *particularum* im Tangeten." Johann Jakob Zimmermann, *Cometo-Scopia oder Himmel-gemäser Bericht* (Stuttgart: Zufinden bei Joh. Gottfridt Zubrodt Druckts Tobias Friederich Coccyus, 1681), 6.
2. Isaac Newton, *The Mathematical Principles of Natural Philosophy*, trans. Andrew Motte (New York: Putnam, 1850), 482, https://www.newtonproject.ox.ac.uk/view/texts/diplomatic/NATP00303.
3. *Abbildung Und Beschreibung Deß Wunderwürdigen Unvergleichlichen Cometen: Der Erstmals Zu Anfang Deß Wintermonats Vor Aufgang Der Sonnen Erschienen, Und Anjetzt Nach Derselben Untergang Sich Entsetzlich Sehen Lässet* (Nuremberg: Schollenberger, 1680), Munich, Bavarian State Library, https://www.digitale-sammlungen.de/de/view/bsb00100510?page=,1 (accessed August 22, 2023).
4. "Die Himmel / Saget Daniel / erziehen Ehre Gottes und die Feste verkündigt seiner hande werct Psalm 19. Wie nun durch dieselbe im *curso ordinario* der Natur / allerfordristt die Ehre Gottlicher zumacht / Weisheit und Gute gepriesen wird; Also lasset Gott auch durch die ausser ordenliche himmlische Phenomena, sonderheitlich die Ehre seiner Justiz Gerechtigkeit herfür leuchten." Zimmermann, *Cometo-Scopia*, 13. The attribution to Daniel might come from several verses, perhaps most likely Daniel 6:27.
5. Mike Zuber, "Johann Jacob Zimmerman and God's Two Books: Copernican Cosmology in Lutheran Germany Around 1700," in *Knowing Nature in Early Modern Europe*, ed. David Beck (London: Pickering & Chatto, 2015), 90.
6. Robin Bruce Barnes, *Prophecy and Gnosis: Apocalypticism in the Wake of the Lutheran Reformation* (Stanford, CA: Stanford University Press, 1988), especially chaps. 4 and 5.
7. Genesis 1:14 KJV.

236 NOTES

8. Edwin M. Good, *Genesis 1–11: Tales of the Earliest World* (Stanford, CA: Stanford University Press, 2011), 8–9.

9. Brian Fagan, *The Little Ice Age: How Climate Made History, 1300–1850* (New York: Basic Books, 2000), xvi.

10. Parker, *Global Crisis*, xx.

11. Parker, *Global Crisis*, xx.

12. Alistair MacBeath, "Meteors, Comets and Millennialism," *WGN: Journal of the International Meteor Organization* 27, no. 6 (1999): 318–326.

13. Parker, *Global Crisis*, 11.

14. Parker, *Global Crisis*, 10–11, 13.

15. Parker, *Global Crisis*, 25.

16. Wedgwood, *The Thirty Years War*, 494. The obvious comparison is the emergence of spiritualism in the wake of the Civil War in the United States.

17. Parker, *Global Crisis*, 227.

18. Brett Grainger, "Vital Nature and Vital Piety: Johann Arndt and the Evangelical Vitalism of Cotton Mather," *Church History* 81, no. 4 (2012): 859.

19. W. R. Ward notes that it is "calumny" to accuse Lutheran orthodoxy of wholesale disinterest in piety, but acknowledges that, in the late seventeenth century, it was "clear that the ordinary faithful needed something simpler and more devotional than the grand theological systems" (*Early Evangelicalism*, 2).

20. Robert Orsi, *History and Presence* (Cambridge, MA: Belknap Press of Harvard University Press, 2016).

21. Winfried Zeller, ed., *Der Protestantismus des 17. Jahrhunderts* (Bremen: Schünemann, 1962).

22. Harmutt Lehmann has previously pointed to the general crisis of the seventeenth century as a circumstance that contributed to the appearance of devotional and evangelical literature during the period. See Harmutt Lehmann, *Das Zeitalter des Absolutismus: Gottesgandemtum und Kriegsnot* (Stuttgart: Kohlhammer, 1980).

23. See Hans Schneider, *German Radical Pietism*, trans. Gerald T. MacDonald (Lanham, MD: Scarecrow Press and Center for the Study of World Christian Revitalization Movements, 2007).

24. Douglas H. Shantz, *An Introduction to German Pietism: Protestant Renewal at the Dawn of Modern Europe* (Baltimore: Johns Hopkins University Press, 2013), 9. Recent general accounts of Pietism also include Johannes Wallmann, *Der Pietismus* (Göttingen: Vandenhoeck & Ruprecht, 2005); Martin Brecht et al., eds., *Geschichte des Pietismus*, 4 vols. (Göttingen: Vandenhoeck & Ruprecht, 1993–2004).

25. For an expanded definition and much more thorough treatment, see Shantz, *Introduction to German Pietism*, 9. Ward, *Early Evangelicalism*, is another excellent introduction in English, with an emphasis on Pietist influence on what would become evangelicalism.

26. On enthusiasm as a theme in German religious history, see Monique Scheer, *Enthusiasm: Emotional Practices of Conviction in Modern Germany* (Oxford: Oxford University Press, 2021). Scheer writes that enthusiasm "derives from the Greek *entheos*, meaning 'filled with a god,' as in a possession or divine inspiration.

English speakers of the seventeenth century adapted this ancient term to describe the adherents of radical religious movements of their time, rooting the concept in the connection between religious belief and the strong emotional and physical excitement which they often displayed at their ritual gatherings" (1).

27. Dorette Seibert, *Glaube, Erfahrung und Gemeinschaft: Der junge Schleiermacher und Herrnhut* (Göttingen: Vandenhoeck & Ruprecht, 2003).

28. Friedrich Schleiermacher, *On Religion: Speeches to Its Cultured Despisers*, trans. and ed. Richard Crouter (Cambridge: Cambridge University Press, 2003), 22.

29. Ward, *Early Evangelicalism*, 2.

30. Wedgwood, *The Thirty Years War*, 20.

31. Frances A. Yates, *The Rosicrucian Enlightenment* (1972; London: Routledge, 2002), xiii.

32. Yates, *The Rosicrucian Enlightenment*, 290. Yates's historiography of Western esotericism has since been rightly revised by figures like Antoine Faivre and Wouter Hanegraaff, but her simple point in *The Rosicrucian Enlightenment* stands: the prewar Palatinate was a major European center of modern Hermetic religion and philosophy.

33. Isaac Causabon's 1614 debunking of the popular notion of an ancient Egyptian origin for the *Hermetica* was only slowly and begrudgingly accepted. See Florian Ebeling, *The Secret History of Hermes Trismegistus: Hermeticism from Ancient to Modern Times*, trans. David Lorton (Ithaca, NY: Cornell University Press, 2007), 91. As we will see in figures like Francis Daniel Pastorius (who accepts Hermes as an ancient Egyptian philosopher) in Chapter 2, Causabon's insights were slow to spread during the seventeenth century.

34. Hanegraaff, *Esotericism and the Academy*.

35. Brian Copenhaver, *The Hermetica: The Greek Corpus Hermeticum and the Latin Asclepius in a New English Translation, with Notes and Introduction* (Cambridge: Cambridge University Press, 2002), xlvii–xlviii.

36. Ebeling, *Secret History*.

37. Hanegraaff, *Esotericism and the Academy*, 371.

38. *Corpus Hermeticum X*, "Discourse of Hermes Trismegistus: The Key," trans. Brian Copenhaver, *The Hermetica*, 33.

39. Hanegraaff, *Esotericism and the Academy*, 371.

40. See Hanegraaff, *Esotericism and the Academy*, 107–114, for a detailed examination of Colberg's heresiology.

41. Hanegraaff, *Esotericism and the Academy*, 108.

42. Hanegraaff, *Esotericism and the Academy*, 108.

43. Quoted in Hanegraaff, *Esotericism and the Academy*, 109.

44. Hanegraaff, *Esotericism and the Academy*, 113.

45. Lawrence Principe, *The Secrets of Alchemy* (Chicago: University of Chicago Press, 2013), 194.

46. Principe, *The Secrets of Alchemy*, 30–31.

47. Principe, *The Secrets of Alchemy*, chap. 3.

48. George Perrigo Conger, *Theories of Macrocosms and Microcosms in the History of Philosophy* (New York: Columbia University Press, 1922), 55–56.

238 NOTES

49. Shantz, *Introduction to German Pietism*, 22.

50. Andrew Weeks, "Introduction," in *Paracelsus (Theophrastus Bombastus Von Hohenheim, 1493–1541): Essential Theoretical Writings*, ed. and trans. Andrew Weeks (Leiden: Brill, 2008), 16.

51. Shantz, *Introduction to German Pietism*, 21. Paracelsus himself is not always consistent on this point—in certain writings the character of "the peasant" stands in as a kind of uneducated person, who only sees the superficial appearance of things, alongside, however, "the experimenter," who is representative of all that is wrong with Galenic traditional medicine. "The Physician" is Paracelsus's ideal, who looks past and through both appearance and tradition to see things as they really are. See Chapter 2, "Paramirum," in Paracelsus, *Essential Theoretical Writings*.

52. Weeks, "Introduction," 11–12.

53. Paracelsus, *Essential Theoretical Writings*, 336.

54. Paracelsus, *Essential Theoretical Writings*, 336.

55. Weeks describes him as a "theorist of the supernatural" ("Introduction," 1), and he refers to the earthquake and rainbow writings on p. 500 of the same text.

56. Paracelsus, "Piramirum, Liber II," in *Essential Theoretical Writings*, 501.

57. Weeks, "Introduction," 15–16.

58. On Paracelsus's resistance to experimental methodology, see Conger, *Theories of Macrocosms*, 59.

59. Paracelsus, *De Potentia et Potentia Gratia Dei* (1533) (G 1:138), quoted in *Essential Theoretical Writings*, 148 note b.

60. Principe, *The Secrets of Alchemy*, 129.

61. Peter Erb, "Introduction," in Johann Arndt, *True Christianity*, trans. and ed. Peter Erb (New York: Paulist Press, 1979), 5.

62. Shantz, *Introduction to German Pietism*, 29.

63. Johannes Wallman, "Johann Arndt (1555–1621)," in *The Pietist Theologians: An Introduction to Theology in the Seventeenth and Eighteenth Centuries*, ed. Carter Lindberg (Malden, MA: Blackwell, 2005), 21.

64. Shantz, *Introduction to German Pietism*, 28.

65. Bernard McGinn, *Mysticism in the Reformation (1500–1650)* (New York: Herder and Herder, 2016), 151.

66. Hans Schneider, *Der fremde Arndt: Studien zu Leben, Werk und Wirkung Johann Arndts (1555–1621)* (Göttingen: Vandenhoeck & Ruprecht, 2006). See also Shantz, *Introduction to German Pietism*.

67. Shantz, *Introduction to German Pietism*, 25.

68. Shantz, *Introduction to German Pietism*, 26.

69. Shantz, *Introduction to German Pietism*, 27–28.

70. Schneider, *Der fremde Arndt*, cited in Shantz, *Introduction to German Pietism*.

71. Phillip Jenkins, *Climate, Catastrophe, and Faith: How Changes in Climate Drive Religious Upheaval* (New York: Oxford University Press, 2021), 36.

72. C. S. Zerefos, P. Tetsis, A. Kazantzidis, V. Amiridis, S. C. Zerefos, J. Luterbacher, K. Eleftheratos, E. Gerasopoulos, S. Kazadzis, and A. Papayannis, "Further Evidence of Important Environmental Information Content in Red-to-Green Ratios as Depicted

NOTES   239

in Paintings by Great Masters," *Atmospheric Chemistry and Physics* 14 (2014): 2987–3015.

73. "Wenn man nun eine Finsternis der Sonne und des Monds anschauet, soll man gedenken, es sei eine Verhinderung ihrer natürlichen Wirkung und Kräfte; denn es ist wider ihre Natur und verkündiget uns eine große vollbrachte Bosheit auf Erden, und derselben Strafe." Johann Arndt, *Sechs Bücher von Wahren Christenthum* (Philadelphia: Georg Menz und Sohn, 1834), 582.

74. "Und wenn der Himmel also brennet, und die Sonne blutrot ist, will er uns sagen: Sehet ihrs, so werde ich einmal im Feuer vergehen. Auf diese Weise reden alle Elemente mit uns, verkündigen uns unsere Bosheit und Strafen. Was ist der schreckliche Donner anders, denn eine gewaltige Stimme des Himmels, davor die Erde zittert, dadurch uns Gott warnet? Was ist das Erdbeben anders, denn eine erschreck-liche Sprache der Erde, die ihren Mund auftut, und große Veränderung verkündiget" (Arndt, *Sechs Bücher*, 582).

75. "Welches Leiden der großen Welt hernach auch im Micro-cosmo, das ist, im Menschen vollbracht wird. Was dem Menschen widerfahren soll, das leidet zuvor die Natur und die große Welt, denn aller Kreaturen Leiden, Gutes und Böses, ist auf den Menschen gerichtet, als auf ein Zentrum, darin alle Linien des Zirkels zusammenschießen. Denn was der Mensch verschuldet, dass muß zuvor die Natur leiden" (Arndt, *Sechs Bücher*, 581–582).

76. "Bedenke allhier die Weisheit und Gütigkeit Gottes: Du wirst an jedem Kraut und Blümlein sonderliche Zeichen finden, welches ist die lebendige Handschrift und Überschrift Gottes, damit ein jedes Kraut gezeichnet ist nach seiner verborgenen Kraft, so künstlich, so wunderbar, so zierlich, dass sie kein Künstler wird so eigentlich nachmalen können. Ja, mit der äußerlichen Form zeigen sie oft an ihre verborgene Kraft. Denn eines hat die Gestalt eines Hauptes, ein anders die Gestalt und Signatur der Augen, das dritte der Zähne, das vierte der Zunge, das fünfte der Hände und Füße, das sechste des Herzens, der Leber, der Blasen, der Nieren, der Wunden und dergleichen. Und das liegt da vor deinen Augen allenthalben. Sobald du auf einen grünen Rasen trittst, so hast du unter deinen Füßen eine Speise und Arznei. Denn in dem allergeringsten Gras und Samen, welches du gar gering und unnütz achtest, ist größere Weisheit Gottes, Kraft und Wirkung, als du ergründen kannst. Denn Gott hat nichts Unnützes geschaffen. Darum siehe zu, dass du Gott in seinen Werken nicht verachtest. Ich sage dir, es ist der tausendste Teil der Kräuter-Kraft noch nicht ergründet" (Arndt, *Sechs Bücher*, 555–556).

77. "Und wer nun ein guter Sternseher ist, der sich mehr auf die Sterne verstehet, denn auf die Rechenkunst, der weiß, wann, wie und wo ein solcher Baum am Himmel blühet, und solche Frucht geben wird. Siehe, also erzählen die Himmel die Ehre Gottes, und die Feste verkündiget seiner Hände Werk" (Arndt, *Sechs Bücher*, 571).

78. 1957.1107 A,B Painting, Portrait, Johann Arndt, Frame, Object card (Winterthur Museum).

79. Shantz, *Introduction to German Pietism*, 28.

80. In my understanding of Böhme, I lean on the two major studies in English: Andrew Weeks, *Boehme: An Intellectual Biography of a Seventeenth-Century Philosopher and Mystic* (Albany: State University of New York Press, 1991); John Joseph Stoudt,

240 NOTES

Sunrise to Eternity: A Study in Jacob Boehme's Life and Thought (Philadelphia: University of Pennsylvania Press, 1957). Ariel Hessayon also provides a worthwhile overview and consolidation of more recent research: "Boehme's Life and Times," in *An Introduction to Jacob Boehme: Four Centuries of Thought and Reception*, ed. Ariel Hessayon and Sarah Apetrei (New York: Routledge, 2014), 13–37.

Finally, Joshua Levi Ian Gentzke's 2016 dissertation "Imaginal Renaissance: Desire, Corporeality, and Rebirth in the work of Jakob Böhme" (Stanford University, 2016) is an essential (re)interpretation. I rely on a few of Gentzke's translations in his analysis of embodiment in the Böhmean corpus.

81. The comparison of Böhme and Dick is an admittedly speculative suggestion on my part, but the similar nature of their initial insight (accidently getting a beam of sunlight reflected into their eyes by a polished metal surface), the volume and extent of their writings attempting to auto-exegete the insights that followed, and the "gnostic" patterns that their readers have pulled out of their work are strikingly similar.

82. Weeks, *Boehme*, 1–2.

83. Weeks, *Boehme*, 1–2.

84. Weeks, *Boehme*, 1.

85. Weeks, *Boehme*, 1–2.

86. Most recently, Kristine Hannak has noted Arndt's and Böhme's unusual emphasis on the contemplation of nature, which she connects with their mutual influence, Paracelsus. "Johann Arndt (1555–1621) and the "Crisis of Piety" of Jacob Böhme's Time" in *Jacob Böhme and His World*, ed. Bo Andersson, Lucinda Martin, Leigh T. I. Penman, and Andrew Weeks (Leiden: Brill, 2019), 145–165.

87. Gentzke, "Imaginal Renaissance," 150.

88. Gentzke, "Imaginal Renaissance," 225.

89. George Fox, *The Journal of George Fox*, ed. John L. Nickalls (New York: Cambridge University Press, 1952), 27. On the comparisons between this specific passage and the writings of Böhme, see Ariel Hessayon's article "Jacob Bohme and the Early Quakers," *Journal of the Friends Historical Society* 60, no. 3 (2005).

90. Gentzke, "Imaginal Renaissance," 229.

91. Mike Zuber, *Spiritual Alchemy: From Jacob Boehme to Mary Anne Atwood* (Oxford: Oxford University Press, 2021).

92. See Patrick Erben, *A Harmony of the Spirits: Translation and the Language of Community in Early Pennsylvania* (Chapel Hill: Published for the Omohundro Institute of Early American History and Culture by the University of North Carolina Press, 2012), for the most complete recent treatment.

93. As mentioned above, Mike Zuber's work on Zimmerman and his connection to esoteric thought is invaluable: "Copernican Cosmotheism: Johann Jacob Zimmermann and the Mystical Light," *Aries* 14, no. 2 (September 2014): 215–245, and Zuber, "Johann Jacob Zimmerman." Basic biographical information on Zimmerman is available in G. Aker, "Johann Jacob Zimmerman 1642–1693: Ein Prophet des Tausendjährigen Reiches," in *Vaihinger Köpfe: Biographische Porträts aus fünf Jahrhunderten*, ed. L. Behr et al. (Vaihingen: Selbstverlag der Stadt Vaihingen an der Enz, 1993), 71–88.

94. Elizabeth Fisher, "'Prophesies and Revelations': German Cabbalists in Early Pennsylvania," *Pennsylvania Magazine of History and Biography* 109, no. 3 (July 1985): 312.
95. See Zuber, "Copernican Cosmotheism," 220–221.
96. Zuber, "Copernican Cosmotheism," 219.
97. Zuber, "Johann Jacob Zimmerman," 89–90.
98. Zuber, "Copernican Cosmotheism," 224.
99. Zuber, "Copernican Cosmotheism," 217, 224.
100. Zuber, "Copernican Cosmotheism," 215.
101. Zuber, "Copernican Cosmotheism," 223.
102. Ambrosius Sehman von Caminiez [Johann Jacob Zimmerman], *Mutmaßliche Zeitbestimmung göttlicher Gerichte über das Europäische Babel und Antichristentum jetziger Seculis* (Frankfurt am Main, 1684), 33.
103. Zimmerman, *Mutmaßliche Zeitbestimmung*, 52.
104. Zimmerman, *Mutmaßliche Zeitbestimmung*, 33.
105. The proceedings are described in Aker, "Johann Jacob Zimmerman 1642–1693," 79–84.
106. Earnest L. Lashlee, "Johannes Kelpius and His Woman in the Wilderness: A Chapter in the History of Colonial Pennsylvania Religious Thought," in *Glaube, Geist, Geschichte: Festschrift fur Ernst Benz*, ed. Gerhard Muller and Winfried Zeller (Leiden: Brill, 1967), 329. See also Fisher, "Prophesies and Revelations," 319.
107. Zuber, "Copernican Cosmotheism," 239; Johann Jakob Zimmerman, *Orthodoxia theosophiae teutonico-Boehmianae contra Holzhausiam defensa, das ist: Christliche Untersuchungen . . . wider Jacob Boehmens Auroram* (Leipzig, 1691).
108. Zuber, "Copernican Cosmotheism," 239.
109. Gerardus Croese, *The general history of the Quakers containing the lives, tenents, sufferings, tryals, speeches and letters of the most eminent Quakers, both men and women: from the first rise of that sect down to this present time* (London: Printed for John Dunton, 1696), 263.
110. Croese, *General History of Quakers*, 263.
111. Croese, *General History of Quakers*, 263.
112. Heinrich Hermelink, *Geschichte der evangelischen Kirche in Württemberg von der Reformation bis zur Gegenwart* (Stuttgart: Wunderlich, 1949), 191.
113. Croese, *General History of Quakers*, 263.
114. Almost all the secondary literature assumes the intermediary to have been Benjamin Furley, a Dutch Quaker with whom Penn worked to recruit German immigrants to Pennsylvania. If so, this would mean that Furley himself anonymously and generously forked over 130 pounds to the group.
115. The documentation surrounding Zimmerman's final moments has been happily, if somewhat surreally, clarified by a recent episode of the American popular genealogy television series *Who Do You Think You Are?* (Season 5, Ep. 7, March 15, 2015) in which the American singer-songwriter Josh Groban is aided by professional genealogists, archivists, and the historians Jonathan Clark and Jan Stevieman in uncovering his ancestry. Groban, it turns out, is a direct descendent of Johan Jacob

242 NOTES

Zimmerman, and the small army of researchers martialed by the producers pulled out all the stops in researching the details of Zimmerman's life and presenting them to a perplexed and delighted Groban. In a subsequent blog post on her website *Dutch Genealogy*, (https://www.dutchgenealogy.nl/the-josh-groban-episode-the-dutch-part/) researcher Yvette Hoitink presents her findings surrounding Zimmerman's death: Zimmerman died in Rotterdam, she found, on or just before September 19, 1693: he is listed as *vremdt*, "stranger" or transient and nonmember of the Dutch Reformed Church of Rotterdam, and buried in the Wijnhaven.

116. Croese, *General History of Quakers*, 264.

117. I am grateful to Anthony Grafton, who pointed out these connections and the inscriptions between Kelpius, Zimmerman, and the LCP holdings to me in a series of personal communications. James Logan records that the books originally belonged to Zimmerman and were bequeathed to Kelpius. After Kelpius's death, Logan acquired them for his library. See Ismael Boulliau, *Astronomia philolaica: Opus novum, in quo motus Planetarum per nouam ac veram hypothesim demonstrantur* (Paris: Sumptibus Simeonis Piget, 1645), Library Company of Philadelphia: Sev Boul., Log 205.F.

118. "Leibniz to Thomasius" (1669) in *The Book of Magic: From Antiquity to the Enlightenment*, ed. and trans. Brian Copenhaver (New York: Penguin, 2017).

119. Aristotle, *The Metaphysics*, trans. Hugh Lawson-Tancred (New York: Penguin, 1998), 375.

120. "Leibniz to Thomasius" (1669) in *The Book of Magic: From Antiquity to the Enlightenment*, ed. and trans. Brian Copenhaver (New York: Penguin, 2017).

121. Johannes Kelpius, *Theologiae Naturalis, Sev Metaphysicae Metamorphosin* (Altdorf: Schönnerstaedt, 1689), 7: "Deum esse magna semper fuit omium gentium consensio...fuisse tam barbaram, neque tam immansuetam, neque tam feram, quae etsi ignorarit qualem DEUM habere deceat, tamen habendum scivisse, docemur."

122. Kelpius, *Theologiae Naturalis*, 7: "Unde vero manifesta erat gentilibus cognitio de DEO? Vocemne e superis immisit illis Deus? Nequaquam! (d) sed quod illos voce validius illicere poterat, id fuit, creaturam suam in medio ponens, ut potuerit sapiens, rudis Scytha, barbarus ex ipso aspectu eorum, quae oculis subjecta erant, pulchritudinem edoctus, ad Deum conscendere."

123. Kelpius, *Theologiae Naturalis*, 7: "Ex hoc jam dogmate veluti perenni errorum scaturigine, per varias diductae sectas Philosophiae Gentilis cisternina promanare videtur."

124. 1 Corinthians 1:17, 2:1, 2:4.

125. Kelpius, *Theologiae Naturalis*, 20: "XVI. Jam ergo Metaphysicam Scholasticorum, qvi ab ea Pnevmaticam, scientiam scilicet de DEO & Spiritibus."

126. Kelpius, *Theologiae Naturalis*, 21–22: "& ipsi DEUM creatorem in unam cum Spiritibus creatis scientiam conjunxere, ut & hodie major pars Recentium, qvi scientiam particularem ab universali sejunctam esse velent, in eadem DEUM cum Angelis scientia vulgo Pnevmatica dicta relinqvant, non animadvertentes cum (5) Perierio, Majorem esse distantiam & diversitatem DEUM inter & Spiritus creatos, qvam inter hos & res naturales; magis etiam distare finitum ab infinito qvam ab

altero finito; plura item esse comunia Spiritibus creatis cum creaturis aliis qvam cum DEO; & haec ipsa quibus a DEO separantur Spiritus creati esse insigniora, &c."

127. Kelpius, *Theologiae Naturalis*, 29: "XXIV. Id tantum dico: Phaenomenorum omnium in causas pure Mechanicas (ne corporibus quidem plantarum animaliumque exceptis) possibilem resolutionem tantam partibus Religionis maxime essentialibus plagam inflixisse, aut infligere posse, ut incauti, qvi illius admiratione capti qvaecunqve ille dictaverit, qvam remotissima etiam fuerint à communi sensu, verisimilia modo sint, vera tamen ac solida sibi esse persvadent; qvorumqve religio sacrarum literarum fundamentis parum inaedificata, qvicqvid rationi suae corruptae consentaneum esse vident, amplectuntur, Existentiam DEI, animaeqve suae immortalitatem turpissimae subrisioni & contemptui exposituri sint."

128. Kelpius, *Theologiae Naturalis*: "Id igitur agamus ut ex visibilibus mundi phaenomenis, seu, ut cum (c) Apostolo loqvar, ut ex creatione mundi per ea qvae facta sunt mirabilia DEI, sempiternam ejus virtutem & Deitatem intelligamus . . . Rom 1:20."

129. Carolyn Merchant, *The Death of Nature: Women, Ecology, and the Scientific Revolution* (San Francisco: HarperCollins, 1980).

130. Weeks "Introduction," 15–16.

131. Andrew Weeks and Bo Andersson, "Jacob Böhme's Writings in the Context of His World," in *Jacob Böhme and His World*, ed. Bo Andersson, Lucinda Martin, Leigh T. I. Penman, and Andrew Weeks (Leiden: Brill, 2019), 18.

132. Weeks and Andersson, "Jacob Böhme's Writings," 17.

Vita I

1. Kelpius's precise date of birth and age has a confused history in the sources. Most of the secondary literature, beginning with Thomas Gordon (1829), dates his birth to 1673. This assumed date and Kelpius's exact age are not insignificant, since an important aspect of his story in the secondary literature is his wildly precocious attainment of a PhD at the age of sixteen and taking on the role of leader of Zimmerman's group at the age of twenty-one. As of the first decade of this century, several online sources were scattered with references to Kelpius's birthday as 1667, and potentially 1670 (Aaron Spencer Fogleman, *Hopeful Journeys: German Immigration, Settlement, and Political Culture in Colonial America, 1717–1775* [Philadelphia: University of Pennsylvania Press, 1996]). By 2019, Patrick Erben had adopted the 1667 date for his Pastorius reader, but there was no documentation provided for the new date. As of the twenty-first century, then, the secondary literature had several birthdays for Kelpius with precisely no primary documentation. For more precise information on Kelpius's birthdate, I turned to genealogy archives, where I was lucky to find the work of the German genealogist (and Kelp family descendant) Richard Ackner's self-published 2010 work *Allerlei von Vorfahren in Siebenbürgen* (*All Kinds of Ancestors in Transylvania*). Ackner had also found Kelpius's childhood attainment of a doctorate suspicious, and he managed to

244 NOTES

locate baptismal records in Denndorf for Kelpius for September 20, 1667, meaning that he was probably born about two days prior. Following up on Richard Acker's genealogical work, I was able to locate Kelpius's baptism records in the archives of Casa Teutsch, the archive of the Meeting and Cultural Center Friedrich Teutsch of the Evangelical Church in Romania (Casa Teutsch, Denndorfer Kirchenbuch, Signatur 980, 20). I am grateful to András Bándi at Casa Teutsch for locating the manuscript for me. Scholars can now confidently cite the year of Kelpius's birth as September 1667. Six years is not an overwhelming change, but the new date makes his earlier life trajectory a bit more sensible. In 2022, Kirby Richards reached similar conclusions, also on the basis of Ackner's work: Kirby Richards, "From Transylvania to Pennsylvania: Johannes Kelpius," *Yearbook of German-American Studies* 55 (2022): 133–162.

2. Levente Juhász, "Johannes Kelpius (1673–1708): Mystic on the Wissahickon," *Cromohs—Cyber Review of Modern Historiography*, 2006, https://oajournals.fupress. net/public/journals/9/Seminar/juhasz_kelpius.html.

3. Parker, *Global Crisis*, 7, 204.

4. Parker, *Global Crisis*, 7.

5. Parker, *Global Crisis*, 209–210.

6. I am grateful to Dr. Frank Trommler for his insights on the Transylvanian Saxons. Having had the chance to visit Siebenburg, he was impressed by the historical depth and contemporary flourishing of this German ethnic community within Romania— a community, he stressed, that was centered on the church.

7. Kirkenburgen Foundation, "Daia, Denndorf," https://kirchenburgen.org/en/locat ion/denndorf-daia/ (accessed December 5, 2023).

8. Karl Kurt Klein, "Magister Johannes Kelpius Transylvanus, der Heilige und Dichter vom Wissahickon in Pennsylvanien," in *Festschrift seiner Hochwürden D. Dr. Friedrich Teutsch gewidmet zu seinem 25 jährigen Bischofs-Jubiläum vom Ausschuß des Vereins für Siebenbürgische Landeskunde* (Hermannstadt: Honterusbuchdruckerei, 1931), 56–77.

9. Schäßburg was coincidentally the birthplace of another Transylvanian whose memory would be taken up by Romantic authors in the nineteenth century: Vlad Tepes the III, better known as Vlad the Impaler or Vlad Dracula, the namesake for the titular Transylvanian vampire in Bram Stoker's 1897 novel.

10. Johann Seivert, *Nachrichten von siebenbürgischen Gelehrten und ihren Schriften* [*Messages from Transylvanian Scholars and Their Writings*] (Pressburg, 1785), 212–214.

11. Johannes Kelpius, *Doctissimum Virum Deum Michael Deli* (Schäßburg, 1687), Manuscript 505, Department of the Library of the City of Sighişoara, Romania. Again, Richard Ackner, the indefatigable genealogist, deserves credit for this discovery, which was written up by Kirby Don Richards: http://kelpius.org/panegyric. html (accessed December 5, 2023).

12. On Kelpius's life in Transylvania, see Klein, "Magister Johannes Kelpius Transylvanus," 56–77.

13. *Archiv des Vereins für Siebenbürgische Landeskunde*, vol. 14 (Hermanstadt, 1872), 397. His name is listed as "Joh. Kelpius, Dalino Transyl." This source appends the

NOTES 245

abbreviation "dep. Et jur.," suggesting his intention to pursue a course of study in law. See also *Die Jüngere Matrikel der Universität Leipzig, 1559–1809* (Leipzig: Giesecke & Devrient, 1909), 214. I am grateful to Petra Hesse of the University Archives at Leipzig for help in accessing this source.

14. Shantz, *Introduction to German Pietism*, 103.

15. See Shantz, *Introduction to German Pietism*, chap. 4.

16. Johannes Kelpius, Letter to Steven Momfort in Rhode Island, December 11, 1699, in Journal, 1694–1708, , Historical Society of Pennsylvania, Ferdinand J. Dreer Autograph Collection (#0175), 50.

17. Kelpius, Letter to Steven Momfort, 49.

18. Kelpius's matriculation at Tübingen on December 22, 1687, is well attested: Matricula universitatis, Matricula Almae Universitatis Tubingensis de Anno MDCXXVIII. 1628–1711, University of Tübingen Archives, 74v, http://idb.ub.uni-tuebingen.de/opendigi/UAT_005_27b#tab=info&p=152 (accessed December 5, 2023). See also "Matricula universitatis VII" (1614–1800, Tübingen), 227r, http://idb.ub.uni-tuebin gen.de/opendigi/UAT_005_29a#p=459 (accessed December 5, 2023).

19. Shantz, *Introduction to German Pietism*, 84, 151.

20. Lashlee, "Kelpius and His Woman," 329. See also Fisher, "Prophesies and Revelations," 319.

21. Differing reasons for Kelpius's expulsion from the Tubingen seem to have persisted in Philadelphia as oral traditions of his life. Richard Mott Gummere described Kelpius as "A German university student, expelled for pietism," in his essay "Apollo on Locust Street," *Pennsylvania Magazine of History and Biography* 56, no. 1 (1932): 68–92. Writing in 1873, Oswald Seidensticker suggests that it was "the French War" that compelled Kelpius to leave Tubingen, presumably the invasion of Louis XIV in the Nine Years War: "More about the Hermit of the Ridge, John Kelpius," in *The American Historical Record* (Philadelphia: Chase & Town, 1873), 127.

22. Kelpius, *Theologiae Naturalis*, 1: "Vos enim estis DOMINI GRATIOSI, qui exclusum me per immanem Christianissimi in Christianos saevitiem a Gratia Wurtembergica, ut vidistis, ita (utinam tanta felicitate dignum!) sub umbra alarum Vestrarum nutrivistis, fovistis, protexistis."

23. Hermann Schüssler, "Fabricius, Johann," in *New German Biography*, vol. 4 (Berlin: Duncker & Humblot, 1959), 735–736.

24. Johannes Fabricius, *Daß zwischen der Augsburgischen Konfession und Katholischen Religion kein sonderlicher Unterschied sei* (Cologne, 1707). As Levente Juhász, "Johannes Kelpius (1673–1708)," relates, there was a political sponsorship behind this work: "This latter work, in which he was to prove that the two religions shared the same basis, was commissioned by Anton Ulrich, Prince of Braunschweig-Lüneburg in an effort to facilitate the marriage of his daughter to the Spanish king."

25. Johannes Kelpius, "Letter to Johannes Fabricius," 1705, in *The Diarium of Magister Johannes Kelpius*, trans. Julius Sachse (Lancaster, PA: New Era Printing Co, 1917; University Park: Metalmark Books, 2012), 83.

26. Johann Herdeegen, *Historische Nachricht von deß löblichen Hirten- und Blumen-Ordens an der Pegnitz Anfang und Fortgang . . .* (Nuremberg, 1744), 218. I am indebted

246　NOTES

to Levente Juhász, "Johannes Kelpius (1673–1708)," for this source, who in turn attributed its original discovery to Harold Jantz, "Deutschamerikanischer Literatur: Einige weitere Perspektiven," in *Amerika und die Deutschen: Bestandsaufnahme einer 300jährigen Geschichte*, ed. Frank Trommler (Opladen: Westdeutscher Verlag, 1986), 279–288.

27. Ernst Benz, *Die protestantische Thebais: Zur Nachwirkung Makarios des Ägypters im Protestantismus des 17. und 18. Jahrhunderts in Europa und Amerika* (Wiesbaden: Verlag der Akademie der Wissenschaften und der Literatur, 1963), 94.

28. Kelpius, *Theologiae Naturalis*.

29. Johannes Fabricius and Johannes Kelpius, *Scylla Theologica aliquot exemplis Patrum and Doctorum Ecclesiae, qui cum alios refutare laborarent, fervore disputationis abrepti in contrarios errores misere inciderunt, ostensa atque in materiam disputationis proposita a Joh. Fabricio S. Theol. Prof. Publ. and M. Joh. Kelpio Dalia-Transylvano Saxone* (Altdorf, 1690).

30. Johannes Kelpius, *Ethicus Ethnicus: Inquisitio an ethicus Etnicus aptus sit Christianae Juventutis Hodegus? sive: An juvenis christianus sit idoneus auditor Ethices Aristotelicae? Resp. Balthas. Blosio* (Nuremberg, 1690).

31. At some point, Kelpius definitely became acquainted with or at least aware of the Christian Kabbalist Christian Knorr Von Rosenroth, since he attributed certain melodies and hymns to Rosenroth's composition in his later hymnody. But whatever influence a figure like Rosenroth may have had on Kelpius is unclear—there is no clear influence of Rosenroth's Christian Kabbalah in Kelpius's later writings. Fisher, "Prophesies and Revelations," suggests that Rosenroth probably introduced Kelpius and Zimmerman on this basis. Sachse (*German Pietists*, 223), meanwhile, suggests that Zimmerman sought out Kelpius on the basis of his excellent university writings. I find both of these explanations unnecessarily speculative and specific. Kelpius and Zimmerman had so much in common and ran in such similar circles between 1687 and 1693 that they would have had countless chances to be introduced and reintroduced. They probably met at a conventicle meeting in or around Nuremberg between 1690 and 1693.

32. Kelpius, Letter to Steven Momfort, 50.

33. Peter James Yoder, "Pietism," in *Miracles: An Encyclopedia of People, Places, and Supernatural Events, from Antiquity to the Present*, ed. Patrick J. Hayes (Santa Barbara, CA: ABC-CLIO, 2016), 321–322.

34. Ernst Benz, *The Theology of Electricity: On the Encounter and Explanation of Theology and Science in the 17th and 18th Centuries*, trans. Wolfgang Taraba (Eugene, OR: Pickwick Publications, 1989).

35. Ernst Benz, *Emanuel Swedenborg: Visionary Savant in the Age of Reason*, trans. Nicholas Goodrick-Clarke (West Chester, PA: Swedenborg Foundation, 2002).

36. Kelpius, Letter to Steven Momfort, 43. The nonstandard spelling of "Penn" here—when he is clearly referring to the writing instrument, but chooses to spell it like the name William Penn—is very interesting. Kelpius did not shy away from criticizing the Quaker founder of the commonwealth, and I think there is good reason to suspect here that he is taking a swing at Penn's approach to the meaning of religious

NOTES 247

freedom, which he criticizes openly in his 1705 letter to Johannes Fabricius. Cryptic and nonstandard spelling and writing practices were common among the early Pietists, and this is *precisely* the way in which we might expect that an early Pietist like Kelpius would discretely criticize Penn. See Lucinda Martin, "The 'Language of Canaan': Pietism's Esoteric Sociolect," *Aries* 12, no. 2 (2012): 237–253.

37. Kelpius, Letter to Steven Momfort, 43–44.
38. Kelpius Letter to Steven Momfort, 46.

Chapter 2

1. "Corpus Hermeticum V: A discourse of Hermes to Tat, his son: That god is invisible and entirely visible," in Brian Copenhaver, trans., *Hermetica: The Greek Corpus Hermeticum and the Latin Asclepius in a New English Translation, with notes and introduction* (Cambridge: Cambridge University Press, 1992), 18.

2. Genesis 49:21.

3. John Joseph Stoudt, *Pennsylvania German Folk Art: An Interpretation* (Allentown, PA: Schletler's, 1966), 229. See also John Joseph Stoudt, *Early Pennsylvania Arts and Crafts* (New York: Bonanza Books, 1964), 316–317. The original German of Schuhmacher's *vorschrift* reads "I: Buch Mose Cap 49 vr 21. Naphtali "ist ein Schneller hirsch und gibt Schöne Rede." On the history and purpose of the *vorschrift*, see Stoudt, *Early Pennsylvania Arts*, 292–313. On misconceptions surrounding the literacy levels among early modern German Protestants, see Richard Gawthrop and Gerald Strauss, "Protestantism and Literacy in Early Modern Germany," *Past & Present*, no. 104 (1984): 31–55. By no means were all or even most Palatinate immigrants in early Pennsylvania illiterate, but many were, and part of pastoral care for a popular country pastor like Schuhmacher would have included techniques like illustrating his sermons.

4. For Schuhmacher's biographical details, see "Daniel Schuhmacher's Baptismal Register," translated and introduced by Frederick S. Weiser in *The Publications of the Pennsylvania German Society*, vol. 1: *The Four Gospels: Translated into the Pennsylvania German Dialect* (Allentown: Pennsylvania German Society, 1968). Mühlenberg's comments are quoted in Weiser, 195.

5. Weiser, *The Four Gospels*, also mentions a telescope being among the effects listed in Schuhmacher's will.

6. Daniel Schumacher (c. 1729–1787). Scrivener (ca. 1769). Drawing (Up to the Judgment [Auf zum Gericht]). "Auf zum gericht Auf säumet nic[ht]:

> "Ein Comet Stern sehr Blasser farb, in Pensylvanien, erschienen im Jahr 1769 im August \ Ihr Menschen fragt euch doch, waß dieser Stern thut deuten Ob Gott euch straffen will \ ach thut doch Buß bey Zeiten." Free Library of Philadelphia, Manuscripts, retrieved from https://libwww.freelibrary.org/digi tal/item/6372.

7. See previous chapter.

248 NOTES

8. Stoudt, *Pennsylvania German Folk Art*, 229.
9. Jacob Böhme, *Mysterium magnum, or An exposition of the first book of Moses called Genesis*, part 3, chap. 77, p. 594. University of Michigan, Early English Books Text Creation Partnership, https://quod.lib.umich.edu/e/eebo/A28529.0001.001/ 1:1?rgn=div1;view=fulltext;q1=naphtali.
10. Stoudt, *Pennsylvania German Folk Art*, 229.
11. Stoudt, *Pennsylvania German Folk Art*, 229.
12. Stoudt, *Pennsylvania German Folk Art*, 229.
13. Frances A. Yates, *The Rosicrucian Enlightenment* (London: Routledge, 2002), xiii. See Chapter 1.
14. For a more detailed analysis of the motivations and periodizations in German immigration to the mid-Atlantic colonies, see Fogleman, *Hopeful Journeys*.
15. *The Papers of Benjamin Franklin*, vol. 4, July 1, 1750, through June 30, 1753, ed. Leonard W. Labaree (New Haven: Yale University Press, 1961), 225–234.
16. John Joseph Stoudt, *Sunrise to Eternity: A Study in Jacob Boehme's Life and Thought* (Philadelphia: University of Pennsylvania Press, 1957). Joshua Levi Ian Gentzke, a leading contemporary Böhme scholar, noted Stoudt's book as remaining among the important studies in English ("Imaginal Renaissance," 16–17).
17. John Greenleaf Whittier, *The Pennsylvania Pilgrim and Other Poems* (Boston: Osgood and Co., 1872), xi.
18. Matthew Stewart. *Nature's God: The Heretical Origins of the American Republic* (New York: Norton, 2014), 15.
19. Alexander Ames, *The Word in the Wilderness: Popular Piety and the Manuscript Arts in Early Pennsylvania* (University Park: Penn State University Press, 2020).
20. The religious studies scholar Arthur Versluis's *The Esoteric Origins of the American Renaissance* (Oxford: Oxford University Press, 2001), and *Wisdom's Children: A Christian Esoteric Tradition* (Albany: State University of New York Press, 1999), have been invaluable to my positioning of esotericism in early American literature and religion. For comprehensive overviews of early American esotericism under the rubrics of "occultism" and "metaphysics," respectively, see Jon Butler, *Awash in a Sea of Faith: Christianizing the American People* (Cambridge, MA: Harvard University Press, 1990), and Catherine L. Albanese, *A Republic of Mind and Spirit: A Cultural History of American Metaphysical Religion* (New Haven: Yale University Press, 2007). David Hall's *Worlds of Wonder, Days of Judgment: Popular Religious Belief in Early New England* (Cambridge, MA: Harvard University Press, 1989), remains a helpful analysis of popular esotericism in early America. Historians of Mormonism have been working in this area for a while, and their works are particularly helpful. Their pursuit of the origins of Joseph Smith's thought has prompted two essential studies of early American esotericism: John L. Brooke's *The Refiner's Fire: The Making of Mormon Cosmology, 1644–1844* (Cambridge: Cambridge University Press, 1994), and D. Michael Quinn's *Early Mormonism and the Magic World View* (Salt Lake City: Signature Books, 1998). All of these texts—and this book—lean on Herbert Leventhal's classic *In the Shadow of the Enlightenment: Occultism and Renaissance Science in Eighteenth-Century America* (New York: New York University Press, 1976).

NOTES 249

21. Bernard Bailyn, *The Barbarous Years: The Peopling of British North America: The Conflict of Civilizations, 1600–1675* (New York: Vintage, 2012), 40–41; Jill Lepore, *The Name of War: King Phillip's War and the Origins of American Identity* (New York: Vintage, 1999), 99–101. On miracles and supernaturalism generally following the Revolution, see Adam Jortner, *Blood from the Sky: Miracles and Politics in the Early American Republic* (Charlottesville: University of Virginia Press, 2017).

22. None of the work in this book would have been possible without substantial reference to a recent wave of interdisciplinary work in what might be called early Pennsylvania studies: see John Smolenski's *Friends and Strangers: The Making of a Creole Culture in Colonial Pennsylvania* (Philadelphia: University of Pennsylvania Press, 2010); Aaron Fogleman, *Hopeful Journeys: German Immigration, Settlement, and Political Culture in Colonial America, 1717–1775* (Philadelphia: University of Pennsylvania Press, 1996); also by Fogleman, *Jesus Is Female: Moravians and Radical Religion in Early America* (Philadelphia: University of Pennsylvania Press, 2007); Erben, *Harmony of the Spirits*; Francis Daniel Pastorious, *The Francis Daniel Pastorius Reader: Writings by an Early American Polymath.*, ed. Patrick Erben, associate editors Alfred L. Brophy and Margo M. Lambert (University Park: Pennsylvania State University Press, 2019); Bach, *Voices of the Turtledoves*; Jean R. Soderlund, *Lenape Country: Delaware Valley Society before William Penn* (Philadelphia: University of Pennsylvania Press, 2015); and of course James Merrell's *Into the American Woods: Negotiators on the Pennsylvania Frontier* (New York: Norton, 1999).

23. Douglas Shantz (*Introduction to German Pietism*, 2) points out that one in four Lutheran congregations in America was of a Pietist bent by the year 1776.

24. Catherine L. Albanese, *A Republic of Mind and Spirit: A Cultural History of American Metaphysical Religion* (New Haven: Yale University Press, 2007), 42.

25. On the influence of modern Jewish esoteric thought in early American religion, see Brian Ogren, *Kabbalah and the Founding of America: The Early Influence of Jewish Thought in the New World* (New York: New York University Press, 2021).

26. The primary source of Arndt's *Wahren Christenthum* that I consulted for the translations in this book was printed in Philadelphia in 1834: *Sechs Bücher von Wahren Christenthum* (Philadelphia: Georg Menz und Sohn, 1834), held at the Horner Library of the German Society of Pennsylvania. The Horner Library has several Arndts printed in Pennsylvania and earlier printings from Germany, further demonstrating the importance of the text for German speakers in early Pennsylvania.

27. *The Journals of Henry Melchior Muhlenberg*, 3 vols, trans. Theodore G. Tappert and John W. Doberstein (Philadelphia: Evangelical Lutheran Ministerium of Pennsylvania and Adjacent States and the Muhlenberg Press, 1945). For a few mentions of Arndt and *True Christianity*, see 1:182, in which Arndt is beside Luther as the "highly enlightened fathers of the church"; 1:415, in which copies of *True Christianity* were given out alongside Bibles to poor Germans in Pennsylvania during the reign of Queen Anne; 2:288, in which Muhlenberg refers to the "blessed Anrd," etc. On the reading of *True Christianity* as a testament to a person's faith, see 1:357.

250 NOTES

28. Joseph Kelley, *Pennsylvania: The Colonial Years, 1681–1776* (Garden City, NY: Doubleday, 1980), 226–229. See also James Merrell, *Into the American Woods: Negotiations on the Pennsylvania Frontier* (New York: Norton, 1999), 24.

29. James Merrell (*Into the American Woods*) compiled the primary source material that shapes my understanding of colonial and Indigenous attitudes toward the nonhuman landscape in early Pennsylvania.

30. Bailyn, *The Barbarous Years*, 15.

31. Soderlund, *Lenape Country*, 7.

32. Soderland, *Lenape Country*, 7.

33. David Hackett Fischer, *Albion's Seed: Four British Folkways in America* (New York: Oxford, 1989), 452.

34. See also Smolenski, *Friends and Strangers*, 91–96, on Penn's interest in Lenape politics and social life.

35. Soderlund, *Lenape Country*, 11.

36. Soderlund, *Lenape Country*, 1.

37. Soderlund, *Lenape Country*, 12.

38. See Chapter 2, "Wicked Liberty," in David Graeber and David Wengrow, *The Dawn of Everything: A New History of Humanity* (New York: Farrar, Straus and Giroux, 2021).

39. Soderlund, *Lenape Country*, 21.

40. Soderlund, *Lenape Country*, 21.

41. Soderlund, *Lenape Country*, 23.

42. Soderlund, *Lenape Country*, 23.

43. Soderlund, *Lenape Country*, 23.

44. Andrew R. Murphy, *William Penn: A Life* (Oxford: Oxford University Press, 2019)

45. Murphy, *William Penn*, 23.

46. Smolenski, *Friends and Strangers*, 45.

47. Smolenski, *Friends and Strangers*, 45.

48. Smolenski, *Friends and Strangers*, 45–46.

49. See Murphy, *William Penn*, chap. 6.

50. Murphy, *William Penn*, 115.

51. *The concessions and agreements of the proprietors, freeholders and inhabitants of the province of West New-Jersey, in America* [1677], https://westjersey.org/ca77.htm.

52. Soderlund, *Lenape Country*, 142.

53. Murphy, *William Penn*, 47.

54. Soderlund, *Lenape Country*, 149.

55. Shantz, *Introduction to German Pietism*, 82.

56. Shantz, *Introduction to German Pietism*, 82; see also Patrick Erben, "Introduction: The Lives and Letters of Francis Daniel Patorius," in Pastorius, *Francis Daniel Pastorius Reader*, 3.

57. Patrick Erben's recent work is the essential entry into understanding Francis Daniel Pastorius, and in the following section I lean on his efforts to translate, interpret, and explore this immensely fascinating but understudied early American polymath. His 2012 monograph *A Harmony of the Spirits* is among the first works since Jeffrey Bach (and before then, John Joseph Stoudt) that really reckon with the task of translating

and understanding the radical Protestant literatures of early Pennsylvania. Equally useful is the critical edition of Pastorius, *Francis Daniel Pastorius Reader*.

58. Erben, "Introduction," 1.

59. Francis Daniel Pastorius, "Sichere Nachtricht auß America, wegen der Landschaft Pennsylvania," March 7, 1684, in *Francis Daniel Pastorius Reader*, 50.

60. Pastorius, "Sichere Nachtricht auß America," 51.

61. Pastorius, "Sichere Nachtricht auß America," 51.

62. Pastorius, "Sichere Nachtricht auß America," 52, 53.

63. Shirley Hershey Showalter, "'The Herbal Signs of Nature's Page': A Study of Francis Daniel Pastorius' View of Nature," *Quaker History* 71, no. 2 (1982): 89–99.

64. Alfred L Brophy, "'Ingenium est Fateri per quos profeceris': Francis Daniel Pastorius' Young Country Clerk's Collection and Anglo-American Legal Literature, 1682–1716," *University of Chicago Law School Roundtable* 3, no. 2 (1996): article 16, 648.

65. Francis Daniel Pastorius, *The Bee-Hive*, Ms. Codex 726, Kislak Center, University of Pennsylvania. Accessed via the Digital Beehive interface. Vol. 2, Image 222.

66. Francis Daniel Pastorius, *A Few Onomastical Considerations enlarged from the Number of Sixty-Six To that of One Hundred, and Presented or rather Re-Presented*, MS, 1700, p. 63. Appended to a photostat copy of Pastorius, *A new primmer, or, Methodical directions to attain the true spelling, reading & writing of English: whereunto are added, some things necessary & useful both for the youth of this province, and likewise for those, who from foreign countries and nations come to settle amongst us* (New York: William Bradford, 1698), German Society of Pennsylvania archives, German American Collection, AM 1.3. See also Smolenski, *Friends and Strangers*, 172, 353.

67. Pastorius, *A Few Onomastical Considerations*, 59–60. See also Smolenski, *Friends and Strangers*, 172, 353.

68. Showalter, "Herbal Signs," 93.

69. Pastorius, *Deliciae Hortenses*, ed. and trans. Christoph E. Schweitzer (Columbia, SC: Camden House, 1982), quoted in Erben, *Harmony of the Spirits*, 154.

70. Showalter, "Herbal Signs," 94.

71. Smolenski, *Friends and Strangers*, 27.

72. Carole Dale Spencer, "James Nayler and Jacob Boehme's 'The Way to Christ,'" *Quaker Religious Thought* 125 (2015), article 7. See also Hessayon, "Jacob Bohme."

73. The first copies of Johann Arndt in the Americas would be much harder to track, given his popularity. Cotton Mather is likely a frontrunner in bringing the first copies of Arndt to North America. See Brett Grainger, "Vital Nature and Vital Piety: Johann Arndt and the Evangelical Vitalism of Cotton Mather," *Church History* 81, no. 4 (December 2012): 852–872.

74. Versluis, *Esoteric Origins*, 23; Brian Regal and Frank J. Esposito, *The Secret History of the Jersey Devil: How Quakers, Hucksters, and Benjamin Franklin Created a Monster* (Baltimore: Johns Hopkins University Press, 2018), 30.

75. Daniel Leeds, *A trumpet sounded out of the wilderness of America . . .* (New York: William Bradford, 1697; London, 1699), preface (pages unnumbered).

76. Leeds, *Trumpet Sounded*.

252 NOTES

77. Leeds, *Trumpet Sounded*, preface.
78. Leeds, *Trumpet Sounded*, preface.
79. Leeds, *Trumpet Sounded*, preface.
80. Leeds, *Trumpet Sounded*, preface.
81. Regal and Esposito, *Secret History*, p. 20
82. Smolenski, *Friends and Strangers*, 54.
83. Regal and Esposito, *Secret History*, 24.
84. Daniel Leeds, *An almanack for the year of christian account 1687. particularly respecting the meridian and latitude of Burlington, but may indifferently serve all places adjacent* (Philadelphia: William Bradford, 1687).
85. Soderlund, *Lenape Country*, 143.
86. Soderlund, *Lenape Country*, 19.
87. Marion Barber Stowell, *Early American Almanacs: The Colonial Weekday Bible* (New York: B. Franklin, 1977), 7
88. Philipp Blom, *Nature's Mutiny: How the Little Ice Age of the Long Seventeenth Century Transformed the West and Shaped the Present*, trans. by the author (New York: Liverwright, 2017).
89. Carolyn Merchant, *Ecological Revolutions: Nature, Gender, and Science in New England* (Chapel Hill: University of North Carolina Press, 2010), 115
90. Daniel Leeds, *An almanack for the year of Christian account 1695 . . .* (New York: Printed and sold by William Bradford at the Bible in New-York, 1695).
91. John Everard, *The Divine Pymander of Hermes Mercurius Trismegistus . . .* (London: Robert White, 1650). The passage that Leeds quotes is found on page 13 of Everard's edition, as indicated. See also Copenhaver's introduction and reception history of the *Hermeticum* in *Hermetica*, xlix–li.
92. John Everard, *The Divine Pymander of Hermes Mercurius Trismegistus . . .* (London: Printed by J.S. for Thomas Brewster, 1657), 74–75
93. Everard, *Divine Pymander*, 20.
94. See also Copenhaver, *Hermetica*, 105, for the astrological breakdown of this passage and its common ancient understandings.
95. Genesis KJV.
96. Peter Brown, *The Cult of the Saints: Its Rise and Function in Latin Christianity* (Chicago: University of Chicago Press, 1981), 12.
97. Butler, *Awash*, 80.
98. Leventhal, *In the Shadow*, 64.
99. Charles Brockden Brown, *On Almanacks. The Monthly Magazine and the American Review*, vol. 1, issue 2 (New York: T. & J. Swords, 1799), 85–88, http://brockdenbrown.cah.ucf.edu/xtf3/view?docId=1799-05085.xml.
100. Brown, *On Almanacks*, 86
101. Brown, *On Almanacks*, 86.
102. Leeds, *Trumpet Sounded*, preface (pages unnumbered)
103. Daniel Leeds, *The temple of wisdom for the little world, in two parts* (Philadelphia: Printed and sold by William Bradford, 1688), https://quod.lib.umich.edu/e/evans/N00365.0001.001/1:2?rgn=div1;view=toc.

NOTES 253

104. Regal and Esposito, *Secret History*, 34.
105. See the section on the Keithian schism in Chapter 3.
106. Jacob Taylor, *Almanac for the Year 1705*, quoted in Regal and Esposito, *Secret History*, 49.
107. Albanese, Catherine L. *A Republic of Mind and Spirit: A Cultural History of American Metaphysical Religion* (New Haven: Yale University Press, 2007) 42
108. John L. Brooke, *The Refiners Fire: The Making of Mormon Cosmology, 1644–1844* (Cambridge: Cambridge University Press. 1994). p. 44.
109. "To Benjamin Franklin from John Peter Miller, 12 June 1771," Founders Online, National Archives, https://founders.archives.gov/documents/Franklin/01-18-02-0087. [Original source: The Papers of Benjamin Franklin, vol. 18, January 1 through December 31, 1771, ed. William B. Willcox. New Haven and London: Yale University Press, 1974, pp. 130–132.]

Vita II

1. Croese, *General History of Quakers*, 263.
2. See the notes 115 and 116 in Chapter 1 for the documentation surrounding Zimmerman's death.
3. In his Journal, 1694–1708, Historical Society of Pennsylvania, Ferdinand J. Dreer Autograph Collection (#0175), Kelpius notes that he was the one who handled the money with which they secured passage to Pennsylvania, a suggestion of some sort of leadership role.
4. Croese, *General History of Quakers*, 263.
5. Schneider, *German Radical Pietism*, 20.
6. Schneider, *German Radical Pietism*, 20.
7. See Schneider *German Radical Pietism*, 19. See also Siglind Ehinger. "German Pietists between the Ancient Unity of Brethren and the Moravian Church: The Case of Württemberg Pastor Georg Konrad Rieger (1687–1743) and His 'History of the Bohemian Brethren,'" *Journal of Moravian History* 14, no. 1 (2014): 55.
8. Schneider, *German Radical Pietism*, 19.
9. *Copia Eines Send-Schriebens auß der Neun Welt*, described in Oswald Seidensticker, "Hermits of the Wissahickon," *Pennsylvania Magazine of History and Biography* 11 (1887): 427–441. See also Erben, "Introduction."
10. Kelpius does say that he was the one who eventually paid the ship in London, meaning that the group trusted him to administer funds, but his journal goes on to say that it was Köster who eventually "excommunicated" Daniel Falckner and Anna Maria Schuchart. This suggests, I think, a more decentralized organization in which several figures were recognized as authoritative.
11. Kelpius, Journal, 1694–1708, 1.
12. Judd Stitziel, "God, the Devil, Medicine, and the Word: A Controversy over Ecstatic Women in Protestant Middle Germany 1691–1693," *Central European History* 29, no. 3 (1996): 309–337.

254 NOTES

13. See Bernard Bailyn, *The Barbarous Years: The Peopling of British North America. The Conflict of Civilizations, 1600–1675* (New York: Vintage, 2012).

14. Friends House Library, Minutes for the Meetings for Sufferings, vol. 9, 1693–1694, 40. The minutes use the pre-1752 Julian calendar, in which the first month of the year would have been March, thus, the "8th month" noted by the minutes refers to October. I am grateful to Levente Juhász for locating this source and establishing the connection to the Kelpius group.

15. Friends House Library, Minutes for the Meetings for Sufferings, vol. 9, 1693–1694, 44.

16. Friends House Library, Minutes for the Meetings for Sufferings, vol. 9, 1693–1694, 75.

17. Friends House Library, Minutes for the Meetings for Sufferings, vol. 9, 1693–1694, 79.

18. Kelpius, Journal, 1694–1708, 4.

19. Croese, *General History of Quakers*, 264.

20. See Chapter 2.

21. In Revelation, the angel has a warning for the Philadelphians, tinged with millennialist meanings, from which the people of Philadelphia would be protected: "Because thou hast kept the word of my patience, I also will keep thee from the hour of temptation, which shall come upon all the world, to try them that dwell upon the earth. Behold, I come quickly: hold that fast which thou hast, that no man take thy crown" (Rev 3:7–13).

22. The best contemporary treatment of Lead, the Philadelphians, and their influence is Ariel Hessayon's edited volume *Jane Lead and Her Transnational Legacy* (London: Palgrave Macmillan, 2016).

23. Two letters to a former colleague by Kelpius have recently surfaced in a European archive from this period of Kelpius's life. See Kelpius 1693 and 1694. I am grateful to Kirby Richards for pointing me toward these letters.

24. Friends House Library, Minutes for the Meetings for Sufferings, vol. 9, 1693–1694, 79.

25. "Septima Jannarii convictus a Dio iter in America institui." Kelpius, Journal, 1694–1708, 1.

26. For the Falckner/Seelig letter, *Copia Eines Send-Schreibens auß der Neun Welt* (Halle and Frankfurt, 1695?) described in Oswald Seidensticker, "Hermits of the Wissahickon," *Pennsylvania Magazine of History and Biography* 11 (1887): 427–441. Patrick Erben (*Harmony of the Spirits*; "Introduction") also attributes the letter to Seelig.

27. Seidensticker, "Hermits of the Wissahickon," 430.

28. Kelpius, *Diarium*, 11–13.

29. "Mens praesaga, mala cum eventu felici mihi praesagiebat. Idem Falckernus de se affirmabat." Kelpius, Journal, 1694–1708, 1.

30. Kelpius, *Diarium*, 13; Journal, 1694–1708, 1.

31. Seidensticker, "Hermits of the Wissahickon," 431.

32. Kelpius, *Diarium*, 14.

33. Kelpius, *Diarium*, 14.

NOTES   255

34. Seidensticker, "Hermits of the Wissahickon," 431.
35. Seidensticker, "Hermits of the Wissahickon," 434.
36. Seidensticker, "Hermits of the Wissahickon," 436.
37. Kelpius, Journal, 1694–1708, 12, "Certantes quasi cursu cum navigio haud Seeus ac igne ferri viderentur." The "Seeus" here shows Kelpius's tendency to slip between German and Latin.
38. Seidensticker, "Hermits of the Wissahickon," 435.
39. Kelpius, Journal, 1694–1708, 14: "sibi naute timerent, praeterae hebet inter nos haud ita procul navis rigens."
40. Seidensticker, "Hermits of the Wissahickon," 438.
41. Kelpius, *Diarium*, 26.
42. Seidensticker, "Hermits of the Wissahickon," 438.
43. Kelpius, Journal, 1694–1708: "Copiae literam ad amicos in & extra Pensylvaniam missas ex deserto."
44. Kelpius, Journal, 1694–1708: "Patriam meam transire non possum, omnium una est, extra hanc nemo projici potest. Non patria mihi inter|dicitur sed locus, in quamcunque terram venio, in meam venio, nulla exilium est, sed altera patria est. Patria est ubicunque bene est. Si enim sapiens est peregrinator, si stultus, exultat." My gratitude to Claire Fanger for her careful help with this passage.

Chapter 3

1. Timothy Pauketat, "Ancient Faith and the Fall of Cahokia," Illinois Program for Research in the Humanities (IPRH) at the Chicago Humanities Festival, November 4, 2017, https://www.youtube.com/watch?v=0LP2m9eYhe8&t=380s.
2. To read a more complete and elegant articulation of this idea, see Sarah McFarland Taylor's 2007 article, "What If Religions Had Ecologies? The Case for Reinhabiting Religious Studies," *Journal for the Study of Religion, Nature, and Culture* 1, no. 1 (2007): 129–138.
3. William Cobbett, *Rural Rides* (London: A. Cobbett. 137, Strand, 1853), 2.
4. Joseph D. Bicknell, *The Wissahickon in History, Song and Story* (Philadelphia: City History Society of Philadelphia, 1906), 23.
5. David R. Contosta and Carol Franklin, *Metropolitan Paradise: The Struggle for Nature in the City. Philadelphia's Wissahickon Valley, 1620–2020*, vol. 1, *Wilderness* (Philadelphia: Saint Joseph's University Press, 2010).
6. Edgar Allen Poe, "Morning of the Wissahickon," in *Poetry & Tales* (New York: Library of America, 1984), 939–944. First published in *The Opal*, 1844.
7. Poe, "Morning of the Wissahickon."
8. Edgar Allen Poe, "The Lake — To ——", in *The Works of the Late Edgar Allan Poe*, vol. 2, *Poems and Miscellanies* (New York: Redfield: Clinton Hall, 1850), 109.
9. Oswald Seidensticker, *Bilder aus der Deutsch-Pennsylvanischen Geschichte* (New York: E. Steiger, 1885), 95–96. ("Hätte Kelpius in den briefen, deren abschrift von

256 NOTES

seiner eigenen hand sich erhalten hat, nur etwas von seinem alltaglichen Leben mit einfliessen lassen, so ware uns jetzt damit beser gedient als mit den weitlaufigen theologischen Grillen, die er darin ausspinnt.")

10. Daniel Falckner, *Falckner's Curieuse Nachricht von Pennsylvania: The Book That Stimulated the Great German Immigration to Pennsylvania in the Early Years of the XVIII Century*, trans. Julius Sachse (1905; University Park: Pennsylvania State University Press, 2012), 159. For the manuscript version of Falckner's report, see "Curiose Nachrichten von Pennsylvania . . . ," MS AFSt/H D85, 469–597, Frankesche Stiftungen, Halle. See also Erben, *Harmony of the Spirits*, 103.

11. Seidensticker, *Bilder*, 441.

12. See Johann Christoph Adelung, *Geschichte der menschlichen Narrheit*, vol. 7 (Leipzig, 1789), 91. The most thorough investigation into the records of the history of the Hermitage is Cissy Scheerer's "A Historical Sketch of Johannes Kelpius and the Hermits of the Wissahickon," Fairmount Park Commission, Park Historians Office, 1979. Scheerer's work is helpful but often intensely speculative, to the point of suggesting that some of the religious beliefs of the group could be attributed to drug use.

13. See Vita II for a detailed overview of the curious extent of Quaker generosity toward the group.

14. Croese, *General History of Quakers*, 264.

15. Cissy Scheerer ("A Historical Sketch of Johannes Kelpius and the Hermits of the Wissahickon,." Fairmount Park Commission, Park Historians Office, 1979) has suggested that Kelpius's correspondence seems "too religious," suggesting that each letter was a unique and understated solicitation of charity on behalf of the Wissahickon group. Kelpius certainly solicited charity on behalf of his group, as we have seen in the records of his time in London (see Vita II), but Sheerer's estimation undercuts the content of the correspondence, which includes no direct solicitation of any kind, and does not seem directed to particularly wealthy individuals—rather, Kelpius seems to write to whoever bothers to reach out to him in the first place.

16. Ruth L. Springer, Louise Wallman, And. Rudman, and Andreas Sandell, "Two Swedish Pastors Describe Philadelphia, 1700 and 1702," *Pennsylvania Magazine of History and Biography* 84, no. 2 (1960): 194–218.

17. Springer et al., "Two Swedish Pastors," 205.

18. Springer et al. also bemoan Sachse's influence on the historiography of Gloria Dei: "Clear view of Gloria Dei's beginnings has been further prevented by a fanciful account of the consecration of the church published in 1895 in *The German Pietists of Provincial Pennsylvania*. Often quoted, this has become widely accepted as sober, historical fact. Fortunately, it is now possible to supply, from the first of the letters which follow, a record of that event written by the person most deeply concerned with it, Andreas Rudman" ("Two Swedish Pastors," 199).

19. Angelus Silesius, *Cherubinischer Wandersmann: oder Geist-reiche Sinn- und Schluss-Reime zur göttlichen Beschauligkeit anleitende. Von dem Urheber aufs neue übersehn und mit dem sechsten Buche vermehrt . . . zum andernmahl herauss gegeben* (Glatz: auss neu auffgerichter Buchdrukkerey Ignatij Schubarthi, 1675), Library Company of

NOTES   257

Pennsylvania, Sev Ang 70122.D, "Johannes Kelpius Transylvanus me sibi comparavit 1696."

20. Albrecht Classen, "The Secret and Universal Relevance of Johann Scheffler' (Angelus Silesius's) Epigrams: Mystico-Philosophical Messages from the World of the Baroque for the Twenty-First Century," *The Comparatist* 44 (2020): 215–234.

21. Silesius, *The Cherubinic Wanderer*, trans. Maria Shrady, introduction and notes by Josef Schmidt (New York: Paulist Press, 1986).

22. Schmidt, "Introduction" to Silesius, *The Cherubinic Wanderer*, 30.

23. Zuber, *Spiritual Alchemy*, 9.

24. I am quoting Maria Schrady's excellent English translation (Silesius, *The Cherubinic Wanderer*, 31). Silesius, *Cherubinischer Wandersmann*, 35: 257. "Die Dreieinigkeit in der Natur. Daß Gott dreieinig ist, zeigt dir ein jedes Kraut, Da Schwefel, Salz, Merkurin in einem wird geschaut."

25. Kelpius, Letter to Hesther Palmer at Flushing, Long Island, May 25, 1706, in Journal, 1694–1707, Historical Society of Pennsylvania, Ferdinand J. Dreer Autograph Collection (#0175), 94. Kelpius spells her name "Hester Pallmer" in the manuscript letter. Sachse's *Diarium* spells it "Hester Palmer." For the sake of clarity, I spell her name Esther Palmer here.

26. See Chapter 2 for a detailed refutation of the idea of early Pennsylvania as a wilderness.

27. Stephanie Grauman Wolf, *Urban Village: Population, Community, and Family Structure in Germantown, Pennsylvania, 1683–1800* (Princeton: Princeton University Press, 1976), 10.

28. Wolf, *Urban Village*, 24–25.

29. *American Weekly Mercury*, September 21–28, 1729. See Wolf, *Urban Village*, 28–29.

30. Revelation 12, KJV.

31. Kelpius, Letter to Elizabeth Gerber, 1704, in Journal, 1694–1707: "Apoc. 12 am Ende, (von Wüste zeichnet so viel als verborgen oder nicht offenb als)" (77–78).

32. There is no reliable list of all forty companions—Sachse claims to have located one, but Willard Martin managed to point out several inconsistencies between the list and a few individuals who were certainly on the ship, yet again casting doubt on another obscure manuscript Sachse claimed to refer to. See Willard Martin, "Johannes Kelpius and Johann Gottfriend Seelig: Mystics and Hymnists on the Wissahickon" (PhD diss., Pennsylvania State University, 1973), 34.

33. For the Spener and Francke correspondence see Philipp Jakob Spener, *Briefwechsel mit August Hermann Francke 1689–1704*, ed. Johannes Wallmann and Udo Sträter (Tübingen: Mohr Siebeck, 2006), 365, in which Seelig is indicated as a theology student. Adelung, *Geschichte der menschlichen Narrheit*, also names Seelig coming from Lemgo.

34. "In den vorigen wochen haben wir fast alle tage etwas ungewohnliches erfahren un einigen studiosis, deren einer nach dem andern in einen sonderlichen zustand gesetzet worden, einige mit ungemeiner und ubernaturlich Freude uberschuttet, andere mit scharffer contrition und vielen thränen mit bezeugung daß ihnen ihr gantzes hertz gleichsam im Leibe zerschmoltzen wäre, oder daß es wäre als wolte

258 NOTES

ihnen das hertz aus dem Leibe springen, oder wenn etwas kräfftiges vom worte Gottes geredet worden, als fuhre es we ein blitz durch alle Glieder, anderer Umstände zu geschweigen, die so kurtz nicht mogen berichtet werden. Ihre Namen, wie sie nacheinander in solchen Zustand, der doch immer bey einem anders ist als bey im den andern, kommen sind, sind folgende: Stophasius, Kohler, Ulrici, Seelig, Kipsch, Schroter. Nun gehen sie in einem stillen wesen fort, zum theil freudig, theils etwas ängstlich; dohc so daß es sich so sonderlich nicht äussert, laßen sonst genug spuren, daß is ihnen ein größer Enrst mit ihrer Gottseeligkeit sey als vorhin. Der Herr wird ja ferner sein werck ze erkennen geben. Sonst sind auch ins gemein die studiosi sehr fein untereinander affgemuntert, und in hertzlicher Liebe verbunden, ind reitzen einander sehr zum wachsthum so wol der Erkentniß, als der Beweisung." Spener, *Briefwechsel*, 86–87.

35. *Copia Eines Send-Schreibens auß der Neun Welt*, described in Seidensticker, "Hermits of the Wissahickon." For Seelig's hymns, see Willard Martin's "Kelpius and Seelig," 239–249.

36. Seelig's letter to Deichmann is in Kelpius's Journal, 1694–1707, 40.

37. Seelig, *Copia Eines Send-Schreibens*; Seelig's letter to Deichmann, 40.

38. Seelig, "Letter to Heinrich Deichmann," 1699, in Kelpius, *Diarium*, 42.

39. Horatio Gates Jones, *The Levering Family, or, A Genealogical Account of Wigard Levering and Gerhard Levering* (Philadelphia: King and Baird, 1858).

40. Jones, *Levering Family*, 19. This passage has also been noted by Owen Davies in *Grimoires: A History of Magic Books* (New York: Oxford University Press, 2009), 140–141.

41. Croese, *General History of Quakers*, 263. Köster's name is spelled "Cöster" in Kelpius's journal, and Heinrich was frequently abbreviated as "Henry."

42. Kelpius, Journal, 1694–1707, 16.

43. Adelung, *Geschichte der menschlichen Narrheit*, 86.

44. Seidensticker, *Bilder*, 440.

45. Seidensticker, *Bilder*.

46. Seidensticker, *Bilder*.

47. Erben, *Harmony of the Spirits*, 100.

48. Kelpius, Journal, 1694–1707, 16. See Vita II. Rosalind J. Beiler's essay "Migration and the Loss of Spiritual Community: The Case of Daniel Falckner and Anna Maria Schuchart," in *Enduring Loss in Early Modern Germany*, ed. Lynne Tatlock (Leiden: Brill, 2010), 369–395, is a well-researched analysis of the life and marriage of Falckner and Schuchart.

49. "So hat Herr Köster Herrn Falcknern dahin gebracht, das er nun keine ecstases mehr habe." Ph. J. Spener to A. H. Francke, Berlin, May 6, 1693, in Spener, *Briefwechsel*, 299.

50. "Auch hat dieser gesagt, wie er daran gekommen, und das ex imaginatione intensa Göttl[icher] dinge er sich die erwecken könne." Spener to Francke, in Spener, *Briefwechsel*, 299.

51. "Wäre ich in dieser materie, die extraordinaria angehend, auff eine oder andre seite gewißer, so deucht mich, solte ein größstes stück der sorgen gehoben sein: da ich jetzt mir in vielem nicht zu helffen weiß." Spener to Francke, in Spener, *Briefwechsel*, 299.

NOTES 259

52. On educated German use of Latin script for foreign ideas, events, and phenomena, see Birte Pfleger's chapter "Ein Schrecklicher Zustand," in *Babel of the Atlantic*, ed. Bethany Wiggin (University Park: Pennsylvania State University Press, 2019), 201.

53. Seidensticker, *Bilder*, 439.

54. Seidensticker, *Bilder*, 439.

55. Keith came to New Jersey Quaker territory in 1685 before moving to Philadelphia in 1688 (see Regal and Esposito, *Secret History*, 39; Erben, "Introduction," 67).

56. On the Keithian schism, see Jon Butler, "Into Pennsylvania's Spiritual Abyss: The Rise and Fall of the Later Keithians, 1693–1703," *Pennsylvania Magazine of History and Biography* 101, no. 2 (April 1, 1977): 151–170.

57. Butler, "Into Pennsylvania's Spiritual Abyss," 153.

58. George Keith, *The Deism of William Penn . . .* (London: Printed for Brab. Aylmer, 1699).

59. Erben, "Introduction," 68.

60. Brian Ogren, *Kabbalah and the Founding of America: The Early Influence of Jewish Thought in the New World* (New York: New York University Press, 2021). See Chapter 1.

61. Daniel Leeds, *A Trumpet Sounded Out of the Wilderness of America Which May Serve as a Warning to the Government and People of England to Beware of Quakerisme* (London: St. Paul's London; New York, William Bradford, 1699); Daniel Leeds, *The Great Mistery of Fox-Craft Discovered* (New York: Printed by William Bradford, 1705).

62. Susan E. Klepp, "Demography in Early Philadelphia, 1690–1860," *Proceedings of the American Philosophical Society* 133, no. 2 (1989): 103.

63. Regal and Esposito also point out the religious and partisan agreements between Leeds and the Wissahickon group (*Secret History*, 35).

64. Francis Daniel Pastorius, "Henry Bernard Koster, William Davis, Thomas Rutter & Thomas Bowyer, four Boasting Disputers of this World briefly REBUKED," 1697, in *Francis Daniel Pastorius Reader*, 66–79.

65. Pastorius, "Henry Bernard Koster," 71.

66. Pastorius, "Henry Bernard Koster," 68.

67. Pastorius, "Henry Bernard Koster," 68.

68. Pastorius, "Henry Bernard Koster," 80.

69. Pastorius, "Henry Bernard Koster," 83–84.

70. Pastorius, "A Missive of Sincere Affection to the So-Called Pietists in Germany," in *Francis Daniel Pastorius Reader* 82,

71. Pastorius, "Henry Bernard Koster," 87.

72. See Shantz, *Introduction to German Pietism*, chap. 5, "Halle Pietism and Universal Social Reform."

73. Seidensticker, *Bilder*, 441.

74. Henry Melchior Mühlenberg, *Nachrichten von den vereingten deutschen Evangelisch-Lutherischen Kurtze nachricht von einigen Evangelischen gemeinen in America, absonderlich in Pensylvanien*, vol. 2 (Halle, 1774; Philadelphia: P.G.C. Eisenhardt, 1895), 639–640. See also Martin, "Kelpius and Seelig," 49. This would have been three years before Seelig's death in 1745.

260 NOTES

75. Daniel Falckner, *A Contribution to Pennsylvania History: Missives to Rev. August Herman Francke from Daniel Falckner and Justus Falckner*, trans. George T. Ettinger (Lancaster, PA: Pennsylvania-German Society, 1909), 13. See also Martin, "Kelpius and Seelig," 50.

76. Falckner, *Contribution to Pennsylvania History*, 5–7.

77. See Kelpius, *Diarium*, 45, 84.

78. Croese, *General History of Quakers*, 263.

79. Seidensticker, *Bilder*, 440.

80. Falckner, *Contribution to Pennsylvania History*, 5–7.

81. Kelpius, *Diarium*, 80.

82. Kelpius, *Diarium*, 80. See Martin, "Kelpius and Seelig," 51. "Maulchristen," literally "mouth-Christians," or Christians only in the words of their own mouths.

83. See Soderlund, *Lenape Country*, 22.

84. Kelpius, *Diarium*, 80–81.

85. Graeber and Wengrow, *The Dawn of Everything*.

86. "Wenn wir einmal macht werde gewürdigt dis viele und [] wohnungen in unser Vater Hause zu sehen (von Wer Wolte so gar einfältig . . . einerlei), so glaube ich wie werden das sehen, wie [] derselben Architectes an unser gemeins. Formula und systematische architektur wenig gelegt habe." Kelpius, Letter to Fabricius, 1705, in Journal, 1694–1707, 85.

87. John 14:2.

88. Belden C. Lane, *The Solace of Fierce Landscapes: Exploring Desert and Mountain Spirituality* (Oxford: Oxford University Press, 2007), 75.

89. Kelpius, *Ethicus Ethnicus*, 1: "Cum nocte nuper astrorum contemplationi sacrata immensam hanc opificis infiniti machinam accuratius aliquanto meditarer, tantoque angustrioribus singula corpora cancellis circumscribi videbam, quantoque liberius in vastissimam illam universi extensionem cogitando excurrere mihi contingeret, ut tandem orbis iste noster instar punctuli penitus evansceret: adeo vere Sapiens ille vidit omnia opera, quae facta sunt sub Sole, & ecce, universa vanitas!"

90. Kelpius, *Diarium*.

91. Seelig, "Letter to Heinrich Deichmann," 44.

92. Falckner, *Curieuse Nachricht*, 219–220.

93. Falckner, *Curieuse Nachricht*, 219–220.

94. See the note on the provenance of these works in Chapter 1.

95. Kelpius, "Letter to Steven Momfort," 1699, in *Diarium*, 48.

96. Kelpius, "Letter to Steven Momfort," 49.

97. Kelpius, "Letter to Hester Palmer at Flushing, Long Island," May 25, 1706, in *Diarium*, 88.

98. Kelpius, "Letter to Steven Momfort," 49–50.

99. Kelpius, "Letter to Steven Momfort," 50.

100. Kelpius, *Diarium*, 25. Kelpius is suspicious that the animal may have not been a real dolphin, and this color pattern would seem to support his suspicions.

101. Kelpius, *Diarium*, 25.

NOTES 261

102. Richard Crawford, "A Historian's Introduction to Early American Music," *Proceedings of the American Antiquarian Society* 89, no. 2 (October 1979): 261.

103. Seidensticker, *Bilder*, 434: "We had, also, prayer meetings and sang hymns of praise and joy, several of us accompanying on instruments that we had brought from London."

104. Christopher Herbert, "Voices in the Pennsylvania Wilderness: An Examination of the Music Manuscripts, Music Theory, Compositions, and (Female) Composers of the Eighteenth-Century Ephrata Cloister" (DMA diss., Juilliard School, May 2018), 167.

105. Martin, "Kelpius and Seelig," 123.

106. Arthur Versluis, "Mysticism and Spiritual Harmonics in Eighteenth-Century England," *Esoterica* 4 (2002), http://www.esoteric.msu.edu/VolumeIV/Harmonic.htm. See also Erben, *Harmony of the Spirits*, 49–50 and 202–220.

107. Versluis, "Mysticism and Spiritual Harmonics."

108. Lucy Carroll, *The Hymn Writers of Early Pennsylvania* (n.p.: Xulon Press: 2008), 15.

109. Johannes Kelpius, "I: N: J: Die Klägliche stimme Der Verborgenen Liebe . . . ," with facing English title, "The Lamenting Voice of the Hidden Love . . . ," Historical Society of Pennsylvania, MS Ac 189, Abraham Cassel Collection, vol. 27, Coll. 1675. See Martin's "Kelpius and Seelig" for complete bibliographic detail and analysis of Wissahickon hymn manuscripts.

110. Carroll, *Hymn Writers*, 28.

111. Kelpius, *Diarium*, 78. Kelpius spells his name "Matthey," and he frequently exchanged *i*'s for *y*'s in his writings in German.

112. "Lamech and Agrippa," *Chronicon Ephratense: A History of the Community of Seventh-Day Baptists at Ephrata, Lancaster County, Penn'a.*, trans. J. Max Hark (Lancaster, PA: S.H. Zahm & Co., 1889; reprint: University Park: Pennsylvania State University Press, Metalmark Books).

113. Lamech and Agrippa, *Chronicon Ephratense*, 14. See also Levin Theodore Reichel, "The Early History of the Church of the United Brethren (Unitas Fratrum) Commonly Called Moravians, in North America, A.D. 1734–1748," *Transactions of the Moravian Historical Society* 3 (1888): 1–241, 50.

114. Bach, *Voices of the Turtledoves*, 14.

115. Bach, *Voices of the Turtledoves*, 16.

116. John Smith, *Hannah Logan's Courtship: A True Narrative*, ed. Albert Cook Myers (Philadelphia: Ferris & Leach, 1904), 225–226. See also Peter Brock, *Pacifism in the United States: From the Colonial Era to the First World War* (Princeton: Princeton University Press, 2015), 178.

117. Bill Porter / Red Pine, *Road to Heaven: Encounters with Chinese Hermits* (1993; Berkeley: Counterpoint Press, 2009).

118. John F. Watson, *Annals of Philadelphia and Pennsylvania* (Philadelphia: A. Hart, J.W. Moore, J. Penington, U. Hunt, and H.F. Anners, 1850), 267.

119. Erben (*Harmony of the Spirits*, 210–211) has justifiably pointed out that the "Lamenting Voice" manuscript does not include Witt's signature as author, but he does not dispute the historicity of Witt's traditional association with the

262 NOTES

manuscript. For my part, based on the identical unique handwriting of the English side of "Lamenting Voice" and a surviving medical diploma from Witt, and the wide attestation of Witt acting as a creative companion of sorts with Kelpius toward the end, Witt is doubtless the author of the facing English side of "Lamenting Voice." See Samuel Pennypacker, *The Settlement of Germantown* (Philadelphia: William J. Campbell, 1899), 224.

120. Christopher Witt, *Johannes Kelpius Portrait*, 1705, Historical Society of Pennsylvania, Abraham H. Cassel Collection (#1610).

121. Julius Sachse (1895, 403–418) seems to have had access to sources that confirm Witt's land dealings after the year 1708, and he assumes that Witt lived with Kelpius on the ridge. Without access to those unnamed Sachse manuscripts while knowing that Witt, unlike Matthai and Seelig, *did* live in Germantown and generally enjoyed a social and civic life as a doctor, I see good reason to doubt that Witt lived on the ridge as a hermit, although it is certainly possible.

122. William Shainline Middleton, "John Bartram, Botanist," *Scientific Monthly* 21, no. 2 (1925): 194.

123. John Bartram, *The Correspondence of John Bartram, 1734–1777*, ed. Edmund Berkeley and Dorothy Smith Berkeley (Gainesville: University Press of Florida, 1992), xiii.

124. Bartram, *Correspondence of John Bartram*. Note the "Witt, Christopher" index entry for the complete reference of letters that mention Witt.

125. William Young to John Stuart, May 15, 1765, Society Miscellaneous Collection, Historical Society of Pennsylvania. See also Erben, *Harmony of the Spirits*, 208.

126. William Bartram commonplace book, private collection, John Bartram Association, Bartram's Garden digital copy. My gratitude to Joel Fry, who first noticed the Star Pill formula, and to Tom Carroll, who brought Fry's discovery to my attention.

127. John Bartram, "To COLLINSON," 1743, in *Correspondence of John Bartram*, 215.

128. William Young to John Stuart, May 15, 1765, Society Miscellaneous Collection, Historical Society of Pennsylvania. See also Erben, *Harmony of the Spirits*, 208.

129. Bartram, "To COLLINSON," 1745, in *Correspondence of John Bartram*, 269.

130. Peter Collinson to John Bartram, 1759, in Bartram, *Correspondence of John Bartram*, 215.

131. "To Benjamin Franklin from Deborah Franklin," February 10–21, 1765, *The Papers of Benjamin Franklin*, vol. 12, January 1–December 31, 1765, ed. Leonard W. Labaree (New Haven: Yale University Press, 1967), 43–46.

132. The Journals of Henry Melchior Muhlenberg, Evangelical Lutheran Ministerium of Pennsylvania and Adjacent States, vol. 2, 183–184.

133. Watson, *Annals*, 267.

134. *Ephemerides of the celestial motions for X. years beginning anno 1672 . . . and ending an. 1681. Calculated according to art from new tables, and compared with the most correct observations of the noble Tycho, Kepler, Mr. Wright, and other approved astronomers* (London: printed by John Macock for the Company of Stationers, 1672), Library Company of Pennsylvania Archives.

NOTES   263

135. The most recent significant work to look closely at Dr. Witt is Ena V. L. Swain's *The Evolution of Abolitionism in Germantown and Its Environs* (self-published, 2018). While Swain's book was not an academic publication, her sourcing and research are rigorous and her work as a community scholar-historian and deep knowledge of Germantown's history make her book very worthwhile.

Chapter 4

1. "Wenn werd ich doch dies *ein* anschauen und Empfinden!
   Wenn werd ich in ihm ganz Zerfliessen und Verschwinden!
   Wenn fält mein fünklein gar in sein Licht-feur ein!
   Wenn wird mein Geist mit ihm nur eine flamme sein."
   Johannes Kelpius, "Das Paradoxe und seltsame vergnügen der göttliche verliebten," in "Lamenting Voice," 19.

   A useful facsimile of the manuscript was published in *Church Music and Musical Life in Pennsylvania in the Eighteenth Century*, vol. 1 (Philadelphia: Printed for the Society of Colonial Dames in America, 1926), 21–163. The manuscript contains an opening note made in 1823 by J. F. Watson, author of *Annals of Philadelphia*, which is covered in more detail in Chapter 6. Watson notes that the hymns in "Lamenting Voice" are not made in Kelpius's own hand; rather, they are copied, and the MS contains facing translations of the hymns in English by Kelpius's friend, Dr. Christopher Witt.

   The authorship of the volume has been thrown into question by the opening dedication page, where the name "Christina Warmerin, 1705, in Germantown, in Pennsylvania" appears. This has led a few scholars to question the attributions to Kelpius and Witt, and instead suggest that the poems are the composition of Mrs. Warmer herself (see Albert Hess, "Observations on the Lamenting Voice of the Hidden Love," *Journal of the American Musicological Society* 5, no. 3 [Autumn 1952]: 211–223). There are several good reasons to doubt the attribution to Warmer and accept the attribution to Kelpius. The first is the title page, which contains the phrase "Composed by one in Kumber," with a footnote that reads, "That Cumber is here above spel'd with a K, & not with a C, has its peculier Reason." As scholars like Patrick Erben (*Harmony of the Spirits*) have noted, this kind of roundabout attribution is exactly what we might expect from Kelpius or his community in collating an edition of his hymns.

   The second is the numerous notes appended to the titles of the hymns that reflect their varied dates of composition, from 1699 to 1706, and the circumstances of the declining health of the author. For example, "A Loving Moan," to which is appended "As I lay in Christian Warmer's house very weak, in a small bed, not unlike a coffin in May 1706" ("Lamenting Voice," 57) and "A Comfortable and Incouraging Song" is appended "By occasion of a great Cold which seized me in July 1706" (63). The note appended to "Loving Moan" is especially interesting for the purposes of attribution, since it would make little sense for Christina Warmer to refer to her own home as "Christian Warmer's house."

264 NOTES

Rather, the "Lamenting Voice" manuscript, along with the portrait of Kelpius attributed to Christopher Witt (which was originally folded and held in the "Lamenting Voice" volume itself, as noted by Watson in his 1823 note), likely represents an attempt by Warmer and Witt to preserve something of Kelpius's legacy as his health began to decline. Christina Warmer, Kelpius's neighbor and end-of-life caregiver, wrote her name and location on the dedication page to ensure the book was never lost.

None of the scholars who have worked with the "Lamenting Voice" text in recent decades have seriously doubted its attribution to Kelpius and Witt, including Albert Hess, who first raised these questions before dismissing them in his own 1952 article. Most recently, the musicologist Christopher Herbert has reconfirmed the suggestion that "Lamenting Voice" represents the oldest extant musical manuscript in the British colonies (Herbert, "Voices," 167).

The earliest attribution of the hymns to Kelpius is the Peter Leibert, ed., publication of *Etliche liebliche und erbaulichen Lieder: von der Herrlichkeit und Ehre Christi, von der starcken und mächtigen Liebe Christi, in der seeligen Jungfrau Agnes, und zwey Lieder von der Nachfolge Jesu Christi, wie sie aufgesetzt sind von zwey Brüddern, die vor einiger Zeit in dem Herrn entschlaffen sind. Nähmlich eines von dem lieben Bruder Grumbacher... und das andere von dem lieben Bruder Christoph Saur . . . Nebst etliche noch niemal im Druck erschienene sehr erbaulichen Liedern, von Joh. Kelpius . . . / Auf Begehren etlicher Liebhaber, und in Hoffnung der Erbauung gedruckt, und heraus gegeben, von Peter Leibert* (Germantown: Gedruckt und zu finden bey Peter Leibert, 1788), making them some of the best-attested primary Kelpius writings in Philadelphia. These printings are covered in Chapter 6.

2. Jeffrey Kripal, "Sexuality and the Erotic," in *Oxford Handbook of Religion and Emotion*, ed. John Corrigan (Oxford: Oxford University Press, 2007), 168.

3. "Während er seine Vorstellung von den letzten Dingen gewöhnlich in biblische Bilder kleidet, bricht einmal eine pantheistische Auffassung durch, die eher an Plotin als an das Christenthum erinnert." Oswald Seidensticker, "Johann Kelpius, Der Einsielder am Wissahickon," in *Bilder*, 97.

4. "In einer antwort an einen brief so voller Liebe trost und demuth." Kelpius, "Lamenting Voice."

5. For more information on Esther Palmer (later Esther Champion), see Rebecca Larson, *Daughters of Light: Quaker Women Preaching and Prophesying in the Colonies and Abroad, 1700–1775* (New York: Knopf, 1999). Kelpius spells her name "Hester Pallmer" in the manuscript letter. Sachse's *Diarium* spells it "Hester Palmer." For the sake of clarity, I spell her name Esther Palmer here.

6. Palmer's diary of her American travels is in the Library of the Society of Friends in London: "Journal of the travels of Susanna Freeborn and Esther Palmer," MS BOX X1/10. It is, unfortunately for our purposes, only an itinerary.

7. Johannes Kelpius, Letter to Hester Pallmer at Flushing, Long Island, May 25, 1706, in Journal, 1694–1708, , Historical Society of Pennsylvania, Ferdinand J. Dreer Autograph Collection (#0175), 91.

8. Kenneth L. Carroll, "Quakerism on the Eastern Shore of Virginia." *Virginia Magazine of History and Biography* 74, no. 2 (1966): 170–189.

9. Erben, *Harmony of the Spirits*, 219.
10. Elizabeth Ashbridge, *Some Account of the Forepart of the Life of Elizabeth Ashbridge, Who Departed This Life . . . : In the County of Carlow, Ireland, the 16th, 5 Mo., 1755* (Philadelphia: Printed for C.C.C. by P.C. Stockhausen, 1886), Historical Society of Pennsylvania, E.42115.
11. Erben, *Harmony of the Spirits*, 220.
12. Kelpius, Letter to Hester Palmer. See also "Letter to Hester Palmer at Flushing, Long Island," May 25, 1706, in Kelpius, *Diarium*, 86–96. Sachse's edition is usable but contains a few errors and exclusions.
13. Seidensticker, *Bilder*, 95–96. "Hätte Kelpius in den briefen, deren abschrift von seiner eigenen hand sich erhalten hat, nur etwas von seinem alltaglichen Leben mit einfliessen lassen, so ware uns jetzt damit beser gedient als mit den weitlaufigen theologischen Grillen, die er darin ausspinnt."
14. Kelpius, Letter to Hester Palmer, 93.
15. Zuber, *Spiritual Alchemy*, 9.
16. Zuber, *Spiritual Alchemy*, 11.
17. Zuber, *Spiritual Alchemy*, 11.
18. D. Johann Ludewig Shulze, *Nachrichten von den vereinigten deutschen evangelisch-lutherischen Gemeinen in Nord-America, absonderlich in Pensylvanien*, ed. William Julius Mann (Allentown: Brobst, Diehl & Company, 1884), 40, "Kelpius, der seltsamen unter jenen seltsamen."
19. Richard Valantasis, "Constructions of Power in Asceticism," *Journal of the American Academy of Religion* 63, no. 4 (1995): 797.
20. Niki Kasumi Clements, *Sites of the Ascetic Self: John Cassian and Christian Ethical Formation* (Notre Dame: University of Notre Dame Press, 2020), 4–5.
21. William Cronon, *Uncommon Ground: Toward Reinventing Nature* (New York: Norton, 1995), 69.
22. Roderick Nash, *Wilderness and the American Mind*, 5th ed. (New Haven: Yale University Press, 2014), 1.
23. Nash, *Wilderness*, 2–3.
24. George H. Williams, *Wilderness and Paradise in Christian Thought: The Biblical Experience of the Desert in the History of Christianity & the Paradise Theme in the Theological Idea of the University* (Harper, 1962; Eugene, OR: Wipf and Stock, 2016), 4.
25. Kelpius, Letter to Hester Palmer, 92.
26. Kelpius, Letter to Hester Palmer, 92.
27. Kelpius, Letter to Hester Palmer, 92.
28. For a few examples, see Isaiah 64:10, 1QM (The War Scroll of the Dead Sea Scrolls) I, 2, and 1QM I, 3.
29. In her 2010 book *Past Renewals*, the Hebrew Bible scholar Hindy Najman puts forth three primary "uses of the concept of wilderness in ancient Judaism." First: a place of exile and suffering. Second: wilderness as purification. Third: wilderness as a locus of revelation. Throughout the Hebrew Bible (and the writings of the early Christians), wilderness was understood to be a location in which hierophanic, revelatory, and

266 NOTES

miraculous episodes clustered and intensified. The stories of Moses and Elijah are two most prominent examples of these Hebrew wilderness traditions. Hindy Najman, *Past Renewals: Interpretative Authority, Renewed Revelation, and the Quest for Perfection in Jewish Antiquity* (Leiden: Brill, 2010), chap. 7, "Towards a Study of the Uses of the Concept of Wilderness in Ancient Judaism."

30. Kelpius, Letter to Hester Palmer, 93.

31. Johannes Kelpius, Letter to Steven Momfort in Rhode Island, December 11, 1699, in Journal, 1694–1708, 44.

32. Kelpius, Letter to Hester Palmer, 93.

33. Kelpius, Letter to Hester Palmer, 93.

34. Kelpius, Letter to Hester Palmer, 93.

35. Kelpius, Letter to Steven Momfort, 42.

36. Kelpius, Letter to Steven Momfort, 43.

37. Kelpius, Letter to Hester Palmer, 94.

38. Kelpius, Letter to Hester Palmer, 94.

39. Kelpius, Letter to Hester Palmer, 95.

40. Kelpius, Letter to Hester Palmer, 95.

41. Jeffrey Bach and Michael Birkel, *Genius of the Transcendent: Mystical Writings of Jakob Boehme* (Boston: Shambhala Press, 2010), 19.

42. Kelpius, Letter to Hester Palmer, 95.

43. Kelpius, Letter to Hester Palmer, 96.

44. Robert Barry Leal, *Wilderness in the Bible: Toward a Theology of Wilderness* (New York: P. Lang, 2004), 105.

45. Leal, *Wilderness in the Bible*, chap. 5, "Critical Encounter in the Wilderness."

46. Kelpius, Letter to Hester Palmer, 96.

47. Mark 1:6.

48. Zechariah 13:4 backs up the general understanding that prophets wore "garments of hair," and it seems Kelpius and Seelig got the message.

49. Seelig's letter to Deichmann in Kelpius, Journal, 1694–1708, 40; see also Kelpius, *Diarium*, 45, 46.

50. Christopher Witt, *Johannes Kelpius Portrait*, 1705, Historical Society of Pennsylvania, Abraham H. Cassel Collection (#1610).

51. "Late Hermits in Pennsylvania," from the *Germantown Telegraph*, collected in *American Penny Magazine, and Family Newspaper*, vol. 3 (New York: No. 112 Broadway, 1847), 491.

52. Kelpius, Letter to Hester Palmer, 97.

53. Kelpius, Letter to Hester Palmer, 97.

54. Mark 9:2–8 and parallels.

55. Exodus 34.

56. Kelpius, Letter to Hester Palmer, 97.

57. Kelpius, Letter to Hester Palmer, 97.

58. H. C. Erik Midelfort, "The Anthropological Roots of Paracelsus' Psychiatry," *Medizinhistorisches Journal* 16, nos. 1–2, "Kreatur und Kosmos: Internationale Beiträge zur Paracelsusforschung" (1981): 67–77.

NOTES   267

59. Kelpius, Letter to Hester Palmer, 98. That bit of proto-feminist biblical criticism is original to the journal.

60. Kelpius, Letter to Hester Palmer, 98; Hebrews 11:38.

61. Kelpius, Letter to Hester Palmer, 98.

62. Kelpius, Letter to Hester Palmer, 98–99.

63. Kelpius, Letter to Hester Palmer, 100; 1 Corinthians 4:9.

64. Kelpius, Letter to Hester Palmer, 100.

65. Kelpius, Letter to Hester Palmer. 100.

66. Kelpius, Letter to Hester Palmer, 101.

67. Williams, *Wilderness and Paradise*, 4.

68. Williams, *Wilderness and Paradise*, 5.

69. John Gill, *An Exposition of the New Testament*, 3 vols. (London: printed for the author; and sold by Aaron Ward, at the King's-Arms in Little-Britain, 1746–48), Revelation, 12.

70. John Wesley, *Journals*, 1740, quoted in Williams, *Wilderness and Paradise*, 89, and see Wesley, Sermon 46, "The Wilderness State."

71. Arthur Versluis, "Jane Lead(e)," in *Dictionary of Gnosis & Western Esotericism*, ed. Wouter J. Hanegraaff with Antoine Faivre, Roelof van den Broek, and Jean-Pierre Brach (Leiden: Brill, 2005), 684.

72. Jane Lead, *The Glory of Sharon in the Renovation of Nature, Introducing the Blessed Kingdom of Christ in the Sealed Number of the First Fruits* (first published in 1700), in *The Wars of David, and the Peaceable Reign of Solomon; Symbolizing the Times of Warfare and Refreshment of the Saints of the Most High God* (London: thomas Wood, 1816), 102. See also Warren Johnston, "Jane Lead and English Apocalyptic Thought in the Late Seventeenth Century," in *Jane Lead and Her Transnational Legacy*, ed. Ariel Hessayon (London: Palgrave Macmillan, 2016), 119–142.

73. Jane Lead, *The Ascent to the Mount of Vision* (London, 1699), 28.

74. M. Ehregott Daniel Colberg, *Das Platonisch-Hermetisches Christenthum: Begreiffend Die Historische Erzehung vom Ursprung und vielerley Secten der heutigen Fanatischen Theologie, unterm Namen der Paracelsisten, Weigelianer, Rosencreutzer, Quäcker, Böhmisten, Wiedertäuffer, Bourignisten, Labadisten und Quieristen* (Frankfurt am Main: Weidmann, 1690).

75. "Irrigen und Platonischen Lehren" (Colberg, *Das Platonisch-Hermetisches Christenthum*, 61).

76. "Der Haubt-Mangel des ganken Wercks bestehet im Methodo der drey Platonischen Wege / darinn die gange Theologia Mystica eingeschlossen wird. Denn da lehren sie / man mille durch die Reinigung zur Erleuchtung / und durch diese zur Vereinigung kommen / welcher Zweck die Vergötterung und Verchristung ist" (Colberg, *Das Platonisch-Hermetisches Christenthum*, 61).

77. "Die *Summa* oder Inhalt dieser 'verborgenen Lehr oder Weißheit belangend / haben die alten Väter dieselbe abgetheilet in die 3 Theile, nemlich: Im 1. die Reinigung /2. Er euchtung / 3. Vereinigung" (Colberg, *Das Platonisch-Hermetisches Christenthum*, 61–62).

78. David Luscombe, "Dionysius Areopagita (Pseudo-), ca. 500," in Hanegraaff, *Dictionary*, 312–313.

268 NOTES

79. "Wir solten anriss die irrigen und Platonischen Lehren / die in der *Theologia Mystica* siecken / herausziehen / und ordentlich vorstellen" (Colberg, *Das Platonisch-Hermetisches Christenthum*, 61).

80. Zuber, "Copernican Cosmotheism," 233.

81. Johann Jakob Zimmerman, *Tergemina lucis mysticae mysteria in tribus lucis corporeae facultatibus, quae sunt: splendor, calor, motus* (Launoy, 1688) Available here: http://resolver.sub.uni-goettingen.de/purl?PPN598772707.

82. Sunt inter Sophia concredita pectora, *Lucem*
    Naturae mediae queis statuisse placet.
    Sic varium in sensum se scindit Turba Sophorum,
    Et pendent animis, quae statuenda forent.
    At quanquam *lucis lateat natura* nitentis,
    Munus in hac massa non tamen omne *latet*,
    Dum *natura latet*, triplici *virtute patescit*
    Hoc jubar aetherium, qua latitare nequit.
    Sunt inquam *tria*, queis gaudet LUX, *munera* certa:
    Cum MOTU SPLENDOR fulgidus atque CALOR."
    Zimmerman, *Tergemina lucis mysticae mysteria*, 6. I am grateful to Claire Fanger for help with this translation.

83. Zuber, "Copernican Cosmotheism," 227.

84. Weeks, *Boehme*, 142–143.

85. Andrew Weeks, "Jacob Boehme," in Hanegraaff, *Dictionary*, 190. See also Zuber, *Spiritual Alchemy*, for an expansive reading of Böhme's spiritual alchemy.

86. Paul Henry, "The Place of Plotinus in the History of Thought," in Plotinus, *The Enneads*, trans. Stephen MacKenna (New York: Penguin, 1991), xlvii.

87. Timothy Cotton Wright, "Hidden Lives: Asceticism and Interiority in the Late Reformation, 1650–1745" (PhD diss., University of California, Berkeley, 2018), 6. Wright is aware of Kelpius but locates him primarily as a practitioner of Madame Guyon's quietism based on the text *Method of Prayer*. Kelpius was no doubt aware of Guyon and likely interested in her notion of inward prayer, but as Chapter 6 will show, Kelpius is not the author of *Method of Prayer*.

88. Gottfried Arnold, *Vitae Patrum, oder Leben der Alt-Väter* (Halle, 1700).

89. Elizabeth Clark, *Reading Renunciation: Asceticism and Scripture in Early Christianity* (Princeton: Princeton University Press, 1999), 17.

90. Clements, *Sites*, 8.

91. Michel Foucault, *History of Sexuality*, vol. 3, *The Care of the Self*, trans. Robert Hurley (New York: Vintage, 1986), 43.

92. Michel Foucault, "Technologies of the Self," in *Ethics: Subjectivity and Truth*, vol. 1 of *Essential Works of Foucault, 1954–1984* (New York: New Press, 1998), 225.

93. Michel Foucault, *Security, Territory, Population: Lectures at the College de France, 1977–1978*, trans. Graham Burchell (New York: Palgrave, 2004), 208.

94. Kelpius, Letter to Hester Palmer, 93.

95. William G. McLoughlin, "Pietism and the American Character," *American Quarterly* 17, no. 2 (1965): 163.

96. Martin, "Kelpius and Seelig," 119.

97. Clements, *Sites*.
98. "Lamenting Voice":
Denck, sprach er, wie zu Nächst der strom in sich verlieffe,
wie / sein gar stiller fluss bezeugte seine Tieffe:
Man kan den Tieffen / Grund der liebe nicht ershen
biss ihrer Sonnen Glantz / kommt über ihr Zu stehn.
99. Denck an Empfindlich Kraut, Wenn diess es wird Berühret,
Wies in Sich kehren traur, wies seine Saat Verlieret:
Es will Vom Himmel Thau allein berühret Sein
und angescheinet nur Vom Reinen Sonnen-schein.
100. Geheime Jesus Lieb ist wie die Tieffen Wunden
Ihr inner / bluten wird im hertzen nur empfunden,
Nichts heilet ihre / Pein, nichts is das sie Versüsst,
bis die sich das hertz des / Liebsten aus ergiesst
101. Kelpius, Letter to Hester Palmer, 94.

Vita III

1. Kelpius, "Lamenting Voice." For example, "A Loving Moan," to which is appended "As I lay in Christian Warmer's house very weak, in a small bed, not unlike a coffin in May 1706" (57) and "A Comfortable and Incouraging Song" is appended "By occasion of a great Cold which seized me in July 1706" (63).

Chapter 5

1. *Providence Gazette and Country Journal*, March 19, 1814, 3. See also Daniel Rolph, "The Strange Death of Richard Elliot and His Encounter with the Balls of Light," October 30, 2013, Historical Society of Pennsylvania Online, https://hsp.org/blogs/hidden-histories/the-strange-death-of-richard-elliott-and-his-encounter-with-the-balls-of-light-a-halloween-story.
2. Adam Jortner, *Blood from the Sky: Miracles and Politics in the Early American Republic* (Charlottesville: University Press of Virginia, 2017), 2.
3. Butler, *Awash*, 225.
4. Peter Kafer, *Charles Brockden Brown's Revolution and the Birth of American Gothic* (Philadelphia: University of Pennsylvania Press, 2004), 114–115, 117–118, 120–121. See also Butler, *Awash*, 225–226. It's not clear if Butler was the very first scholar to connect Kelpius with the character of the elder Wieland, since he does not specify that his claim is original, but his 1990 claim is the earliest that I have located. Peter Kafer cites Butler's earlier article, "Into Pennsylvania's Spiritual Abyss," but he does not cite *Awash in a Sea of Faith*, published in 1990, where Butler first makes the connection between *Wieland* and Kelpius, raising the possibility that Kafer and Butler reached their conclusions about the connection independently.

270 NOTES

5. See Lisa West, "Early Years: 1771–1795," in *Oxford Handbook of Charles Brockden Brown*, ed. Philip Barnard, Hilary Emmett, and Stephen Shapiro (Oxford: Oxford University Press, 2019), 7–23.

6. Jeffrey Andrew Weinstock, *Charles Brockden Brown* (Cardiff: University of Wales Press, 2011), 11. See also Bryan Waterman, "Later Years, 1795–1810," in Barnard, Emmett, and Shapiro, *Oxford Handbook*, 24–43.

7. Brown studies have consistently punched above their weight in American literary studies, and it was a challenge to digest this entire literature for the purposes of situating the relationship of one author with Kelpius. My own analysis leans most heavily on Kafer's *Charles Brockden Brown's Revolution* for his special emphasis on the influence of the Kelpius community in the novel. Weinstock's *Charles Brockden Brown* has helped with much of the biographical and literary background on Brown and his work. Other works like Bill Christopherson's *The Apparition in the Glass: Charles Brockden Brown's American Gothic* (Athens: University of Georgia Press, 1993) and Mark L. Kamrath's *The Historicism of Charles Brockden Brown: Radical History and the Early Republic* (Kent, OH: Kent State University Press, 2010) were invaluable in synthesizing and interpreting Brown's whole corpus and locating him in his eighteenth-century American context. The recent *Oxford Handbook of Charles Brockden Brown*, edited by Barnard, Emmett, and Shapiro, was a clarifying assessment of the author in light of the voluminous work on Brown in various academic journals. Finally, I have also made extensive use of the Charles Brockden Brown Electronic Archive and Scholarly Edition to access some of Brown's less widely available works for magazines, including his work on almanacs.

8. Charles Brockden Brown, *Wieland and Memoirs of Carwin the Biloquist* (New York: Penguin, 1991), x. All page numbers referring to the text of *Wieland* refer to the Penguin edition. This edition preserves Brown's nonstandard spellings and English throughout, as I do throughout this chapter. I also use the Norton edition, *Wieland and Memoirs of Carwin the Biloquist*, ed. Bryan Waterman (New York: Norton, 2011), for additional primary texts and interpretations.

9. Brown, *Wieland*, xxxvii; Charles Brockden Brown, Letter to Thomas Jefferson, December 25, 1798, Charles Brockden Brown Electronic Archive and Scholarly Edition, https://brockdenbrown.cah.ucf.edu/xtf3/view?docId=1798-L-108.xml.

10. Christopherson, *Apparition in the Glass*, 2.

11. Kafer, *Charles Brockden Brown's Revolution*, 248.

12. Kafer, *Charles Brockden Brown's Revolution*, 115–116.

13. Brown, *Wieland*, 5.

14. Brown, *Wieland*, 8–9.

15. Brown, *Wieland*, 10–11.

16. Kafer, *Charles Brockden Brown's Revolution*, 114. There were fewer distinct neighborhoods at the time of Brown's writing: checking Kafer's measurements and looking at the map today, one can determine that "Mettingen" is positioned roughly in the Wissahickon neighborhood of lower northwest Philadelphia, adjacent to the neighborhoods of Roxborough and Manayunk—indeed, the very place where the Wissahickon hermitage was located.

17. Kafer, *Charles Brockden Brown's Revolution*, 226.
18. Brown, *Wieland*, 53–54.
19. Brown, *Wieland*, 11.
20. Brown, *Wieland*, 11.
21. Brown, *Wieland*, 12.
22. Brown, *Wieland*, 13.
23. Brown, *Wieland*, 113.
24. Brown, *Wieland*, 13.
25. Brown, *Wieland*, 14.
26. Brown, *Wieland*, 14.
27. Brown, *Wieland*, 12.
28. Brown, *Wieland*, 13.
29. Caleb Crain, "The Awful Truth," *Commonplace: The Journal of Early American Life* 5, no. 4 (July 2005), http://commonplace.online/article/the-awful-truth/ (accessed August 26, 2021).
30. Brown, *Wieland*, 14.
31. Brown, *Wieland*, 17.
32. Brown, *Wieland*, 17.
33. Brown, *Wieland*, 17.
34. Brown, *Wieland*, 18.
35. Brown, *Wieland*, 18.
36. Brown, *Wieland*, 19.
37. Brown, *Wieland*, 19.
38. Brown, *Wieland*, 21.
39. Brown, *Wieland*, 21.
40. Brown, *Wieland*, 21.
41. "Letter respecting an Italian priest, killed by an electric commotion, the cause of which resided in his own body," *American Museum, or, Universal Magazine* (Philadelphia) 11, no. 4 (April 1792): 146–149, reproduced in the Norton *Wieland*, 282–286.
42. In an apparent recognition of this ambiguity, the Norton edition of *Wieland* includes the *American Museum* article with an inserted title: "[A Case of Spontaneous Combustion]," despite the article's suggestion of electrical anomalies as the cause of death in the cases described.
43. Bernard Rosenthal, "The Voices of *Wieland*," in *Critical Essays on Charles Brockden Brown*, ed. Bernard Rosenthal (Boston: G.K. Hall, 1981), 87–103.
44. Kafer, *Charles Brockden Brown's Revolution*, 121
45. Johannes Kelpius, Letter to Hester Palmer at Flushing, Long Island, May 25, 1706, in Journal, 1694–1708, , Historical Society of Pennsylvania, Ferdinand J. Dreer Autograph Collection (#0175), 93.
46. Erben, *A Harmony of the Spirits*, 219.
47. Johannes Kelpius, Letter to Steven Momfort in Rhode Island, December 11, 1699, in Journal, 1694–1708.
48. See Sachse, *German Pietists*, 152–153. See also Versluis, *Wisdom's Children*, 94–95.

272 NOTES

49. John Woolman, *The Works of John Woolman; in two parts* (Philadelphia: Printed by Joseph Crukshank, in Market-Street, between Second and Third Streets, 1774), 52–53, Library Company of Philadelphia, Am 1774 Woolm 1118.O.
50. Brown, *Wieland*, 21.
51. Brown, *Wieland*, 26.
52. Brown, *Wieland*, 27.
53. Kelpius, "Letter to Steven Momfort" in *Diarium*, 47.
54. Brown, *Wieland*, 28.
55. Brown, *Wieland*, 28.
56. Brown, *Wieland*, 28.
57. Brown, *Wieland*, 40.
58. Brown, *Wieland*, 40.
59. Brown, *Wieland*, 41.
60. Brown, *Wieland*, 50.
61. Brown, *Wieland*, 51.
62. Brown, *Wieland*, 52.
63. Jeffrey Kripal, *Authors of the Impossible: The Paranormal and the Sacred* (Chicago: University of Chicago Press, 2010), 116.
64. Brown, *Wieland*, 52.
65. Brown, *Wieland*, 57.
66. Brown, *Wieland*, 113.
67. The Hermetic and alchemical influences on Brown's construction of Carwin are further illustrated in Evert Jan van Leeuwen's essay "'Though Hermes Never Taught Thee': The Anti-patriarchal Tendency of Charles Brockden Brown's Mercurial Outcast Carwin, the Biloquist" (online).
68. See van Leeuwen, "Though Hermes Never Taught," again, on the local alchemical and Hermetic stereotypes that would have made Carwin's Spanish travel more conspicuous to Brown's audience.
69. Brown, *Wieland*, 85.
70. Another resonance with Paracelsus and Arndt is found in Brown's fragmented sequel, *The Memoirs of Carwin the Biloquist*, in which Carwin hears the sound of thunder as a divine rebuke: "I could not divest myself of secret dread. My heart faultered with a consciousness of wrong. Heaven seemed to be present and to disapprove my work; I listened to the thunder and the wind, as to the stern voice of this disapprobation" (Brown, *Wieland*, 291).
71. Brown, *Wieland*, 85.
72. Brown, *Wieland*, 69.
73. Brown, *Wieland*, 102–103.
74. Brown, *Wieland*, 168.
75. Brown, *Wieland*, 169–170.
76. Brown, *Wieland*, 168.
77. Brown, *Wieland*, 187.
78. "A fiery stream issued and came forth from before him: thousand thousands ministered unto him, and ten thousand times ten thousand stood before him: the judgment was set, and the books were opened." Daniel 7:10, KJV.

NOTES 273

79. Brown, *Wieland*, 190.
80. Anonymous. "An Account of a Murder Committed by Mr. J.—— Y——, upon His Family, in December A.D. 1781," *New York Weekly Magazine; or Miscellaneous Repository*, July 20 and 27, 1796, reprinted in Philadelphia *Minerva*, August 20 and 27, 1796. Reproduced in the Norton *Wieland*, 267.
81. On the radical religious and esoteric cultural climate of early New York, see Josclyn Godwin, *Upstate Cauldron: Eccentric Spiritual Movements in Early New York State* (Albany: Excelsior Editions, 2015).
82. Brown, *Wieland*, 205–206.
83. Brown, *Wieland*, 226.
84. Brown, *Wieland*, 226.
85. Joannes Baptista de La Chapelle, *Le Ventriloque, ou l'engastrimthye* (London: Duchense, 1772). See also Leigh Eric Schmidt, *Hearing Things: Religion, Illusion, and the American Enlightenment* (Cambridge, MA: Harvard University Press, 2000), 144.
86. Schmidt, *Hearing Things*, 144.
87. Schmidt, *Hearing Things*, 144.
88. Brown, *Wieland*, 226.
89. Brown, *Wieland*, 278.
90. Brown, *Wieland*, xlii.
91. Shirley Samuels, "Patriarchal Violence, Federalist Panic, and *Wieland*," *Early American Literature* 25, no. 1 (1990): 46–66.
92. Kafer, *Charles Brockden Brown's Revolution*, 123.
93. E. J. Clery, *The Rise of Supernatural Fiction, 1762–1800* (Cambridge: Cambridge University Press, 1995), 1.
94. Clery, *Rise of Supernatural Fiction*, 1.
95. Charles Brockden Brown, "Terrific Novels," *Literary Magazine and American Register* 3, issue 19 (Philadelphia: John Conrad & Co., 1805), 288–289. Accessed via the Charles Brockden Brown Electronic Archive and Scholarly Edition, https://brockdenbrown.cah.ucf.edu/xtf3/view?docId=1805-04288.xml.
96. Clery, *Rise of Supernatural Fiction*, 18.
97. John Greenleaf Whittier, *The Supernaturalism of New England* (1847; Norman: University of Oklahoma Press, 1969), 37.
98. Whittier, *Supernaturalism of New England*, 37.
99. Brown, *Wieland*, x.
100. Timothy Morton, *Ecology without Nature: Rethinking Environmental Aesthetics* (Cambridge, MA: Harvard University Press, 2007), 31.
101. Morton, *Ecology without Nature*, 33.
102. Amitav Ghosh, *The Great Derangement: Climate Change and the Unthinkable* (Chicago: University of Chicago Press, 2016), 16.
103. Ghosh, *The Great Derangement*, 19.
104. Robert Carroll and Stephen Prickett, "Introduction," in *The Bible: Authorized King James Version* (Oxford: Oxford University Press, 1997), xliv. It is worth mentioning that the "queerer" quotation is not from Einstein.
105. Ghosh, *The Great Derangement*, 10.

274 NOTES

106. As I have written elsewhere, these cultural connections between nonhumans and paranormal phenomena are more than superficial: "The Night Side of Nature: Environmental Meanings of the Modern Paranormal," *Journal for the Study of Religion, Nature, and Culture* 15, no. 2 (2021): 229–254.
107. Kelpius, Letter to Steven Momfort, 43.

Chapter 6

1. Michel Foucault, "Of Other Spaces, Heterotopias," *Architecture, Mouvement, Continuité*, no. 5 (1984): 46–49.
2. The earliest mention of Kelpius in the primary literature is in Gottfried Arnold's *Unparteyische Kirchen- und Ketzer -Historie*, 2 vols. (Frankfurt am Main: Thomas Fritsch, 1699–1700). Kelpius and company appear on 2:624–625, 774–775. Arnold's information is quite limited: he confirms the names of Kelpius, Falckner, Koster, and Schaeffer and that the group was composed of men and women who numbered about forty.
3. At the beginning of a new century of Pietist and Lutheran thought, we dip our toes into another vast and unwieldy historiography: Craig Atwood's article " 'The Hallensians Are Pietists; Aren't You a Hallensian?': Mühlenberg's Conflict with the Moravians," *Journal of Moravian History* 12, no. 1 (2012): 47–92, sums up this particular conflict very well.
4. Mühlenberg, *Nachrichten*, 639–640. See also Martin, "Kelpius and Seelig," 49. This would have been three years before Seelig's death in 1745.
5. Mühlenberg, *Nachrichten*, 640: "Eswurde vor etlichen Jahren aus Teutschland bei mir nach gewissen *Canditatis Theologiä* gefragt. . . . So viel ich übrigens von ein und andern unpartheiischen alten Bekannten Nach richt einziehen können, scheint mirs, daß die meisten von diesen ehemaligen Candidaten sonst wenig oder nichts von denen von Christo verordneten heiligen Sacramenten, der Taufe und Abendmahl, gehalten, das vom Geiste Gottes eingegebene, und durch die Propheten, Evangelisten und Apostel aufgeschriebene Wort Gottes als todte Buchstaben geachtet, und dagegen viel mit der himmlischen Sophia, mit Beschaulichkeiten wie auch zugleich mit der Alchymie zu thun gehabt."
6. Kelpius, Letter to Esther Palmer at Flushing, Long Island, May 25, 1706, in Journal, 1694–1707, Historical Society of Pennsylvania, Ferdinand J. Dreer Autograph Collection (#0175), 93.
7. Kelpius, *Diarium*, 50–51, 89.
8. Mühlenberg, *Nachrichten*, 640: "Von dem ältesten und vornehmsten dieser *Candidaten* Herr G, gab mir vor acht und zwanzig Jahren ein glaubwürdiger Mann der über sechzig Jahr alt war, auch bei Herr G. verschiedene Jahre gewohnt und sein vertrauter Freund gewesen, folgende Nachricht."
9. Mühlenberg, *Nachrichten*, 640: "Herr G habe unter andern fest geglaubt, daß er nicht sterben, sein Leib nicht verwesen, sondern verwandelt, verflärt, überfleidet, und er, wie Elijah, hingenommen werden sollte."

NOTES   275

10. Mühlenberg, *Nachrichten*, 640: "Als er zurückgekommen, habe Herr G. ihm scharf nach den Augen gesehen, und gesagt: Ihr habt die Schachtel nicht ins Wasser geworfen, sondern am Ufer versteckt, worüber der ehrliche Daniel erschrocken, und geglaubt, daß seines Freundes Geist einiger maßen allwissend sein müßte, sei wieder zum Wasser gesprungen, und habe die Schachtel wirklich hineinge worfen, und mit Erstaunen gesehen und gehöret, daß das Arcanum im Wasser, wie er es ausdrückte, geblitzet und gedonnert. Nachdem er nun zurückgekommen, habe ihin Herr G. entgegen gerufen: Nun ists vollbracht, was ich euch aufgetragen hatte."

11. "Philadelphia Girl Owns Stone of Wisdom," *Philadelphia Evening Star*, August 14, 1900, 6.

12. Horatio Gates Jones, *The Levering Family, or, A Genealogical Account of Wigard Levering and Gerhard Levering* (Philadelphia: King and Baird, 1858), 19.

13. Leibert, *Etliche liebliche*.

14. Leibert, *Etliche liebliche*.

15. Peter Leibert, ed., *Ernst Christoph Hochmanns von Hochenau Glaubens-Bekänntniss...* (Germantown: Gedruckt bey Peter Leibert, 1800).

16. See previous chapter.

17. Philip Freneau, *The Poems of Philip Freneau*, ed. Fred Lewis Pattee (Princeton, NJ: University Library, 1902), 84–85.

18. Philip Freneau, "The Philosopher of the Forest. Numb. I.," in *The miscellaneous works of Mr. Philip Freneau containing his essays, and additional poems* (Philadelphia: Printed by Francis Bailey, at Yorick's Head, in Market Street, 1788), 286. First printed in the *Freeman's Journal*, November 1781.

19. Freneau, "Philosopher of the Forest," 286.

20. On Freneau's complex and idiosyncratic religious and philosophical ideas, see Nelson Frederick Adkins, *Philip Freneau and the Cosmic Enigma: The Religious and Philosophical Speculations of an American Poet* (New York: New York University Press, 1949).

21. Freneau, *Miscellaneous Works*, 76.

22. Philip Freneau, "The Philosopher of the Forest Num. VIII.," in *Miscellaneous Works*, 334.

23. Freneau, "Philosopher of the Forest Num. VIII.," 337–338.

24. Schmidt, *Restless Souls*, chap. 2.

25. Coby Dowdell, "The American Hermit and the British Castaway: Voluntary Retreat and Deliberative Democracy in Early American Culture," *Early American Literature* 46, no. 1 (2011): 121–156.

26. Dowdell, "American Hermit," 121.

27. Literature on Ephrata and Beissel is voluminous, and much of it relies uncritically on Julius Sachse. The standard work is Bach's *Voices of the Turtledoves*. Patrick Erben's *A Harmony of the Spirits* is also an excellent recent work.

28. Bach, *Voices of the Turtledoves*, 14.

29. Lamech and Agrippa, *Chronicon Ephratense*, 14.

30. D. Michael Quinn, *Early Mormonism and the Magic World View*, rev. ed. (Salt Lake City: Signature Books, 1998).

276 NOTES

31. Todd Kontje, "Private Life in the Public Sphere: Heinrich Jung-Stilling's 'Lebensgeschichte,'" *Colloquia Germanica* 21 (1988): 276. See also a very useful section on Jung-Stilling as a Pietist in F. Ernest Stoeffler's *German Pietism during the Eighteenth Century* (Leiden: Brill, 1973).

32. Johann Heinrich Jung-Stilling, *Theory of pneumatology, in reply to the question, what ought to be believed or disbelieved concerning presentiments, visions, and apparitions, according to nature, reason and scripture*, trans. Samuel Jackson, ed. George Bush (1808; London: Longman, Rees, Orme, Brown, Green, and Longman, 1834). Reverend Bush (1796–1859) was a biblical scholar, pastor, and abolitionist who would later embrace the work of Emmanuel Swedenborg.

33. Jung-Stilling, *Theory of Pneumatology*, 46–47. In Jung-Stilling's original German, he writes of the solitary man "daß er einem verborgene Sachen entdecken könne," "that he could discover hidden things." Jung-Stilling, *Theorie der Geister-Kunde* (Reading, PA: Heinrich B. Sage, 1816), 79, German Society of Pennsylvania Archives.

34. Jung-Stilling, *Theorie der Geister-Kunde*, 47.

35. Jung-Stilling, *Theorie der Geister-Kunde*, 47.

36. Jung-Stilling, *Theorie der Geister-Kunde*, 47.

37. Sachse, *German Pietists*, 394.

38. Andrew Steinmetz, "Kelpius: Mystic on the Wissahickon," *German-American Review*, August 1941, 11.

39. Steinmetz, "Kelpius," 11.

40. Not to mention the erroneous date of 1759 for *Pneumatology*, first published in German in 1808.

41. See Chapter 3.

42. Johannes Kelpius, *A Method of Prayer*, ed. Gordon Alderfer (New York: Harper Brothers, 1951). The most recent example is *A Method of Prayer: A Mystical Pamphlet from Colonial America*, ed. and trans. Kirby Don Richards (Philadelphia: Schuylkill Wordsmiths, 2006).

43. A note on the early American imprints database points out some inconsistencies with the attribution. This edition was advertised in Christopher Sauer's *Pensylvanische Berichte*, on June 1, 1756, and ascribed to the press of Franklin and Armbruster by Seidensticker, Hildeburn, and Evans. Franklin, however, had disposed of his German printing house to the Trustees of the Charitable Scheme two years earlier. This edition tentatively ascribed to the press of Christopher Sower of Germantown by Miller, q.v. *Kurtzer Begriff oder leichtes Mittel zu beten oder mit Gott zu reden* (Germantown, PA?: Gedruckt bey Christoph Saur?, 1756?], Evans 7693. Since this attribution is clearly lacking in detail and corroboration, I am inclined to think that this edition may, in fact, have been printed in Europe and distributed in the Americas.

44. *A Short, Easy, and Comprehensive Method of Prayer; Translated from the German; and Published for a Farther Promotion, Knowledge, and Benefit of Inward Prayer, by a Lover of Internal Devotion* (Philadelphia: Henry Miller, 1761), and *A Short, Easy, and Comprehensive Method of Prayer; Translated from the German; and Published for a Farther Promotion, Knowledge, and Benefit of Inward Prayer, by a Lover of Internal Devotion*, 2nd ed. (Germantown: Christopher Sower, 1763).

NOTES   277

45. Oswald Seidensticker, "Deutsch-amerikanisde Bibliographie bis zum Schlusse des leßten Jahrhunderts," *Der Deutsche Pioner* (Cincinnati, 1878), 199.

46. Oswald Seidensticker, *The First Century of German Printing in America, 1728-1830* (Philadelphia: Schaefer & Koradi, 1893), 62.

47. Kelpius, *A Method of Prayer*, 8.

48. See Martin, "Kelpius and Seelig," 99–101.

49. "The Hymnal of the Pietists of the Wissahickon," 1709, Free Library of Philadelphia.

50. Jeanne-Marie Bouvier de la Motte-Guyon, *Geistreiche Discourse über verschiedene Materien, welche das Innere Leben betreffen und gröstentheils aus der heiligen Schrift genommen sind*, vol. 2 (Leipzig: Samuel Benjamin Walter, 1730), 101.

51. *Short Method of Prayer*, 1st ed.

52. In 2022, Kirby Richards reached similar conclusions, on the basis of different evidence: Kirby Richards, "From Transylvania to Pennsylvania: Johannes Kelpius," *Yearbook of German-American Studies* 55 (2022): 133–162.

53. Hanegraaff, *Esotericism and the Academy*, 136–137.

54. Hanegraaff, *Esotericism and the Academy*, 136–137.

55. Adelung, *Geschichte der menschlichen Narrheit*, 7:86.

56. "Nachgehends reisete er nach Pensilwanien, und sein Vaterland hat nichts mehr von im gehört." Seivert, *Nachrichten von siebenbürgischen Gelehrten*, 212.

57. Thomas F. Gordon, *A History of Pennsylvania, from its Discovery by Europeans to the Declaration of Independence in 1776* (Philadelphia: Carey, Lea, & Carey, 1829).

58. Gordon, *History of Pennsylvania*, 578.

59. Gordon also suggests that Matthai and Witt traveled together from Europe to join the Wissahickon group.

60. Gordon, *History of Pennsylvania*, 578.

61. Gordon, *History of Pennsylvania*, 579.

62. John F. Watson, *Historic Tales of Olden Time, Concerning the Early Settlement and Progress of Philadelphia and Pennsylvania* (Philadelphia: E. Littell and T. Holden, 1833), 53.

63. John F. Watson, *Annals of Philadelphia*, 2 vols. (Philadelphia: A. Hart, J.W. Moore, J. Pennington, U. Hunt, and H.F. Anners, 1850), 2:20–22.

64. George Lippard, *Paul Ardenheim, the Monk of the Wissahikon* (Philadelphia, 1848).

65. Carsten Seecamp, "The Chapter of Perfection: A Neglected Influence on George Lippard," *Pennsylvania Magazine of History and Biography* 94, no. 2 (April 1, 1970): 192–212.

66. Seecamp, "The Chapter of Perfection," 204.

67. Seecamp, "The Chapter of Perfection," 212.

68. Michael Cohen, "Whittier, Ballad Reading, and the Culture of Nineteenth-Century Poetry," *Arizona Quarterly* 64, no. 3 (2008): 1.

69. Cohen, "Whittier, Ballad Reading," 1.

70. Edmund Clarence Stedman, *Poets of America* (Boston: Houghton, Mifflin, 1885), 113.

71. John Greenleaf Whittier, *The Pennsylvania Pilgrim and Other Poems* (Boston: Osgood and Co., 1872), 33.

278 NOTES

72. John Greenleaf Whittier, *The Supernaturalism of New England* (1847; Norman: University of Oklahoma Press, 1969), ix.

73. Whittier, *Supernaturalism of New England*, 70.

74. Lewis H. Miller, "The Supernaturalism of 'Snow-Bound,'" *New England Quarterly* 53, no. 3 (1980): 291–307.

75. Angela Sorby, *Schoolroom Poets: Childhood, Performance, and the Place of American Poetry, 1865–1917* (Durham, NH: University of New Hampshire Press, 2005), 37.

76. John Greenleaf Whittier, "Snow-Bound: A Winter Idyl," in *The Complete Poetical Works of John Greenleaf Whittier*, ed. H. E. S. (Boston: Houghton Mifflin, 1894), 398–406.

77. "Agrippa" was a name with a certain cachet in the esoteric literatures of the Americas for several centuries. One of the authors of the internal history of the Ephrata Community, the *Chronicon Ephratense*, wrote under the pseudonym "Agrippa."

78. Whittier, "Snow-Bound," 402.

79. Falckner, *Curieuse Nachricht*, 159. For the manuscript version of Falckner's report, see "Curiose Nachrichten von Pennsylvania . . . ," MS AFSt/H D85, 469–597, Frankesche Stiftungen, Halle. See also Erben, *Harmony of the Spirits*, 103.

80. Whitter, "Snow-Bound," 398–406.

81. Sorby, *Schoolroom Poets*, 37.

82. Jones, *Levering Family*. The Kelpius material is located in appendix note A, p. 186. Also very useful in tracing the trajectory of the letters, diary, and hymns is a letter in the *Acts and Proceedings of the Pennsylvania Federation of Historical Societies, Twelfth Annual Meeting* (Harrisburg, 1917), from Edwin C. Jillet on his attempts to locate and authenticate various primary documents related to the Kelpius group and the Warmer family (80–84). Jones's major article on the subject, which used some of Seidensticker's 1870 research alongside his own work, was "John Kelpius, the Hermit of the Ridge," in *The American Historical Record*, vol. 2, no. 13 (Philadelphia: Chase & Town, January 1873), 1–6.

83. Lillian M. Evans, "Oswald Seidensticker, Bibliophile," *Pennsylvania History* 7, no. 1 (January 1940): 8–19.

84. Oswald Seidesticker, "Johann Kelpius, der Einfiedler am Wissahickon," in *Der Deustche Pioner*, ed. G. Bruhl (Cincinnatti, 1870), 67–75. *Copia Eines Send-Schriebens auß der Neun Welt* is described in Seidensticker, "Hermits of the Wissahickon."

85. Marcy Silver Flynn, "Amateur Experiences: Julius Sachse and Photography," *Pennsylvania History* 64, no. 2, "History of Photography in Pennsylvania" (Spring 1997): 333–348.

86. "The writer has heard it stated that Lippard's informant had in his youth frequently seen and been about the ruins of the old structure" (Sachse, *German Pietists*, 71).

87. *The German Pietists of Provincial Pennsylvania, 1694–1708* (1895); *The German Sectarians of Pennsylvania, 1708–1742* (1899) on the early Ephrata community; and *The German Sectarians of Pennsylvania, 1742–1800* (1901), on decline and end of Ephrata.

88. Bach *Voices of the Turtledoves*, 197.

89. Sachse, *German Pietists*, 246–247.

NOTES 279

90. Sachse, *German Pietists*, vi.

91. Hans Kippenberg, *Discovering Religious History in the Modern Age* (Princeton: Princeton University Press, 2001), 89.

92. Mitch Horowitz, *Occult America: White House Seances, Ouija Circles, Masons, and the Secret Mystic History of Our Nation* (New York: Bantam Books, 2009); Fisher, "Prophesies and Revelations."

93. *Allgemeine und General Reformation der gantzen weiten Welt* (Universal and General Reformation of the Whole Wide World), *Fama Fraternitatis, Deß Löblichen Ordens des Rosenkreutzes, an alle Gelehrte und Häupter Europae geschrieben* (The Fame of the Fraternity of the Praiseworthy Order of the Rose-Cross, Written to All the Learned and Rulers of Europe), and *Auch einer kurtzen Responsion* (Also a Short Response). See Roland Edighoffer, "Rosicrucianism I: First Half of the 17th Century," in *Dictionary of Gnosis & Western Esotericism*, ed. Wouter J. Hanegraaff with Antoine Faivre, Roelof van den Broek, and Jean-Pierre Brach (Leiden: Brill, 2005), 1009.

94. As Roland Edighoffer writes, "The 'true philosophy' that the *Confessio* extols is Hermetist; the reference to the theological and medical sources of this "philosophy" reflect its Paracelsian origin" ("Rosicrucianism I," 1011).

95. On the origin of the Rosicrucian myth, Edighoffer writes: "The manifestoes originated in the 'Learned and Christian Society' established by Johann Valentin Andreae in Tübingen in 1610. This small group of bosom friends of Andreae's, notably Christoph Besold and Tobias Hess (his *amici secretissimi*), together conceived of and constructed the Rosicrucian myth. In all likelihood the *Fama Fraternitatis* and the *Confessio* resulted from the cooperation of several authors, whereas the Chemical Wedding was written by Andreae alone" ("Rosicrucianism I," 1009).

96. Edighoffer, "Rosicrucianism I," 1014.

97. Massimo Introvigne, "Rosicrucianism III: 19th–20th Century," in Hanegraaff, *Dictionary of Gnosis*, 1018.

98. It is possible that this label arose in the work of John Watson, in whose correspondence we are told that Christopher Witt's library contained volumes of "Rosecution philosophy." Watson does not mention precisely which volumes or indicate a specific understanding of "Rosecution," further complicating this suggestion. See the letter from Watson to Darlington, May 8, 1848, MS in the American Philosophical Society microfilm of selections from the Darlington papers filmed by the New York Historical Society, film no. 627.

99. Sachse, *German Pietists*, 37–38.

100. Yates, *The Rosicrucian Enlightenment*, xiv.

101. Arthur Edward Waite, *The Brotherhood of the Rosy Cross, Being Records of the House of the Holy Spirit in Its Inward and Outward History* (1924; New Hyde Park, NY: University Books, 1961), 600–610.

102. R. Swinburne Clymer, "The Mystics in America," *A Magazine Issued by Authority of the Rosicrucian Fraternity and Devoted to Mysticism, Occultism, and the Well-Being of Man* 4 (May–June 1931 to May–June 1932): 115–123.

103. Introvigne, "Rosicrucianism III," 1019.

280 NOTES

104. Harvey Spencer Lewis, *Rosicrucian Questions and Answers: With Complete History of the Rosicrucian Order* (San Jose: Supreme Grand Lodge of AMORC, 1959), 160–164.
105. Martin, "Kelpius and Seelig."
106. Donald E. Durnbaugh, "Work and Hope: The Spirituality of Radical Pietist Communitarians," *Church History* 39 (March 1970): 74–76.
107. Benz, *Die Protestantische Thebais.*
108. Fisher, "Prophesies and Revelations."
109. Bach, Voices of the Turtledoves, 197.
110. http://kelpius.org (accessed December 9, 2023).
111. http://kelpius.org/marker.html (accessed December 9, 2023).
112. Gaston Bachelard, *The Poetics of Space*, trans. Maria Jolas (Boston: Beacon Press, 1994), 32.
113. Bachelard, *The Poetics of Space*, 32.
114. Schmidt, *Restless Souls*, 79–80.
115. Bachelard, *The Poetics of Space*, 36–37.
116. Bachelard, *The Poetics of Space*, 33.

Conclusion

1. "Ford Go Further Presents: A Trip to the Hideout of America's First Doomsday Cult," 6abc Action News, September 2018, https://6abc.com/fyi-philly-wissahickon-park-walk/4202683/.
2. Wolfson, *Through a Speculum*, 29.
3. Jenkins, *Climate, Catastrophe, and Faith*, 23.
4. See Ebeling, *Secret History*; Hanegraaff, *Esotericism and the Academy.*
5. Stephen J. Fleming, Egil Asprem and Ann Taves, "Refiner's Fire and the Yates Thesis: Hermeticism, Esotericism, and the History of Christianity," *Journal of Mormon History* 41, no. 4 (October 2015): 198–209.
6. Quoted in Wouter J. Hanegraaff, *Hermetic Spirituality and the Historical Imagination* (Cambridge: Cambridge University Press, 2022), 357.
7. Michel Foucault, *The Order of Things: An Archaeology of the Human Sciences*, trans. Alan Sheridan (New York: Vintage, 1994), 26.
8. Foucault, *The Order of Things*, 20–21.
9. Amitav Ghosh, *The Nutmeg's Curse: Parables for a Planet in Crisis* (Chicago University of Chicago Press, 2021), 38.
10. Hanegraaff, *Hermetic Spirituality.*
11. Hanegraaff, *Hermetic Spirituality*, 194.
12. Hanegraaff, *Hermetic Spirituality*, 195.
13. See Chapter 2.
14. Kelpius, Letter to Esther Palmer at Flushing, Long Island, May 25, 1706, in Journal, 1694-1707, Historical Society of Pennsylvania, Ferdinand J. Dreer Autograph Collection (#0175), 94.

NOTES 281

15. Ghosh, *The Nutmeg's Curse*, 244.
16. "September 14, 1839," in *Journals of Ralph Waldo Emerson 1838–1841*, ed. Edward Waldo Emerson and Waldo Emerson Forbes, 252 (Boston: Houghton Mifflin Company, 1911). "A primrose by the brim of the river" is quoting Wordsworth, "Peter Bell: A Tale."
17. See Chapter 1.
18. Emerson, *Journals,* 252.
19. Robert Richardson, *Emerson: The Mind on Fire* (Berkeley: University of California Press, 1996).
20. Richardson, *Emerson*, 197.
21. Emerson, "Nature," in *The Complete Works of Ralph Waldo Emerson*, vol. 1: *Nature, Addresses and Lectures* (Boston: Houghton, Mifflin, 1903–4), 41–42.
22. Weeks and Andersson, "Jacob Böhme's Writings," 17.

References

Abbildung Und Beschreibung Deß Wunderwürdigen Unvergleichlichen Cometen: Der Erstmals Zu Anfang Deß Wintermonats Vor Aufgang Der Sonnen Erschienen, Und Anjetzt Nach Derselben Untergang Sich Entsetzlich Sehen Lässet. Nuremberg: Schollenberger, 1680. Munich, Bavarian State Library. https://www.digitale-sammlun gen.de/de/view/bsb00100510?page=,1. Accessed August 22 2023.

Ackner, Richard. *Allerlei von Vorfahren in Siebenbürgen.* Self-published, 2010.

Adkins, Nelson Frederick. *Philip Freneau and the Cosmic Enigma: The Religious and Philosophical Speculations of an American Poet.* New York: New York University Press, 1949.

Aker, G. "Johann Jacob Zimmerman 1642–1693: Ein Prophet des Tausendjährigen Reiches." In *Vaihinger Köpfe: Biographische Porträts aus fünf Jahrhunderten,* edited by L. Behr et al., 71–88. Vaihingen, Selbstverlag der Stadt Vaihingen an der Enz, 1993.

Albanese, Catherine. *America: Religions and Religion.* Belmont: Thomson/Wadsworth, 1981.

Albanese, Catherine. *America: Religions and Religion.* 5th ed. Belmont: Thomson/ Wadsworth, 2013.

Albanese, Catherine. *A Republic of Mind and Spirit: A Cultural History of American Metaphysical Religion.* New Haven: Yale University Press, 2007.

Ames, Alexander. *The Word in the Wilderness: Popular Piety and the Manuscript Arts in Early Pennsylvania.* University Park: Penn State University Press, 2020.

Andersson, Bo, Lucinda Martin, Leigh T. I. Penman, and Andrew Weeks, eds. *Jacob Böhme and His World.* Leiden: Brill, 2019.

Archiv des Vereins für Siebenbürgische Landeskunde. Vol. 14. Hermanstadt, 1872.

Aristotle. *The Metaphysics.* Translated by Hugh Lawson-Tancred. New York: Penguin, 1998.

Arndt, Johann. *Sechs Bücher von Wahren Christenthum.* Philadelphia: Georg Menz und Sohn, 1834. Horner Library of the German Society of Pennsylvania.

Arndt, Johann. *True Christianity.* Translated and edited by Peter Erb. New York: Paulist Press, 1979.

Arnold, Gottfried. *Unparteyische Kirchen- und Ketzer -Historie.* 2 vols. Frankfurt am Main: Thomas Fritsch, 1699–1700.

Arnold, Gottfried. *Vitae Patrum, oder Leben der Alt-Väter.* Halle, 1700.

Ashbridge, Elizabeth. *Some Account of the Forepart of the Life of Elizabeth Ashbridge, Who Departed This Life . . . : In the County of Carlow, Ireland, the 16th, 5 Mo., 1755.* Philadelphia: Printed for C.C.C. by P.C. Stockhausen, 1886. Historical Society of Pennsylvania, E.42115.

Atwood, Craig. "'The Hallensians Are Pietists; Aren't You a Hallensian?': Mühlenberg's Conflict with the Moravians." *Journal of Moravian History* 12, no. 1 (2012): 47–92.

Bach, Jeffrey. *Voices of the Turtledoves: The Sacred World of Ephrata.* University Park: Pennsylvania State University Press, 2003.

284 REFERENCES

Bach, Jeffrey, and Michael Birkel. *Genius of the Transcendent; Mystical Writings of Jakob Boehme*. Boston: Shambhala Press, 2010.

Bachelard, Gaston. *The Poetics of Space*. Translated by Maria Jonas. Boston: Beacon Press, 1994.

Bailyn, Bernard. *The Barbarous Years: The Peopling of British North America: The Conflict of Civilizations, 1600–1675*. New York: Vintage, 2012.

Barnes, Robin Bruce. *Prophecy and Gnosis: Apocalypticism in the Wake of the Lutheran Reformation*. Stanford, CA: Stanford University Press, 1988.

Bartlett, Robert. *The Natural and the Supernatural in the Middle Ages*. Cambridge: Cambridge University Press, 2008.

Bartram, John. *The Correspondence of John Bartram, 1734–1777*. Edited by Edmund Berkeley and Dorothy Smith Berkeley. Gainesville: University Press of Florida, 1992.

Bartram, William. William Bartram commonplace book. Philadelphia: Private collection, John Bartram Association, Bartram's Garden digital copy.

Beiler, Rosalind J. "Migration and the Loss of Spiritual Community: The Case of Daniel Falckner and Anna Maria Schuchart." In *Enduring Loss in Early Modern Germany*, edited by Lynne Tatlock, 369–396. Leiden: Brill, 2010.

Benz, Ernst. *Die protestantische Thebais: Zur Nachwirkung Makarios des Ägypters im Protestantismus des 17. und 18. Jahrhunderts in Europa und Amerika*. Wiesbaden: Verlag der Akademie der Wissenschaften und der Literatur, 1963.

Benz, Ernst. *Emanuel Swedenborg: Visionary Savant in the Age of Reason*. Translated by Nicholas Goodrick-Clarke. West Chester, PA: Swedenborg Foundation, 2002.

Benz, Ernst. *The Theology of Electricity: On the Encounter and Explanation of Theology and Science in the 17th and 18th Centuries*. Translated by Wolfgang Taraba. Eugene, OR: Pickwick Publications, 1989.

Bicknell, Joseph D. *The Wissahickon in History, Song and Story*. Philadelphia: City History Society of Philadelphia, 1906.

Blom, Philipp. *Nature's Mutiny: How the Little Ice Age of the Long Seventeenth Century Transformed the West and Shaped the Present*. Translated by the author. New York: Liverwright, 2017.

Boehme, Jacob. *Mysterium magnum, or An exposition of the first book of Moses called Genesis*. Translated by John Sparrow. London: University of Michigan, Early English Books Text Creation Partnership, 1656. https://quod.lib.umich.edu/e/eebo/A28 529.0001.001/1:1?rgn=div1;view=fulltext;q1=naphtali.

Boulliau, Ismael. *Astronomia philolaica: Opus novum, in quo motus Planetarum per nouam ac veram hypothesim demonstrantur*. Paris: Sumptibus Simeonis Piget, 1645.

Brecht, Martin, et al., eds. *Geschichte des Pietismus*. 4 vols. Göttingen: Vandenhoeck & Ruprecht, 1993–2004.

Brock, Peter. *Pacifism in the United States: From the Colonial Era to the First World War*. Princeton: Princeton University Press, 2015.

Brooke, John L. *The Refiner's Fire: The Making of Mormon Cosmology, 1644–1844*. Cambridge: Cambridge University Press, 1994.

Brophy, Alfred L. "'Ingenium est Fateri per quos profeceris': Francis Daniel Pastorius' Young Country Clerk's Collection and Anglo-American Legal Literature, 1682–1716." *University of Chicago Law School Roundtable* 3, issue 2, Article 16 (1996): 637–734.

Brown, Charles Brockden. "On Almanacks." *Monthly Magazine and the American Review*, vol. 1, issue 2 (New York: T. & J. Swords, 1799), 85–88. Accessed via the Charles

REFERENCES   285

Brockden Brown Electronic Archive and Scholarly Edition, https://brockdenbrown. cah.ucf.edu/xtf3/view?docId=1805-04288.xml.

Brown, Charles Brockden. "Terrific Novels." *Literary Magazine and American Register*, vol. 3, issue 19 (Philadelphia: John Conrad & Co., 1805), 288–289. Accessed via the Charles Brockden Brown Electronic Archive and Scholarly Edition, https://brockd enbrown.cah.ucf.edu/xtf3/view?docId=1805-04288.xml.

Brown, Charles Brockden. *Wieland and Memoirs of Carwin the Biloquist*. New York: Penguin, 1991.

Brown, Charles Brockden. *Wieland and Memoirs of Carwin the Biloquist*. Edited by Bryan Waterman. New York: Norton, 2011.

Brown, Peter. *The Cult of the Saints: Its Rise and Function in Latin Christianity*. Chicago: University of Chicago Press, 1981.

Butler, Jon. *Awash in a Sea of Faith: Christianizing the American People*. Cambridge, MA: Harvard University Press, 1990.

Butler, Jon. "Into Pennsylvania's Spiritual Abyss: The Rise and Fall of the Later Keithians, 1693–1703." *Pennsylvania Magazine of History and Biography* 101, no. 2 (April 1, 1977): 151–170.

Carroll, Kenneth L. "Quakerism on the Eastern Shore of Virginia." *Virginia Magazine of History and Biography* 74, no. 2 (1966): 170–189.

Carroll, Lucy. *The Hymn Writers of Early Pennsylvania*. N.p.: Xulon Press, 2008.

Carroll, Robert, and Stephen Prickett "Introduction." In *The Bible: Authorized King James Version*, edited by Robert Carroll and Stephen Prickett, xi–xlvi. Oxford: Oxford University Press, 1997.

Christopherson, Bill. *The Apparition in the Glass: Charles Brockden Brown's American Gothic*. Athens: University of Georgia Press, 1993.

Clark, Elizabeth. *Reading Renunciation: Asceticism and Scripture in Early Christianity*. Princeton: Princeton University Press, 1999.

Classen, Albrecht. "The Secret and Universal Relevance of Johann Scheffler'[s] (Angelus Silesius's) Epigrams: Mystico-Philosophical Messages from the World of the Baroque for the Twenty-First Century." *The Comparatist* 44 (2020): 215–234.

Clements, Niki Kasumi. *Sites of the Ascetic Self: John Cassian and Christian Ethical Formation*. Notre Dame, IN: University of Notre Dame Press, 2020.

Clery, E. J. *The Rise of Supernatural Fiction, 1762–1800*. Cambridge: Cambridge University Press, 1995.

Clymer, R. Swinburne. "The Mystics in America." *A Magazine Issued by Authority of the Rosicrucian Fraternity and Devoted to Mysticism, Occultism, and the Well-Being of Man* 4 (May–June 1931 to May–June, 1932): 115–123.

Cobbett, William. *Rural Rides*. London: A. Cobbett. 137, Strand, 1853.

Cohen, Michael. "Whittier, Ballad Reading, and the Culture of Nineteenth-Century Poetry." *Arizona Quarterly* 64, no. 3 (2008): 1–29.

Colberg, M. Ehregott Daniel *Das Platonisch-Hermetisches Christenthum: Begreiffend Die Historische Erzehung vom Ursprung und vielerley Secten der heutigen Fanatischen Theologie, unterm Namen der Paracelsisten, Weigelianer, Rosencreutzer, Quäcker, Böhmisten, Wiedertäuffer, Bourignisten, Labadisten und Quieristen*. Frankfurt am Main: Weidmann, 1690.

The concessions and agreements of the proprietors, freeholders and inhabitants of the province of West New-Jersey, in America [1677]. https://westjersey.org/ca77.htm.

286 REFERENCES

Conger, George Perrigo. *Theories of Macrocosms and Microcosms in the History of Philosophy*. New York: Columbia University Press, 1922.

Contosta, David R., and Carol Franklin. *Metropolitan Paradise: The Struggle for Nature in the City: Philadelphia's Wissahickon Valley, 1620–2020*. Vol. 1, *Wilderness*. Philadelphia: Saint Joseph's University Press, 2010.

Copenhaver, Brian. *The Hermetica: The Greek Corpus Hermeticum and the Latin Asclepius in a New English Translation, with Notes and Introduction*. Cambridge: Cambridge University Press, 1992.

Crain, Caleb. "The Awful Truth." *Commonplace* 5, no. 4 (July 2005). https://commonpl ace.online/article/the-awful-truth/

Crawford, Richard. "A Historian's Introduction to Early American Music." *Proceedings of the American Antiquarian Society* 89, no . 2 (October 1979): 261–298.

Croese, Gerardus. *The general history of the Quakers containing the lives, tenents, sufferings, tryals, speeches and letters of the most eminent Quakers, both men and women: from the first rise of that sect down to this present time*. London: Printed for John Dunton, 1696.

Cronon, William. *Uncommon Ground: Toward Reinventing Nature*. New York: Norton, 1995.

"Daia, Denndorf." Kirkenburgen Foundation. https://kirchenburgen.org/en/location/ denndorf-daia/. Accessed December 10, 2023.

Daston, Lorraine, and Katharine Park. *Wonders and the Order of Nature, 1150–1750*. New York: Zone Books, 2001.

Davies, Owen. *Grimoires: A History of Magic Books*. New York: Oxford University Press, 2009.

Denndorf Baptism Records. Casa Teutsch, Denndorfer Kirchenbuch, Signatur 980.

Die Jüngere Matrikel der Universität Leipzig, 1559–1809. Leipzig: Giesecke & Devrient, 1909.

Dowdell, Coby. "The American Hermit and the British Castaway: Voluntary Retreat and Deliberative Democracy in Early American Culture." *Early American Literature* 46, no. 1 (2011): 121–156.

Durnbaugh, Donald E. "Work and Hope: The Spirituality of Radical Pietist Communitarians." *Church History* 39 (March 1970): 74–76.

Ebling, Florian. *The Secret History of Hermes Trismegistus: Hermeticism From Modern to Ancient Times*. Translated by David Lorton. Ithaca, NY: Cornell University Press, 2007.

Edighoffer, Roland. "Rosicrucianism I: First half of the 17th Century." In *Dictionary of Gnosis & Western Esotericism*, edited by Wouter J. Hanegraaff with Antoine Faivre, Roelof van den Broek, and Jean-Pierre Brach, 1009–1014. Leiden: Brill, 2005.

Ehinger, Siglind. "German Pietists between the Ancient Unity of Brethren and the Moravian Church: The Case of Württemberg Pastor Georg Konrad Rieger (1687–1743) and His 'History of the Moravian Brethren.'" *Journal of Moravian History* 14, no. 1 (2014): 51–72.

Emerson, Ralph Waldo. *The Complete Works of Ralph Waldo Emerson*. Vol. 1, *Nature, Addresses and Lectures*. Boston: Houghton, Mifflin, 1903–4.

Emerson, Ralph Waldo. *Journals of Ralph Waldo Emerson 1838–1841*. Edited by Edward Waldo Emerson and Waldo Emerson Forbes. Boston: Houghton Mifflin Company, 1911.

Ephemerides of the celestial motions for X. years beginning anno 1672 . . . and ending an. 1681. Calculated according to art from new tables, and compared with the most correct observations of the noble Tycho, Kepler, Mr. Wright, and other approved astronomers.

London: printed by John Macock for the Company of Stationers, 1672. Library Company of Pennsylvania Archives.

Erben, Patrick. *A Harmony of the Spirits: Translation and the Language of Community in Early Pennsylvania*. Chapel Hill: Published for the Omohundro Institute of Early American History and Culture, Williamsburg, Virginia, by the University of North Carolina Press, 2012.

Erben, Patrick. "Introduction: The Lives and Letters of Francis Daniel Pastorius." In *The Francis Daniel Pastorius Reader: Writings by an Early American Polymath*, edited by Patrick Erben, associate editors Alfred L. Brophy and Margo M. Lambert, 1–32. University Park: Pennsylvania State University Press, 2019.

Evans, Lillian M. "Oswald Seidensticker, Bibliophile." *Pennsylvania History* 7, no. 1 (January 1940): 8–19.

Everard, John. *The Divine Pymander of Hermes Mercurius Trismegistus . . .* London: Robert White, 1650.

Fabricius, Johannes. *Daß zwischen der Augsburgischen Konfession und Katholischen Religion kein sonderlicher Unterschied sei*. Cologne, 1707.

Fabricius, Johannes, and Johannes Kelpius. *Scylla Theologica aliquot exemplis Patrum and Doctorum Ecclesiae, qui cum alios refutare laborarent, fervore disputationis abrepti in contrarios errores misere inciderunt, ostensa atque in materiam disputationis proposita Joh. Fabricio S. Theol. Prof. Publ. and M. Joh. Kelpio Dalia-Transylvano Saxone*. Altdorf, 1690.

Fagan, Brian. *The Little Ice Age: How Climate Made History, 1300–1850*. New York: Basic Books, 2000.

Falckner, Daniel. *A Contribution to Pennsylvania History: Missives to Rev. August Herman Francke from Daniel Falckner and Justus Falckner*. Translated by George T. Ettinger. Lancaster, PA: Pennsylvania-German Society, 1909.

Falckner, Daniel. *Falckner's Curieuse Nachricht von Pensylvania: The Book That Stimulated the Great German Immigration to Pennsylvania in the Early Years of the XVIII Century*. Translated by Julius Sachse. 1905; University Park: Pennsylvania State University Press, 2012. For the manuscript version of Falckner's report, see Curiose Nachrichten von Pennsylvania . . . MS AFSt/H D85, 469-597, Frankesche Stiftungen, Halle, 1702.

Fischer, David Hackett. *Albion's Seed: Four British Folkways in America*. New York: Oxford University Press, 1989.

Fisher, Elizabeth W. "'Prophesies and Revelations': German Cabbalists in Early Pennsylvania." *Pennsylvania Magazine of History and Biography* 109 (July 1985): 299–333.

Fleming, Stephen J., Egil Asprem, and Ann Taves. "Refiner's Fire and the Yates Thesis: Hermeticism, Esotericism, and the History of Christianity." *Journal of Mormon History* 41, no. 4 (October 2015): 198–209.

Flynn, Marcy Silver. "Amateur Experiences: Julius Sachse and Photography." *Pennsylvania History* 64, no. 2, "History of Photography in Pennsylvania" (Spring 1997).

Fogleman, Aaron Spencer. *Hopeful Journeys: German Immigration, Settlement, and Political Culture in Colonial America, 1717–1775*. Philadelphia: University of Pennsylvania Press, 1996.

Fogleman, Aaron Spencer. *Jesus Is Female: Moravians and Radical Religion in Early America*. Philadelphia: University of Pennsylvania Press, 2007.

Foucault, Michel. *History of Sexuality*. Vol. 3, *The Care of the Self*. Translated by Robert Hurley. New York: Vintage, 1986.

288 REFERENCES

Foucault, Michel. "Of Other Spaces, Heterotopias." *Architecture, Mouvement, Continuité*, no. 5 (1984): 46–49.

Foucault, Michel. *The Order of Things: An Archaeology of the Human Sciences*. Translated by Alan Sheridan. New York: Vintage, 1994.

Foucault, Michel. *Security, Territory, Population, Lectures at the College de France, 1977–1978*. Translated by Graham Burchell. New York: Palgrave, 2004.

Foucault, Michel. "Technologies of the Self." In *Ethics: Subjectivity and Truth*, vol. 1 of *Essential Works of Foucault, 1954–1984*, edited by Paul Rabinow, 223–251. New York: New Press, 1998.

Fox, George. *The Journal of George Fox*. Edited by John L. Nickalls. New York: Cambridge University Press, 1952.

Franklin, Benjamin. *The Papers of Benjamin Franklin*. Vol. 4, July 1, 1750, through June 30, 1753. Edited by Leonard W. Labaree. New Haven: Yale University Press, 1961.

Franklin, Benjamin. *The Papers of Benjamin Franklin*. Vol. 12, January 1, through December 31, 1765. Edited by Leonard W. Labaree. New Haven: Yale University Press, 1967.

Freneau, Philip. *The miscellaneous works of Mr. Philip Freneau containing his essays, and additional poems*. Philadelphia: Printed by Francis Bailey, at Yorick's Head, in Market Street, 1788.

Freneau, Philip. "The Philosopher of the Forest Num I." In *The miscellaneous works of Mr. Philip Freneau containing his essays, and additional poems*. Philadelphia: Printed by Francis Bailey, at Yorick's Head, in Market Street, 1788. Early English Books Online Text Creation Partnership. http://name.umdl.umich.edu/N16424.0001.001.

Freneau, Philip. "The Philosopher of the Forest Num. VIII." In *The miscellaneous works of Mr. Philip Freneau containing his essays, and additional poems*. Philadelphia: Printed by Francis Bailey, at Yorick's Head, in Market Street, 1788. Early English Books Online Text Creation Partnership. http://name.umdl.umich.edu/N16 424.0001.001.

Freneau, Philip. *The Poems of Philip Freneau*. Edited by Fred Lewis Pattee. Princeton, NJ: University Library, 1902.

Friends House Library. *Minutes for the Meetings for Sufferings*. Vol. 9, 1693–94. London.

Gawthrop, Richard, and Gerald Strauss. "Protestantism and Literacy in Early Modern Germany." *Past & Present*, no. 104 (1984): 31–55.

Gentzke, Joshua Levi Ian. "Imaginal Renaissance: Desire, Corporeality, and Rebirth in the Work of Jakob Böhme." PhD dissertation, Stanford University, 2016.

Ghosh, Amitav. *The Great Derangement: Climate Change and the Unthinkable*. Chicago: University of Chicago Press, 2016.

Ghosh, Amitav. *Gun Island*. New York: Farrar, Straus and Giroux, 2019.

Ghosh, Amitav. *The Nutmeg's Curse: Parables for a Planet in Crisis*. Chicago University of Chicago Press, 2021.

Gill, John. *An Exposition of the New Testament*. 3 vols. London: printed for the author; 1746–48.

Godwin, Josclyn. *Upstate Cauldron: Eccentric Spiritual Movements in Early New York State*. Albany: Excelsior Editions, 2015.

Good, Edwin M. *Genesis 1–11: Tales of the Earliest World*. Stanford, CA: Stanford University Press, 2011.

Gordon, Thomas F. *A History of Pennsylvania, from its Discovery by Europeans to the Declaration of Independence in 1776*. Philadelphia: Carey, Lea, & Carey, 1829.

REFERENCES 289

Graeber, David, and David Wengrow. *The Dawn of Everything: A New History of Humanity*. New York: Farrar, Straus and Giroux, 2021.

Grainger, Brett. "Vital Nature and Vital Piety: Johann Arndt and the Evangelical Vitalism of Cotton Mather." *Church History* 81, no. 4 (2012): 852–872.

Grieve-Carlson, Timothy. "The Night Side of Nature: Environmental Meanings of the Modern Paranormal." *Journal for the Study of Religion, Nature, and Culture* 15, no. 2 (2021): 229–254.

Gummere, Richard Mott. "Apollo on Locust Street." *Pennsylvania Magazine of History and Biography* 56, no. 1 (1932): 68–92.

Guyon, Jeanne-Marie Bouvier de la Motte. *Geistreiche Discourse über verschiedene Materien, welche das Innere Leben betreffen und gröstentheils aus der heiligen Schrift genommen sind*. Vol. 2. Leipzig: Samuel Benjamin Walter, 1730.

Hall, David. *Worlds of Wonder, Days of Judgment: Popular Religious Belief in Early New England*. Cambridge, MA: Harvard University Press, 1989.

Hanegraaff, Wouter J. *Esotericism and the Academy: Rejected Knowledge in Western Culture*. Cambridge: Cambridge University Press, 2012.

Hanegraaff, Wouter J. *Hermetic Spirituality and the Historical Imagination*. Cambridge: Cambridge University Press, 2022.

Hannak, Kristine. "Johann Arndt (1555–1621) and the 'Crisis of Piety' of Jacob Böhme's Time." In *Jacob Böhme and His World*, edited by Bo Andersson, Lucinda Martin, Leigh T. I. Penman, and Andrew Weeks, 145–165. Leiden: Brill, 2019.

Harper, Kyle. *The Fate of Rome: Climate, Disease, and the End of an Empire*. Princeton: Princeton University Press, 2017.

Hazard's Register of Pennsylvania. Vol. 3, no. 4. Philadelphia, Jan 24, 1829.

Hazard's Register of Pennsylvania. Vol. 4, no. 3. Philadelphia, July 18, 1829.

Henry, Paul. "The Place of Plotinus in the History of Thought." In Plotinus, *The Enneads*, translated by Stephen MacKenna, xlii–lxxxiii. New York: Penguin, 1991.

Herbert, Christopher. "Voices in the Pennsylvania Wilderness: An Examination of the Music Manuscripts, Music Theory, Compositions, and (Female) Composers of the Eighteenth-Century Ephrata Cloister." DMA dissertation, Juilliard School, May 2018.

Herdeegen, Johann. *Historische Nachricht von deß löblichen Hirten- und Blumen-Ordens an der Pegnitz Anfang und Fortgang . . .* Nuremberg, 1744.

Hermelink, Heinsrich. *Geschichte der evangelischen Kirche in Württemberg von der Reformation bis zur Gegenwart*. Wunderlich: Stuttgart, 1949.

Hess, Albert G. "Observations on 'The Lamenting Voice of the Hidden Love.'" *Journal of the American Musicological Society* 5, no. 3 (1952): 211–223.

Hessayon, Ariel. "Boehme's Life and Times." In *An Introduction to Jacob Boehme: Four Centuries of Thought and Reception*, edited by Ariel Hessayon and Sarah Apetrei, 13–37. New York: Routledge, 2014.

Hessayon, Ariel. "Jacob Bohme and the Early Quakers." *Journal of the Friends Historical Society* 60, no. 3 (2005): 191–223.

Hessayon, Ariel, ed. *Jane Lead and Her Transnational Legacy*. London: Palgrave Macmillan, 2016.

"Historical Pageant, Friday, October 9, 1908." In folder Oberholtzer, Ellis Paxson, Box 3, Marion Dexter Learned Collection, Archives and Special Collections, Boyd Lee Spahr Library, Dickinson College, Carlisle, PA.

Horowitz, Mitch. *Occult America: White House Seances, Ouija Circles, Masons, and the Secret Mystic History of Our Nation*. New York: Bantam Books, 2009.

290 REFERENCES

"The Hymnal of the Pietists of the Wissahickon." Free Library of Philadelphia. Manuscript. 1709.

Introvigne, Massimo. "Rosicrucianism III: 19th–20th Century." In *Dictionary of Gnosis & Western Esotericism*, edited by Wouter J. Hanegraaff with Antoine Faivre, Roelof van den Broek, and Jean-Pierre Brach, 1018–1020. Leiden: Brill, 2005.

Jakobsson, Ármann. *The Troll inside You: Paranormal Activity in the Medieval North.* Brooklyn, NY: Punctum Books, 2017.

Jantz, Harold. "Deutschamerikanischer Literatur: Einige weitere Perspektiven." In *Amerika und die Deutschen: Bestandsaufnahme einer 300jährigen Geschichte*, edited by Frank Trommler, 279–288. Opladen: Westdeutscher Verlag, 1986.

Jenkins, Phillip. *Climate, Catastrophe, and Faith: How Changes in Climate Drive Religious Upheaval.* New York: Oxford University Press, 2021.

Jillet, Edwin C. *Acts and Proceedings of the Pennsylvania Federation of Historical Societies, Twelfth Annual Meeting.* Harrisburg, 1917.

Johnston, Warren. "Jane Lead and English Apocalyptic Thought in the Late Seventeenth Century." In *Jane Lead and Her Transnational Legacy*, edited by Ariel Hessayon, 119–142. London: Palgrave Macmillan, 2016.

Jones, Horatio Gates. *The Levering Family, or, A Genealogical Account of Wigard Levering and Gerhard Levering.* Philadelphia: King and Baird, 1858.

Jortner, Adam. *Blood from the Sky: Miracles and Politics in the Early American Republic.* Charlottesville: University of Virginia Press, 2017.

Juhász, Levente. "Johannes Kelpius (1673–1708): Mystic on the Wissahickon." *Cromohs: Cyber Review of Modern Historiography*, 2006. https://oajournals.fupress.net/public/journals/9/Seminar/juhasz_kelpius.html.

Jung-Stilling, Johann Heinrich. *Theorie der Geister-Kunde.* Reading, PA: Heinrich B. Sage, 1816. German Society of Pennsylvania archives.

Jung-Stilling, Johann Heinrich. *Theory of pneumatology, in reply to the question, what ought to be believed or disbelieved concerning presentiments, visions, and apparitions, according to nature, reason and scripture.* Translated by Samuel Jackson. 1808; London: Longman, Rees, Orme, Brown, Green, and Longman, 1834.

Kafer, Peter. *Charles Brockden Brown's Revolution and the Birth of American Gothic.* Philadelphia: University of Pennsylvania Press, 2004.

Kamrath, Mark L. *The Historicism of Charles Brockden Brown: Radical History and the Early Republic.* Kent, OH: Kent State University Press, 2010.

Kazal, Russell A. "The Lost World of Pennsylvania Pluralism: Immigrants, Regions, and the Early Origins of Pluralist Ideologies in America." *Journal of American Ethnic History* 27, no. 3 (Spring 2008): 7–42.

Keith, George. *The deism of William Penn . . .* London: Printed for Brab. Aylmer, 1699.

Kelley, Joseph. *Pennsylvania: The Colonial Years, 1681–1776.* Garden City, NY: Doubleday, 1980.

Kelpius, Johannes. "Briefe von Johannes Kelpius an Jacob Wilhelm Imhof." December 1693. Bayerische Staatsbibliothek, Munich.

Kelpius, Johannes. "Briefe von Johannes Kelpius an Jacob Wilhelm Imhof." February 1694. Bayerische Staatsbibliothek, Munich.

Kelpius, Johannes. *The Diarium of Magister Johannes Kelpius.* Translated by Julius Sachse. Lancaster, PA: New Era Printing Co, 1917; University Park: Metalmark Books, 2012.

Kelpius, Johannes. "Doctissimum Virum Deum Michael Deli." Schäßburg, 1687. Manuscript 505, Department of the Library of the City of Sighișoara, Romania.

REFERENCES   291

Kelpius, Johannes. *Ethicus Ethnicus: Inquisitio an ethicus Etnicus aptus sit Christianae Juventutis Hodegus sive: An juvenis christianus sit idoneus auditor Ethices Aristotelicae? Resp. Balthas. Blosio.* Nuremberg, 1690.

Kelpius, Johannes. "I: N: J: Die Klägliche stimme Der Verborgenen Liebe Zur Zeit da Sie Elend und Verlassen Darneider Lag und Von Der Menge ihrer Feinde Gedrenget und Geängstiget Wurder Von einem in kuñers Schwebenden Entworffen," with facing English title: "The Lamenting Voice of the Hidden Love, at the time when she lay in Misery & forsaken; and oprest by the multitude of her enemies, Composed by one in Kumber 1705." Historical Society of Pennsylvania, MS Ac 189, Abraham Cassel Collection, vol. 27, Coll. 1675.

Kelpius, Johannes. *Journal, 1694–1707.* Historical Society of Pennsylvania, Ferdinand J. Dreer Autograph Collection (#0175).

Kelpius, Johannes. *A Method of Prayer.* Edited by Gordon Alderfer. New York: Harper Brothers, 1951.

Kelpius, Johannes. *A Method of Prayer: A Mystical Pamphlet from Colonial America.* Edited and translated by Kirby Don Richards. Philadelphia: Schuylkill Wordsmiths, 2006.

Kelpius, Johannes. *Theologiae Naturalis, Seu Metaphysicae Metamorphosin.* Altdorf: Schönnerstaedt, 1689.

Kippenberg, Hans. *Discovering Religious History in the Modern Age.* Princeton: Princeton University Press, 2001.

Klein, Karl Kurt. "Magister Johannes Kelpius Transylvanus, der Heilige und Dichter vom Wissahickon in Pennsylvanien." In *Festschrift seiner Hochwürden D. Dr. Friedrich Teutsch gewidmet zu seinem 25 jährigen Bischofs-Jubiläum vom Ausschuß des Vereins für Siebenbürgische Landeskunde,* 56–77. Hermannstadt: Honterusbuchdruckerei, 1931.

Klepp, Susan E. "Demography in Early Philadelphia, 1690–1860." *Proceedings of the American Philosophical Society* 133, no. 2 (1989): 85–111.

Kontje, Todd. "Private Life in the Public Sphere: Heinrich Jung-Stilling's 'Lebensgeschichte.'" *Colloquia Germanica* 21 (1988): 275–287.

Kripal, Jeffrey. *Authors of the Impossible: The Paranormal and the Sacred.* Chicago: University of Chicago Press, 2010.

Kripal, Jeffrey. "Sexuality and the Erotic." In *Oxford Handbook of Religion and Emotion,* edited by John Corrigan, 162–180. Oxford: Oxford University Press, 2007.

La Chapelle, Joannes Baptista de. *Le Ventriloque, ou l'engastrimthye.* London: Duchense, 1772.

"Lamech [Jacob Gass], and Agrippa." *Chronicon Ephratense: A History of the Community of Seventh-Day Baptists at Ephrata, Lancaster County, Penn'a.* Translated by J. Max Hark. Lancaster, PA: S.H. Zahm & Co., 1889; reprint: University Park: Pennsylvania State University Press, Metalmark Books.

Lane, Belden C. *The Solace of Fierce Landscapes: Exploring Desert and Mountain Spirituality.* Oxford: Oxford University Press, 2007.

Larson, Rebecca. *Daughters of Light: Quaker Women Preaching and Prophesying in the Colonies and Abroad, 1700–1775.* New York: Knopf, 1999.

Lashlee, Earnest L. "Johannes Kelpius and His Woman in the Wilderness: A Chapter in the History of Colonial Pennsylvania Religious Thought." In *Glaube, Geist, Geschichte: Festschrift für Ernst Benz,* edited by Gerhard Muller and Winfried Zeller, 327–338. Leiden: Brill, 1967.

292 REFERENCES

"Late Hermits in Pennsylvania." In *American Penny Magazine, and Family Newspaper*, edited by Theodore Dwight, 491–492. New York: No. 112 Broadway, 1847.

Lead, Jane. *The Ascent to the Mount of Vision*. London, 1699.

Lead, Jane. *The Glory of Sharon in the Renovation of Nature, Introducing the Blessed Kingdom of Christ in the Sealed Number of the First Fruits, in The Wars of David, and the Peaceable Reign of Solomon; Symbolizing the Times of Warfare and Refreshment of the Saints of the Most High God*. 1700; London: Thomas Wood, 1816.

Leal, Robert Barry. *Wilderness in the Bible: Toward a Theology of Wilderness*. New York: P. Lang, 2004.

Leeds, Daniel. *An almanack for the year of christian account 1687. particularly respecting the meridian and latitude of Burlington, but may indifferently serve all places adjacent*. Philadelphia: William Bradford, 1687.

Leeds, Daniel. *An almanack for the year of Christian account 1695. . . .* Printed and sold by William Bradford at the Bible in New-York, 1695.

Leeds, Daniel. *The great mistery of Fox-craft discovered*. New York: Printed by William Bradford, 1705.

Leeds, Daniel. *The temple of wisdom for the little world, in two parts*. Philadelphia: Printed and sold by William Bradford, 1688.

Leeds, Daniel. *A trumpet sounded out of the wilderness of America . . .* New York: Printed by William Bradford, 1697; London, 1699.

Leeuwen, Evert Jan van. "'Though Hermes Never Taught Thee': The Anti-patriarchal Tendency of Charles Brockden Brown's Mercurial Outcast Carwin, the Biloquist." *European Journal of American Studies* 5, no. 1 (2010). https://journals.openedition.org/ejas/7791.

Lehmann, Harmutt. *Das Zeitalter des Absolutismus: Gottesgandemtum und Kriegsnot*. Stuttgart: Kohlhammer, 1980.

Leibert, Peter, ed. *Ernst Christoph Hochmanns von Hochenau Glaubens-Bekänntniss . . .* Germantown: Gedruckt bey Peter Leibert, 1800.

Leibert, Peter, ed. *Etliche liebliche und erbaulichen Lieder . . .* Germantown, 1788. Library Company of Pennsylvania.

Leibniz, Gottfried. "Leibniz to Thomasius" (1669). In *The Book of Magic: From Antiquity to the Enlightenment*, edited and translated by Brian Copenhaver, 565–566. New York: Penguin, 2017.

Lepore, Jill. *The Name of War: King Phillip's War and the Origins of American Identity*. New York: Vintage, 1999.

Leventhal, Herbert. *In the Shadow of the Enlightenment: Occultism and Renaissance Science in Eighteenth-Century America*. New York: New York University Press, 1976.

Lewis, Harvey Spencer. *Rosicrucian Questions and Answers: With Complete History of the Rosicrucian Order*. San Jose: Supreme Grand Lodge of AMORC, 1959.

Lippard, George. *Paul Ardenheim, the Monk of the Wissahikon*. Philadelphia, 1848.

MacBeath, Alistair. "Meteors, Comets and Millennialism." *WGN: Journal of the International Meteor Organization* 27, no. 6 (1999): 318–326.

Malm, Andreas. *Corona, Climate, Chronic Emergency: War Communism in the Twenty-First Century*. London: Verso, 2020.

Martin, Lucinda. "The 'Language of Canaan': Pietism's Esoteric Sociolect." *Aries* 12, no. 2 (2012): 237–253.

Martin, Willard. "Johannes Kelpius and Johann Gottfried Seelig: Mystics and Hymnists on the Wissahickon." PhD dissertation, Pennsylvania State University, 1973.

REFERENCES   293

"Matricula universitatis, Matricula Almae Universitatis Tubingensis de Anno MDCXXVIII." 1628–1711, University of Tübingen Archives. http://idb.ub.uni-tuebin gen.de/opendigi/UAT_005_27b#tab=info&p=152. Accessed December 10, 2023.

Matricula universitatis VII, 1614–1800, Tübingen. http://idb.ub.uni-tuebingen.de/opend igi/UAT_005_29a#p=459. Accessed December 10, 2023.

McGinn, Bernard. *Mysticism in the Reformation (1500–1650)* Vol. 6, Part 1 of *The Presence of God: A History of Western Christian Mysticism*. New York: Herder and Herder, 2016.

McLoughlin, William G. "Pietism and the American Character." *American Quarterly* 17, no. 2 (1965): 163–186.

Merchant, Carolyn. *The Death of Nature: Women, Ecology, and the Scientific Revolution*. New York: HarperCollins, 1980.

Merchant, Carolyn. *Ecological Revolutions: Nature, Gender, and Science in New England*. Chapel Hill: University of North Carolina Press, 2010.

Merrell, James. *Into the American Woods: Negotiators on the Pennsylvania Frontier*. New York: Norton, 1999.

Middleton, William Shainline. "John Bartram, Botanist." *Scientific Monthly* 21, no. 2 (1925): 191–216.

Midelfort, H. C. Erik. "The Anthropological Roots of Paracelsus' Psychiatry." *Medizinhistorisches Journal* 16, no. 1/2 (1981): 67–77.

Miller, John Peter. "To Benjamin Franklin from John Peter Miller, 12 June 1771." Founders Online, National Archives, https://founders.archives.gov/documents/Franklin/01-18-02-0087. Original source: *The Papers of Benjamin Franklin*, vol. 18, January 1 through December 31, 1771, ed. William B. Willcox. New Haven: Yale University Press, 1974.

Miller, Lewis H. "The Supernaturalism of 'Snow-Bound.'" *New England Quarterly* 53, no. 3 (1980): 291–307.

Morton, Timothy. *Ecology without Nature: Rethinking Environmental Aesthetics*. Cambridge, MA: Harvard University Press, 2007.

Mühlenberg, Henry Melchior. *The Journals of Henry Melchior Muhlenberg*. 3 vols. Translated by Theodore G. Tappert and John W. Doberstein. Philadelphia: Evangelical Lutheran Ministerium of Pennsylvania and Adjacent States and the Muhlenberg Press, 1945.

Mühlenberg, Henry Melchior. *Nachrichten von den vereingten deutschen Evangelisch-Lutherischen Kurtze nachricht von einigen Evangelischen gemeinen in America, absonderlich in Pensylvanien*, Vol. 2. Philadelphia: P.G.C. Eisenhardt, 1895.

Murphy, Andrew R. *William Penn: A Life*. Oxford: Oxford University Press, 2019.

Najman, Hindy. *Past Renewals: Interpretative Authority, Renewed Revelation, and the Quest for Perfection in Jewish Antiquity*. Leiden: Brill, 2010.

Nash, Roderick. *Wilderness and the American Mind*. 5th ed. New Haven: Yale University Press, 2014.

Newton, Isaac. *The Mathematical Principles of Natural Philosophy*. Translated by Andrew Motte. New York: Putnam: 1850.

Ogren, Brian. *Kabbalah and the Founding of America: The Early Influence of Jewish Thought in the New World*. New York: New York University Press, 2021.

Orsi, Robert. *History and Presence*. Cambridge, MA: Belknap Press of Harvard University Press, 2016.

Paracelsus. *Paracelsus (Theophrastus Bombastus Von Hohenheim, 1493–1541): Essential Theoretical Writings*. Edited by and translated by Andrew Weeks. Leiden: Brill, 2008.

294 REFERENCES

Parker, Geoffrey. *Global Crisis: War, Climate Change and Catastrophe in the Seventeenth Century*. New Haven: Yale University Press, 2013.

Pastorius, Francis Daniel. "The Bee-Hive." Ms. Codex 726, Kislak Center, University of Pennsylvania. Accessed via the Digital Beehive interface.

Pastorius, Francis Daniel. "A Few Onomastical Considerations enlarged from the Number of Sixty-Six To that of One Hundred, and Presented or rather Re-Presented." 1700, p. 63. Appended to a photostat copy of Pastorius, *A new primmer, or, Methodical directions to attain the true spelling, reading & writing of English: whereunto are added, some things necessary & useful both for the youth of this province, and likewise for those, who from foreign countries and nations come to settle amongst us*. New York: William Bradford, 1698. German Society of Pennsylvania archives, German American Collection, AM 1.3.

Pastorius, Francis Daniel. *The Francis Daniel Pastorius Reader: Writings by an Early American Polymath*. Edited and translated by Patrick Erben, Alfred L. Brophy, and Margo M. Lambert. University Park: Pennsylvania State University Press, 2019.

Pauketat, Timothy. "Ancient Faith and the Fall of Cahokia." Illinois Program for Research in the Humanities (IPRH) at the Chicago Humanities Festival, November 4, 2017. Accessed here: https://www.youtube.com/watch?v=0LP2m9eYhe8&t=380s.

Pennypacker, Samuel. *The Settlement of Germantown*. Philadelphia: William J. Campbell, 1899.

Pfleger, Birte. "Ein Schrecklicher Zustand Race, Slavery, and Gradual Emancipation in Pennsylvania." In *Babel of the Atlantic*, edited by Bethany Wiggin, 199–227. University Park: Pennsylvania State University Press, 2019.

"Philadelphia Girl Owns Stone of Wisdom." *Philadelphia Evening Star*, August 14, 1900.

Poe, Edgar Allen. "The Lake — To ——." In *The Works of the Late Edgar Allan Poe*, vol. 2, *Poems and Miscellanies*, edited by Rufus Wilmot Griswold, 109. New York: Redfield: Clinton Hall, 1850.

Poe, Edgar Allen. "Morning of the Wissahickon." In *Edgar Allan Poe: Poetry & Tales*, 939–944. New York: Library of America, 1984. First published in The Opal (1844).

Porter, Bill. *Road to Heaven: Encounters with Chinese Hermits*. 1993; Berkeley: Counterpoint Press, 2009.

Principe, Lawrence. *The Secrets of Alchemy*. Chicago: University of Chicago Press, 2013.

Providence Gazette and Country Journal, March 19, 1814, 3.

Quinn, D. Michael. *Early Mormonism and the Magic World View*. Rev. ed. Salt Lake City: Signature Books, 1998.

Regal, Brian, and Frank J. Esposito. *The Secret History of the Jersey Devil: How Quakers, Hucksters, and Benjamin Franklin Created a Monster*. Baltimore: Johns Hopkins University Press, 2018.

Reichel, Levin Theodore. "The Early History of the Church of the United Brethren (Unitas Fratrum) Commonly Called Moravians, in North America, A.D. 1734–1748." *Transactions of the Moravian Historical Society* 3 (1888): 1–241.

Richards, Kirby Don. "From Transylvania to Pennsylvania: Johannes Kelpius." *Yearbook of German-American Studies* 55 (2022): 133–162.

Richardson, Robert. *Emerson: The Mind on Fire*. Berkeley: University of California Press, 1996.

Rosenthal, Bernard. "The Voices of Wieland." In *Critical Essays on Charles Brockden Brown*, edited by Bernard Rosenthal, 87–103. Boston: G.K. Hall, 1981.

REFERENCES 295

Sachse, Julius. *The German Pietists of Provincial Pennsylvania*. 1895; University Park: Metalmark Books, 2012.

Sachse, Julius. *The German Sectarians of Pennsylvania: A Critical and Legendary History of the Ephrata Cloister and the Dunkers*. Philadelphia: Printed for the author, 1899.

Samuels, Shirley. "Patriarchal Violence, Federalist Panic, and *Wieland*." *Early American Literature* 25, no. 1 (1990): 46–66.

Schaffer, Simon. "Late Enlightenment Crises of Facts: Mesmerism and Meteorites." *Configurations* 26, no. 2 (Spring 2018): 119–148.

Scheer, Monique. *Enthusiasm: Emotional Practices of Conviction in Modern Germany*. Oxford: Oxford University Press, 2021.

Scheerer, Cissy. "A Historical Sketch of Johannes Kelpius and the Hermits of the Wissahickon." Fairmount Park Commission, Park Historians Office, 1979.

Schleiermacher, Friedrich. *On Religion: Speeches to its Cultured Despisers*. Translated and edited by Richard Crouter. Cambridge: Cambridge University Press, 2003.

Schmidt, Leigh Eric. *Hearing Things: Religion, Illusion, and the American Enlightenment*. Cambridge, MA: Harvard University Press, 2000.

Schmidt, Leigh Eric. *Restless Souls: The Making of American Spirituality*. San Francisco: HarperSanFrancisco, 2005.

Schneider, Hans. *Der fremde Arndt: Studien zu Lehen, Werk und Wirkung Johann Arndts (1555—1621)*. Göttingen: Vandenhoeck 81 Ruprecht, 2006.

Schneider, Hans. *German Radical Pietism*. Translated by Gerald T. MacDonald. Lanham, MD: Scarecrow Press and Center for the Study of World Christian Revitalization Movements, 2007.

Schumacher, Daniel (c. 1729–1787). Scrivener. (ca. 1769). Drawing (Up to the Judgment [Auf zum Gericht]). Free Library of Philadelphia.

Schüssler, Hermann. "Fabricius, Johann." In *New German Biography*, vol. 4, 735–736. Berlin: Duncker & Humblot, 1959.

Seecamp, Carsten. "The Chapter of Perfection: A Neglected Influence on George Lippard." *Pennsylvania Magazine of History and Biography* 94, no. 2 (April 1, 1970): 192–212.

Seelig, Johann [?]. *Copia Eines Send-Schreibens auß der Neun Welt*. Halle [1695?].

Seibert, Dorette. *Glaube, Erfahrung und Gemeinschaft: Der junge Schleiermacher und Herrnhut*. Göttingen: Vandenhoeck & Ruprecht, 2003.

Seidensticker, Oswald. *Bilder aus der Deutsch-Pennsylvanischen Geschichte*. New York: E. Steiger, 1885.

Seidensticker, Oswald. *The First Century of German Printing in America, 1728–1830*. Philadelphia: Schaefer & Koradi, 1893.

Seidensticker, Oswald. "Johann Kelpius, der Einfiedler am Wissahickon." *Der Deustche Pioner*. Ed. G. Bruhl. (Cincinnatti, 1870): 67–75.

Seidensticker, Oswald. "Hermits of the Wissahickon." *Pennsylvania Magazine of History and Biography* 11 (1887): 427–441.

Seidensticker, Oswald. "More About the Hermit of the Ridge, John Kelpius." In *The American Historical Record*, 127. Philadelphia: Chase & Town, 1873.

Seivert, Johann. *Nachrichten von siebenbürgischen Gelehrten und ihren Schriften*. Pressburg, 1785.

Shantz, Douglas H. "German Pietism." In *Oxford History of Modern German Theology*, edited by Grant Kaplan and Kevin M. Vander Schel, vol. 1, *1781–1848*. Online ed. Oxford: Oxford Academic, 2023.

296 REFERENCES

Shantz, Douglas H. *An Introduction to German Pietism: Protestant Renewal at the Dawn of Modern Europe.* Baltimore: Johns Hopkins University Press, 2013.

A Short, Easy, and Comprehensive Method of Prayer; Translated from the German; and Published for a Farther Promotion, Knowledge, and Benefit of Inward Prayer, by a Lover of Internal Devotion. Philadelphia: Henry Miller, 1761. Library Company of Philadelphia.

A Short, Easy, and Comprehensive Method of Prayer; Translated from the German; and Published for a Farther Promotion, Knowledge, and Benefit of Inward Prayer, by a Lover of Internal Devotion. 2nd ed. Germantown: Christopher Sower, 1763. Library Company of Philadelphia.

Showalter, Shirley Hershey. "'The Herbal Signs of Nature's Page': A Study of Francis Daniel Pastorius' View of Nature." *Quaker History* 71, no. 2 (1982): 89–99.

Shulze, D. Johann Ludewig. *Nachrichten von den vereinigten deutschen evangelisch-lutherischen Gemeinen in Nord-America, absonderlich in Pensylvanien.* Edited by William Julius Mann. Allentown, PA: Brobst, Diehl & Company, 1884.

Silesius, Angelus. *The Cherubinic Wanderer.* Translated by Maria Shrady. Introduction and notes by Josef Schmidt. New York: Paulist Press, 1986.

Silesius, Angelus. *Cherubinischer Wandersmann: oder Geist-reiche Sinn- und Schluss-Reime zur göttlichen Beschaulichkeit anleitende. Von dem Urheber aufs neue übersehn und mit dem sechsten Buche vermehrt ... zum andernmahl herauss gegeben.* Glatz: auss neu auffgerichter Buchdrukkerey Ignatij Schubarthi, 1675. Library Company of Pennsylvania, Sev Ang 70122.D.

Smith, John. *Hannah Logan's Courtship: A True Narrative.* Edited by Albert Cook Myers. Philadelphia: Ferris & Leach, 1904.

Smolenski, John. *Friends and Strangers: The Making of a Creole Culture in Colonial Pennsylvania.* Philadelphia: University of Pennsylvania Press, 2010.

Soderlund, Jean R. *Lenape Country: Delaware Valley Society before William Penn.* Philadelphia: University of Pennsylvania Press, 2015.

Sorby, Angela. *Schoolroom Poets: Childhood, Performance, and the Place of American Poetry, 1865–1917.* Durham, NH: University of New Hampshire Press, 2005.

Spencer, Carole Dale. "James Nayler and Jacob Boehme's 'The Way to Christ.'" *Quaker Religious Thought* 125 (2015), article 7: 43–56.

Spener, Philipp Jakob. *Briefwechsel mit August Hermann Francke 1689–1704.* Edited by Johannes Wallmann and Udo Sträter. Tübingen: Mohr Siebeck, 2006.

Springer, Ruth L., Louise Wallman, And. Rudman, and Andreas Sandell. "Two Swedish Pastors Describe Philadelphia, 1700 and 1702." *Pennsylvania Magazine of History and Biography* 84, no. 2 (1960): 194–218.

Stedman, Edmund Clarence. *Poets of America.* Boston: Houghton, Mifflin, 1885.

Steinmetz, Andrew. "Kelpius: Mystic on the Wissahickon." *German-American Review,* August 1941.

Stewart, Matthew. *Nature's God: The Heretical Origins of the American Republic.* New York: Norton, 2014.

Stitziel, Judd. "God, the Devil, Medicine, and the Word: A Controversy over Ecstatic Women in Protestant Middle Germany 1691–1693." *Central European History* 29, no. 3 (1996): 309–337.

Stoudt, John Joseph. *Early Pennsylvania Arts and Crafts.* New York: Bonanza Books, 1964.

Stoudt, John Joseph. *Pennsylvania German Folk Art: An Interpretation*. Allentown, PA: Schletler's, 1966.

Stoudt, John Joseph. *Sunrise to Eternity: A Study in Jacob Boehme's Life and Thought*. Philadelphia: University of Pennsylvania Press, 1957.

Stowell, Marion Barber. *Early American Almanacs: the Colonial Weekday Bible*. New York: B. Franklin, 1977.

Swain, Ena V. L. *The Evolution of Abolitionism in Germantown and Its Environs*. Self-published, 2018.

Taylor, Sarah McFarland. "What If Religions Had Ecologies? The Case for Reinhabiting Religious Studies." *Journal for the Study of Religion, Nature, and Culture* 1, no. 1 (2007): 129–138.

Valantasis, Richard. "Constructions of Power in Asceticism." *Journal of the American Academy of Religion* 63, no. 4 (1995): 775–821.

Vallee, Jacques, and Chris Aubeck. *Wonders in the Sky: Unexplained Aerial Objects from Antiquity to Modern Times*. New York: Tarcher/Penguin, 2009.

Verschuier, Lieve. *Staartster (komeet) boven Rotterdam*, Museum Rotterdam 11028-AB. 1680. https://museumrotterdam.nl/collectie/item/11028-A-B.

Versluis, Arthur. *The Esoteric Origins of the American Renaissance*. Oxford: Oxford University Press, 2001.

Versluis, Arthur. "Jane Lead(e)." In *Dictionary of Gnosis & Western Esotericism*, edited by Wouter J. Hanegraaff with Antoine Faivre, Roelof van den Broek, and Jean-Pierre Brach, 683–685. Leiden: Brill, 2005.

Versluis, Arthur. "Mysticism and Spiritual Harmonics in Eighteenth-Century England." *Esoterica* 4 (2002). http://www.esoteric.msu.edu/VolumeIV/Harmonic.htm.

Versluis, Arthur. *Wisdom's Children: A Christian Esoteric Tradition*. Albany: State University of New York Press, 1999.

Waite, Arthur Edward. *The Brotherhood of the Rosy Cross, Being Records of the House of the Holy Spirit in its Inward and Outward History*. 1924; New Hyde Park, NY: University Books, 1961.

Wallman, Johannes. "Johann Arndt (1555–1621)." In *The Pietist Theologians: An Introduction to Theology in the Seventeenth and Eighteenth Centuries*, edited by Carter Lindberg, 21–37. Malden, MA: Blackwell, 2005.

Ward, W. R. *Early Evangelicalism: A Global Intellectual History, 1670–1789*. Cambridge: Cambridge University Press, 2006.

Warde, Paul, Libby Robin, and Sverker Sörlin. *The Environment: A History of the Idea*. Baltimore: Johns Hopkins University Press, 2021.

Watson, John F. *Annals of Philadelphia. in two vols*. Philadelphia: A. Hart, J.W. Moore, J. Pennington, U. Hunt, and H.F. Anners, 1850.

Watson, John F. *Historic Tales of Olden Time, Concerning the Early Settlement and Progress of Philadelphia and Pennsylvania*. Philadelphia: E. Littell and T. Holden, 1833.

Waterman, Bryan, "Later Years, 1795–1810." In *The Oxford Handbook of Charles Brockden Brown*, edited by Philip Barnard, Hilary Emmett, and Stephen Shapiro, 24–43. Oxford: Oxford University Press, 2019.

Wedgwood, C. V. *The Thirty Years War*. 1938; New York: New York Review of Books, 2005.

Weeks, Andrew. *Boehme: An Intellectual Biography of a Seventeenth-Century Philosopher and Mystic*. Albany: State University of New York Press, 1991.

298 REFERENCES

Weeks, Andrew. "Jacob Boehme." In *Dictionary of Gnosis & Western Esotericism*, edited by Wouter J. Hanegraaff with Antoine Faivre, Roelof van den Broek, and Jean-Pierre Brach, 185–192. Leiden: Brill, 2005.

Weeks, Andrew, and Bo Andersson. "Jacob Böhme's Writings in the Context of His World." In *Jacob Böhme and His World*, edited by Bo Andersson, Lucinda Martin, Leigh T. I. Penman, and Andrew Weeks, 1–20. Leiden: Brill, 2019.

Weinstock, Jeffrey Andrew. *Charles Brockden Brown*. Cardiff: University of Wales Press, 2011.

Weiser, Frederick S. *The Publications of the Pennsylvania German Society Vol. 1: The Four Gospels: Translated into the Pennsylvania German Dialect*. Allentown, PA: Pennsylvania German Society, 1968.

West, Lisa. "Early Years: 1771–1795." In *Oxford Handbook of Charles Brockden Brown*, edited by Philip Barnard, Hilary Emmett, and Stephen Shapiro, 7–23. Oxford: Oxford University Press, 2019.

Whittier, John Greenleaf. *The Pennsylvania Pilgrim and Other Poems*. Boston: Osgood and Co., 1872.

Whittier, John Greenleaf. "Snow-Bound: A Winter Idyl." In *The Complete Poetical Works of John Greenleaf Whittier*, edited by H. E. S., 398–406. Boston: Houghton Mifflin, 1894.

Whittier, John Greenleaf. *The Supernaturalism of New England*. 1847; Norman: University of Oklahoma Press, 1969.

Williams, George H. *Wilderness and Paradise in Christian Thought: The Biblical Experience of the Desert in the History of Christianity & The Paradise Theme in the Theological Idea of the University*. Harper, 1962; Eugene, OR: Wipf and Stock, 2016.

Witt, Christopher. *Johannes Kelpius portrait by Dr. Christopher Witt*. 1705. Historical Society of Pennsylvania. Permanent ID: 5975.

Wolf, Stephanie Grauman. *Urban Village: Population, Community, and Family Structure in Germantown, Pennsylvania, 1683–1800*. Princeton: Princeton University Press, 1976.

Wolfson, Elliot R. *Through a Speculum That Shines: Vision and Imagination in Medieval Jewish Mysticism*. Princeton: Princeton University Press, 1994.

Woolman, John. *The Works of John Woolman; in two parts*. Philadelphia: Printed by Joseph Crukshank, in Market-Street, between Second and Third Streets, 1774. Library Company of Philadelphia. Am 1774 Woolm 1118.O.

Wright, Timothy Cotton. "Hidden Lives: Asceticism and Interiority in the Late Reformation, 1650–1745." PhD dissertation, University of California, Berkeley, 2018.

Yates, Frances. *Giordano Bruno and the Hermetic Tradition*. Chicago: University of Chicago Press, 1964.

Yates, Frances. *The Rosicrucian Enlightenment*. 1972; London: Routledge, 2002.

Yoder, Peter James. "Pietism." In *Miracles: An Encyclopedia of People, Places, and Supernatural Events, from Antiquity to the Present*, edited by Patrick J. Hayes, 321–322. Santa Barbara: ABC-CLIO, 2016.

Young, William. "William Young to John Stuart, May 15, 1765." Society Miscellaneous Collection, Historical Society of Pennsylvania.

Zeller, Winfried, ed. *Der Protestantismus des 17. Jahrhunderts*. Bremen: Schünemann, 1962.

Zerefos, C. S., P. Tetsis, A. Kazantzidis, V. Amiridis, S. C. Zerefos, J. Luterbacher, K. Eleftheratos, E. Gerasopoulos, S. Kazadzis, and A. Papayannis. "Further Evidence of Important Environmental Information Content in Red-to-Green Ratios as Depicted in Paintings by Great Masters." *Atmospheric Chemistry and Physics* 14 (2014): 2987–3015.

Zimmermann, Johann Jakob. *Cometo-Scopia oder Himmel-gemäser Bericht.* Stuttgart: Zufinden bei Joh. Gottfridt Zubrodt Druckts Tobias Friederich Coccyus, 1681.

Zimmermann, Johann Jakob [writing as Ambrosius Sehman von Caminiez]. *Mutmaßliche Zeitbestimmung göttlicher Gerichte über das Europäische Babel und Antichristentum jetziger Seculis.* Frankfurt am Main, 1684.

Zimmerman, Johann Jakob. *Orthodoxia theosophiae teutonico-Boehmianae contra Holzhausiam defensa, das ist: christliche Untersuchungen . . . wider Jacob Boehmens Auroram.* Leipzig, 1691.

Zimmerman, Johann Jakob. *Tergemina Lucis Mysticae Mysteria In Tribus Lucis Corporeae Facultatibus, Quae Sunt: Splendor, Calor, Motus.* Launoy: 1688. http://resolver.sub.uni-goettingen.de/purl?PPN598772707.

Zuber, Mike. "Copernican Cosmotheism: Johann Jacob Zimmermann and the Mystical Light." *Aries* 14, no. 2 (September 2014): 215–245.

Zuber, Mike. "Johann Jacob Zimmerman and God's Two Books: Copernican Cosmology in Lutheran Germany around 1700." In *Knowing Nature in Early Modern Europe*, edited by David Beck, 83–100. London: Pickering & Chatto, 2015.

Zuber, Mike. *Spiritual Alchemy: From Jacob Boehme to Mary Anne Atwood.* Oxford: Oxford University Press, 2021.

Index

For the benefit of digital users, indexed terms that span two pages (e.g., 52–53) may, on occasion, appear on only one of those pages.

Figures are indicated by *f* following the page number

Albanese, Catherine, 6, 7, 67–68, 87, 210
alchemy
  appeal of, 32
  ascetic alchemy, 136, 138, 139, 143–44, 146, 148–50, 155–57, 160
  early modern Europe and, 31–34
  environmental knowledge and, 33–34
  Hermeticism and, 31–35
  Kelpius and, 108, 109, 136, 137, 142–44, 151, 158
  spiritual alchemy, 108, 109, 136, 137, 142–44, 151, 158
  Threefold Wilderness State and, 137, 139, 142–44, 148–50, 155–57, 160
Alderfer, Gordon, 204–5
"Almanack, An" (Leeds), 80
almanacs, 80–82, 83, 84–85, 164, 178, 228–29
America (Albanese), 7
American Kelpius legend
  Chronicon Ephratense and, 200–1, 222
  devotional literature and, 197
  Enlightenment and, 9, 106, 208, 232
  failure to understand Kelpius in, 208
  growth of, 191–92, 210
  historical accounts and, 207–9, 212, 215–21
  History of Human Folly and, 207–9
  Kelpius Society and, 222
  method of prayer and, 204–6
  Mühlenberg's report and, 192–97
  novels and poems and, 209–15
  overview of, 191–92, 222–25
  philosopher of the forest and, 197–200
  Rosicrucians and, 215–21
  scattered sources on, 197–200
  spiritual travel of Conrad Matthai and, 201–4
Ames, Alexander, 66
Ancient and Mystical Order Rosae Crucis (AMORC), 7–8, 220–21
Andersson, Bo, 232

apocalypse
  biblical sources for, 110, 151
  comets and, 26–27, 35–36
  definition of, 16–17, 226–27
  environmental knowledge and, 16–17, 63–64
  Kelpius and, 16–17, 110, 140, 208, 212, 216, 222, 226–28
  Little Ice Age and, 38
  Philadelphia and, 95
  political meaning of, 227
  prediction of, 46
  Threefold Wilderness State and, 154–55
  wilderness and, 110, 140, 154–55
Aristotle, 47–48, 50–51, 57, 81–82, 136
Arndt, Johann
  apocalypse and, 38–39
  cosmos as intelligent and communicative, 39
  education of, 37–38
  environmental knowledge and, 39–40
  influence of, 13, 35, 40, 68
  light compared to God by, 44
  Little Ice Age and, 39–40
  meaning and, 39
  mysticism and, 40
  paintings by, 69*f*
  popularity of, 37
  practical nature of writings of, 38
  Protestantism and Hermeticism integrated by, 40
  suffering and, 39
Arnold, Gottfried, 10, 156
Ascent to the Mount of Vision, The (Lead), 152
ascetic alchemy. *See* alchemy
asceticism, 57, 119, 136, 137–38, 146, 148–50, 155–57, 160, 211
Ashbridge, Elizabeth, 134–35
Asprem, Egil, 227–28
Assman, Jan, 11–12, 229
astrology, 32, 82–84, 122, 131

302 INDEX

Astronomica philolaica (Bouillau), 122
Awash in a Sea of Faith (Butler), 5–6

Bach, Jeff, 7, 9, 217–18, 221
Bailyn, Bernard, 14–15
Bartram, John, 128–29
Bartram, William, 130–31
Beissel, Conrad, 88, 200
Benz, Ernst, 59
Blom, Phillip, 81
Böhme, Jacob
　accessibility of works of, 42
　anxieties of, 40
　changing cosmologies and, 40
　conflict avoided by, 42
　early life and upbringing of, 79
　environmental knowledge and, 41–42
　feminine aspect of God and, 87
　influence of, 10, 35, 40, 41
　self-teaching of, 41
　spiritual alchemy and, 137
　stages of history and, 64
　visionary episodes of, 40–42
Book of Nature, 16, 24, 33–34, 215
Book of Nature (Arndt), 228
Brooke, John L., 88, 227–28
Brown, Charles Brockden
　almanacs and, 84–85, 164
　birth and upbringing of, 164–65
　death of, 165
　difficulty of writing of, 165
　Enlightenment critiqued by, 166
　family history of, 166
　genre-straining nature of writing of, 165, 185
　paranormal in literature and, 185–87
　productive period of, 165
Brown, Peter, 83
Brunnquell, Ludwid, 55–56
Bruno, Giordano, 43–44
Burlington Friends, 166
Butler, Jon, 83–84, 164
Byllynge, Edward, 73

Cambridge Platonists, 34–35, 52
Campanius, Johan, 71–72
Carrol, Lucy, 125–26, 222
Carroll, Robert, 188
Cartesian mechanism, 43, 51
Cassian, John, 138
Castle of Otranto, The (Walpole), 185–86
Cave of Kelpius, 8, 218, 219*f*
celestial phenomena, 2–3, 5, 38, 39–40, 87, 110,
　121–23, 147–48, 173–74, 230

Cherubinic Wanderer, The (Silesius), 108
Chronicon Ephratense (1786), 126, 200–1, 222
Clements, Niki Kasumi, 138, 156–57
Clery, E. J., 185
Climate, Catastrophe, and Faith (Jenkins), 227
climate change, 9, 11, 12–13, 14–15, 18–19. *See
　also* Little Ice Age
Colberg, Ehregott Daniel, 33–34, 67–68, 152–
　53, 158
Comet of 1680, 23–25, 25*f*, 44, 226
Cometo-Scopia (Zimmerman), 24–25, 44
comets and meteors, 1–5, 11, 13–14, 21–22,
　23–28, 25*f*, 35–36, 44–46, 63–64, 81,
　153–54, 161–62, 226
*Concessions and Agreements of the Proprietors,
　The* (Penn), 73
Confession of Faith (Hochmanns von
　Hochenau), 197
Corpus Hermeticum, 31–33, 62, 76–77, 82–
　83, 229
cosmotheism, 11–12, 32–33, 44–45, 77–78, 81–
　82, 83, 86, 87–88, 95, 154–55, 229
Crain, Caleb, 170
Crawford, Richard, 124
crisis of piety, 10, 29, 155–56
Croese, Gerardus, 112
Cronin, William, 139
Curieuse Nachricht von Pennsylvania (Falkner),
　105, 112–13

Death of Nature, The (Merchant), 12
Deichman, Johann, 151–52
Deichmann, Heinrich, 124–25
Deli, Michael, 54
De Potentia et Potentia Gratia Dei
　(Paracelsus), 36–37
devotional poetry, 108–9
Divine Pymander (Everard), 82

early modern Europe
　alchemy and, 31–34
　Cartesian mechanism and, 51
　climate change and, 27–29
　crises of, 27–29
　crisis of piety and, 29
　ecology and, 30–31
　enthusiasm and, 30–31, 33
　environmental knowledge and, 33–42, 47
　esotericism and, 30–31
　extraordinary heavenly phenomena
　　and, 23–27
　Hermeticism and, 31–42
　Little Ice Age and, 27–29, 32, 34

metamorphosis of the metaphysics and, 49–52
nature is the interpreter of scripture and, 42–47
Pietism and, 28, 30–31, 42–43
Protestantism and, 29
sola scriptura and, 47–48
Thirty Years War and, 28, 30, 33
wisdom in nature and, 47–49
Ebeling, Florian, 32
Ecology without Nature (Morton), 187
Ein verliebtes Girren der trostlosen Seele in der Morgendammerung (Kelpius), 161
Elijah, 145–49, 150
Elliot, Richard, 163
Emerson, Ralph Waldo, 199, 230–31
the Enlightenment
American Enlightenment, 67, 106, 177
American Kelpius legend and, 9, 106, 208, 232
Cartesian mechanism and, 43
comets and, 3
critique of, 165–66
disenchantment through, 182
distorting effects of, 9, 106, 208, 232
epistemic rupture of, 208
hubris of, 189–90, 230
literature of, 207
paranormal and, 216
Pietism and, 14, 201–2
rationalism of, 165–66, 175–76, 182, 184–85, 187–88, 199
skepticism of religious experience of, 175–76, 182–83, 184–85, 187–88, 199
Wieland and, 175–76, 186, 187–88
wisdom in nature and, 49, 52
enthusiasm, 20, 30–31, 33, 45–46
environmental knowledge
alchemy and, 33–34
apocalypse and, 16–17, 63–64
changes in environment and, 11–12
comets and meteors and, 1–5
definition of, 13
early modern Europe and, 33–42, 47
esotericism and, 228–29
global crisis and, 17–22
God's role in, 12–17, 26
Hermeticism and, 33–42, 229
Kelpius's transformation of, 5–6, 13–14, 19
meaning and, 16, 25–26
miracles and, 13–14
modern scientific knowledge distinguished from, 13

overview of, 5–9
paranormal and, 15–16
Protestantism and, 34–42
structure of current volume on, 19–22
Wissahickon community and, 105
Ephrata Cloister of Conrad Beissel, 88
Erben, Patrick, 135
esotericism
almanacs and, 85
ancient wisdom as basis of, 7
early modern Europe and, 30–31
environmental knowledge and, 228–29
Hermeticism and, 11–12
Pietism and, 10–11
scholarship on, 10–11, 12, 227–29
Western form of, 11, 152–53, 221
Europe. *See* early modern Europe
Exegesis (Dick), 40
Exegesis of the Comet (Paracelsus), 35–36
extraordinary heavenly phenomena, 23–27, 122–23

Fabricus, Johannes, 8–9, 57
Fairman, Thomas, 107
Falckner, Daniel
contemplation of the stars and, 122
education of, 112–13
excommunication of, 112, 113
Pietism of, 112–13
primary of scripture subverted by, 105
return to Germany of, 105
social reform and, 118–19
upbringing of, 112–13
Fate of Rome, The (Harper), 18
Few Onomastical Considerations, A (Pastorius), 76
Ficino, Marsilio, 31–32, 76–77
First Century of German Printing in America, The (Seidensticker), 205
Fischer, David Hackett, 70
Fleming, Stephen J., 227–28
Fliegelmen, Jay, 165, 184
Fort, Charles, 176–77
Foucault, Michel, 136, 156–58, 191, 228
Fox, George, 41–42, 71, 78, 79, 99
Francke, August Herman, 30, 43–44, 54–55, 92, 105, 111, 112–13, 169
Franckenberg, Abraham von, 41
Frankfurt Land Company, 106
Franklin, Benjamin, 65–66, 67, 88, 114, 131, 201, 217, 220–21
Freneau, Phillip, 198–200, 212, 216, 224
Furley, Benjamin, 93

304 INDEX

Garrison, William Lloyd, 210
German Pietists of Provincial Pennsylvania, The
  (Sachse), 173–74, 203–4, 217–18
Germantown, Philadelphia
  economy of, 110
  environmental context of, 110
  as extensive mission field, 119
  immigrant community of, 75
  Kelpius's experiences in, 99, 106, 161–62
  settling of, 75
  Wieland representation of, 168
Germantown Telegraph, 147
Ghosh, Amitav, 15, 187–89, 228–30
Golden Bough, The (Frazer), 218
Good, Edwin, 26
Gordon, Thomas F., 207–8
Graeber, David, 71, 120
Grainger, Brett, 29
Great Comet of 1680, 23–25, 25f, 44, 226
Great Derangement, The (Ghosh), 187–88
Gun Island (Ghosh), 15

Hamburg group, 45–46
Hanegraaff, Wouter, 7, 10–12, 32–33, 152–53,
  207, 208, 228, 229
Harper, Kyle, 18
Hazard's Register of Pennsylvania, 1–5
Helmont, Francis Mercurius van, 42–43
Henry, Paul, 155–56
Herbert, Christopher, 124
Hermes Trismegistus, 31–32, 75–76, 82, 84, 178
Hermetica, 31–33, 62, 76–77, 82–83, 229
Hermeticism
  alchemy and, 31–35
  as ancient spirituality, 229
  appeal of, 32
  change in environment and, 11
  cosmotheism and, 11–12
  definition of, 227–28
  development of, 31–32
  early modern Europe and, 31–42
  environmental knowledge and, 33–42, 229
  esotericism and, 11–12
  golden age of, 42–43, 65
  Mormonism and, 227–28
  overview of, 31–34
  Pietism and, 60, 63–64, 87
  scholarship on, 227–28
  terminology of, 227–28
Hermetic Protestantism
  definition of, 40, 41, 228
  early American form of, 66–68
  environmental knowledge and, 228

Little Ice Age and, 40, 84, 231–32
  overview of, 34–42
  pantheism and, 77–78
  proliferation of, 66–68, 87
  relation to Christianity and, 228
  structure of current volume on, 19–21
  vernacular nature of, 87
  women as receptive to, 87
*Hermetic Spirituality and the Historical
  Imagination* (Hanegraaff), 229
"Hermit of Saba, The" (Freneau), 198
Hessayon, Ariel, 78
Historic Tales of Olden Time (Watson), 208
History of Human Folly (Adelung), 112, 207–9
History of Pennsylvania (Gordon), 207–8
Hohenheim, Theophrastus von. *See* Paracelsus
  (Theophrastus von Hohenheim)
Holm, Alvin, 222–24
Hume, David, 188

*Illustration and Description of the Wonderful
  Incomparable Comet*, 23–24, 24f
Indigenous critique, 71, 120
Isaac, Jacob, 112
Italian Renaissance, 34–35, 43–44

Jakobsson, Ármann, 15–16
Jefferson, Thomas, 220–21
John the Baptist, 139, 146–47
Jones, Horatio Gates, 216
Jortner, Adam, 163
Jung-Stilling, Johann Heinrich, 202–4

Kafer, Peter, 166, 169–70, 173, 184
Keith, George, 114–17
Kelpius, Johannes. *See also* American Kelpius
  legend; Kelpius group; Threefold
  Wilderness State; Wissahickon
  community
  alchemy and, 108, 109, 136, 137, 142–44,
    151, 158
  ancient philosophers distinguished
    from, 50–51
  anti-institutionalism of, 157
  apocalypse and, 16–17, 110, 140, 208, 212,
    216, 222, 226–28
  asceticism of, 57, 111–12, 119, 136, 137–38,
    146, 155–57, 211
  biblical approach to history of, 122–23
  birth and upbringing of, 9–12, 27–28, 53
  Cartesian mechanism and, 51
  Cave of, 8, 218, 219f
  character of, 6

community writing of, 134–35
contemplation of the stars by, 121–23
crisis of piety and, 9–12
devotional poetry and, 108–9
ecstatic states and, 122–23
education of, 5, 9, 54, 57
environmental knowledge transformed
    through, 5–6, 13–14, 19
erotic devotion of, 133–34
Europe experiences of, 53–61
expulsion from Tübingen of, 56–57
Fabricius's mentorship of, 57
family of, 5, 53–54
Germantown experiences of, 99, 106, 161–62
hidden memoir and, 58–59
hymns and, 124, 133–34
inner revelation and environmental wonders
    and, 13–14
inspiration for current volume on, 5–7
Keithian schism and, 115, 116
legacy of, 7–9, 135, 201
legends about celestial phenomena following
    death of, 173–74
Lenape and, 119–21
Little Ice Age and, 53, 146
metamorphosis of the metaphysics and, 49–52
miracles and, 13–16
misinformation on, 7–9
missionizing efforts and, 119–21
modern news segment on, 226
motivations for current volume on, 19
music and, 124–26
near ship wreck of, 97
overview of, 5–9, 19–22, 226–32
pagan awareness of God and, 49–51
paranormal and, 15–16, 59–61, 142, 201–2
perception as starting "doomsday cult," 226
Philadelphians and, 95, 151–52
Pietism of, 10–12, 30–31, 54–56, 58–60
Pillar of Cloud and, 122–23
portrait of, 128, 147, 161
rejection of mixing theology and philosophy
    and, 57
relation between physics and metaphysics
    and, 50–52
Rotterdam, London, and the Atlantic
    experiences of, 90–100
scholarship on, 5–9
scholasticism critiqued by, 49–52
silent period of, 58
source material for, 8–9
spiritual alchemy of, 108, 109, 136, 137, 142–
    44, 151, 158

stone monument to, 8*f*
structure of current volume on, 19–22
telepathy and, 15–16
Thirty Years War's effects on, 28
trip to America of, 96–98
unmute gospel of, 226–32
Wieland and, 166, 169–70, 180, 189
wilderness and, 68, 110
wisdom in nature and, 49–52
withdrawal from public life of, 118–19
Kelpius group
    characteristics of companions in, 92–93
    decentralized nature of, 92
    definition of, 92
    formation of, 90–92
    fundraising of, 93–94
    Germantown experiences of, 106
    hymns and, 205–6
    London experiences of, 93
    members of, 92
    misperception as doomsday cult of, 226
    missionizing efforts of, 119
    Pennsylvania trip of, 94, 107
    Rotterdam experiences of, 94
Kelpius Society, 222
Kemble, Fanny, 102
knowledge, environmental. *See* environmental
    knowledge
Köster, Heinrich Bernard, 92, 97, 112–13, 115–
    17, 119, 166, 204
Kripal, Jeffrey, 133, 176–77

"Lake, The" (Poe), 103
"Lamenting Voice of the Hidden Love, The"
    (Kelpius), 125–26, 125*f*, 158–60, 161,
    193–94, 208–9
Lapidem, 194–96
Lead, Jane, 95, 151–52
Lee, Frances, 124
Leeds, Daniel
    agricultural practice of, 80–81
    almanacs and, 80–82, 86
    America travels of, 79–80
    astrology and, 82–84
    Böhme's work printed by, 78
    cosmotheism and, 83, 86
    environmental knowledge and, 81
    family and upbringing of, 78–79
    increase in religiosity of, 79
    Keithian schism and, 115
    Lenape and, 80–81
    precocious and spiritual childhood of, 78–79
    Quakerism of, 78–79, 86

306 INDEX

Leeds, Daniel (*cont.*)
    self and environment blurred in writings of, 80
    visions of God of, 78–79
legends about Kelpius. *See* American Kelpius legend
Leibniz, Gottfried, 47–49, 50, 51–52, 229–30
Le Morte d'Arthur (Mallory), 195, 217–18
Lenape
    astronomical expertise of, 80–81
    attempts to Christianize, 71–72
    cosmology of, 71
    decentralized authority of, 70–71
    diplomacy and conflict resolution
        emphasized by, 70
    environmental knowledge and, 81
    Kelpius and, 119–21
    Pennsylvania and, 70, 73–74
    wilderness and, 70
Leventhal, Herbert, 84
Le Ventriloque, ou l'engastrimthye (La
    Chapelle), 182–83
Lewis, Harvey Spencer, 220–21
Linnaeus, Carolus, 128
Lippard, George, 217
Little Ice Age
    apocalypse and, 38
    definition of, 11
    development of, 27
    early modern Europe and, 27–29, 32, 34
    Hermetic Protestantism and, 40, 84, 231–32
    Kelpius and, 53, 146
Louis XIV, 56–57, 65
Luther, Martin, 40, 43

Malm, Andreas, 18
Markham, William, 68
Martin, Willard, 124, 158
Matthai, Conrad
    birth and upbringing of, 126
    communal housing and, 127
    connective presence of, 126–27
    disembodied abilities of, 127–28
    legends about, 127–28
    responses to meeting with, 127
McLoughlin, William G., 157
Medici, Cosimo de', 31–32
Merchant, Carolyn, 52
Metamorphosis of the Metaphysics (Kelpius),
    49–52, 57, 140, 146
Metaphysics (Aristotle), 48, 50
meteors and comets, 1–5, 11, 13–14, 21–22,
    23–28, 25*f*, 35–36, 44–46, 63–64, 81,
    153–54, 161–62, 226
Miller, Henry, 205

Miller, Peter, 88
miracles, 13–16, 44, 60, 113, 142, 148, 178–79,
    187–89, 199–200
modern Europe. *See* early modern Europe
Mormonism, 227–28
"Morning on the Wissahiccon" (Poe), 102–3
Moses, 145–49, 150
Mühlenberg, Heinrich Melchior
    decline in accuracy in reporting over time
        of, 194
    Lapidem and, 194–96, 196*f*
    limitations of information provided
        to, 193–94
    report of, 192–97
    sources of, 192–93, 196–97
    suspicion of Kelpius of, 137–38, 194
Muir, John, 140, 200
Mumford, Stephen, 58
Mysteries of Udolpho, The (Radcliffe), 185
Mysterium Magnum (Böhme), 64
Mystical Theology (pseudo-Dionysius), 153

Name of War, The (Lepore), 14–15
Nash, Roderick, 139
Natural Theology (Kelpius), 49–52, 57, 140, 146
Nature's Mutiny (Blom), 12
Nayler, James, 78
"New Theory of Musick, A" (Lee), 124–25
Newton, Isaac, 5, 23–24, 43, 52, 122, 161–
    62, 230–31

Oetinger, Friedrich Christoph, 59
Of True Christianity (Arndt), 37
Ogren, Brian, 115
On Religion (Schleiermacher), 30–31
"On Retirement" (Freneau), 198
"On the Honorable Emmanuel Swedenborg's
    Universal Theology" (Freneau), 198–99
Order of Things, The (Foucault), 228

Pagan Ethics (Kelpius), 57, 121–22
Palmer, Esther, 135
Paracelsus (Theophrastus von Hohenheim)
    alchemy and, 34–35, 36–37, 108
    apocalypse and, 35–36
    astronomy as primary for, 35–36
    comets and, 35–36
    divine presence in nature and, 36–37
    environmental knowledge and, 13, 36, 41–
        42, 81
    extraordinary phenomena and, 36
    as father of toxicology, 34
    Hermeticism and, 34–35

influence of, 10, 37–38
Little Ice Age and, 38
methodological approach of, 36
motivation for, 34
peasantry and, 35
relationship between individual and divine, 35
spiritual alchemy and, 137
theorica and, 34, 36, 44, 81, 122
"Paradox and Strange Pleasure of the Divine
    Lovers, The" (Kelpius), 133
paranormal
definition of, 15–16
Enlightenment and, 216
environmental knowledge and, 15–16
Kelpius and, 15–16, 59–61, 142, 201–2
miracles distinguished from, 16
overview of, 15–17
Pietism and, 59–61, 113, 142
terminological use of, 15–16
Threefold Wilderness State and, 142
Wieland and, 170–73, 176, 179–80, 182–83,
    185–88, 189–90
Parker, Geoffrey, 11, 17–18, 27, 28, 53
Pastorius, Francis
cosmotheism of, 77
Germantown settled by, 75
Indigenous peoples and, 75
influences on, 75–76
Keithian schism and, 116–17
legacy of, 77
Lenape and, 77, 120
motivations of, 74
pantheism and, 77–78
Pennsylvania trip of, 75
poem on, 211
sources used by, 76–77
Pauketat, Timothy, 101–2
Paul Ardenheim, the Monk of the Wissahikon
    (Lippard), 209–10, 220
Penn, William
childhood and upbringing of, 72
founding of Pennsylvania by, 67, 70–71, 74
Germany trip of, 74
governing style of, 70–71
Lenape and, 70, 119–21
perception of, 72
political work of, 72–73
Quaker conversion of, 72
zoning of Philadelphia and, 94
Pennsylvania. *See also* Germantown,
    Philadelphia
blurred lines between dissenting
    groups in, 78

early American Hermetic Protestantism
    and, 66–68
founding of, 70–71, 74
German immigration to, 65–66
holy experiments and, 72–74
Lenape and, 70, 73–74
Platonic-Hermetic Christianity and, 67–68
Quakers and, 73–74
religious and cultural pluralism of, 67
scholarship on American religion and, 67
uniquely receptive audiences in, 87
whiteness and, 65–66
as wilderness, 68–72
Pennsylvania Pilgrim, The (Whittier), 66
"Pennsylvania Pilgrim, The" (Whittier), 211–12
Petersen, Johanna Eleonora, 16
Philadelphia. *See* Germantown
"Philadelphia Girl Owns Stone of Wisdom"
    (*Philadelphia Evening Star*, 1900), 196f
Philadelphians, 95
"Philosopher of the Forest, The" (Freneau), 198
Physics (Aristotle), 50–51
Pietism
affective dimensions of, 30–31
anti-institutionalism and, 157
camps within, 91
church response to, 91
concerns about the ecstasies of followers of, 113
crisis of, 9–12
definition of, 10
development of, 10, 17–18, 55–56, 58–
    60, 201–2
early modern Europe and, 28, 30–31, 42–43
Enlightenment and, 14, 201–2
esotericism and, 10–11
Hermeticism and, 60, 63–64, 87
Kelpius and, 10–12, 30–31, 54–56, 58–60
as manifestation of more general religious
    awakening, 17–18
marginalization of, 201–2
miracles and, 14–15
missionizing efforts of, 119
motivations for, 10
overview of, 10, 30–31
paranormal and, 59–61, 113, 142
Protestantism and, 9–12
radical forms of, 28, 30, 91, 207–8
social reform and, 117–18
Thirty Years War and, 30
Pillar of Cloud, 122–23, 142
Piramirum (Paracelsus), 36
Platonic-Hermetic Christianity (Colberg), 33,
    67–68, 152–53

308 INDEX

Pliny, 81–82
Poe, Edgar Allen, 102–4
Poetics of Space, The (Bachelard), 191, 224
Pordage, John, 95
Pray, Mary, 14–15
Precise Mathematical Determination of the Time (Zimmerman), 44–45
Prickett, Stephen, 188
Principe, Lawrence, 34
Principia Mathematica (Newton), 23, 122, 161–62
Printz, Johan, 71
Protestantism. *See also* Hermetic Protestantism
    crisis of piety and, 9–12
    early modern Europe and, 29
    environmental knowledge and, 34–42
    Pietism and, 9–12
    radical forms of, 9–10, 32, 41–42, 76, 78, 87–88, 95, 134–35, 167, 178
    sola scriptura and, 32–33, 43–44, 47–48
pseudo-Dionysius the Areopagite, 153
Ptolemy, 81–82

Quakerism, 41–42, 71, 115–16, 164, 166

Reading Renunciation (Clark), 156–57
Report on Transylvanian Scholars and Their Writings (Seivert), 207
Republic of Mind and Spirit, A (Albanese), 5–6
Restless Souls (Schmidt), 5–6
Revelation 12, 110, 135–36, 140, 151–52, 200–1
Reyes, Jeanette, 226
Ritchie, Jean, 191
Road to Heaven (Porter), 127
Rosenthal, Bernard, 173
Rosicrucian Enlightenment, The (Yates), 219
Rosicrucianism, 218–21
Rural Rides (Cobbett), 102

Sachse, Julius, 6, 106, 217, 220
Samuels, Shirley, 184
Sauer, Christopher, Jr., 205
Schaffer, Simon, 3
Schleiermacher, Friedrich, 10, 30–31
Schmidt, Leigh Eric, 170, 200
Schneider, Hans, 91
Schuchart, Anna, 92, 111, 112, 113
Schuhmacher, Daniel
    apocalypse and, 62–66, 63*f*
    audience of, 64–65
    comets and, 63–64
    environmental knowledge and, 63–64
    illustration by, 63*f*, 64
    influences on, 65

scriptural references
    2 Kings
        1:8, 146–47
        19, 146
    Joel 2:30, 163
    John 14:2, 121
    Matthew 11:7, 133
    Numbers
        14, 141
        14:38, 141
    Proverbs 10:24, 141
    Revelation 12, 110, 135–36, 140, 151–52, 200–1
    Threefold Wilderness State and, 140–42, 143, 151, 156
Seelig, Johan
    ascetic commitments of, 111–12
    biographical details scarce on, 111
    birth and upbringing of, 111
    contemplation of the stars and, 122
    doctrinal disputes and, 114
    hymns and, 124
    Keithian schism and, 114–15
    missionizing efforts and, 119
    Sarah Mariah Hopewell described by, 96
    social reform and, 118
    withdrawal from public life of, 118
Seidensticker, Oswald, 104–5, 134, 136, 205, 216
Seneca, 100
Seventh Day Baptists, 58
Seven Years War, 88
Several Lovely and Edifying Songs (1788), 197
Shantz, Douglas, 30, 37, 40
Short and Easy Method of Prayer, A, 204–6
Short and Easy Method of Prayer, A (Motte-Guyon), 205–6
Short and Easy Method of Prayer or Speaking with God (attributed Sauer), 205
Showalter, Shirley, 77–78
Smith, Joseph, 227–28
Smith, J. Z., 218
Smolenski, John, 78
"Snow-Bound: A Winter Idyll" (Whittier), 213–14
Soderlund, Jean R, 70–72, 73–74
Soffa, Kris, 226
sola scriptura, 32–33, 43–44, 47–48
Spencer, Carole Dale, 78
Spener, Philipp Kakob, 30, 54–55, 113
spiritual alchemy. *See* alchemy
spontaneous human combustion, 173
Steinmetz, Andrew, 203–4
Stewart, Matthew, 66

Stoudt, John, 64, 66
Supernaturalism of New England (Whittier), 212
Swedenborg, Emmanuel, 59

Taves, Ann, 227–28
telepathy, 15–16, 130
Temple of Wisdom for the Little World, The
(Böhme/Leeds), 85–86, 115
Tergemina lucis mysticae mysteria
(Zimmerman), 154
Tharpe, Sister Rosetta, 1
Theory of Pneumatology (Jung-Stilling), 202–3
Thirty Years War, 19, 28, 30, 33, 53, 65
Thirty Years War, The (Wedgewood), 14–15,
18–19, 44
Thomasius, Jacob, 11, 47
Thoreau, Henry David, 110
Threefold Wilderness State
apocalypse and, 154–55
ascetic alchemy and, 139, 143–44, 148–50,
155–57, 160
Barren Wilderness stage, 136–37, 141, 155
definite spiritual objective and, 158
definition of, 141–51
devotional crisis and, 156
Elijah as example for, 145–46, 148–49, 150
environment as medium of revelation
and, 154–55
Fruitful Wilderness stage, 136–37, 141–42
hesitation, doubt, and failure in first stage
of, 141
Jesus as example for, 147–48
John the Baptist as example for, 146–47
meaning of wilderness and, 139–40, 144–45,
151, 154–55
monasticism and, 149, 155–56
Moses as example for, 145–46, 150
overview of, 133–40
paranormal and, 142
Pillar of Cloud and, 142
scriptural references and, 140–42, 143,
151, 156
sources of, 151–55
as spiritual alchemy, 137, 142–44
stages of, 136–37
technology of self-negation and, 155–60
tripartite nature of, 152–54
uniqueness of, 137–38
visible presence of God in the second state
of, 142
Wilderness of the Elect of God stage, 136–37,
144–45, 194
"To the Wissahickon" (Kemble), 102

True Christianity (Arndt), 37, 38–39, 40, 44,
63–64, 68

unmute gospel, 226–32
"Up to the Judgment" (Schumacher), 4f

Valantasis, Richard, 138
Verluis, Arthur, 85–86
Verschuier, Lieve, 24
Versluis, Arthur, 7
Vitae Patrum, 101
Von Rosenroth, Christian Knorr, 42–43

Waite, Arthur E., 220
Ward, W. R., 31
Washington, George, 217
Watson, John F., 131
Wedgewood, C. V., 14–15, 31
Weeks, Andrew, 232
Wengrow, David, 71, 120
Whittier, John Greenleaf
abolitionism of, 210
attention to esoteric dimensions of rural life
and, 213
background and upbringing of, 211
book of nature and, 214–15
career of, 210
Enlightenment and, 213
environmental knowledge and, 212–15
language use by, 215
occult interests of, 212
paranormal and, 212
reputation of, 210
spiritual power and, 213–14
stern duty to expose error and, 212
Wieland (Brown)
class consciousness in, 177–78
difficulty of writing of, 165
ecomimesis and, 187–88
effects without cause and, 175–77
Enlightenment and reason critiqued in, 175–
76, 186, 187–88
Germantown represented in, 168
God represented in, 173
Hermetic farmer in, 178–79, 183
hubris critiqued in, 184–85
intellectual context of, 176–77
intermediatism and, 176–77
Kelpius in, 166, 169–70, 180, 189
as long-form exercise in philosophical
problem, 186
meaning of, 184–85
"nature" and, 188

310   INDEX

Wieland (Brown) (*cont.*)
  overview of, 163–67, 189–90
  paranormal in, 170–73, 176, 179–80, 182–83, 185–88, 189–90
  political interpretations of, 184
  prefatory statement in, 188–89
  Schuylkill tabernacle in, 170–71
  secularizing agenda subverted in, 165
  source material for, 174–75
  spontaneous human combustion in, 173
  subject of, 164
  summary of, 167–75
  ventriloquy in, 182–84
  Yates family murders in, 180–81
wilderness. *See also* Threefold Wilderness State
  apocalypse and, 110, 140, 154–55
  Kelpius and, 68, 110
  Lenape and, 70
  meaning of, 139–40, 144–45, 151, 154–55
  Pennsylvania as, 68–72
Wilderness and paradise in Christian Thought (Williams), 151
wisdom in nature, 36–37, 47–50, 51–52, 229–30
Wissahickon community
  beauty of environment and, 102–4, 109, 144
  communal housing and, 127
  contemplation of the stars and, 121–23
  environmental context of, 109–10
  environmental knowledge and, 105
  establishment of, 106–7
  funding challenges of, 107–8
  humanizing of, 102
  Keithian schism and, 114–17
  members of, 111–13
  methodological considerations for Kelpius's life with, 104–6
  missionizing efforts and, 119–21
  overview of, 102
  poems about, 102–4
  social reform and, 117–19
  sources for Kelpius's life at, 104–6
Witt, Christopher
  death of, 131
  house of, 130

  mysteriousness of, 131
  oil portrait of Kelpius by, 128, 129*f*
  physical decline of, 131
  spiritual conversation and, 130–31
  translation work of, 128
Wolf, Stephenie Grauman, 110
Wolfson, Eliot, 17, 226
Wonders of the Invisible World (Mather), 14
Wright, Timothy, 155–56

Yates, Frances, 11–12, 13, 31, 42–43, 65, 181
Yates family murders (1781), 180–81
Yoder, Peter, 59

Zeller, Winnfried, 29
Zimmerman, Johann Jacob
  anti-institutionalism and, 157
  apocalypse and, 25, 26–27, 44–46, 55–56, 153–54
  burial of, 90
  character and faith of, 45
  comets and, 24–27, 44–46
  death of, 90
  distinctness of approach of, 26–27
  environmental knowledge and, 25–26, 154
  expulsion of, 44–46, 91
  heresy attributed to, 44–46
  legacy of, 46–47
  meaning of comets and, 24–27
  measurements made by, 23–24
  metaphysical approach to the nature world and, 43
  music and, 124
  nature is the interpreter of scripture and, 42–47
  Pietism of, 30–31, 43, 55–56, 91
  sola scriptura revised by, 43
  Spiritual Babel of Europe and, 74
  Threefold Wilderness State and, 154–55
  timing of divine judgment and, 44–45
Zinzendorf, Nicolaus, 169, 192
Zosimos of Panopolis, 34–35
Zuber, Mike, 42, 44–45, 108, 137, 154–55

The manufacturer's authorised representative in the EU for product safety is Oxford
University Press España S.A. of El Parque Empresarial San Fernando de Henares,
Avenida de Castilla, 2 – 28830 Madrid (www.oup.es/en or product.safety@oup.com).
OUP España S.A. also acts as importer into Spain of products made by the manufacturer.

Printed in the USA/Agawam, MA
August 15, 2025

892047.015